The New Testament
and Literature

D1566275

Books by Stephen Cox

"The Stranger Within Thee": Concepts of the Self in Late Eighteenth-Century Literature (1980)

Love and Logic: The Evolution of Blake's Thought (1992)

The Titanic Story: Hard Choices, Dangerous Decisions (1999)

The Woman and the Dynamo: Isabel Paterson and the Idea of America (2004)

The New Testament and Literature: A Guide to Literary Patterns (2006)

The New Testament and Literature

A Guide to Literary Patterns

STEPHEN COX

OPEN COURT
Chicago and La Salle, Illinois

To order books from Open Court, call toll-free 1-800-815-2280, or visit our website at www.opencourtbooks.com.

Open Court Publishing Company is a division of Carus Publishing Company.

Copyright ©2006 by Carus Publishing Company

First printing 2006

All rights reserved. No part of this publication may be reproduced, stored in a retrieval system, or transmitted, in any form or by any means, electronic, mechanical, photocopying, recording, or otherwise, without the prior written permission of the publisher, Open Court Publishing Company, a division of Carus Publishing Company, 315 Fifth Street, P.O. Box 300, Peru, Illinois, 61354-0300.

Permission to reprint "The Gardener," by Rudyard Kipling, has been granted by A.P. Watt Ltd, on behalf of the National Trust for Places of Historic Interest or Natural Beauty.

Printed and bound in the United States of America.

Library of Congress Cataloging-in-Publication Data

Cox, Stephen D., 1948-
    The New Testament and literature : a guide to literary patterns / Stephen Cox.
        p. cm.
    Includes bibliographical references (p.   ) and indexes.
    ISBN-13: 978-0-8126-9591-5 (trade pbk. : alk. paper)
    ISBN-10: 0-8126-9591-7 (trade pbk. : alk. paper)
    1. Christianity and literature—Great Britain—History. 2. Christianity and literature—United States—History 3. Bible.N.T.—Influence. 4. Bible as literature. 5. Bible and literature. 6. English literature—History and criticism. 7. American literatur—History and criticism I. Title.
    PR145C69 2006
    809'.935225—dc22

                                                    2005029993

To Paul Beroza and Paul Hochstetler

Contents

Preface

This book is not primarily theological, historical, or devotional. It does something uncommon, something often mentioned or recommended but rarely attempted in a serious way. It looks at the New Testament both as a distinctive work of literature and as a productive influence on later works of literature.

Many books have been written about "the Bible as literature." For some, the phrase means, in effect, the Old Testament as literature. For many others, it means the study of historical issues that have little to do with the special characteristics of New Testament writing. Few books are willing to assess the literary quality of the New Testament. Fewer still are written for intelligent readers who may not already be very familiar with the Bible or Christian teachings.

Making the New Testament accessible as literature does not mean examining its techniques in abstraction from its vital message. Nor does it mean tracing its themes in abstraction from its literary methods. *The New Testament and Literature* approaches its subject by identifying certain patterns, certain combinations of ideas and methods, that give the New Testament its distinctiveness and coherence and its ability to create resemblances to itself in later literature. I call these patterns the DNA of the New Testament.

Part I (my first eight chapters) explores these patterns, identifying specific elements of the New Testament's DNA, and examining their effects on the four major types of New Testament literature: gospel, epistle, church history, and apocalypse. The chief examples are the gospels of Luke and John, the Acts of the Apostles, the epistles of Paul to the Galatians and the Corinthians, and the Revelation.

Part II (Chapters 9–16), examines the influence of New Testament patterns on a wide range of English and American literature.

Chapter 9 shows the persistence of the New Testament DNA in one of the earliest works in the English language, *The Dream of the Rood*, and in a story written twelve centuries later, Rudyard Kipling's "The Gardener."

Chapter 10 samples the vast popular literature of Christian revival, with special reference to George Foxe's *Book of Martyrs*, a work of the Protestant Reformation, and Christian hymns of the eighteenth and nineteenth centuries.

Chapter 11 discusses the importance of the New Testament DNA in the seemingly opposed religious movements represented by John Bunyan's *Pilgrim's Progress* and the poetry of John Donne and George Herbert.

Chapter 12 explores the tradition of New Testament individualism, as represented especially in the work of William Blake and Emily Dickinson.

Chapter 13 takes up the influence of the book of Revelation, particularly in American culture. It looks at a variety of popular American writers, including Dickinson, Julia Ward Howe, James Baldwin, and Vachel Lindsay.

Chapter 14 analyzes literary challenges to Christianity, exposing their ironic tendency to assimilate Christian patterns of thought and writing. This chapter considers works by John Adams and Thomas Jefferson, D.H. Lawrence, Harold Frederic, Sinclair Lewis, and others.

Chapter 15 follows some of the many literary responses that Christians and non-Christians have made to attacks on Christianity and the New Testament. The authors considered here include Thornton Wilder, Ernest Hemingway, William Faulkner, John Betjeman, Martin Luther King, C.S. Lewis, and Robert Browning.

Chapter 16 studies two distinguished examples of twentieth-century literature, the fiction of J.F. Powers and the poetry of T.S. Eliot—vivid illustrations of the way in which the same New Testament patterns can renew themselves in works that seem radically different in approach and style.

For the reader's convenience, Part III presents the texts of some of the works discussed in the book.

Acknowledgments

This book grew out of the courses I teach in New Testament literature at the University of California, San Diego. I am grateful to my enthusiastic and perceptive students, who gave me a great deal of help in identifying what intelligent people want to know about the Bible.

Paul Beroza provided the first opportunity to talk through my ideas. Tim Beals and Michael Travers offered expert advice and the kind of support that one never forgets. Garrett Brown, Chris Capen, and the Reverend Lawrence Waddy gave me encouragement at exactly the right times. Paul Hochstetler not only advised me about Christian music but also helped me plan the figures in the first two chapters.

I wish that every author could have the chance to work with my editor, David Ramsay Steele—a generous colleague and a superbly talented man of letters.

Part I

The Patterns
Identified

1

"The Most Difficult Book in the World"?

A great authority on literature once called the New Testament "the most difficult book in the world."[1] It is also, perhaps, the most influential book in the world. It has placed an indelible stamp on Western culture.

Yet the literary qualities of the New Testament and their effects on later works are far from widely understood. Even devout Christians often confess their difficulty in understanding the Bible as a work of art as well as a work of religious teaching. And when they think about later Christian literature, they often cannot identify anything that distinguishes it, or anything that connects it with the New Testament, besides particular doctrinal messages.

The New Testament itself can seem overwhelmingly complex. It is brief—about the size of a medium-length modern novel—but its materials are extraordinarily rich and diverse. The word "Bible" (Greek "biblia" = "books") emphasizes this diversity. The Bible is not just one work but a library of sixty-six works. The first thirty-nine of them, the Old Testament or Hebrew Scriptures, are sacred to both Jews and Christians.[2] They were scripture in Jesus's day. Then the New Testament, the specifically Christian part of the Bible, was added. It consists of twenty-seven books, written by a variety of authors, using a variety of literary techniques.

The literature influenced by the New Testament is still more diverse. There is no limit to the variety of Christian literature. One naturally wonders: Is there anything distinctive, in a literary way, about the New Testament and the works it has inspired? Beneath the diversity, is there also a continuity? One may also wonder about another basic issue—the literary merit of the New Testament. Apart from its teachings, is it "really any good"? Finally, can one learn anything significant about the intellectual content of the New Testament by examining its literary qualities?

My answer is Yes to all these questions. I believe that one of the best ways to learn about "the most difficult book in the world" is to study it from a literary perspective. That does not mean ignoring its teachings. The literary methods of the New Testament are inseparably connected with its religious ideas. The more one understands the methods, the more one understands the character and reach of the ideas. The teachings of the New Testament are part of a literary fabric of great complexity and beauty, a fabric created by literary strategies designed to give those teachings the strongest expression possible.

Essential to this fabric are certain closely related, frequently recurring patterns of religious ideas and literary devices, patterns important enough to be called the DNA of the New Testament. These patterns are the means by which New Testament Christianity identified and expressed itself, and reproduced itself in later literature. They appear throughout the New Testament and the writing it has helped to shape. They give that literature its special character and coherence, and they are a major source of the New Testament's continuing influence on our literary culture.

That is the central conception of this book. For readers who are not deeply familiar with the New Testament, or later Christian literature, I think the idea will provide a convenient way of approaching the subject. For professional students of this literature, I think it will suggest a new perspective to consider and debate.[3] For all, I hope it will offer a new occasion to follow the advice that the future St. Augustine once received from the excited voice of a child: "Take it and read! Take it and read!"[4] Take the Book and read it, with increased pleasure and appreciation.

In the next chapter I will discuss the New Testament patterns I've mentioned, identifying them individually and detailing their relationships. To prepare for that discussion, the present chapter will offer a brief—and necessarily general—account of what we know, and don't know, about the way in which the New

Testament texts were written and assembled. It will also notice some of the ways in which the New Testament has been viewed and used.

The Writing of the New Testament

The more complicated a text appears, the more important it is to start with the simple things about it. One place to start is the basic types or "genres" of writing that it includes. The New Testament's twenty-seven books can be divided among four main genres: four "gospels" or statements of the "good news" about Jesus (the gospels of Matthew, Mark, Luke, and John), one history of the early Christian church (the Acts of the Apostles), one apocalypse (Revelation), and twenty-one letters or "epistles" attributed to five of Jesus's followers (James, John, Jude, Paul, and Peter).[5] Some of the twenty-seven books are less than a page in length; others are as long as an ancient scroll could conveniently accommodate. All are written in "koiné" or common Greek, the major commercial language of the Roman empire.[6] Twenty-five of them were produced by Jewish Christians, and two (Luke and Acts) by a "gentile" (non-Jewish) author.

The New Testament was written within a relatively short period of time. Most scholars agree that, with one or two possible exceptions,[7] all of its books appeared in the first century, within a few decades of Jesus's crucifixion, which occurred around the year 30. There is also scholarly agreement on the idea that the first books to be written were some or all of Paul's epistles. His first epistle to the church in Thessalonica can be dated to about the year 50. It shows that Christianity had acquired, by that time, a significant body of beliefs and believers, and that it had spread far beyond its place of origin on the eastern shore of the Mediterranean.

Controversy continues about the dating of the four gospels and their relationship to one another. The gospel of John seems to have been written last, perhaps as a complement to one or more than one of the others. It is usually dated to the last decade of the first century. But none of the gospels is clearly datable by reference to external events. In the year 70, a Roman army devastated Jerusalem and destroyed its temple. The destruction was a religious event of the first importance, but one that is never directly reported in the New Testament. Even the "late" gospel of John refers to a landmark in Jerusalem as if it still existed: "Now there is at Jerusalem . . . a pool, which is called in the Hebrew tongue Bethesda, having five porches" (John 5:2). The question of how much of the New Testament was produced before the year 70 has no definitive answer.[8]

None of the gospels says explicitly who wrote it, but by the middle of the second century the names Matthew, Mark, and Luke were firmly associated with the first three texts; no other possibilities seem to have been considered. The fourth gospel has its own subtle means of identifying its author as John, the disciple "whom Jesus loved" (John 21:7, 24; see Chapter 4, below). Early Christians believed that the author of Matthew's gospel was the man whose calling by Christ is described at Matthew 9:9, that the author of Luke's gospel was one of Paul's most respected friends (Colossians 4:14), and that the author of Mark's gospel was John Mark, an associate of both Paul and Peter (Acts 12:11–12, 25). According to the early-second-century writer Papias, Mark compiled his gospel from Peter's recollections; and this may be true, although it is impossible to prove it, and many other explanations have been proposed.[9]

Twentieth-century critics made determined attempts to trace each of the gospels to a particular group of early Christians, either in the sense that the text was written for the benefit of that group or in the sense that it was "produced" by the group's special conception of the resurrected Christ.[10] It must always be remembered, however, that communities do not actually write books—individual people do—and although the gospel was preached and taught within communities of believers, the communities were created in the first place by the preaching and teaching of the gospel.[11] Virtually the only direct evidence we have about the early decades of the Christian movement comes from the New Testament writings themselves. The attempt to explain the texts by reference to their social and religious circumstances leads inevitably back to the literary features of the texts and our ability to find similarities and differences among them.[12] What shows most clearly in the gospels is the effect of authors working in individual but often closely related ways with the great store of memory and testimony about Jesus that was present in the years following his death. The gospel of John remarks that if everything that Jesus did were written down,

FIGURE 1
Key Sources for the Life of Jesus

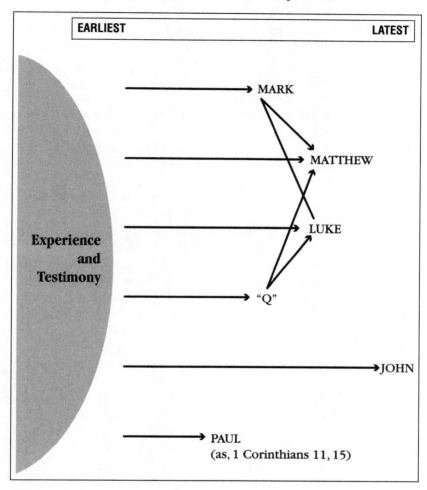

"even the world itself could not contain the books that should be written" (John 21:25). The New Testament as a whole presents at least six independent sources of information about his life (see Figure 1). Each gospel writer undoubtedly had access to a variety of documents, stories, and recollections and could select what he regarded as the most authentic and effective material.

The greatest puzzle of the New Testament is the unity and individuality of the first three gospels, Matthew, Mark, and Luke. These books share so many features that they are called the "synoptic" gospels, the word "synoptic" indicating that they have a common viewpoint (common "optics"). One way of seeing how much they share is to divide them into separable literary units, technically called "pericopes." Jesus's story of the Good Samaritan (Luke 10:29–37) is a pericope; the immediately succeeding story of Martha and Mary (Luke 10:38–42) is another pericope. Of the approximately five hundred pericopes that can be clearly classified, about four hundred represent sharing by two or more of the synoptic gospels; of these, eighty-six represent sharing by all three (see Figure 2).[13] The shared pericopes are full of verbal similarities and identities; they were produced by a common use of documents, not by a common reception of oral accounts.

Many theories have attempted to explain how this sharing happened. The most popular and plausible theory suggests that the gospel of Mark was written first, then used as a source by Matthew and Luke. Mark's gospel is the shortest of the three synoptics, and its material is almost entirely contained in one or both of the other two. Supposing that the theory is correct, Matthew and Luke took what they wanted from the text of Mark, which was almost all of it, then added a good deal of material (fifty pericopes) that is common to them alone, material that they derived from another written source, or, more likely, a number of such sources. These sources—if they existed—have disappeared. Scholars call the hypothetical document or documents "Q," for "Quelle," the German word for "source."

One might think that Matthew could have copied the Q material from Luke, or vice versa. But if one writer copied from the other, why aren't the two gospels even more similar than they are? Each, for example, presents its own narrative of Jesus's birth. The gospel of Matthew includes forty pericopes that are

FIGURE 2
Overlapping Gospels

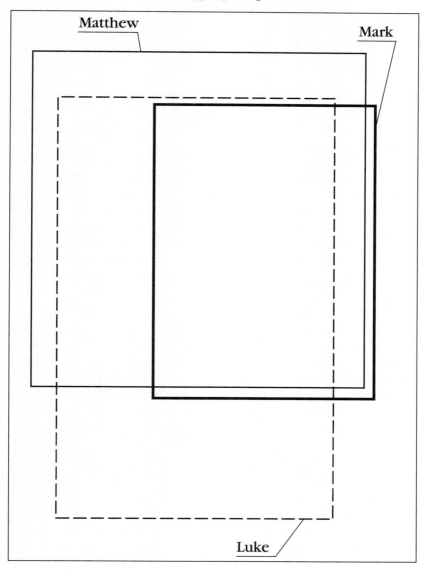

unique to it and for which the author presumably had his own independent sources, unknown to Luke. Luke includes sixty-one pericopes that are not found in Matthew or Mark. To most students of the synoptic problem, this indicates that Matthew and Luke developed their gospels separately from one another, though with mutual aid from Q and the gospel of Mark. Luke then continued the story of Christianity after the death and resurrection of Jesus by writing a second volume, the Acts of the Apostles.

It is possible that some of the New Testament books were written in a number of stages or "editions." The gospel of John includes comments about itself, apparently written after its author's death (John 21:24). The gospel of Mark (and the Q documents) may conceivably have appeared in more than one version, with Matthew and Luke using somewhat different texts. If that is true, it would help to explain certain features of the gospels. Yet it is remarkable that none of the hypothetical earlier versions has survived. If one or more gospels resulted from an extensive "editorial" process, we can study only the final results.

Of course, the question of *how* the texts were written makes little difference to the theological issue of whether the writing was inspired or directed by God. And it makes almost as little difference to the issue of the literary character of the texts as we have them. We may not know precisely where, when, and how the gospels were produced, but we do know that they possess the integrity, individuality, and decisive patterning that we expect from finished works of literature. Even the differences among the gospels provide strong reasons for respecting the wholeness and integrity of each one of them. As more than one critic has emphasized, each has a clearly identifiable "perspective," expressed in its author's choice of material and his way of working with it.[14] We are not dealing with nondescript committee work. Neither are we dealing with work that was edited to smooth away all the rough edges. If systematic smoothing had been accomplished, it would have left none of the "problems" and "hard sayings" that we find in the gospels. In time, perhaps only one well synthesized gospel would have remained.[15] In any event, there is no reason why mysteries of origins, in a Bible text or any other, should distract attention from the literary patterns that the text itself presents.[16]

The gospels are not the only New Testament books whose writing retains an element of mystery. The epistle to the Hebrews, for example, is traditionally attributed to Paul, but it is unusual in several ways: it does not specify its author or occasion, and to many people it reads less like an epistle than like a treatise or sermon. The writer of the epistle of James, "a servant of God and of the Lord Jesus Christ," is often, but not certainly, identified with an important member of the early church whom Paul calls "the Lord's brother" (James 1:1, Galatians 1:19). The two epistles that are self-attributed to Jesus's friend Peter are so different from each other that most scholars doubt they were written by the same hand. Some observe that it was not uncommon in the ancient world for disciples of an important person to write "on behalf of" or "in continuation of" the master. Whether this improves our understanding of the two epistles remains unclear. The three epistles traditionally attributed to John, author of the fourth gospel, show close affinities to one another and to that gospel; but Revelation, which is also attributed to John, is written in a very different manner, and its self-identification as the work of Christ's "servant John" does not specify which John is meant (Revelation 1:1).

Some New Testament authors reveal little of their personalities. The opposite is true of Paul, the most prolific among them, and the most dynamic writer. Originally a violent opponent of Christianity, he underwent a dramatic conversion in which, as he said, the resurrected Jesus manifested himself by a light and a voice from heaven, demanding to know why Paul was persecuting him. As a result of that experience, Paul became Christianity's greatest intellectual exponent and Christ's most adventurous apostle ("apostle" = messenger, advocate, person "sent forth"). Paul's voice is one of the strongest that reverberate from the ancient world. His letters present an enormous range of moods and styles, concepts and arguments; he is alert to every possible way of communicating his ideas; yet his approach to writing is very difficult to confuse with anyone else's. His authorship of the epistles to Timothy and Titus is often disputed, but the conflict of attributions is between him and a hypothetical follower who succeeds in imitating his manner.[17]

Christianity has always been a highly literary faith, a faith that thrives on scripture and propagates itself by the written word. In Paul, we see how important literary gifts can be. His task was

to maintain the integrity and unity of the tumultuously expanding Christian church, in a world that was very much larger than
ours in terms of the time required to travel from one part of it
to another. He could not keep visiting and revisiting local congregations, influencing them with his presence. He had to concentrate all the strength of his message and his personality into
a few sheets of papyrus and send them across the world, hoping that his written words would fully project his meanings. In
the service of his organizational mission, Paul became one of
the world's great writers.

Devout Bible readers often fail to appreciate the literary gifts
of people like Paul, and therefore miss a good deal of what is
actually present in the Bible, because they unconsciously put its
authors in a separate, non-literary category. Dorothy Sayers, the
mystery writer, complained that for Christians Jesus was no
longer "'really' real . . . and the taint of unreality has spread to
His disciples and friends and to His biographers: they are not
'real' writers, but just 'Bible' writers."[18] Paul's work is one example of the way in which "Bible writing" attains the depth and
scope and personal interest of "real writing."

The Continuity of the New Testament

But however good its authors may be, the New Testament is
much more than the sum of its individual parts. As the collection grew, the story of Christianity extended itself across history, from the gospel accounts of Jesus's life, death, and
resurrection, through the commentaries on the early church in
the epistles and the book of Acts, and at last to Revelation's
prophecies of the church's final triumph and the ages to come.
Despite the New Testament's diversity of books and writers, its
stories could now be seen as one grand, continuous narrative.[19]
The vital elements of the Christian message could be found
both in the New Testament as a whole and in each of its longer
books, making the degree of literary coherence among the
parts of the collection more than sufficient for them to serve as
a common inspiration for later Christian literature. That literature would, in turn, possess its own continuity as a series of
echoes from the same New Testament source. Period styles and
local customs might vary wildly, new societies, new problems,
and new communities of Christians might arise and express

themselves forcefully in new literary texts, but the underlying patterns would persist.

Any work of Christian literature is likely to recall ideas from many parts of the New Testament. Figure 3 presents a convenient example: "The Church's One Foundation," a nineteenth-century hymn that remains popular in traditional Christian churches.[20] The left column of the figure reproduces the song; the right column cites its New Testament sources. Gospels, Acts, epistles, Revelation—all join to create a single modern text. The text, once created, retells the story of Christianity, repeating both the individual parts of the New Testament and its overarching plot, from the coming of Christ to the victory of his church. The text has integrity; it exists on its own; it is not just a string of Bible quotations; yet it carries all the weight of scripture with it, presenting itself as one more set of variations on the great New Testament themes.

It's important to mention that for every New Testament source I have listed in Figure 3, I could have provided a dozen more. Basic ideas and literary devices are endlessly repeated and re-emphasized in the New Testament. This pattern of re-emphasis has been recognized from very early times. It appears to have been important in the decisions that believers made about what documents belong in the "canon" of authoritative writings. They expected each candidate for inclusion to be patterned in certain basic respects like the others.

Treatments of the New Testament by modern media and popular literature have led many people to suppose that its canon must have been constructed by a church official, council, or committee, many centuries after the contents were written, and that eligible books were excluded for what would now be called political reasons. This is untrue. The essential decisions were made in the second century by local Christian churches that had to choose, from the evidence before them, which documents were worthy of being read and copied. Their decisions were made on historical, doctrinal, and literary—not political—authority, and the individual judgments thus reached were so much in agreement with one another that by the end of the second century comparatively few disputes remained. There is even some interesting evidence that by the latter part of that century an edition of the whole New Testament had been published, containing the twenty-seven books that we

FIGURE 3
The Church's One Foundation
(Samuel Stone, 1866)

The Church's one Foundation
Is Jesus Christ her Lord:
She is His new creation
By water and the Word;
From heaven He came and
    sought her
To be His holy Bride,
With His own Blood He
    bought her,
And for her life He died.

- This is the stone which . . . is become the head of the corner.   ACTS 4:11
- If any man be in Christ, he is a new creature.   2 COR. 5:17
- And I John saw the holy city, new Jerusalem, coming down from God out of heaven, prepared as a bride adorned for her husband.   REV. 21:2
- The church of God, which he hath purchased with his own blood.   ACTS 20:28

Elect from every nation,
Yet one o'er all the earth,
Her charter of salvation
One Lord, one Faith, one Birth;
One Holy Name she blesses,
Partakes one Holy Food,
And to one Hope she presses,
With every grace endued.

- He . . . shall gather together his elect from the four winds.   MARK 13:27
- One Lord, one faith, one baptism.   EPH. 4:5
- By the name of Jesus . . . doth this man stand here before you whole.   ACTS 4:10
- This is the bread which came down from heaven.   JOHN 6:58
- I press toward the mark for the prize of the high calling of God in Christ Jesus.   PHIL. 3:14
- But unto every one of us is given grace according to the measure of the gift of Christ.   EPH. 4:7

The Church shall never perish!
Her dear Lord to defend,
To guide, sustain, and cherish,
Is with her to the end.
Though there be those who
    hate her,
And false sons in her pale,
Against or foe or traitor
She ever shall prevail.

- Lo, I am with you alway, even unto the end of the world.   MATT. 28:20
- Such are false apostles, deceitful workers, transforming themselves into the apostles of Christ.   2 COR. 11:13
- I will build my church, and the gates of hell shall not prevail against it.   MATT. 16:18

Though with a scornful wonder
Men see her sore opprest
By schisms rent asunder,
By heresies distrest;
Yet saints their watch are
    keeping,
Their cry goes up, "How long?"
And soon the night of weeping
Will be the morn of song.

- And they laughed him to scorn.
  LUKE 8:53
- I hear that there be divisions among
  you . . . heresies among you.
  1 COR. 11:18–19
- If any man preach any other gospel
  unto you than that ye have received,
  let him be accursed.   GAL. 1:9
- They cried with a loud voice, saying,
  How long, O Lord . . .?   REV. 6:10
- And they sung as it were a new
  song.   REV. 14:3

Mid toil and tribulation,
And tumult of her war,
She waits the consummation
Of peace for evermore;
Till with the vision glorious
Her longing eyes are blest,
And the great Church victorious
Shall be the Church at rest.

- In the world ye shall have tribulation:
  but be of good cheer; I have
  overcome the world.   JOHN 16:33
- To wait for his Son from heaven.
  1 THESS. 1:10
- The weapons of our warfare are not
  carnal. . . . 2 COR. 10:4
- Now we see through a glass, darkly;
  but then face to face.   1 COR. 13:12
- And God shall wipe away all tears
  from their eyes.   REV. 21:4

Yet she on earth hath union
With God the Three in One,
And mystic sweet communion
With those whose rest is won:
Oh, happy ones and holy!
Lord, give us grace that we
Like them, the meek and lowly,
On high may dwell with thee.
Amen.

- God was in Christ, reconciling the
  world unto himself.   2 COR. 5:19
- Baptizing them in the name of the
  Father, and of the Son, and of the
  Holy Ghost.   MATT. 28:19
- And every creature which is in
  heaven, and on the earth . . . heard I
  saying, Blessing, and honour, and
  glory, and power, be unto him that
  sitteth upon the throne, and unto the
  Lamb for ever and ever.   REV. 5:13
- By grace are ye saved through
  faith.   EPH. 2:8
- Blessed are the meek, for they shall
  inherit the earth.   MATT. 5:5
- And he will dwell with them, and they
  shall be his people.   REV. 21:3

have today, with their now-familiar titles ("The Gospel According to Matthew," "Acts of the Apostles," and so on). Although that edition would necessarily have been produced, in the first instance, by one person or a small group of persons, it evidently became the model for succeeding arrangements of the sacred library.[21] To exert that influence, it must have won the independent assent of the great majority of readers or at least buyers of manuscripts, and be seen as reflecting their preexisting views. Ratification of the canon by church council was not required, and it did not happen until late in the fourth century.

Several issues were crucial in the process of canon-formation. Was there evidence that a given work had been written by an apostle or another early disciple of Christ? That was one important question. But many works that people claimed to have been written by the apostles were rejected. Why? Some were known to have appeared too recently to verify the claim. Some, however, simply lacked the right literary stuff. They didn't have the same features as a "real" gospel, a "real" revelation, or a "real" apostolic epistle, with a strong history of acceptance by the Christian community. The real scriptures were diverse, but their literary approaches seemed to be congruent with one another. Works that were judged "apocryphal" ("hidden," non-canonical) either failed to use similar methods or failed to balance and integrate them in the ways in which more trusted works did.[22]

One interesting example is the so-called Gospel of Thomas, which is fairly early (second century) and is, from a literary point of view, by far the best of the apocryphal writings. It consists of 114 sayings attributed to Jesus. Many of them appear in the canonical gospels as well, and others may also be authentic in some way. But Thomas is not a gospel as Matthew, Mark, Luke, and John are gospels. It provides no connected story and only small fragments of narrative; and as I will emphasize throughout this book, story-telling is a dominant characteristic of the canonical books of the New Testament. There is no evidence that the Gospel of Thomas was ever seriously considered for inclusion in any canon.[23]

Decisions about what belonged in the New Testament were guided by a sense of literary continuity. A similar sense of continuity is important in interpreting the works it inspired. If you miss the continuity, you generally miss the meaning. Glance, for a moment, at another nineteenth-century hymn, this time an apparently simple product of American revivalism, "Are You Washed in the Blood?" (Figure 4).[24] A hundred years ago, everyone in America knew this song; most Americans can still read its lyrics without difficulty. But how would they look to people who had no acquaintance with the literary features of the New Testament, as they appear in gospels, epistles, Acts, and Revelation? Such people would see a curious collection of fragments—ideas and pictures with no obvious relationship to one another: the strange image of washing oneself in blood; the even stranger image of "resting in the crucified"; the demand to know whether "you" have actually done these things; the assumption that doing them has some relationship to being "ready" for another world, or to some kind of journey in quest of "power" . . . What could all this possibly mean?

The song begins to make sense when one notices its repetition of Revelation 7:14, where the saints in heaven are said to have "washed their robes, and made them white in the blood of the Lamb." But that passage, in turn, makes sense only when one catches the song's echoes of other passages in the New Testament: the symbolism, in the gospel of John and Acts, of Christ as the Lamb of God (John 1:29, Acts 8:32–35); the idea of the atonement or reconciliation between God and humanity through the sacrifice of Christ, especially as this idea is presented in Paul's epistles (Galatians 3); Paul's emphasis on the irony of Christ's crucifixion as the source of power and purity (1 Corinthians 1:17–31; 6:1–11); the New Testament's response, throughout, to the death of the man who said, "Come unto me . . . and I will give you rest," yet who challenged his friends to pick up their crosses and follow him (Matthew 11:28, Luke 14:27).

Such diverse conceptions grew together as the New Testament was formed out of texts of many kinds. Paul pictures the Christian church as a body in which every part, though unique, contributes to the good of the whole (1 Corinthians 12). The picture also applies to Christian literature. Creatures from some other planet, who had never beheld a human body, would not know what to make of a hand, an eye, or an ear when they first encountered it. They wouldn't immediately recognize what each organ contributed to make the body what it is. And unless these creatures investigated carefully, they would not know that

FIGURE 4
Are You Washed in the Blood?
(Elisha Hoffman, 1878)

Have you been to Jesus for the cleansing pow'r?
Are you washed in the blood of the Lamb?
Are you fully trusting in His grace this hour?
Are you washed in the blood of the Lamb?

Chorus
Are you washed in the blood,
In the soul-cleansing blood of the Lamb?
Are your garments spotless? Are they white as snow?
Are you washed in the blood of the Lamb?

Are you walking daily by the Saviour's side?
Are you washed in the blood of the Lamb?
Do you rest each moment in the Crucified?
Are you washed in the blood of the Lamb?

When the Bridegroom cometh will your robes be white?
Are you washed in the blood of the Lamb?
Will your soul be ready for the mansions bright,
And be washed in the blood of the Lamb?

Lay aside the garments that are stained with sin,
Are you washed in the blood of the Lamb?
There's a fountain flowing for the soul unclean,
O be washed in the blood of the Lamb.

the same genetic material can be found throughout the body, however diverse its parts may be in other respects. The New Testament is like the human body in that way, and so is Christian literature. No single text fully explains itself, but once a person begins to see the continuity among the texts, the explanatory process has begun.

Chapter 2 will attempt to identify the ideas and literary devices that are especially important in uniting the New Testament and the literary works that have followed it. But although this book is focused on the continuity of Christian literature, it is not a survey of that literature in all its major languages and periods. No one could live long enough to prepare such a survey. Even my selections from the New Testament are just that—selections, samples of the most interesting writing in the work's various genres. All my examples of Christian literature, besides those from the New Testament itself, were written in English. I think—since selection must be made—that there is some value in targeting a single literary lineage, and in analyzing texts that do not require translation. Something is inevitably lost when one translates, and historical developments are easier to grasp when one compares works written at different times but in the same tongue.

Because I am not writing a comprehensive history of English literature, any more than I am writing a comprehensive history of Christian literature, I have felt free to draw most of my examples from comparatively recent periods—the past five hundred years. After all, the most convincing tests of continuity can be expected to come from comparisons between ancient and modern works, between the twenty-seven short books of New Testament scripture and the astonishingly varied literature of modern England and America. The exception to my policy is a discussion of the Old English poem *The Dream of the Rood*, which does need to be read in translation. The *Rood* poem is a literary masterpiece, by any standard, one that deserves a place in any book on this subject; and it demonstrates the continuity of Christian literature in a particularly dramatic way. Composed seven hundred years after the birth of Christ and 1,300 years before the present century, in circumstances as different as one can imagine from those of either modern or early Christianity, and inspired by none of the sophisticated traditions of medieval Christian learning, it still exhibits the basic methods and concerns of Christian literature as they are likely to manifest themselves at any place or time.

Some of the literary works that I discuss are readily available in stores and libraries; others are hard to find, at least in early, unmodernized form. Part III of this book presents a number of these texts, together with a translation of *The Dream of the Rood.* Page references to Part III are provided in the sections where these works are discussed.

The Bible translation I use is the one most familiar to English-speaking people, the King James version (KJV) of 1611. This translation of the Bible is the greatest monument of English prose. It has exerted a stronger influence on English language and literature than any other book. It is, indeed, the only English version of the Bible that enjoys any literary influence. A twenti-eth-century critic spoke for many other writers and readers when she argued that there could not be a "more useful" trans-lation of the Bible, because the King James version was written in "the language of poets, scholars and thinkers," and the Bible "cannot be truly 'translated' in any other terms."[25] Since 1611, earlier manuscripts have been discovered than those used by the translators of the KJV, and the study of manuscript evidence has vastly improved. This does not mean that the KJV is, on the whole, either inaccurate or outmoded. Newer translations have replaced many of its readings with more accurate ones, but the great majority of these improvements have been of minor importance. When there is any substantial question about the difference between a New Testament passage cited from the KJV and the passage as currently established by modern textual research, I will provide a clarification in my text or notes.[26]

This book, however, makes no attempt to reveal the final meaning of the New Testament, or any part of it. The meanings of the Bible are inexhaustible. My book presents one way of approaching them. I will be pleased if it helps its readers explore Christian literature with greater interest and confidence, returning with a continual sense of expectation to the New Testament itself—a book that always repays the attention one gives it.

2
The DNA of the New Testament

Teachers of the Bible as literature often complain that their task is difficult because "the doctrines keep getting in the way": the ideas in the text are so compelling and controversial that students are interested only in them, not in the literary methods used to communicate them. But the solution should not be to ignore the ideas and concentrate on the methods. As the critic Leopold Damrosch said, "Attempts to study the Bible 'as literature' are always disappointing because finally it has to be studied as what it is—as a Bible."[1] What distinguishes the New Testament as a particular kind of literary work, a Bible, is neither its message nor its methods, taken in isolation, but its combinations of ideas and methods[2]—the patterns that constitute what I have called its "DNA."

The elements of this DNA (as many as can be usefully distinguished) are listed in Figure 5, where the New Testament's intellectual emphases occupy the left column and the literary devices[3] that are commonly used to express them occupy the right.

There is a great deal of continuity among the items on these lists. The ideas in the left column have many close associations, one with another; and several of the devices are naturally adapted to the expression of more than one of the ideas. Some highly characteristic devices, such as paradox, irony, and reversal of perspective—devices that respond directly to the challenge of representing the effects of God's astonishing convergence with human history in the person of Jesus Christ—might be listed in many more places than the primary locations where I have entered them. In fact, all the elements of the New Testament DNA are so closely related that when we look at any one of them we can easily discover its connection to the next one and the next, until we see, in outline, the broad anatomy of Christian ideas and forms of expression. It is because of their many associations, indeed, that we should not be surprised to see these elements occurring together throughout the New Testament, regardless of the genre or authorship of the texts in which we find them. One idea leads very conveniently to another, and to the literary devices that communicate it.

None of the elements is unique to Christian literature. Other kinds of literature use paradox and irony, and other kinds of literature teach the concept of a providential God—to cite just three examples. But even the DNA described by biologists is a combination of constituents that exist elsewhere as well. What counts is the *combination*, the distinctive set of relationships among these basic building blocks. Similarly, when one sees the ideas and devices mentioned in Figure 5 appearing prominently, working together, and heightening one another's effects, one is very likely to be looking at a work inspired by Christianity.

History, Providence, and Progress

But now is the time to discuss these elements individually, beginning with the first and most fundamental group of ideas shown in Figure 5: the concepts of *history* and *providence*.

Christianity is a "historical religion." It is founded on the idea that certain events—specifically, the life, death, and resurrection of Jesus—actually took place in history, in accordance with the "providence" or provision of God. The New Testament places a heavy emphasis on events, and on the connection of human events with God's plans for humanity. The emphasis is on events, and not just thoughts.[4] There's a difference between a religion that begins with events and a religion that begins with an abstract philosophy. Paul says in his first epistle to the church at Corinth, "I determined not to know anything among you, save [except] Jesus Christ, and him crucified" (1 Corinthians 2:2). In other words, Paul presented the Corinthians, not with a system of philosophical ideas, but with an account of historical events, a story of what Jesus did and suffered. Certainly the story contained ideas, ideas that Paul affirmed as true, but it was a story,

FIGURE 5
The DNA of the New Testament

IDEAS	LITERARY DEVICES
History, providence	Story, journey, progress, change of perspective
Reconciliation, unity	Unification, symbolism, paradox
Conversion	Transformation
Separation, division	Distinction
Priority of the inside to the outside	Reversal, irony, symbolism
Priority of the "lower" to the "higher"	Reversal, irony, change of perspective
Revelation	Symbolism, prophecy
Individualism	Transformation, distinction, irony
Discipleship	Repetition

not a philosophy. It was an account of ideas in action, of events in time and space.

This emphasis on specific events in their concrete, real-life framework can be found even in the New Testament's most symbolic book, Revelation. The revelation is rendered not in abstract terms but in stories full of things that are visible and familiar in human life—streets and houses, clothing and food, buying and selling, mourning and rejoicing, dying and giving birth. The New Testament writers would agree with Christian novelist Flannery O'Connor, who said that literature can "reinforce our sense of the supernatural by grounding it in concrete observable reality."[5] An absence of "concrete observable reality" may have been a major reason why early Christian congregations excluded from their canon of accepted works such apocryphal books as the so-called Gospel of Truth, which is almost wholly composed of abstract philosophy, and the Gospel of Thomas, which is composed of teachings without a surrounding history.

Corresponding to Christianity's emphasis on history (as the right column of Figure 5 indicates) is its constant use of *story* or narrative. You can read the New Testament for a long time without encountering any systematic philosophical discourse, much less any sustained passage of description or social commentary; but you cannot read very far without encountering a story. Again, this does not mean that New Testament storytellers see themselves as *just* telling stories; it means that they prefer a literary method that reveals truth in both thought and action. New Testament stories often take the form of a spiritual *journey* or *progress*, a movement of people along the course of God's plan. This movement can be pictured in many ways. It can be represented as a slow struggle across a landscape, or as a footrace— the faster the better (this is Paul's image at 1 Corinthians 9:24–26). The people who are on this journey may not see exactly where their path is leading, because it was laid out by providence, not by human knowledge; still, the journey has an end and aim. The journey-image that appears so frequently in Christian literature allows the events of human life to be visualized as purposeful and definite, as a sequence that starts someplace and goes someplace.

Everyone who has hiked through difficult terrain has had the experience of wondering whether one is walking along a path or merely wandering in the wilderness. A character in one of Robert Browning's poems describes a road leading over a mountain, a track that anyone "who stands upon / Is apt to doubt if it be meant for a road." But the road is really there, and it can be seen distinctly if one attains a better perspective. When one consults a map or (with God's help) travels over the mountain and looks back on it, one understands what was always true:

> Up goes the line there, plain from base to brow,
> Not vague, mistakable![6]

So Christian literature habitually challenges travelers to a *change of perspective*—often a reversal of perspective, from confusion to clarity, doubt to belief, entrapment by the natural to liberation by the supernatural. The challenge is, in a way, the reason for the literature's existence. By showing other people's journeys, other people's conflicts, other people's doubts and hesitations, Christian literature offers a new perspective on the reader's own journey. When we see that other people's experience had a shape, that it wasn't simply a path twisting aimlessly through a tortured wasteland, we may be prepared to look for evidence of a similarly providential shape in our own lives. Literary devices that (like Browning's image of the path over the mountain) produce a change of perspective on the journey of life have been part of the DNA of Christian literature from the New Testament on.

Many New Testament stories depict more than one journey. In Jesus's story of the Prodigal Son, the child who has lost everything journeys back toward his father, but "when he [is] yet a great way off," the merciful father sees him and journeys toward his child (Luke 15). The incident, which marks a dramatic change of perspective from ordinary views about "losing" and "winning," exemplifies the great story-theme of the New Testament, God's providential quest for humanity—the idea, as Paul puts it, that "God was in Christ, reconciling the world unto himself" (2 Corinthians 5:19). Here, certainly, is a story that starts someplace and goes someplace, but it is a double story, and it can be redoubled, as Paul goes on to say: "Now then we are ambassadors for Christ, as though God did beseech you by us: we pray you in Christ's stead, be ye reconciled to God"

(2 Corinthians 5:20). God in Christ seeks to *reconcile* the world to himself, and his human "ambassadors" repeat his action, inviting other people to begin their own journeys in quest of God. Someone could rewrite the New Testament as simply the story of God or simply the story of human beings, and many writers have tried to do so, with theologians telling the first kind of story and historians telling the second. But both approaches are foreign to the New Testament itself. New Testament stories are about God *and* humanity, time *and* eternity.

The doubleness of these stories, which includes the fact that they are accounts of human life that take us beyond human life, means that the New Testament often refuses to give us things that we might reasonably expect to find, while giving us other things, which we might never expect. It provides little "biographical" information about Jesus or his first disciples, apart from information directly related to their journey with God. Biographical details would fill out the human story, but they might divert attention from its relationship to the story of God. So they are omitted. Another example: in the New Testament we frequently hear about heaven, but heaven is never really described, even when Paul mentions that on one occasion he was "caught up into paradise" (2 Corinthians 12:4). Pictures of heaven have to wait until the last book of the New Testament, where we see the persecution of God's people on earth provoking a reaction and a revelation from heaven. Then we are allowed to "see" the heavenly rewards of the saints—which, as presented, are more than enough to astonish and fulfill the literary imagination. Yet what we see is largely an array of *symbols.* The pictures are clear and concrete; in the nature of things, however, they can only indicate; they cannot literally describe.

This gap between the picture and what is depicted reminds us that the New Testament stories are not just about the encounter of God and humanity; they are also about the difficulties of the latter in coming to terms with the former—difficulties that include not just the incomplete or false perceptions of people living in the world of time, but also the presence of sin in their lives and perceptions of reality. The dramatic reversals that one comes to expect in Christian stories are motivated by the crucial idea that something must change, or the reconciliation will not take place.

Division and Unity

The New Testament's symbolism and religious terminology respond to the same idea. An interesting New Testament word for the encounter of the divine and the human is καταλλαγή ("katallagé"), which has the basic meaning of "change" or "exchange," as in an "exchange of money," or a "change from enmity to friendship." In translations, this word is generally rendered as "reconciliation." In one instance, the King James version translates it with the English word "atonement," a word that conveys an even stronger image: "We also joy in God through our Lord Jesus Christ, by whom we have now received the atonement" (Romans 5:11). Divide "atonement" into its segments, and you see what it literally means: at-one-ment; God makes humanity "at one" with himself. Other, even more important New Testament terms cluster around the concept of reconciliation: "salvation," "faith," and "grace." To summarize a complicated set of ideas: God *saves* human beings by offering his Son as an atoning sacrifice for their sins; this salvation is an act of *grace*, the act of a gracious God, reaching out to humanity; its acceptance is an act of *faith*, the act of a grateful humanity, reaching up to God. The effect is a regained *unity*.

One of the ways in which the New Testament distinguishes itself from the Old is the pressure it puts on the idea of unity and on the literary means of expressing that idea. As Robert Louis Wilken says, "In the Old Testament the term *Father* appears only occasionally as a term for God, but in the New Testament it is used by Jesus more than 170 times."[7] The New Testament constantly uses symbols and visual images to *unify* diverse entities. We are invited not only to picture God, in this intimate way, as our father but also to see ourselves as members of his united family. The Christian church is represented as a band of brothers, as a human body, and as a building, a structure of diverse materials miraculously organized by his Spirit and his Son.

Paradox, the joining of apparently contradictory ideas, is one of the New Testament's favorite means of unifying what would otherwise seem separate. We see the joining of apparently contradictory conceptions in Christianity's great historical paradox, the idea that the child born in Bethlehem was at once the Son of God and the son of Mary; and in Christianity's great metaphysical paradox, the idea that Christ is both "with God" and "God" (John 1:1). These paradoxes are complemented by others. The gospel of John teaches that Jesus is "in" the Father, but the Father is also "in" him; and his followers ought always to be "in" him, too (John 14:11, 15:4). Paul pictures the followers of Christ, by virtue of their relationship to him, as "having nothing, and yet possessing all things," as "unknown, and yet well known; as dying, and, behold, we live" (2 Corinthians 6:9–10). Those who are "in Christ" can "glory" even in their "infirmities" (2 Corinthians 12:2, 5). Some New Testament paradoxes are readily resolvable, and some are not; but the effort to grasp their meaning is always part of the Christian intellectual journey, a way of understanding that "the foolishness of God is wiser than men" (1 Corinthians 1:25). Paradox draws readers in, invites them to explore the complexities of thought that lie behind it. It is also a way of making sure that the New Testament's human stories do not fall out of unity with the story of the God "in" whom "we live, and move, and have our being" (Acts 17:28).

For humans, as we have seen, unity with God requires a "change" or "exchange" of one thing for another. We are told that Jesus gave his life as a "ransom" in exchange for people kidnapped by sin; he "redeemed" humanity like someone paying off another person's debt; he transformed himself, being "made a curse" on our behalf (Mark 10:45, Ephesians 1:7–14, Galatians 3:13). Paul describes the way in which Christians participate in the process of change that accomplishes their reconciliation with God:

> Know ye not, that so many of us as were baptized into Jesus Christ were baptized into his death? Therefore we are buried with him by baptism into death: that like as Christ was raised up from the dead by the glory of the father, even so we should also walk in newness of life. (Romans 6:3–4)

The concept of reconciliation with God will always be challenging, but literary images and accounts of *transformation* help to elucidate it. They are visible signs that eternity is working in the world of time. The gospel of John identifies Jesus's first miracle as the transformation of water into wine (John 2). The book of Acts describes the way in which Saul, the persecutor of the church, is transformed into Paul, its foremost proponent (Acts 9,

13).[8] Finally, Revelation pictures the time when creation itself will be transformed into "a new heaven and a new earth" (Revelation 21:1).

On the personal level, transformation is what it was for Paul—the result of *conversion* to faith in Jesus. From the New Testament perspective, this is the central episode of the spiritual journey. For Christians it continues to be a very literary moment, the moment when one accepts the New Testament stories as one's own. Often it is accompanied by a transformed view of some particular passage in the Bible. Augustine, the most important of the early church philosophers, was educated in Christian theology but did not achieve conversion until, in a moment of spiritual agony in the garden of the house where he was staying, he heard the child's voice chanting, "Take it and read!"[9] He followed the suggestion, opened the epistles of Paul, and was converted. In the New Testament itself, the first conversions in the early church are inspired by Peter's citation of key passages from the Old Testament and his incorporation of their meanings into the story of Christ (Acts 2). The church finds its first politically important convert when the disciple Philip crosses the path of an Ethiopian official who is riding in his chariot, reading a passage from the prophet Isaiah. Philip asks whether he understands what he is reading. No, the man says, and Philip interprets the passage for him as a prophecy of Jesus. The official converts and is baptized and goes "on his way rejoicing," his life suddenly changed by a discussion of scripture (Acts 8:26–39).

The proper accompaniment of a transformed view of a Bible story is a transformation of the self, such as the Ethiopian official achieved. Ordinarily the transformation is from gloom or bewilderment, as in his case, to the joy or "glory" that promises more glories to come. In this way, the believer's story comes to resemble the story of the Lord whom he or she is following: "Like as Christ was raised up from the dead by the glory of the father . . ." Paul compares the Christian's progress to the reproduction of an image seen in a mirror, thus emphasizing the power of likenesses, visual or verbal, to transform those who take them to heart:

> [W]e all, with open face beholding as in a glass the glory of the Lord, are changed into the same image from glory to glory, even as by the Spirit of the Lord. (2 Corinthians 3:18)[10]

Transformation, unification, and paradox all herald the convergence of God and humanity. But the other side of the story also needs to be told. There could be no at-one-ment if the original unity had not been broken. The differences between God and humanity, and the differences among humans themselves, appear very clearly in the New Testament's frequent emphasis on *separation* or *division*, especially divisions among persons or things that one would expect to be closely connected.

The great separation is between God and his children. Humanity has left God, its father, and needs to come home. That is the gospel message. Yet the message itself can lead to further divisions, as people decide to accept or reject its uncompromising terms. Jesus said,

> I came not to send peace, but a sword. For I am come to set a man at variance against his father, and the daughter against her mother, and the daughter in law against her mother in law. (Matthew 10:34–35)

Christianity is often, to use the contemporary American idiom, a "divisive" issue. And with its coming, divisions open in the soul as well as society. Faith contests with doubt, and one part of the self stands in judgment of the spiritual condition of the other.

The self in the New Testament is chronically a divided, disputed self. From the point of view of the New Testament writers, that is not necessarily bad; it may be a means of transformation. In any event, religious and psychological divisions, and the many kinds of literary *distinctions* that bear them out, are an important part of the New Testament DNA. Christian literature tends to set one thing "at variance" with another, making distinctions even when they do not appear necessary. The gospel of Luke might simply have reported Jesus's words to Mary of Bethany, telling her what a good thing she did when she dropped her daily work to sit at his feet and listen to his teachings; instead, the story emphasizes the distinction between Mary and her sister Martha, who, though a sibling and a fellow disciple, is busy doing housework instead of listening to the Master (Luke 10:38–42). It's significant that Martha is not performing some routine task; she's working hard to make Jesus comfortable in her home. That could well be considered a spiritual concern—which is the point of mentioning it in the story. Mundane concerns can easily be mistaken for spiritual ones; readers must be encouraged to make distinctions between matters that, on the surface, seem very much alike.

Insides and Outsides

One interesting thing about the Mary-Martha story is that Martha *reproves* Mary for neglecting her housework, and Jesus for allowing her to do so. She thus suggests, unconsciously, that she may not have such kind intentions as she appears to have. New Testament distinctions draw attention to the fact that the insides of people and events are often very different from the outsides, and to the idea that the insides are much more important. The Mary-Martha distinction is one example of the New Testament's constant interest in the *priority of the inside to the outside.* In the words of the first epistle of Peter, it is the things associated with "the hidden man of the heart" that are "in the sight of God of great price" (1 Peter 3:4). This idea shapes the perspectives of Christian literature and generates many of its devices of *reversal* and *irony* (a pointed reversal of normal understandings or expectations). Jesus often uses these literary strategies. They respond to his insight that the journey of life is different from what most people assume it is, and that the significant things in life are those that, for good or ill, are hidden from human sight:

> "Whosoever will save his life shall lose it: and whosoever will lose his life for my sake shall find it. For what is a man profited, if he shall gain the whole world, and lose his own soul?" (Matthew 16:25–26)

> "There are last which shall be first, and there are first which shall be last." (Luke 13:30)

> "Beware of false prophets, which come to you in sheep's clothing, but inwardly they are ravening wolves." (Matthew 7:15)

> "When thou prayest, enter into thy closet, and when thou hast shut thy door, pray to thy Father which is in secret; and thy Father which seeth in secret shall reward thee openly." (Matthew 6:6)

Reversals of insides and outsides are typical of Christian literature throughout its history. The Old Testament account of Adam and Eve's expulsion from Eden suggests no very optimistic view of their future lives, but in *Paradise Lost* (1667), John Milton's Christian epic, Adam is told that if he possesses faith, patience, temperance, and love, he will not be "loath / To leave" the outward, visible paradise of Eden. Why? Because "thou . . . shalt possess / A paradise within thee, happier far."[11] Who would have guessed that the loss of Eden could lead to increased happiness? But the story of the "hidden man of the heart" can be—and usually is, in Christian literature—dramatically different from the story of the outer man.

That means that the hidden man may fare far better, or far worse, than the outward and visible one. Jesus's most blistering judgments are directed against religious leaders whom he calls "whited sepulchres." They "appear beautiful" on the outside "but are within full of dead men's bones" (Matthew 23:27). Religious institutions also have an inside and an outside, and as the book of Revelation shows, it's important to distinguish the first from the second. Revelation opens with seven letters to Christian churches, letters that give sevenfold emphasis to the idea that Jesus is "he which searcheth the reins [emotions] and hearts." In the letters, Jesus makes it clear that Christians who consider themselves "rich, and increased with goods" are actually "poor, and blind, and naked" and that they desperately need to "repent" of being that way (Revelation 2:23, 3:17–19). Churches that change will be united with him; churches that refuse will be divided away.

Partly because of the Bible's influence on our culture, we are used to the idea that the inside is more significant than the outside. Few modern parents tell their children, "It's fine to be a hypocrite; what people see on the surface is the only thing that counts." Few respond to their children's dilemmas about whom to marry or what career to choose by advising them that it makes no difference how you feel, so long as you have a respectable role in society. Many parents would probably be inclined to say such things, but our cultural assumptions are all against them. Yet the Christians who are criticized in Revelation undoubtedly held the same assumptions. They were undoubtedly familiar with Jesus's condemnations of the hypocrite's trust in appearances. Evidently, however, they were not used to "searching" their own "reins and hearts." In the passage just cited, Jesus says,

> Behold, I stand at the door, and knock: if any man hear my voice, and open the door, I will come in to him, and will sup with him, and he with me. (Revelation 3:20)

An encouraging message—but it may have come as a surprise. Its recipients probably assumed that Jesus was already "inside" their doors, communing with them, simply because they were outwardly and officially Christian. They needed to be told that their "door" wasn't even "open."

It often takes irony to wake people up, especially if their scale of values has become reversed without their knowing it. They need to see that what they regard as enormously important is in fact ridiculously unimportant. They need to understand not just the priority of the inside to the outside but also the *priority of the "lower" to the "higher."* As Paul told the church at Corinth, God "called" few people who were "mighty" or "wise" or "noble," by the world's scale of values. Instead, he chose people who were "foolish" and "weak" and "base," so he could "confound" those who were "wise" according to "the flesh" (1 Corinthians 1:26–27). Once more, the literary effect is that of *reversal* and *irony*, with a *change of perspective* that encourages the reader to look "downward" and "inward" instead of "upward" and "outward."

But if it is so vital, from a Christian point of view, to see beneath the surface of things, what means do we have of doing it? That is a general problem of human life, one we confront every time we want to discover what other people are "really like," "deep inside." Our usual approach (although we may not use these words for it) is to look for *symbols*. We notice what clothes people wear, what gestures they make, what objects they have in their homes. We treat these things as clues and signs, as symbolic indications of our acquaintances' inner worlds. We also look for symbols when we try to express our conclusions about people. We say, "She has a heart of gold," or, "I've discovered that he's actually a very small person." We don't mean that her heart is literally made of metal or that he is only three feet tall; we are creating symbolic images to describe realities that aren't literally visible.

And symbols, as I've said, are even more important when one tries to represent a state of being that transcends the merely human. The New Testament never attempts to analyze Jesus's presence in the soul and the enjoyment that the soul has of him. Instead, it creates a visual image; it says that he is *like* a loving shepherd, or a bridegroom, or a friend who knocks at the door, then enters and shares a meal. These are characteristic examples of New Testament symbolism, which is a natural expression of Christianity's emphasis on inner, spiritual, and often hidden realities. They remind us that the New Testament always sees God and Christ as persons, and persons are never directly and completely knowable. As Martin Luther King said, "There is and always will be a penumbra of mystery surrounding God."[12] Symbolism helps us to visualize—literally to *see*—how much can still be known, despite the mystery.

There is nothing daunting, in principle, about this necessary device of symbolism, although the richness and variety of New Testament symbols is truly formidable. They range from the small but precise details of speech and action that reveal the personalities of the people we meet in Acts and the gospels, to the symbolic stories or "parables" that Jesus tells, to the vast, mysterious pictures of the book of Revelation. But even the grandest apocalyptic symbolism can repeat the themes of the "easiest" gospel stories, and the symbolism of one of those stories can suggest as many hidden meanings as a chapter of the Apocalypse itself. *Revelation*, in the fundamental sense of that word, can happen anywhere in the New Testament. The Greek word for "revelation," "apocalypse," literally signifies an "uncovering" of what was hidden or otherwise unknown. In this connection, all the New Testament uncoverings of Jesus's identity as Messiah, Lord, Son of Man, and Son of God are "apocalyptic"; and so is much else in the New Testament and Christian literature.

Scriptural revelations have a literary as well as a doctrinal component: the reader is expected to be concerned both with the truth being uncovered and with the literary means of uncovering it—with, for instance, the use and interpretation of *symbols*. The New Testament not only uses symbols but also dramatizes the process of interpreting them. In that process, as in most other aspects of Christian experience, knowing something about literature is important. When, in the gospels, Jesus refers to himself as the Son of Man, he is using a symbol from an earlier work of literature, the Old Testament book of Daniel (Daniel 7:13–14); and readers need to know that, if they want to understand what he means. The various ways in which his original audience responded to his stories and sayings show how difficult it can be to understand him if one lacks the literary ability to recognize symbolism and interpret it appropriately. The New Testament demonstrates its own literary power by the variety of revelations it includes, each of them requiring a specific kinds of literary skill to interpret: revelation by discourse and argument, revelation by symbol and allusion ("Son of Man"); revelation by symbolic story (Jesus's parables); revelation by the statements of witnesses ("thou art the Christ, the Son of the living God" [Matthew 16:16]); revelation by action, as in Jesus's resurrection of Lazarus, which proclaims his own identity as the Lord of life and death (John 11).

In the New Testament, as in the Old, the most specialized means of "uncovering" is *prophecy* and its associated "visions." These flourished so mightily in the early church that Paul had to advise the congregation at Corinth not to overdo prophetic discourse (1 Corinthians 14). They are part of the New Testament's narrative of first-century events, but they are also one of its ways of showing what lies beyond all literal events. They include the great complex of visions related at large in the book of Revelation and, at the other end of the spectrum, the short, sharp vision that provokes Stephen's martyrdom in the book of Acts: "Behold, I see the heavens opened, and the Son of man standing on the right hand of God" (Acts 7:56). Stephen's vision is brief and intense, yet it is a repetition of two other revelations—Jesus's disclosure that he is the Son of Man, and Daniel's much earlier vision of the Son of Man. Further, Stephen's prophetic vision is introduced by his reference to the many prophets who were persecuted in the past and whose lives were known from literary sources (Acts 7:52–53). As is often the case, broad literary knowledge is essential to the reader's appreciation of a particular moment of New Testament story.

Stephen's vision of "the heavens opened, and the Son of man standing on the right hand of God" shows that prophecy is not simply the uncovering of the future. Its other function, less noticed by modern people, is the uncovering of the realities of the present. Although only Stephen sees the Son of Man, the Son of Man is really there, standing in the here and now. In the

Old Testament book of Samuel, the prophet Nathan forecasts the future (this is our ordinary sense of the prophet's job), but he is just as prophetic, in the biblical sense, when he visits King David, tells him a parable about a sinful man, hears his expressions of moral outrage, then announces, "*Thou* art the man" (2 Samuel 7:4–17, 12:1–7). Nathan uncovers what David really is, at this present moment. Bible-based communities continue to respect this understanding of prophecy as an intense revelation of what exists at present. Such an understanding inspired the work of William Blake and Martin Luther King, modern Christian authors who were, in many other respects, as different from one another as any two authors could be. Its basis is the idea that there are meanings inside the events we see, meanings that individuals with a commanding gift of words and an understanding of preceding acts of prophecy are appointed to reveal.

Uniqueness and Repetition

Christianity has been analyzed so frequently as a social and intellectual phenomenon that it is important to stress that the New Testament's stories are largely concerned with individuals, not with philosophical ideas or social concepts. For the New Testament writers, Jesus is not a diffuse God-power or the expression of a people's religious and social aspirations; he is a unique individual. All the New Testament's significant figures are portrayed as individuals, often as curious and eccentric ones; and conversion, like salvation, is presented as an individual matter. *Individualism*—a respect for the individual life and a commitment to studying it—is a major emphasis of Christian literature. It is much more important than it was even in the prophetic literature of the Old Testament, where the individuality of the prophets and heroes is always framed and sometimes overshadowed by the great story of God's relationship with Israel as a people. Individualism expresses itself in many ways in Christian literature; it does so with special clarity in *conversion* and *transformation* narratives, in the *distinctions* that are constantly being drawn among people who would otherwise appear similar or identical, and in the *irony* of a universal God who cherishes such individual distinctions.

In *The Screwtape Letters*, C.S. Lewis, the twentieth century's most popular intellectual advocate of Christianity, describes

God's attitude toward humanity. Lewis, who relished irony; calls on one of Satan's servants to deliver the description. God "really likes the little vermin," the demon says, "and sets an absurd value on the distinctness of every one of them."[13] He's right; that is exactly what the New Testament reports (minus the word "vermin"). To be sure, the New Testament's interest in individuals should not be equated with the individualism of the modern West, which often has no moral content or religious orientation. Christianity clearly influenced modern assumptions about the dignity of the individual, but its own individualism is a harder and tougher variety. It has asserted itself, in one way or another, even in Christendom's most authoritarian regimes.[14] It's hard for Christian literature to avoid some degree of individualism, connected as this is to other Christian concepts—the idea of a providential God, personally interested in his creatures; the idea that the hidden things of the self are more important than its socially defined roles; the idea of personal conversion and transformation; and the idea, central to Christian writing, that everyone should be capable of reading God's word and sharing the experience of Christ as his disciple.

The New Testament's emphasis on *discipleship*, the Christian's ability to "walk" with Jesus "in newness of life," balances and complements its emphasis on individualism (Romans 6:3–4). Jesus is the great individual whose "history or story" other individuals can use to define their own.[15] The gospels represent Jesus's life as a journey on which he calls others to follow him, despite the certainty of conflicts with the world around them. "Whosoever doth not bear his cross, and come after me," he says, "cannot be my disciple" (Luke 14:27). The book of Revelation shows the glorious end of the story: Christ and his disciples, crowned in heaven (Revelation 4:4, 14:14). The journey has an inner as well as an outer dimension. To follow Christ, one must be like him on the inside. "Let this mind be in you," Paul says, "which was also in Christ Jesus" (Philippians 2:5).

This focus on the imitation of Christ is a crucially important key to understanding how the New Testament literature differs from the scriptures that preceded it. The Old Testament teaches many of the same things as the New Testament, starting with the concept of a providential God; and it uses many of the same literary devices. Ultimately, however, it is the New Testament's focus on the figure of Christ that unites its ideas and devices into its special set of patterns. The idea of following God's providential guidance is present throughout the Old Testament; the idea of following Jesus, the Son of Man "in" whom we see God and unite ourselves with him, gives a peculiarly New Testament edge to the concept, associating it with the New Testament's unusually rigorous ironies and paradoxes, with its insistence on the revelation of new truths and unexpected possibilities of progress, and with its dramatic demand that individuals be converted and assimilate into their own lives the paradoxes and reversals of values that attend discipleship to Christ.[16] Because Christianity places such a strong emphasis on individual acceptance of an ensemble of supremely challenging ideas, the New Testament never retires from the intellectual battlefield. Unlike the Old Testament, it keeps reiterating a self-conscious demand for belief in its central figure and the central narrative of his life and work. The Old Testament often takes belief in its central history for granted; the New Testament does not.

The literary expression of discipleship (which is the constant re-enactment of Christ's story by his followers) is constant reminder and *repetition*. The story of Jesus is repeated in the fourfold gospel, in the many speeches about him in the book of Acts, at special moments in the epistles, and in symbolic form in the book of Revelation. One of Paul's methods is to tell and retell the story of his own following of Christ, recommending it as an example for his readers to follow. No significant Christian teaching is established by one passage only. The New Testament offers, besides, a frequent repetition of Old Testament teachings, prophecies, and providential narratives— repetitions of the literature on which Jesus and his earliest disciples relied. A common New Testament method is to circle around a favorite theme, returning to it many times, so it can be viewed from many perspectives. The book of Revelation is especially fond of saying the same thing in many ways, exemplifying the church's opposition to the world in a variety of stories and availing itself (like Paul's epistles) of every opportunity to indulge in the splendor of lists.[17]

Strictly speaking, Christianity does not *need* to have its messages ceaselessly reiterated. One time may be enough, as in the case of people who, like the Ethiopian official, are converted after only one hearing of the word. But conversion is not the end of the Christian life. The practice of Christianity is supposed to be continuous, and continuous reminders are not out of place. A popular hymn of the nineteenth century frankly admits the reason why "the Old, Old Story" needs to be repeated so often. It is because Christians easily lose the intensity of the experience:

> Tell me the Story often,
> For I forget so soon;
> The "early dew" of morning
> Has passed away at noon.[18]

Whenever part of the old, old story is repeated, the rest is prepared to follow—and the DNA of the New Testament reproduces itself again.

Curiously, this tends to happen in anti-Christian as well as Christian writing. One can write a novel or a poem from a *non*-religious or a *non*-Christian perspective—one can even write a work that incidentally criticizes Christianity—and easily keep from involving oneself with the New Testament's DNA. Yet it is apparently very hard to write a work of literature that has a positively anti-Christian theme without becoming attached to Christian ways of doing things. A recent novel takes as its protagonist a man who is writing an attack on Christianity. He argues with a friend, forcefully declaring that for him, the Christian God "doesn't exist." But the friend, who has his own doubts about religion, sees a problem: "He palpably does exist for you . . . because you can't stop talking about 'God'."[19] Christianity itself has always been a talkative, argumentative faith, if only because it is a *faith*, not just a set of external customs, and demands a final decision about belief. Christianity argues, and provokes arguments, urging that the arguments end in decisions and actions—ideally, in acts of conversion and discipleship. Those who argue against Christianity tend to respond to its demand for a Yes or No with a similarly argumentative demand of their own. So, in the novel in question, when someone shows up who is willing simply to state the reasons for belief and the reasons for unbelief, without committing himself to either side, the protagonist's reaction is, "But that won't do, in the end, will it? We have to *decide*."[20]

That is the voice of Christianity—a religion that insists on individual choice and internal commitment, a religion that looks to "the end" of the intellectual journey. Anti-Christian literature is ordinarily just as preoccupied as Christian literature with the revelation of hidden truths, the priority of insides to outsides, and the experience of conversion, transformation, and alteration of normal perspectives that people experience as they proceed on spiritually significant journeys. Anti-Christian literature appropriates Christian symbols and story forms and reverses their values, exploiting the irony of its relationship to Christianity. In short, it exploits the New Testament DNA for its own purposes. Often, it does the best it can to bring Jesus over to its own side, reworking his story to express its own arguments and making his teachings stand in judgment against Christianity itself.

Just as anti-Christian literature tends to assume the patterns of Christian literature, so masterpieces of Christian literature have been written by men and women who were not themselves fully Christian, but who knew how to work with Christianity's DNA. Paul was perhaps the first person to notice that people can use Christian ideas and literary practices, such as the preaching of the gospel, and use them well, without being complete Christians themselves (Philippians 1:15–18). As readers, we rightly require that literature be authentic, that it treat ideas and experiences honestly; but we do not require proof that authors believe, consistently and without reservation, in all the ideas they use. If we did, we could have no respect for Shakespeare, whose personal beliefs are notoriously difficult to determine. In like manner, we reserve the right to criticize even the greatest heroes of faith if their literary works fail to project Christian ideas effectively.

Here is the problem of Christian literature. If the Christian story becomes mere pious repetition, it fails as literature, on its own terms. It is the old, old story, but it is no longer an effective story. Jesus told many parables with similar themes, but he did not tell precisely the same parable over and over again. Paul allowed his letters to be read by more than one church (Colossians 4:16), but he did not simply write a single letter and send it to every group of Christians who asked his advice; he made each letter authentic in its own right and in its own situation. All human beings have the same *kind* of DNA, but individual variations are necessary to make us authentically human. All violins have the same number of strings; it's what you do with them that makes the music good or bad.

The Completed Journey

This book is concerned with Christian literature that succeeds, and with what makes it succeed. In the chapters that follow, I will try to show how that happens, and what the presence of the New Testament DNA has to do with it. I think that the subject is best developed by drawing attention to many very specific examples of Christian authors' use of that DNA. Yet merely to identify those elements, again and again, would be far too repetitive; and it would not give an adequate account of the creative variations that renew the life of Christian literature. Indeed, it would be impossible even to mention every expression of every element of the New Testament DNA that appears in the works or passages I discuss. There are far too many of these expressions. But I won't need to mention them all. Readers will have no difficulty seeing "discipleship" in certain passages in which I emphasize "conversion," or seeing "providence" in certain works in which I emphasize the picture of life as a "journey" guided by God.

At times, however, I will want to show in detail how all the elements come together to shape a single literary text; and this may be a good time to offer an example. One of the best is Jesus's parable of the Prodigal Son (Luke 15). I have already used this story to illustrate some particular features of the New Testament DNA. More significantly, the story shows what can result when a superb literary artist brings those features together.

The story is one of the best-known episodes in the Bible. Most people recall it as a lesson about repentance from sin. Correct—but the story is much more than that. It begins with a young man asking his father for an early payment of his inheritance. He gets it, then leaves home and spends his wealth on sinful entertainment. When the money runs out, he repents, returns to his father, and receives forgiveness. So far, we have a typically Christian *story* about a *journey* that includes *progress* and a *change of perspective*. But the significance of the story increases greatly when one recognizes it as *symbolic* of *recon-*

ciliation between God and humanity. The Father is not content to wait until humanity returns to him; he takes action to bring his children home. That is the point Jesus makes when he says that when the prodigal was still far away, his father "ran, and fell on his neck, and kissed him." God in his *providence* runs to meet the needs of humanity. There could be no finer symbol of *division* and *unity*, of people first *separated* from God, then united with him, than the picture of the father seeing his son at a distance and running happily to meet him.

Not everyone notices that the story contains a journey by the father as well as a journey by the son. People are more likely to notice this when they consider the story from a literary point of view and see that it could have been told in another way. The father could have been represented as waiting passively for his child to do everything himself. But that would have made it more a story of humanity than a *unifying* account of God's relationship to humanity. And God might not have been represented as a father at all; he might have been portrayed as a judge who cares very much about justice and righteousness but very little about the lives of *individual* people. But that is not the kind of story that the DNA of the New Testament produces.

That fact becomes still more noticeable when one thinks about the story's literary setting. The Prodigal Son is the culmination of three stories that Jesus tells in response to the complaints of other religious teachers, people who murmur against him for talking and even eating with sinners and tax collectors. His first story describes the natural reaction of a man who has lost a sheep. The man goes to find it and calls his friends to celebrate when he succeeds. The individual sheep is that important to him, even though he has ninety-nine others, which did not wander off. Jesus's second story describes the natural reaction of a woman who has lost a coin. It is only one coin, but she goes after it, sweeping her house "diligently" until she discovers it, then celebrates with her friends. "Likewise," Jesus says in comment on his stories, there is joy in heaven over God's seeking and finding "one sinner that repenteth"—"more" joy than there is over all the "just persons" who do not need to repent.

Put in this way, the message seems *paradoxical*; but Jesus is working to change his audience's *perspective*, leading us to see that the seeming paradox may be perfectly "natural" for God. He also suggests a new perspective on his own relations with sinners: he is seeking them, just as anyone seeks for something valuable that has been lost. By replying to objections with a pair of *symbolic* stories, each of which conveys his message in its own way, he has drawn attention to the literary skills we use when we interpret symbols, recognize parallels, *unify* things that seem different from one another. Attentive members of the audience may already see that they can learn more about God if they look more closely at the literary methods that are used to teach about him.

Some degree of literary perceptiveness is certainly helpful in appreciating the final story, that of the Prodigal Son. Jesus might have demonstrated the prodigal's alienation from his father by simply saying that the son took the money and started spending it as he wished. Instead, Jesus shows humanity's degree of detachment from God by having the prodigal "journey into a far country." This *journey*, like many others in the New Testament, is accompanied by *reversals* of values, emphasized with the help of *irony*. The young man's pride and pleasure turns into something exactly the opposite—abject humiliation. Instead of feasting, he is reduced to wishing that he could feed on "the husks that the swine did eat." He concludes that he can survive only if he journeys back to his father and begs to be received as one of his "hired servants." This is an irony of *individualism*: the prodigal claimed the right to make his own decisions; now, it seems, he is sinking into the crowd of people who are dependent on someone else's good will.

But the irony also cuts in a hopeful direction. Jesus says that at the prodigal's great moment of decision, when he recognizes his need for his father, "he came to himself." There is something precious about the individual self, after all. The self is an important thing to "come to." At least that is true about one version of the self. "*He* came to *himself*" suggests that there is more than one version, and that the prodigal is now recovering the true one.[21] His dramatic reversal from "higher" to "lower" is followed by a typically Christian *reversal* in which he discovers that the "*lower*" is better than the "*higher*," the *inner* has priority to the *outer*. In his shame, the prodigal looks inside, discovers something more important in "himself" than his lust for pleasure, and decides to humble himself and go home. This is a moment of *revelation* and *conversion*, and it is accompanied by a *change of perspective* and a *transformation* of circumstances. The repentant prodigal is rewarded, not punished; the father whom he spurned runs to welcome him home; his journey returns to its beginning, but returns on an incomparably higher level of understanding and feeling.

We also need to return, and take another look at the beginning of Jesus's discourse. Again, the Prodigal Son is one of a series of stories, all responding to the question suggested at the start, How should we deal with sinners? Jesus's answer is now clear: *Repeat* God's example—help them, find them, run to meet them. So the prodigal's story is an implicit command to *discipleship*. But the importance of the command appears most clearly in the second half of the story, the part that virtually no one remembers.

This second part has to do with the prodigal's brother, the "good" son who stayed at home while the prodigal went forth and "wasted his substance with riotous living." It is an *ironic repetition* of the first part, ironic because it repeats the first part, pointedly, but in an opposite way, showing what happens when the father's example is *not* repeated. When the good son sees his father celebrating the prodigal's return, his mind fills with envy. I served you many years, he says, and you never celebrated my work; but as soon as my delinquent brother came home, you "killed for him the fatted calf." The good son refuses to join the celebration: "he was angry, and would not go in."

By choosing brothers as his examples of opposing courses of action, Jesus re-emphasizes the importance of the *individual* and the importance of making *distinctions* among individuals who are superficially similar. But this is not exactly the story of Mary and Martha, one of whom chooses a better course than the other. This is the story of siblings who are *divided* from each other, and from their father, because they have both taken spiritual journeys in the wrong direction, each in his own way. Ironically, it is their wrongness that *unites* them. The good son is no more God's disciple than the bad son was; he just has his own way of refusing to be one. True, the good son never departs for any distant countries or commits any obvious sins; but as usual in the New Testament, what happens on the *inside* is more important than what happens on the *outside*. The good son's anger shows the spiritual distance he has traveled from his home. He has grown too "good" even for his father. While the father is *transforming* evil into good, the son is transforming good into evil. He claims that he has always been about his father's business, but he's doing nothing at the moment except skulking and pouting—a vivid picture of a person who is not *united* with his father at all.

One sees more of the parable's meaning when one asks the literary question, Why does Jesus end with the "good" brother, ironically reserving the climax of the Prodigal Son for the son who is not a prodigal? As with many Bible texts, the key to the ending can be found by going back, again and again, to the beginning. Jesus's sequence of stories started with his critics' questions about his dealings with sinners. The story of the bad son provided a sufficient answer: Jesus is repeating the example of the Father, seeking sinners so that they can be forgiven and reconciled. But now he takes the next step, rounding on his critics with the story of the good son, which is a symbolic *revelation* of their own motives, their reasons for asking questions to begin with. They believe that they are God's disciples, just as the good son believes that he is working faithfully for his father. Some sins, however, are not so obvious as those of the prodigal son. The sin of self-righteousness can be detected only by looking for outward *symbols* of people's inward states, and interpreting those symbols accurately and fearlessly. The symbolic evidence of sinfulness is the refusal—both of the good son and of Jesus's antagonists—to journey toward the lost or rejoice in their reclamation.

Jesus's *prophetic* uncovering of motives shows that the critics who worry so much about sinfulness are actually worrying about themselves. They are "good" people like the "good" son, and they are being answered as prophets typically answer such people, with a symbolic story about themselves and their real spiritual condition: "Thou art the man!" The story of the good son provides as strong a climax as Nathan's words to David, and it takes the same literary form, a *reversal* in status of the *"lower"* (here, the overt though repentant sinner) and the *"higher"* (the covertly sinful advocates of morality).

Now that we have read the story repeatedly and noticed the parallel between Jesus's critics and the good son—and ourselves, if we consider ourselves good—we can see precisely what God's attitude toward such "good" people is. They are criticized, but they are not cast off. Just as the father ran to meet the prodigal son, so now he hastens to meet the self-righteous son and "intreat him" with reasons, assurances, and reminders: "Son, thou art ever with me . . . ." The story of the "good" son turns into yet another *repetition* of the story of God's seeking something that is lost: the lost sheep, the lost coin, the prodigal son, and at last the self-righteous son. The same attention is offered to all—and this, if we are still following the literary parallels, includes even the critics of Christ, the people whom he is seeking, even now, by the apparently simple, merely literary act of telling a *story*.

How will the good people respond? Will they continue to pout and whine, or will they repeat the story of the prodigal in their own lives, repenting and seeking reconciliation with the Father? That question is never answered. The episode ends without showing the reaction either of the good son or of Jesus's critics. Jesus, the expert story-teller, knows when to stop. Certain modern authors are famous for refusing to "resolve" their stories; Jesus can use the same method, when it works with his other methods. He says what he means to say; the rest depends on the individual responses of his listeners. If they are good enough interpreters of his literary devices, they will view the story of sin and reconciliation from a new *perspective*, and apply the lesson to themselves. And that will be the final literary *transformation*, the change of the audience from critics of others into critics of themselves.

What we see in the story of the prodigal son is what we see throughout Christian literature. The DNA, the generative and reproductive essence of this literature, is more than a list of doctrines or literary devices. It is a pattern that individual writers and readers can make their own. It is like the keys and stops of a great organ, an instrument that is perpetually ready to be brought to life by the composer's art and the performer's insight.

To understand Christian literature, of course, one cannot simply read a few passages here and there, or rely on a summary. One must go back to the beginning and read the New Testament books themselves, as one would read any work of literature. Most people start with the gospels.

3
The Gospel of Luke

Luke is the longest of the three synoptic gospels; of the three, it offers the greatest variety of material and the greatest literary complexity. If a person were to read only one synoptic gospel, Luke would probably give the best impression of the scope and interest of such a work.

The first verses provide an excellent idea of what a gospel is. Their theme is the importance of history to the Christian church. The author addresses his gospel to a reader, Theophilus, who appears to be interested in determining whether the ideas taught in the church are historically true. Luke says he is writing so that Theophilus can "know the certainty of those things, wherein thou hast been instructed." He recognizes that many accounts of Jesus are already in circulation—referring, very likely, to such works as the gospel of Mark and the Q document(s), on which much of his own gospel is based. He does not disparage these accounts, but he believes it is time for him "to set forth in order" a statement of the facts conveyed by "eyewitnesses, and ministers of the word" (Luke 1:1–4). To put this in a more modern way, Luke has conducted research that he believes can confirm the truth of the Christian story. "Gospel" means "good news," but in order for news to be good, it has to be true.

The writer of the gospel of Luke also identifies himself as the writer of the Acts of the Apostles, a second book addressed to Theophilus—Volume 2 in a historical narrative that begins before the birth of Jesus and ends with the development of his church. Acts includes an additional self-identification of its author. In Chapter 16, where he is discussing one of Paul's missionary journeys, he begins speaking of "we" as well as "he," indicating that he was a companion of the apostle. Early Christian sources are certain that this author was Paul's friend Luke. Paul, writing to the church at Colossae, classes Luke with his non-Jewish friends and calls him "the beloved physician" (Colossians 4:14).

In the early days of Christianity, it must have been easier for Jews than for gentiles to understand the claim that Jesus was the messiah or "appointed one" whom God sent to do his will in fulfillment of Jewish prophecy. As a gentile, Luke may have been especially curious about the evidence for this claim; and as a physician, he may have been especially impressed by the value of setting facts "in order." He is one of two gospel writers (Matthew is the other) who present a genealogy of Jesus. He is the only one who attempts to identify the year when Jesus was born and the year when his prophetic predecessor, his cousin John the Baptist, began his ministry (Luke 2:1–2, 3:1–3).

Luke is determined that everything in his gospel should be true, but he does not imply that everything should be fully explicable. He has too much respect for the evidence to insist on that. He reports, for instance, that Jesus once said to a disciple, "He that is not against us is for us"; but two chapters later, he records Jesus as saying something different: "He that is not with me is against me, and he that gathereth not with me scattereth" (Luke 9:50, 11:23). If we knew more about the contexts of these sayings, we might find them perfectly reconcilable, but they appear contradictory.[1] A writer with less concern for truth would simply omit one of them. Luke includes them both, without comment. This is important. Any policeman will tell you that two witnesses who give identical accounts are probably not both telling the truth; some variations are expected, and not all of them may be readily explicable. Luke appears to realize that, too. He is reluctant to meddle with his "witnesses" by risking his own speculative explanations or reconciliations of varying testimony.

Indeed, there is a long list of matters on which Luke, along with the other gospel writers, refuses any comment. What did Jesus look like? How many languages did he speak? None of the gospels tells us. With what tone of voice did he say to the foreign woman who sought a miracle of healing, "I am not sent but unto the lost sheep of the house of Israel"? And when she continued to entreat him, with what tone did he reply, "It is not meet [appropriate] to take the children's bread, and to cast it to the dogs" (Matthew 15:22–28)? When she persists, he grants the miracle: "O woman, great is thy faith: be it unto thee even as thou wilt." But in what way did he initially refuse her—"sternly," "testingly," "ironically, with a hint of encouragement"? Was he smiling or frowning? That is not reported. The gospels seldom provide such stage directions, evidently for two reasons: first, the writers do not want to make up facts they do not possess; second, they consider some facts irrelevant to their task, which is to provide "good news," not simply information.

Again, the only "good" news is news that can be believed. And belief, for a gospel writer, must be beyond the assent one gives to an ordinary work of history. In English, the difference is well expressed by the distinction between believing and believing *in*. To believe what someone tells you does not reach as far as believing *in* that person, fully appreciating that person's significance and authority and submitting to his leadership. A gospel writer wants you to believe his story so that you will believe *in* Jesus. Knowing what Jesus looked like has nothing to do with that. Knowing what tone of voice he used can be just as irrelevant. Jesus's true individuality emerges in his teachings and actions, the remarkable things he did, the remarkable demands he made on other individuals, and the remarkable reactions they had to him.

Christ and Character

Luke is especially attentive to the ways in which the reactions of Jesus's audience can be used to emphasize his significance. Narrating the young Jesus's talks with learned men in the temple at Jerusalem, Luke pictures him "sitting in the midst of" them, the focus of attention, while they respond with astonishment "at his understanding and answers" (Luke 2:46–47). Still more effective is the episode in which Jesus journeys to Nazareth to make a public announcement of his mission (Luke 4:16–30). Luke first notes that Nazareth was the place where Jesus "had been brought up." Then he shows, by word and gesture, that Jesus no longer fits in. He enters the synagogue and stands up to read, one young man rising out of the crowd. We see him waiting silently until the scroll of the prophet Isaiah is brought to him; we see him turning to the right place, his *own* place, in the scroll, and reading the self-referential passage—"The Spirit of the Lord God is upon me; because the Lord hath anointed me to preach good tidings" (Isaiah 61:1–2). He closes the book and sits down. Naturally, "the eyes of all them that were in the synagogue [are] fastened on him" when he says, after a dramatic pause, "This day is this scripture fulfilled in your ears."

His listeners do not agree. They are impressed, but they cannot understand Isaiah's words as prophetically symbolic of what they have seen. "Is not this Joseph's son?" they ask. Isn't he just a normal member of a normal family? How is it that he's playing the prophet? But Jesus is much better than they are at interpreting symbolism. For him, the Nazarenes symbolize all those people who have the ironic habit of rejecting any prophet who emerges from among themselves. That is why, as he tells them, prophets in scripture worked miracles for people who were *not* their neighbors. In other words, his listeners (like him) are repeating stories from scripture, but they are unconsciously casting themselves in the least favorable roles. Hearing this, they rise up "full of wrath" and try to kill him, thus confirming the truth of what he has just said to them.

Several great gospel chords have been touched in this scene: the repetition of sacred texts, the providentially conducted journey, the convergence of God with humanity ("the Spirit of the Lord is upon me"), the transformation of an obscure young man into the declared (and rejected) representative of God, the ironies and reversals surrounding this event, the distinction it reveals between people who can, and people who cannot, grasp prophetic symbolism . . . Luke dramatizes it all by throwing Jesus's individualism into high relief, showing him standing fearless and alone amid the uncomprehending citizens of Nazareth.

The incident at Nazareth is followed immediately by another confirmation of his significance. He continues his journey to the synagogue at Capernaum and there expels an "unclean devil" from an afflicted man. The devil, objecting, cries with the man's voice, "I know thee who thou art: the Holy One of God" (Luke 4:34). The irony could hardly be more emphatic: even devils are better than Jesus's fellow countrymen at understanding the meaning of events. Nevertheless, some discerning people can be found—because this is the point at which Jesus begins gathering his circle of disciples.

The first followers are fishermen, James and John and Simon (Peter). When Peter complains about having worked all night without a catch, Jesus tells him where to lower his net, and so many fish come into it that the net breaks. Everyone is "astonished," but then Jesus does something still more astonishing. "From henceforth," he announces, "thou shalt catch men." We are not told whether Peter and his friends understood the meaning of that strange, symbolic phrase, but their actions distinguish them from the passive or hostile onlookers who so often gather in Jesus's vicinity: "they forsook all, and followed him" (Luke 5:1-11). Here is living symbolism. The disciples shed their old, external signs of identity, abandoning their home and occupation like broken nets and finding a new identity in an internal, invisible source, their belief in Jesus and their desire to journey with him. They are the first people to be "caught"—caught, transformed, separated from their old associations and united with the Lord whose journey has converged with theirs.

Virtually all the DNA of Christianity is in these scenes, and it is *in* them, not just applied to their surface as an explanatory comment. From Luke's perspective, no external explanation is required: it's all there in the story, if you are prepared to read the story carefully. And as frequently happens, Luke is the gospel writer most alert to the literary possibilities. It is he, not Matthew or Mark, who includes the miraculous haul of fish and the broken net.

One might think that Jesus's distinctness from all other men would be established simply by his miracles. But that is not the gospel writers' view. Their final emphasis is on Jesus's inner significance, not his externally visible actions. If that emphasis were lacking, even the import of his healings might be lost. When patients leave the hospital, their minds are usually on their recovery, not on the physician who made it possible. The gospels show that this was true of many of the people whom Jesus healed (Luke 17:11–19). In any event, miracles do not speak for themselves; they need to be interpreted. The gospel writers want them to be read as signs of the miracle worker's unique character and his unique position amid humanity, a humanity in turmoil over rival ways of interpreting him. But great narrative skill is required if readers' interpretations are to be guided, not merely dictated, by the scenes they find in the gospels.

Consider the striking episode in which Jesus restores to life the young daughter of the Jewish official Jairus. Mark and Luke, the gospel writers who relate it in the most detail, turn the episode into a vivid illustration of Jesus's relations with humanity (Mark 5:21–43, Luke 8:40–56; see also Matthew 9:18–26). Quietly, steadily, they convey Jesus's stature by his contrast with the surging, clutching, smothering mob around him. Jesus is called to the deathbed of the twelve-year-old girl. To get there, he has to make his way through the crowd. These are men and women who "gladly received him" and are "all waiting for him," but even they are difficult, unruly, obstructive. A woman with a loathsome illness touches him from behind, trying to be healed. Jesus turns in the crush of people, asking who touched him. The woman falls at his feet, announcing a miracle: she is well! Jesus blesses her ("go in peace") and prepares to go on; he is still trying to reach Jairus's house. Then a messenger rushes up. It's no use, he says; the girl is dead. Undeterred, Jesus pursues his journey; but at Jairus's house he is greeted by another mob, a "tumult" of people weeping and wailing over the girl's death. When he contradicts them—"she is not dead, but sleepeth"—they laugh at him. He manages to "put them all out" and at last reaches the bedroom, taking with him only the parents and three of his disciples. There he finds the little girl, lifeless. In the moment of calm he has created, he speaks to her simply and clearly, as one person to another: "Maid, arise." And she rises. One is not surprised that he commands the witnesses not to tell the crowd outside what has happened. The sense of an ignorant, demanding, volatile humanity is overwhelming—or would be, if Jesus were not such a commanding presence.

To such scenes Luke adds others, unique to him. He is the only gospel writer who includes any incident of Jesus's life between his infancy and the beginning of his ministry around age thirty. The incident he uses is Jesus's discourse at age twelve with the wise men of the temple. The episode begins with a family trip to Jerusalem, where Jesus is left behind by people who have other matters to worry about. Like most things that happen in the gospels, this is understandable in ordinary human terms, yet provides a symbolic indication that Jesus transcends those terms. One somehow knows that *he* would never have left anyone behind.

When Mary and Joseph return to look for him and find him in the temple, his separation from his family acquires a definite symbolic value. He responds to his mother's anxious complaint—don't you know we've been looking for you?—with a remark so individual that the audience misses his meaning: "Wist [knew] ye not that I must be about my Father's business?" (Luke 2:41–51). Yet for the discerning reader, this is a revelation and a prophecy. It indicates that Jesus's true father is not of this world; he is God, the Lord of the temple, and the "business" of his son's life will be with spiritual, not material things. It also suggests that to be divided from a visible family is to be united with an invisible one, and that such dividing and uniting will be important to Jesus's mission.

Matthew and Luke both relate Jesus's later declaration that he "came not to send peace, but a sword," to make "division," as Luke has it, even within families, as people divide from one another over the choices they make about uniting or not uniting with him (Matthew 10:34–37, Luke 12:51–53). But only Luke relates the incident in which an enthusiast interrupts Jesus while he is speaking to a crowd. "Blessed is the womb that bare thee," she shouts, "and the paps which thou hast sucked." Jesus does not welcome this kind of enthusiasm. He advises her to say instead, "blessed are they that hear the word of God, and keep it" (Luke 11:27–28). It is the same point made by the episode in the temple—the distinction between the heavenly and the earthly family, with the same emphasis on showing by one's actions what one's true family connections are: keep your Father's word, do your Father's business.

Only Luke offers the story of Mary and Martha, the two sisters with very different characters, one preoccupied with the things of earth, the other with the things of heaven (Luke 10:38–42). Only Luke records the full sequence of symbolic stories about the lost sheep, the lost coin, and the prodigal son, in each of which the thing that was lost is distinguished from everything that might seem similar to it (Luke 15:4–32).[2] Nothing is more uniform than coins, unless it is sheep, or sinners (when seen from a distance). But in each of these stories the seeker remembers and cares for the lost as something individual and uniquely valuable; remember that the prodigal had a brother who was also "lost," but in his own individual way. And it is only Luke who records Jesus's story of the good Samaritan (Luke

10:30–37). The point of this story is not that all Samaritans are good or that all Jews, priests, or Levites are bad. It is that praise or blame attaches to individuals, not to groups.

Luke's appreciation of individuality is a major factor in the "realism" for which his gospel has often been praised. This realism stems from an interest in the everyday lives of individual men and women, without regard to social status or group identification. The chief emphasis, however—here, as in the other gospels—is on the transformation of the everyday, or on the way in which we view the everyday. That woman, sweeping her house at night—she isn't performing a routine chore; she is seeking a lost treasure; she is a symbol of God, looking for a soul that is lost (Luke 15:8). That other woman, sitting at Jesus's feet, letting her sister prepare the meal—she isn't passive or irresponsible; she is on a spiritual journey, looking for something more valuable than an orderly home (Luke 10:39–40). Those miserable Samaritans—perhaps some of them are actually our "neighbors," from God's point of view; perhaps some of them are closer to him than we are (Luke 10:29).

The Perils of Interpretation

All three synoptic gospels present Jesus's parables, and Luke presents more of them than Matthew or Mark. Jesus's stories are signs of what Thomas Jefferson called his "fine imagination,"[3] and they offer training for his audience's imagination, training in the interpretation of symbols and situations. Few of them are hard to understand, if you are content with a general meaning; but imagining yourself inside the stories and applying their meanings to your own life is one of the "difficult" things about the New Testament. Jesus's parable of the sower (Matthew 13:3–23, Mark 4:3–29, Luke 8:5–18) emphasizes the differences among his listeners: some hear the word but fail to grasp it; others hear "with joy" and believe, but lose their belief just as quickly; still others believe but wander off and are lost amid the cares and pleasures of normal life. Only a few retain the word and translate it into action, use it to "bring forth fruit." Jesus concludes by advising, "Take heed therefore how ye hear" (Luke 8:18). But whether one really "hears" or not is an individual thing.

Jesus's disciples had already demonstrated how difficult "hearing" can be. They had missed the meaning of his story, despite its relative simplicity and the hint he gave them ("He that hath ears to hear, let him hear") that it was about the problems of listening. They still asked him, "What might this parable be?" So he explained. But first he commented:

> Unto you it is given to know the mysteries of the kingdom of God: but to others in parables; that seeing they might not see, and hearing they might not understand. Now the parable is this . . . (Luke 8:8–11)

Again, the New Testament DNA is plainly visible. The kingdom of God is known through *stories.* To grasp their inner meaning, you must interpret their *symbolism.* But symbols, however easy they may seem, are not interpretable by everyone. Everyone has literal ears and literal eyes, but not everyone has an *inner,* spiritual perception, or is willing to use it. *Paradoxically,* there is a "seeing" that is not seeing, and a "hearing" that is not hearing. *Individuals* are *distinguished* from one another by their varying degrees and types of interest in seeking God's "mysteries." What happens in the telling of God's story is similar to what we see in the story of the Prodigal Son. There is a double movement or *progress:* God seeks to be known in the telling of a parable, and his children seek to find him in the "hearing" of it. Those who seek God in this way are *united* to the kingdom and become part of its story; these are the real *disciples.* The others, as Jesus says in the parable of the sower, are *divided;* they fall "by the way side."

Further insight into the second group of people is offered by Jesus's parable of the wicked tenants (Matthew 21:33–46, Mark 12:1–12, Luke 20:9–19; I follow Luke's version). It shows, in an especially grim way, what can occur when a parable is actually "understood," in one sense of that word, anyway; and it shows further effects of the New Testament DNA. In this story, a man plants a vineyard and rents it out. Then the renters refuse to pay. They beat up the agents he sends to them. Finally he sends his son, and the son is murdered. In retribution, the father "destroy[s]" the murderous tenants and "give[s] the vineyard to others." That is the story. Most of the people who hear Jesus tell it make a correct, if superficial, response. "God forbid," they say—God forbid that something like that should ever happen.

They convert the parable into a platitude. But the religious authorities show a deeper comprehension:

> [T]he chief priests and the scribes the same hour sought to lay hands on him; and they feared the people: for they perceived that he had spoken this parable against them[selves]. (Luke 20:19)

The priests and scribes have no trouble identifying the point of this particular parable. What they lack is an understanding of the deepest level and purpose of parables, the intention to *transform* their hearers. The parable of the vineyard moves them to act, but it does not move them closer to God. It accomplishes the work of *division*. Jesus's friends can no longer be confused with his enemies. The enemies are, *ironically*, the very people whom one might expect to follow him, since they are the most outwardly religious men in the community. But as often occurs in the New Testament, a *reversal* takes place. The *outside* turns out to be exactly the opposite of the *inside*; the "great" people are actually small inside. The itinerant rabbi from Nazareth has gained *priority* over the established religious leaders, and they begin, in a dangerous way, to understand that he has. They resent his parable, but (further irony) they grant its truth, by preparing to *re-enact* it—to murder the Son, as the evil tenants did in the parable.

Keeping Perspective

The gospels are so full of story and incident that it would easy to lose perspective if larger patterns were not built into their structure—the steady development, for instance, of the divisions and conflicts that result from listening, interpreting, and responding, conflicts that rise to crisis in the events leading to Jesus's crucifixion. Another way in which the gospels maintain perspective is by presenting episodes that reveal the whole of their story in outline, together with the significance of the story.

Such an episode appears midway in the gospel of Luke, in four of the pericopes that it shares with the other synoptic gospels (Matthew 16:13–17:9, Mark 8:27–9:9, Luke 9:18–36; unless otherwise indicated, I follow Luke's version). The episode answers the fundamental question, Who is Jesus, after all—is he merely a teacher, or is he the messiah, the divinely appointed redeemer? This question could be handled directly, in a simple statement by Jesus or the gospel writer, but it is introduced indirectly, by a question Jesus asks of his disciples: "Whom say the people that I am?" (Luke 9:18) Jesus, like the gospel writers, is interested in people's reactions to him and in their ability to interpret the signs and symbols associated with him. He recognizes the fact that his story is the story of God *and* humanity, not just the story of God. He does not simply announce that he is God's anointed, the messiah or (to use the Greek word) Christ; he allows the conception to arise in people's minds and express itself in dialogue. His disciples report that people say he must be some prophet from the past, restored from the grave or brought down from heaven. Well, Jesus says, who do *you* think I am? "Peter answering said, The Christ of God" (Luke 9:20).

This is the turning point in the story of Jesus and his disciples. It shows that the disciples have the ability to interpret the symbolism of his words and actions, and by doing so, to transform their own parts in the story. They started as the followers of a man who appeared to be a teacher and prophet; now they become the followers of Jesus as he understands himself to be, "the Christ of God." This, therefore, is the appropriate place for him to reveal the special shape of the story they have entered. He does so in one remarkable sentence:

> The Son of man must suffer many things, and be rejected of the elders and chief priests and scribes, and be slain, and be raised the third day. (Luke 9:22)

It is the world's most astonishing plotline, and it is bound to inspire critical comments. Matthew and Mark show Peter objecting—saying, according to Matthew, "This shall not be unto thee"; that is, you must not allow yourself to be slain! And they show Jesus rejecting this attempt at revising the plot: "Get thee behind me, Satan" (Matthew 16:22–23). He will stay with the story till the end.

Luke proceeds directly to the next step, Jesus's statement of what is required if one wants to maintain one's own role in the story:

> If any man will come after me, let him deny himself, and take up his cross daily, and follow me. For whosoever will save his life

shall lose it, but whosoever will lose his life for my sake, the same shall save it. For what is a man advantaged, if he gain the whole world, and lose himself, or be cast away. (Luke 9:23–25)

This ironic description of discipleship, in which Jesus's followers learn that they can win only by losing, changes the topic from Jesus to us, "the people," "any man." At issue now is our concept of ourselves. We ordinarily think of the self as one thing, indivisible. But as the book of Hebrews says, "the word of God is quick, and powerful, and sharper than any two-edged sword, piercing even to the dividing asunder of soul and spirit, and of the joints and marrow . . ." (Hebrews 4:12). Beneath the paradox of losing one's life while saving it are two opposing conceptions of the self. One relates to the outer, bodily self that our friends see and greet, and our enemies believe that they can kill. The other relates to the inner self, a self that God is able to "save," no matter what happens outside and around it. Jesus's priority is the inner self. He insists that it be his disciples' priority too. His picture of a person taking up a cross and bearing it "daily" shows his expectation, not simply that his followers will be willing to risk their lives in crisis, but that the whole of their lives will be transformed, reversed from the normal course of the outer self.

It is fitting that the idea of a mysteriously transformed life should be followed by the eerie grandeur of the transfiguration, the sudden transformation of Jesus's appearance that reveals his true nature. As Jesus prays, his form is suffused with light, and two men appear, talking with him—the ancient prophets Moses and Elijah. In Luke's gospel, they are discussing "his decease which he should accomplish at Jerusalem." Past and future unite in the present moment, a moment that thus announces the convergence of eternity with space and time. It is too much of a paradox for Peter to grasp. Tired and confused, he congratulates Jesus on the fact that his disciples are there, because they can build shelters for him and his visitors. It's a case of Peter's "not knowing what he said" (Luke 9:33); eternity needs no shelter. But even as he speaks, his misinterpretation is rendered irrelevant. A cloud descends, like the clouds that encircled God when Moses treated with him at Mt. Sinai (Exodus 24:15–16), "[a]nd there came a voice out of the cloud, saying, This is my beloved Son: hear him."

So the scene ends. The gospel writers decline to specify the transfiguration's effect on its witnesses, outside of Peter's bewildered response. They do not record any conversations like those that followed Jesus's stilling of the storm, when the disciples said to one another, "What manner of man is this! for he commandeth even the winds and water, and they obey him" (Luke 8:25). Now there is only silence, and the figure of Jesus: "And when the voice was past, Jesus was found alone" (Luke 9:36). The scene is a symbolic revelation of the "good news": here is the Christ, Jesus in his unique character, Jesus alone. He is the goal of the journey. Find him, believe in him, and you have found the transforming glory of God. Nothing else is important.

The Achievement of Faith

Of course, there would be no point in spending as much time as the gospel writers spend on the issue of belief if belief were an easy thing. Belief is not simply a matter of changing one's mind about a set of religious propositions; it is a matter of converting one's whole perspective. A change like this doesn't just happen; it's an achievement. Quite naturally, the gospels pay as much attention to the problems of faith as they do to faith itself.

One problem of faith is that the gospel story is socially divisive; it brings not "peace, but a sword . . ." Another is that it is psychologically divisive. It reveals the uncomfortable differences among various versions of the "self." In one provocative episode (Matthew 16:1–4, Luke 12:54–57; I follow Luke's version), Jesus, who has been performing miracles, considers the question of why his opponents still fail to accept him. He notices that they have no trouble reading symbols when it is simply a matter of interpreting external phenomena: "When ye see a cloud rise out of the west, straightway ye say, There cometh a shower; and so it is." But they seem incapable of reading the visible signs of his own significance. Matthew calls his opponents "wicked"; Luke goes farther. In his account, Jesus calls his opponents "hypocrites."[4] To read one set of symbols and not to read others, equally visible, indicates that there is something wrong with the reader. There is a self that sees and a self that hypocritically refuses or pretends not to see.

In a parable that appears only in Luke, the story of the rich man and Lazarus (who is not to be confused with Jesus's friend

Lazarus, the brother of Mary and Martha), Jesus makes another observation about psychology. The story involves a request from the rich man, a soul suffering for its sins in the afterlife, that a messenger be sent to his relatives to exhort them to repentance. But he is told, "If they hear not Moses and the prophets, neither will they be persuaded, though one rose from the dead" (Luke 16:31). The parable amounts to a prophecy of Jesus's own resurrection—and of the continued refusal of many to believe in him, no matter what. As such, it introduces that higher perspective on the present moment that Luke always wants to find. Its specific meaning, however, is psychological. How could someone not be persuaded by the knowledge that a man rose from the dead? The refusal could happen only if some part of the self was refusing to pay attention, despite the availability of evidence.

Perhaps this is why Jesus commands his followers to make such firm distinctions between their life with him and the patterns of ordinary life:

> Jesus said unto another, Follow me. But he said, Lord, suffer me first to go and bury my father. Jesus said unto him, Let the dead bury their dead: but go thou and preach the kingdom of God. (Matthew 8:21, 22; Luke 9:59–60)

Family obligations, religious customs, practical concerns, momentary wishes and fears and angers and loves, respect for the small things of life—all of these can obliterate one's ability to see the large issues behind and above them. If people do not see and follow Jesus, it is often because they cannot achieve or somehow do not want to achieve an unobstructed point of view.

After the transfiguration, emphasis continues to intensify on the distinction between what is important and what is not, and on the necessity for a reversal of normal priorities. Jesus seats a child beside him and tells his disciples, "He that is least among you all, the same shall be great" (Luke 9:47–48; see also 18:15–17). The disciples complain that some people have treated them rudely: "Lord, wilt thou that we command fire to come down from heaven, and consume them . . . ?" Punishment would be the normal thing to expect. No, no, Jesus says; your fervor is misdirected. What's important is saving lives, not destroying them (Luke 9:54–56).[5] Jesus dines with another reli-

gious teacher, and his host "marvel[s]" that he has not followed
the custom of washing before he eats. If you make an issue of
customs like that, Jesus replies, your values are upside down.
You want to "make clean the outside of the cup and the plat-
ter," while the "inward part is full of ravening and wickedness"
(Luke 11:37–39). The invisible inside is more important than the
visible outside.

That is true of social considerations generally. The people
who, in Jesus's vivid phrase, "love the uppermost seats in the
synagogues, and greetings in the markets" are missing the really
important things in life (Luke 11:37–44). Jesus tells the parable
of the man who had many visible possessions but was "not rich
toward God"; contrast the lilies, which "toil not" and "spin not,"
but "Solomon in all his glory was not arrayed like one of these"
(Luke 12:16–21, 27). The kingdom of God seems small, but it
has a tremendous hidden power. It is like leaven that swells the
whole loaf, or a mustard seed that becomes "a great tree" (Luke
13:18–19). Jesus goes so far in reversing normal priorities as to
say that "that which is highly esteemed among men is abomi-
nation in the sight of God" (Luke 16:15). Then he enforces that
message with the parable of the Pharisee and the publican, in
which the respected religious teacher (the Pharisee) thanks God
that he is sinless, while the detested tax-collector (the publican)
laments the fact that he is a sinner. God favors the publican
(Luke 18:9–14).

Jesus says that the nearly invisible contribution, the "two
mites," that a poor widow makes to the temple treasury is worth
more than all the gifts of the rich, because her gift means so
much more to her (Luke 21:1–4). Then he prophesies that even
the great temple itself will be "thrown down," but the inward joy
of his followers will survive the end of the world as they know
it (Luke 21:6, 28). At his last supper, he recurs to his emphasis
on reversal: "he that is greatest among you, let him be as the
younger; and he that is chief, as he that doth serve." In a
moment of quiet self-revelation that balances the glory of the
transfiguration scene, he confides, "I am among you as he that
serveth" (Luke 22:24–27). The transfiguration showed his heavenly glory, despite the humility of his earthly role; the last supper shows the humility within the glory. With the implied
pairing of last supper and transfiguration, the pattern of ironic
reversals and paradoxes is nearly complete.

The concluding revelations in the gospel of Luke come not in a pair but in a triad: crucifixion, resurrection, ascension. The first fulfills Jesus's role as human, as the suffering servant of Old Testament prophecy.[6] The second demonstrates that he is much more than human. The third is the final confirmation of his glory.

All the gospels evoke the heightening of tensions, the increasing strain of social and psychological division, leading to Jesus's death, as disputes about the meaning of his work intensify. The issue is perhaps most subtly drawn by Luke. We have seen the difficulties that, according to his gospel, the religious leaders find in interpreting Jesus's words and actions. They are distracted by wrong priorities; they find some of his meanings but miss his significance. Now, however, they are actively trying to "take hold of his words" so they can get him into legal trouble (Luke 20:20). At last, when Jesus has been arrested and is on trial before their council, they ask him plainly, "Art thou the Christ?" He can only respond, "If I tell you, ye will not believe." As in the parable of the rich man and Lazarus, they will not "be persuaded." But whether they are persuaded or not, he says, "[h]ereafter shall the Son of man sit on the right hand of the power of God" (Luke 22:66–69).

His accusers easily follow the sequence of terms associated with Jesus: Messiah (Christ), Son of Man, Son of God: "Then said they all, Art thou then the Son of God?" It is they, in fact, who bring up the last term. When Jesus responds, "Ye say that I am," they come directly to their conclusion: "What need we any further witness? for we ourselves have heard of his own mouth" (Luke 22:70–71). They didn't hear it; they are inferring it from his silence, but their inference is correct: he is identifying himself as the Son of God. Ironically, they have finally become excellent interpreters. The problem, as Luke presents it (the sequence of sayings appears just this way only in his gospel), is that their own perspective has not been changed by any of the things they have heard. It is a negative confirmation of the importance of individuality: how you respond to Jesus depends on who Jesus is, but also on who you are.

This truth is expressed in the grim pairings of the crucifixion narrative. The mob is given the opportunity to choose which of two people to release: Jesus or the criminal Barabbas. The mob chooses Barabbas, and Jesus is led off to be crucified (Luke

23:13–24). He hangs on the cross between two "malefactors" who, according to the other synoptic gospels, merely "reviled" him (Mark 15:32, Matthew 27:44). Luke continues the scene, showing one of Jesus's fellow-sufferers repenting and asking to be remembered when Jesus comes into his kingdom (Luke 23:39–43). Even in crucifixion, individuality, the importance of the inner person, asserts itself; it is the individual who recognizes the special significance of the other individual.

The same emphasis on the individual's response, or failure to respond, emerges in the events that show the risen Christ (Luke 24). In Luke's account, Jesus's women disciples discover the empty tomb, but the apostles at first do not believe them, even though the women recall Jesus's prophecy that he would rise on the third day. Peter nevertheless visits the tomb and finds it empty. In the second act of the post-resurrection drama, Jesus encounters two disciples journeying to the village of Emmaus, and he joins them as they travel. Nothing could be more appropriate: being a disciple of Christ means walking along with Christ. But these disciples do not recognize him: "their eyes were holden that they should not know him." The question (to appropriate some words later used by Paul) is whether they walk by faith or just by sight (2 Corinthians 5:7). They literally *see* Jesus, but they do not perceive his significance. They know the reports of the resurrection but are reluctant to credit what they've heard. He is forced to remind them—"O fools, and slow of heart to believe"—that both his death and his resurrection have been prophesied. It is only when they sit down to eat and he vanishes, at the breaking of the bread, that they recognize him. Then they recall the previously ignored evidence of the inner self: "Did not our heart burn within us, while he talked with us by the way . . .?"

The meeting on the road to Emmaus, like the transfiguration and many other gospel episodes, is a symbolic model of the world as viewed from a Christian perspective. From this perspective, what matters is the reality of the Christ and one's ability to believe in him. It is one's way of responding to that central reality that determines one's own role in the story—antagonist, skeptic, or ardent disciple. But because this is a story of God's search for humanity as well as humanity's search for God, there is still plenty of room for supernatural intervention. Back at Jerusalem, the two disciples have barely started to report their

experience when Jesus appears "in the midst of them." Some of
his followers are frightened, thinking that they have seen a ghost
instead of a real person; so he shows them his mutilated hands
and feet, and goes so far as to eat "a piece of broiled fish, and
a honeycomb." He could not have chosen a homelier or more
human, yet also more dramatically superhuman, means of veri-
fying his existence.

Nor could there be a clearer verification of his heavenly origin than his ascent to heaven, some days later. Only Luke
describes the ascension; only Luke provides its climactic emphasis on joy and glory—the full gospel organ, with trumpet rank
engaged. But he presents the scene with beautiful economy:
"And it came to pass, while he blessed them, he was parted
from them, and carried up into heaven." Luke's brevity about
the event itself allows the focus to rest on its witnesses, on the
representatives, within the gospel, of the audience to whom it is
addressed: "And they worshipped him, and returned to
Jerusalem with great joy: and were continually in the temple,
praising and blessing God" (Luke 24:46–53). That, Luke implies,
is how things should happen in the world that is influenced by
the gospel he is recording, a world in which the signs of Jesus's
unique significance are welcomed with joy, and Jesus's true disciples share, by the transformation of their perspective, in both
transfiguration and ascension.

The scene is now set for Acts, Luke's second volume, which
tells the story of the disciples, the "witnesses of these things"
(Luke 24:48) whom Jesus, in his last sayings before the ascension, designates to preach the gospel. From now on, they cannot depend on the direct evidence of his presence among them;
they will have to depend on the gospel itself, and do their best
to interpret it and retell it in the right ways.

One of those ways is that of Luke and the other synoptics; the
other is the approach we find in the fourth gospel, the gospel of
John—a work in which the synoptics' patient accumulation of
evidence and insight, action and response, arranged in a steady
account of events in the life of Jesus, gives way to a more
provocative handling of Christian ideas and literary methods.

4
The Gospel of John

The fourth gospel is one of the subtlest yet one of the most direct books in world literature. For directness, nothing can match its introduction, which announces Jesus's cosmic significance: "In the beginning was the Word, and the Word was with God, and the Word was God . . . All things were made by him" (John 1:1–3) Nothing can match it, that is, except the Old Testament passage that the gospel, without saying so explicitly, is repeating in its own manner: "In the beginning God created the heaven and the earth" (Genesis 1:1). Reading the introduction to John, one simultaneously sees the brilliant surface and senses the underlying depths of allusion and implication. This literary combination of directness and subtlety—almost as paradoxical, in its way, as the theology of John 1:1—also appears in the gospel's identification of its author. The gospel is attributed to John because he is the one member of Jesus's inner circle whom it does *not* mention by name.

"The Disciple Whom Jesus Loved"

Turn to the book's final chapter. Here is a complex account of an apparently simple event, a morning meeting of Jesus and his disciples beside the Sea of Galilee. Everything is informal. The disciples catch fish; Jesus cooks breakfast for them on the beach. "Come and dine," he says. But the event is miraculous; the Jesus whom we meet for breakfast is the Jesus who has just been crucified. He died and was buried; then he rose again. This is an appearance of the resurrected Christ. And after breakfast, a strange dialogue occurs. Jesus takes one of his friends aside and questions him as if the friend were suffering from a remarkable inability to understand his words. Three times Jesus asks Peter if he loves him; three times Peter insists that he does; three times Jesus tells him to "feed" his "sheep." Obviously, the phrase means "minister" to his "disciples"; the seemingly unnecessary repetition is striking, and very vexing to Peter. Jesus then grimly prophesies the kind of death by which Peter will "glorify God."

While this extraordinary conversation continues, one of Jesus's other friends is hovering in the background, eavesdropping. Peter suddenly "turn[s] about" and sees "the disciple whom Jesus loved" trailing along behind. From a literary point of view, this other disciple is showing the right instinct. He is caught up in the story, he wants to find out more about it, and his eavesdropping makes the story itself more interesting, as Peter—evidently irritated, as anyone in these circumstances might be—turns to Jesus and asks, "Lord, and what shall this man do?": how will *this* man glorify God? Jesus responds by suggesting that Peter mind his own business. Don't worry about what will happen to that other man: "follow thou me."

That is good advice, surely, but the gospel then turns to another subject, of crucial importance to the identification of its author. "This," it says, "is the disciple which testifieth of these things, and wrote these things: and we know that his testimony is true." In other words, the eavesdropping disciple, "the disciple whom Jesus loved," is the author of the fourth gospel. He must be someone very close to Jesus, but someone whom the gospel prefers not to name. The only candidate is Jesus's disciple John.

But who are the "we" who "know that his testimony is true"? Perhaps they are disciples to whom the author dictated his gospel. Perhaps, as some have argued, they are disciples who put his writings or recollections into literary shape after his death (if so, achieving an amazingly high degree of coherence and distinctiveness). And the end of John's last chapter provides additional grounds for speculation. Rebuking Peter for his curiosity about what will happen to the beloved disciple, Jesus says, "If I will that he tarry till I come, what is that to thee?" The next verse explains that these words were passed along in the early Christian community, and many people concluded that the beloved disciple would "tarry" and not die; but in fact "Jesus said not unto him, He shall not die"; he simply reproved Peter in an ironic way. It's not hard to guess what this explanation may mean: John is dead, his disciples are publishing his gospel, and they are vouching in this way for its authenticity. They are saying it is fully trustworthy, despite the fact that it includes a famous saying that, if misinterpreted, appears to have been contradicted by events.[1]

That is one implication we can derive from the complex literary dance in the gospel's final chapter. In identifying the author, however, the last passages continue a dance that started in the earlier chapters, which by refusing to name this one important disciple already suggested that there must be something still more important about him. Other meanings emerge, besides the identification of authorship. One is the beloved disciple's ideal of humility, signified by his reluctance to be known by name, a humility that is ironically entwined with the pride he shows in identifying himself by his close relationship to Jesus. The Lord's special love for him appears in more than one passage (John 13:23; 20:2; 21:7, 20). On a less ideal level, we find evidence of his rivalry with Peter, the kind of rivalry that one would expect to see in a close, family-like group consisting mainly of young men. We know from Luke's gospel (22:24) that the disciples contested for superiority even at the last supper.

There are many endearingly human qualities about the John of John's gospel, and one of them is the pattern of words by which he projects himself as the winner of his long struggle with Peter. Describing what happened when Jesus, at the last supper, said that someone present would betray him, John notes that Peter was reclining at such a distance from the Master that he had to signal to the disciple "whom Jesus loved" and who was "lying on Jesus's breast" and ask him to ask Jesus whom he had in mind (John 13:21–25). The gospel makes sure to tell us that on that breakfast morning in Galilee it was the beloved disciple who first recognized Jesus and told Peter, "It is the Lord" (John 21:7). It gives a detailed account of the way in which, on resurrection day, the beloved disciple—here modestly called "the other disciple"—raced Peter to Jesus's tomb, "and the other disciple did outrun Peter, and came first to the sepulchre" (John 20:2-8). John never fully describes the tensions among Jesus's disciples; he lets them be known, nonetheless.

However endearing and amusing this may be to us, it would probably not have been received as well by Peter. But as the final chapter of the gospel implies, Peter had already been martyred when the fourth gospel finally appeared. He had, at times, worked together with John, as Luke's history of the early church suggests (Acts 3–4). Paul refers to both "Cephas [Peter], and John" in his sarcastic comments about people "who seemed to be somewhat" in the church leadership. Paul calls them both "pillars" of the church at Jerusalem, although he cannot resist adding, "Whatsoever they were, it maketh no matter to me: God accepteth [respects] no man's person" (Galatians 2:6, 9). Despite continued, perhaps lifelong tensions, Jesus's disciples managed to co-operate. Peter, Paul, and John left their names to three great streams of New Testament writing: the Pauline literature, represented by Paul's epistles; the Petrine literature, represented by the epistles attributed to Peter and by the second gospel, in its traditional attribution to Peter's assistant Mark; and the Johannine literature, represented by the fourth gospel and the four other New Testament books attributed to John. Despite some rocky passages, the three streams flowed together. "They gave to me," Paul says of the other "pillars," "the right hands of fellowship" (Galatians 2:9). A contentious group of disciples was the means by which a single Christian church was created. John knows that—but he does not forget the contentions, either.

His gospel is very different from the synoptics. It is the most intellectual of the gospels, the one that has the most of what we would call "theology." I will come to that topic a little later—but leaf through the gospel of John, and you will see many signs of its difference from the other three. It gives more space than they do to speeches and prayers, and less to stories. It provides few strong transitions between episodes and (apart from the big things, such as the bold commencement of Jesus's ministry, the last supper, the crucifixion, and the resurrection) refrains from repeating episodes that the synoptics have already related. This is the main reason why many scholars regard it as intentionally supplemental to one or more of the synoptic gospels, which almost everyone assumes were already in circulation by the time it was written.[2]

Some of the indications that the fourth gospel was intended as supplemental have great literary interest. John uses eating and drinking, and everything having to do with wine and grapes, as symbols of Christ's closeness to humanity. In this gospel, Jesus's first miracle is the changing of water into wine, to assist the celebration of a wedding. Jesus tells his disciples that he is the vine and they are the branches. He refers to himself as "the bread of life" and tells them that they must eat his flesh and drink his blood (John 2:1–10, 15:1–7; 6:48–58). These passages offer more than striking symbolism. They explain the importance of the communion meal of bread and wine that has been a feature of the Christian church from the earliest times, a ceremony with which John's audience would have been familiar. More than a sixth of his gospel is devoted to the scene at the last supper, where, according to the synoptics, Jesus instituted the practice of communion. Everything in the gospel seems to prepare for that symbolic sharing of food and drink. John prepares so well for it that many Bible readers believe it is actually present in his gospel. It isn't. Neither ceremonial bread nor ceremonial wine appears in John's last-supper narrative. The most plausible explanation is the one that accords with the author's evident delight in saying things by *not* saying them. Knowing that other gospel writers had already provided the actual bread and wine, he feels free to take a subtler, more symbolic, and more provocative position, suggesting that people keep their eyes on Jesus himself as the Christian's holy food and drink, instead of dwelling on the literal terms of a ritual observance. In Luke's last supper, Jesus gives his disciples the emblems of communion and says, "[T]his do in remembrance of me" (Luke 22:19). In John's last supper, the emphasis is not on remembering Jesus but on Jesus's continuing presence, on his role as the teacher and sustainer who is always "the true vine" (John 15:1).

John's subtlety and ingenuity make his gospel notoriously difficult to generalize about. What is clear, however, is that his portrait of Jesus is more severely divine ("In the beginning was the Word") and more severely human ("Jesus wept") than the portraits in the other gospels (John 1:1, 11:35). It is John who depicts Jesus suddenly standing in the temple and crying out, "If any man thirst, let him come unto me, and drink" (John 7:28, 37). That is a vivid picture, and a good story, as good as many stories in the synoptics. It shows that despite John's fondness for speeches and prayers, he can tell a story when he wants to.

Some of the most memorable stories in the New Testament are found only in his gospel: the woman at the well (Chapter 4), the healing of the man born blind (Chapter 9), the raising of Lazarus (Chapter 11), the doubt and recognition of Thomas (Chapter 20), the appearance to the disciples at the Sea of Galilee (Chapter 21). One of the things that make these stories memorable is their wealth of concrete detail, detail that can be as specific as the number of fish (153!) that the disciples catch (John 21:11). Indeed, the kind of details that John likes are those that are starkly, even a little grotesquely, concrete. John allows Thomas to declare his doubts about Jesus's resurrection at morbid length: "Except I shall see in his hands the print of the nails, and put my finger into the print of the nails, and thrust my hand into his side, I will not believe" (John 20:25). Telling the story of the man born blind, John does not think it beneath him to record that Jesus used clay mixed with spittle as his instrument of healing (John 9:6). Telling the story of Lazarus, he includes the objection that is voiced at the supreme moment when Jesus commands that the tomb be opened—the objection that the dead body "stinketh" (John 11:39). John's choice of detail brings out the irony of God's encounter with humanity: from the common and even repulsive things of this world, "the glory of God" shines forth (John 11:40).

Reading the Signs

While it is easy to appreciate the glory of Jesus's triumphs over death, John insists that glory can also be detected in much less obvious circumstances, if one is willing to admit the possibility that eternity is in touch with time and look carefully for symbolic indications of God's presence. Like the gospel of Luke, the gospel of John can be read throughout as an education in the use of symbols—a literary education, if you will. Leland Ryken has observed that action in John's gospel is ordinarily symbol as well; the acts of Jesus are "signs" of spiritual principles.[3] In the words of a hymn that is annually sung in Christian churches in commemoration of the miracle at Cana, where Jesus transformed water into wine:

> The water reddening into wine
> Proclaimed the present Lord.[4]

John calls this miracle "the beginning of the signs" (John 2:11).[5] It's a sign of what Jesus always does, from the Christian point of view: he transforms the water of this world into the wine of life, demonstrating that external or "natural" appearances are subsidiary to the inner reality of God's providence.

Ryken points to an important feature of John's narrative, the use of "dramas in miniature" that "unfold in three stages":

> Jesus makes a pronouncement, a bystander expresses a misunderstanding of the utterance, and Jesus proceeds to explain the meaning of His original statement. This narrative pattern occurs no fewer than nine times in the book. Usually the misunderstanding arises when Jesus's statement calls for a figurative or symbolic interpretation and is given a literal meaning by the bystander . . .[6]

It is by signs and symbols that Jesus distinguishes perceptive from imperceptive bystanders, and confirms the faith that believers have in him.

Yet, as we saw in Luke, even believers can misread the signs. In the story of Lazarus's resurrection, which prepares for the greater story of Jesus's own resurrection, John emphasizes the failure of the disciples to understand the rudimentary metaphor of death as sleep. When Jesus tells them that he is going to wake Lazarus up, they suggest that it's better that he be allowed to sleep: "Lord, if he sleep, he shall do well." Jesus finally has to tell them bluntly that "Lazarus is dead" (John 11:11–14). As usual, John seizes the detail he needs in order to show the mystery, and the irony, of the moments when humanity comes close to God. The divine expresses itself in human terms, but humanity finds even these terms difficult to understand. Their literal meaning is just too plain; it obscures the symbolic one.

John is a close observer of the reactions of Jesus's audience, and of the frequent silliness, wrongness, and irrelevance of those reactions. By allowing the Lazarus story to develop at luxuriant length, he gives himself plenty of opportunities to illustrate inadequate responses. Jesus weeps at Lazarus's death, and John catches the spectators' soap-opera sentimentalism: "Behold how he loved him!" Nothing is seen beyond Jesus's obvious and normal reaction. Some of the spectators are even willing to interpret his tears as a sign of weakness. His grief gives them an excuse to raise the theological problem: "Could not this man [Jesus], which opened the eyes of the blind, have caused that even this man [Lazarus] should not have died?" (John 11:35–37).

It is a question that every philosophical skeptic asks about providence: Why can't God behave in a way that we understand?
John recognizes that such questions can be asked; anyone can
ask them: they are obvious. They can be asked even by people
who know that Jesus "opened the eyes of the blind." But he
doesn't try to answer them. He shows that while the question-
ing proceeds, so does the work of providence. Jesus walks past
the questioners to Lazarus's tomb, and there the resurrection
takes place.

Strictly speaking, both the sentimentalists and the philosophers are irrelevant to the story, which is about Jesus's resurrection of his friend. Of course, these people do not regard
themselves as irrelevant, and it is precisely that attitude that
earns them a place in John's narrative. They represent the whole
class of bad interpreters, the whole class of people who
approach the encounter of God and humanity with the determination to make it either something purely human, a matter of
mere emotion, or something purely theological, an occasion for
philosophical speculation. For John, the point of the story is the
resurrection itself, the effect of God's power to bring human
beings to life. "Lazarus, come forth," Jesus shouts, and he comes
forth, bound in his grave clothes. Then Jesus says, "Loose him,
and let him go," and that is the end of the story (John 11:43–44).
Were you expecting Lazarus to come from the dead, like the
character in T.S. Eliot's poem, and "tell you all" about life and
death?[7] Nothing could be farther from John's intention (or,
apparently, from that of Lazarus), despite the fact that John is
the most intellectually curious among the gospel writers. He
ends the story when his own point is made.

He remains curious, however, about the various ways in
which other people react to the stories he tells. He says that as
a result of the miracle, "many of the Jews . . . believed" in Jesus.
But others went so far as to report him to the religious authorities, who were morally concerned about his miracles and his
manner of performing them (John 11:45–46; compare 9:13–16).
John, the intellectual, provides insight into the kind of intellectuals in whose mind ethical ideals and political expediency are
constantly chasing each other. Some of the religious leaders are
terrified that Jesus will gather a following, become a political
force, and attract the unwelcome interest of the Roman over-
lords: "The Romans shall come and take away both our place

and nation." Caiaphas, the high priest, has another thought: "[I]t is expedient for us, that one man should die for the people, and that the whole nation perish not." He has a murky idea, which happens to be true in ways he does not understand, that Jesus's death will redeem the people. The high-minded moralists and the panicky politicians can unite on one program: "[F]rom that day forth they took counsel together for to put him to death" (John 11:45–53). John lets the spiritual significance of Jesus's opponents register on the reader, unobscured by abstract analysis. Whatever their motives, their partially correct opinions, or even their accidental accordance with God's plan, which is for Jesus to die a sacrificial death, their plot against him is a revelation of the mind's capacity for evil. They plot to kill him *because* he works miracles.

John is still impressed, however, by people's ability simply to deny what they see. The next chapter of his gospel shows Jesus wrestling with the thought of approaching crucifixion. Jesus's humanity, his struggle with the story of which he is, in effect, the author, is touchingly evident:

> Now is my soul troubled; and what shall I say? Father, save me from this hour: but for this cause came I unto this hour.

Then he prays that his father will use him to glorify his own name. The Father replies, "I have both glorified it, and will glorify it again." The voice is a miraculous proof of Jesus's relationship to God. But the people who hear it are anxious to rationalize the evidence away. Some say, "An angel spake to him." Others imagine that "it thundered" (John 12:27–29). There is something inside people that looks for reasons not to believe. John does not say that in so many words, but he continues assembling a gallery of characters whose outward actions symbolize their incapacity for belief.

The final and best exhibit is the Roman governor, Pontius Pilate. When Pilate hears Jesus say that he "came to bear witness unto the truth," he answers like a modern relativist: "What is truth?" He denies the connection between the visible evidence or "witness" and the inward truth, the connection on which the gospel writer's own ideas are based. Whatever one thinks of Pilate's intellectual method, his response is irrelevant to the situation, which calls for no abstract philosophical speculation. He knows very well that Jesus isn't guilty of the crimes of which he is accused: "I find in him no fault at all" (John 18:38). Yet he allows Jesus to be crucified, partly because he is intimidated by the people who are accusing him and partly because he isn't determined to live up to the standard of truth anyway. In both respects, he functions as a judge while lacking the inner character of a judge. He is an excellent example of the New Testament's concern with reversals of inner and outer and of "higher" and "lower": the judge (as he appears in his outward, official capacity) is in this case the criminal.

John is as sensitive as Luke to the individuality of the people he portrays, and as interested in revealing their inner nature by their differing responses to the events in which they participate. As Jesus speaks and acts, some people recognize and receive him, while others try to explain him away or divert their attention with irrelevancies. Jesus remains the same; the difference lies in the individuals around him. He tells Pilate, "Every one that is of the truth heareth my voice"—meaning, of course, "understands," "grasps the true significance of" what he says (John 18:37). In John's gospel as in Luke's, people are divided by their ability or lack of ability to "hear" in this way. It is a major issue in a book that takes division (from God, and among people) and unity (with God and Christ, and among the followers of Christ) as fundamental themes. In John as in Luke, the literary devices that serve these themes—such devices as distinction, unification, paradox, and irony—are fully deployed. The same DNA appears in John and the synoptic gospels; John's literary contribution is his use of those devices in the most surprising and dramatic ways possible.

Surprised by God

He begins his gospel with the central paradox of the Christ, who is the Word that is "with" God and yet "is" God. But John is far from isolating the idea of Christ's divinity in a separate "prologue": it echoes throughout the gospel, in Jesus's many statements about his unity with the Father: "[H]e that hath seen me hath seen the Father"; "I am in the Father, and the Father in me"; "I and my Father are one" (John 14:9, 11; 10:30). When Jesus makes that last statement, some of his listeners react in an appropriately (though misguidedly) dramatic fashion. They try to stone him, thus justifying what he said to them immediately before: "[Y]e are not of my sheep . . . My sheep hear my voice" (John 10:22–42). Radical expressions of unity are emphasized by the radical divisions they create.

So the believers are distinguished from the unbelievers, but division always leads back to some kind of unification. The unbelievers unite in their own group, the group of opponents who demand the death of Jesus. Paradoxically, his death at their hands will unite the believers in a relationship with him that is as true as his relationship with the Father. He and his followers will share the same life:

> Yet a little while, and the world seeth me no more; but ye see me: because I live, ye shall live also. At that day ye shall know that I am in my Father, and ye in me, and I in you. . . . He that loveth me shall be loved of my Father, and I will love him, and will manifest myself to him. (John 14:19–21)

Even while in "the world," however, Jesus often prefers to manifest himself in symbolic words and actions. In the gospel of John, the manifestation tends, as I have suggested, to take a very concrete and earthy form, using the common things of life as symbols—as if indications of the strange and the spiritual could not be grounded too deeply in the familiar and the natural, or as if symbols and their referents must be as distinct from each other as possible, so that the drama of their final unity can emerge. But not just any earthy symbolism will do. John, like his Master, prefers the kind of symbolism that both unites and divides. Light is one of his favorite symbols. From the start of his gospel, the Word is a "light" that "shineth in darkness" (John 1:1-14). Light, like thought, reason, speech, and discourse (the Greek noun *lógos* ["Word"] can mean all these things), acquaints us with the world around us and unites us to that world, makes us part of it, able to understand and act in it. Light also shows us where the darkness lies. When Jesus announces that he is "the light of the world," he prompts rival religious leaders to show that they prefer to dwell in darkness (John 8:12 and following).

There is nothing more basic than light and darkness, unless it be the food that nourishes this life in which we see the light. When we eat and drink, we unite our own substance with the substance of the world outside us. If we reject food and drink, we divide ourselves from that world; we die. Those are the fundamental facts of our physical existence, and it is almost embarrassing to state them plainly. According to John, Jesus does something even more embarrassing. He calls himself "the bread which came down from heaven." He says to his disciples, "Whoso eateth my flesh, and drinketh my blood, hath eternal life . . . For my flesh is meat indeed, and my blood is drink indeed." At this, many of the disciples rebel. "This is a hard saying," they exclaim; "who can hear it?" Their reaction is natural, in every sense of the word. But by responding in this way, they unite themselves with the unbelievers who refuse to understand the force of Jesus's symbolic speech and action, speech and action that point beyond the distinctions of the natural world to the paradoxical unities of spiritual existence. The symbol of unity, flesh and blood—"He that eateth my flesh, and drinketh my blood, dwelleth in me, and I in him"—becomes the source of conflict and religious division. Jesus identifies the problem: his words "are spirit," but his listeners are interpreting them according to "the flesh" (John 6:35–63). They live in a world of material phenomena instead of spiritual understanding. They are incapable of the imaginative leap that would take them from earth to heaven.

In this sense, at least, Jesus's kingdom is what he told Pilate it was: "not of this world" (John 18:36). The events of John's gospel are meant to lead readers' minds from the concrete things of earth to the highest level of generalization and unification, so they can see that there are, fundamentally, two different "worlds," the fleshly and the spiritual, with two corresponding sets of inhabitants. On the one hand, there are those who really "hear" the meaning of Jesus's words, who are willing to see the spiritual light and eat the spiritual food. On the other hand, there are those who cannot or will not "hear his voice," even though, ironically, they are in a good position to do so, having him literally there before them. Few of John's readers could ever have had that privilege; but by emphasizing the idea that people could be with Jesus in the flesh and still have no insight at all into what he said, regardless of the familiar words with which he spoke, John suggests that being united with him is not dependent on the face-to-face experiences that we ordinarily associate with "knowing" another person.

In the episode of doubting Thomas, John uses multiple ironies to develop the theme of seeing and knowing. Jesus's disciple Thomas hears of the resurrection but refuses to believe that the reports could be literally true, unless he is shown the literal evidence: "Except I shall see in his hands the print of the nails, and put my finger into the print of the nails . . . ." Then suddenly Jesus is with him, inviting him to touch his hands and thrust his own hand into Jesus's wounded side. Thomas, seeing him, exclaims, "My Lord and my God." The fact that the declaration comes, ironically, from the least likely source, a radical skeptic, earns it the climactic place in John's evidence for the reality of the resurrection. But the declaration is important in another way as well. It suggests that literalism can be pushed too far. John does not say that Thomas actually touched Jesus, as he said he needed to do. Sight alone was enough to tell him that the resurrection had occurred, and to inspire the bold flight of deduction that carried him from He Is Risen to He Is God. As always, John is more interested in where the story is going than in the various steps of the journey, which in any case can be undertaken in a variety of ways. But Jesus turns the discussion of evidence in an unexpected direction. He replies to his formerly doubting disciple by saying, "Thomas, because thou hast seen me, thou hast believed: blessed are they that have not seen, and yet have believed" (John 20:29). We may take that as John's assurance that, by another irony, readers who have had no fleshly sight of Jesus at all may be even more favored in their belief than Thomas was.

Certainly they can journey, intellectually, to the same place where Thomas has gone, if they are individually prepared to go there—and "there" is back to the start of the gospel, where the writer himself declared that "the Word was God." Once again in the New Testament, the reader's journey forward becomes a repetition, a circling back. "Spiraling back" might be a better phrase, because one understands the significance of Christ's unity with God much better at the end of the gospel than one did at the beginning. The circle, the journey that bends back on itself, is an age-old literary form. Luke also provides circular structures. We saw one such structure in the stories culminating in the Prodigal Son, stories that returned us repeatedly, with fresh insights, to their point of origin. A larger circle appears in the structure of Luke's gospel as a whole. It begins with angelic

visitors from heaven, busy in the preparation and announcement of Jesus's birth; it shows the inauguration of Jesus's ministry with a voice from heaven that proclaims him the Son of
God; it progresses to the revisitation of his heavenly glory at the
transfiguration; and it ends with his glorious return to his heavenly home (Luke 1, 2, 3, 9, 24).

John's narrative is still more insistent on the paradox of arriv-
ing at the unity that has always been present. John has many
ways, subtle as well as obvious, of suggesting the continuous,
underlying presence of this spiritual unity. One of the statements that nearly leads to Jesus's death at the hands of outraged
listeners is his declaration of pre-existence: "Before Abraham
was, I am" (John 8:58). He says the same thing, in an intimately
reassuring way, when he prays to the Father for the welfare of
his disciples, speaking of them as people who "have kept
[God's] word," asking that they remain in unity, as he remains in
unity with the Father, and associating that unity with the glory
he had with the Father "before the world was" (John 17:5). A
similar, though much earthier effect, appears in his promise, "In
my Father's house are many mansions . . . I go to prepare a
place for you . . . that where I am, there ye may be also" (John
14:2–3). The central image is the journey, but it is a journey
home: the simple, commonplace image unfolds a double meaning. And there are much subtler moments. In the breakfast scene
in the gospel's last chapter, Jesus manifests his identity by his
miraculous advice about fishing: he tells the disciples where to
cast their net, and they achieve an enormous catch. But when
they land it, they find that Jesus is already cooking their meal
(John 21:6–13). Everything has been prepared for them; they
were home before they knew it.

Experience and Reflection

Since very early in the Christian tradition, the author of the
fourth gospel has been called St. John the Divine—"divine"
meaning "theologian." Clearly, he is more "theological" than the
authors of the synoptic gospels. It is true, of course, that the
story of Jesus, as they relate it, cannot be pictured merely as that
of a wandering preacher of righteousness. Attempts have been
made to do so, but the picture that results is not intelligible; the
gospels' supernatural frame keeps coming back to dispute it: in

the reports of Jesus's miracles; in the use of titles ("Messiah" ["Christ"], "Son of Man") that identify him with Old Testament prophecies, and go beyond them ("Son of God"); and finally in the testimonies of his transfiguration and resurrection. But the synoptics offer little *reflection* on the philosophical meaning of what they report, or on the shape of the cosmos revealed by it. There is nothing in the synoptics like "In the beginning was the Word . . . "

An interesting historical incident is connected with this fact, an incident showing the need for caution in reaching conclusions about the New Testament and the development of its ideas. The gospel of John contains such advanced theological reflections that some modern "scientific" scholars of scripture were certain that its ideas could not have evolved in anything less than a century or even a century and a half after Jesus's death. But the evolutionary assumptions of the physical and biological sciences can be hazardous when imported into other fields. The mind can sometimes find its home in one bold movement of thought, with no long evolution of ideas behind it. In 1935 a fragmentary manuscript of the eighteenth chapter of John, preserved by the dry weather of Egypt, was published for the first time. It was reliably dated to the early years of the second century. So the gospel had been copied and was in circulation by then. It was a product of the first century after all.

This product of the first century became the cornerstone of Christianity's intellectual self-definition. The prologue ("In the beginning was the Word") and the declaration of Thomas ("My Lord and my God") testified that Jesus was not merely the messiah, and not merely pre-existent. He was with the Father in eternity, and he was simultaneously man and God. Other features of the gospel (Jesus's power to forgive people's sins, the more than merely messianic intimacy of his prayers to the Father, such statements as "I am the light of the world") bore out the identification. The crisis of Christian theology was reached in the fourth century, in the great contest between trinitarian and Arian ideas. The Arians (followers of Arius) taught that Christ was a created being—the most important of such beings, but created nonetheless. The trinitarians (followers of Athanasius) held that Christ was fully God (no one could be "God" if not *fully* God), along with the Father and the Holy Spirit, the other two persons of a triune deity. At a church council at Nicaea, a town near the imperial capital of Constantinople, a decision was rendered, and it went overwhelmingly against the Arians. The concept endorsed at Nicaea and, later in the fourth century, at the First Council of Constantinople is embodied in the Nicene Creed, the statement of belief on which virtually all branches of Christianity are agreed: there is one God, in three persons.

The doctrine of the trinity is one of the most paradoxical concepts in the world. In it, however, one can see, not just the philosophical developments of the fourth century, but the New Testament's characteristic attitudes toward history and human experience—in a word, the New Testament's DNA. As we have seen, history is an inseparable part of that DNA, which "starts" with the idea of a providential God, manifesting himself historically. When writers like John and Paul concern themselves with the theology of Christianity, they assume that whatever is true in history must continue to be true in philosophical reflection, however paradoxical one's deductions from historical experience may seem, or however many reversals of perspective they may require (1 Corinthians 1:22–31). Christianity began with the heritage of Judaism—the belief in a single, providential God. There was no question of denying that belief, which was held and taught by Jesus himself. But the historical experience reported by the gospel writers and especially by John suggested that the Son as well as the Father was divine. As for the Holy Spirit (or Holy Ghost), he is treated as a person in a number of important Bible passages (for instance, John 15:26, 16:7–8, 13–14; Acts13:2; Romans 8:26); and in the Great Commission, where Jesus says to his disciples: "Go ye therefore, and teach all nations, baptizing them in the name of the Father, and of the Son, and of the Holy Ghost" (Matthew 28:19).

A Platonic idea, most influentially stated by Augustine, the greatest philosopher of the age that immediately followed the Nicene Creed, helps to clarify its logic. Augustine specifies the distinction between time and eternity: eternity is not endless time; it is the absence of time.[8] But if time, like everything else that pertains to the natural world, was created by God "in the beginning," and the Word, according to John, was there "in the beginning," then the Word must have existed before time.[9] Therefore, he existed in eternity, which means that he has been "with" God forever. This brings us home again to John's para-

dox. According to the principles of monotheism, there is but
one uncreated being, and that is God; therefore, Jesus must be
God. Yet John's gospel shows that Jesus suffered death and was
buried, while God the Father remained on high. Impossible! But
John leaves Christians no option except to affirm the paradox,
as he does, and rejoice in it. The interplay of experience and
reflection, and the continuing re-affirmation of paradox, became
permanent features of Christianity.

One way of mapping the literary history of Christianity is to
describe it as a series of experiences and reflections rippling
outward from a central historical event and experience. The life
of Jesus was like a great stone cast into the water. Something
important had clearly happened, but what did it mean? The synoptic gospels record Jesus's teachings; they also provide complex, though introductory, interpretations of his significance.
John's gospel goes farther. Other books of the New Testament
add their own ripples of interpretation. The interpretations that
Paul provides in his epistles would give decisive shape to large
areas of Christian teaching. And Luke followed his gospel with
a history of the early church that has never ceased to shape the
experience of the church itself.

5
Making a Church

The shaping effect of the fifth book of the New Testament, the Acts of the Apostles, can be attributed to the fact that Christianity is embodied in a literature as well as an institution, and that the institution, the church, has always honored literature as fundamental to its existence. While telling the early history of the church, Acts shows the importance of the Word and words to its creation and perpetuation, demonstrating in words the kind of institution it must continue to be—an institution that reproduces the same literary DNA that was present at its birth.

The Aesthetic Problem

Acts is a strange and complex work. Its introduction addresses Theophilus, who was the recipient of the gospel of Luke, and indicates that it is the second "treatise" prepared for him. So Luke and Acts share authorship, but that is where the mystery begins. The gospel of Luke is a literary masterpiece; in purely literary terms, it is much better than the book of Acts—and this raises interesting questions about how Acts was composed and what its author's intentions for it were. But let me state the problem of quality in a more precise way. Acts isn't a badly written book; the interesting thing is that its quality is so uneven.

It has its great literary moments. One example is the incident in which Peter and John, walking through the Beautiful Gate of the temple in Jerusalem, encounter a crippled man who lies there every day, asking for alms. Seeing the two apostles approaching, the beggar makes his usual request. He could not have anticipated the result.

> Peter, fastening his eyes upon him with John, said, Look on us. And he gave heed unto them, expecting to receive something of them. Then Peter said, Silver and gold have I none; but such as I have give I thee: In the name of Jesus Christ of Nazareth rise up and walk. And he took him by the right hand, and lifted him up: and immediately his feet and ankle bones received strength. And he leaping up stood, and walked, and entered with them into the temple, walking, and leaping, and praising God. And all the people saw him walking and praising God. (Acts 3:3–9)

The episode is an especially powerful example of that familiar New Testament device, the reversal of normal expectations. The repetitions in the two final sentences emphasize the effect: the man who a moment before was lying on the pavement is now leaping and praising God. Presumably, he wasn't praising God before, but now there has been a transformation of perspectives—both his perspective and the reader's. When we first saw him, he was just one more professional beggar whom someone carried to the gate every morning to enact his public role. Luke stresses the impersonality and passivity of the ritual. The beggar is "a certain man . . . whom *they laid* daily at the gate" (Acts 3:2). He is a regrettable but familiar sight, a sight that one might easily walk by without noticing. But suddenly there occurs an odd, private interval, the rare occasion on which someone makes a distinction between the beggar and his situation, on which someone actually recognizes him as an individual and imagines that he could be something other than what he is.

To spotlight the moment, Luke introduces a significant detail. It isn't necessary to the basic story, but it's another powerful expression of the New Testament DNA. Most of us try to avoid eye contact with beggars, whether we intend to give them anything or not. But Peter and John fasten their eyes on this particular person and demand that he fasten his eyes on them: "Look on us." With those few words, the typical New Testament effect recurs: the impersonal is transformed into the personal, the external into the internal, and ordinary ideas of value are ironically reversed. Peter confesses that he can offer nothing of external value; he has no more money than the beggar (perhaps less). His real wealth, the ability to work a miracle, lies inside—

as Peter knows. He savors the irony. "*Such as I have* give I thee," he says, as if he considered this hidden wealth as of no account.

But there is something hidden inside the beggar, too, something that is about to be dramatically revealed. No one could have guessed this man's ability to serve, not as evidence of God's neglect or indifference, but as evidence of God's providence, the providence that has brought John and Peter there to heal him. What Peter does next is a vivid symbol of the way in which providence acts. He grasps the beggar by the right hand, the hand with which he probably does whatever he is able to do for himself. So far, that is very little; he cannot use his hand to reach out, steady himself, and rise to his feet. So Peter reaches out to him, as God reached out to the world through "Jesus Christ of Nazareth," and pulls him to his feet. That gesture embodies the New Testament idea of God's relationship to humanity. The beggar "expect[s] to receive something," but what he receives is very different from anything he could have expected. He could not come to God, yet God came to him.

Unfortunately, however, Acts does not always possess the brevity and the resonance of the healing at the Beautiful Gate. In that passage, nothing is redundant; every detail carries symbolic weight; elsewhere, one often finds the kind of redundancy that good writers try to avoid. One example is the episode in which Peter is commanded by God to visit Cornelius, a Roman soldier, and convert him and his household to Christ (Chapter 10). Peter does so, then meets with other Christians at Jerusalem, where he "rehearse[s] the matter from the beginning" (Chapter 11). One would think that a good author, such as Luke clearly was, on the evidence of his gospel, would have eliminated this repetition at the editing stage.[1]

A greater literary problem is presented by the end of the book. Acts doesn't conclude; it simply stops. The last eight chapters follow the legal difficulties that Paul gets into while preaching the gospel: he is arrested in Jerusalem, appeals to the central government at Rome, and journeys there as a prisoner, pursuing his appeal. Then Acts simply breaks off, leaving him in Rome under house arrest, waiting for his trial: "And Paul dwelt two whole years in his own hired house . . ." (Acts 28:30). No one knows whether the trial resulted in the martyrdom that, as tradition reports, he ultimately suffered at Rome. There is no account of those events in Acts, or anywhere else in the New Testament—although one would think that a writer as interested in literary effects as Luke has shown himself to be would not abandon his story without getting to its climax.

But the non-conclusion of Acts suggests a reason for the book's uneven quality. The abrupt ending might make sense if Acts were the second book of a three-book sequence. Acts, like the gospel of Luke, is about as long as a first-century book could conveniently be. There is a point at which a scroll gets too large. The rest of Paul's story might have been saved for volume three. It is possible that Acts was finished in draft form, then put aside by an author who intended to write a third volume before returning to revise the second.

Another literary clue appears in those places in the second half of Acts where the author, having joined Paul as a companion, begins writing in the first person: "And after he had seen the vision, immediately we endeavoured to go into Macedonia . . ."; "These going before tarried for us at Troas . . . "; "And when we came to Rome . . . " (Acts 16:10, 20:5, 28:16). The "we" passages contain accounts of ancient travel that read at times like passages from a diary: "And we sailed thence, and came the next day over against Chios; and the next day we arrived at Samos . . . " (Acts 20:15). The immediacy of these passages imparts a strong sense of authenticity, yet they are the kind of passages that we would expect the author of Luke's gospel to edit severely. Why didn't he do so? One plausible speculation is that death intervened before he completed his work on Acts or came close to completing the conjectured three-volume history meant to include it.[2] (It's hard to believe that a third volume would ever have been lost, once it had been put in usable form.) If this theory is correct, then Acts is one of the ancient world's rare surviving examples of an important though "uncompleted" literary text.

Anyone interested in the ways in which New Testament authors work with their material will be interested in Acts, just as anyone who is curious about the methods of Renaissance painting will profit by examining a Correggio that was left without its final application of color. But much more important is what we can learn from Acts—in its completed or uncompleted form—about the nature of the church and the importance of speech and literary communication in the early Christian community. On these matters, Acts offers insights that are fascinating enough for a hundred books.

Acts dates the institutional origin of the church to events occurring at the Jewish feast of Pentecost, fifty days after Jesus's crucifixion and ten days after his ascension. Devout people from many countries gathered at Jerusalem to celebrate the feast. Jesus's disciples were there, obeying his command to remain in Jerusalem until they were "endued with power from on high" (Luke 24:49). Luke describes the advent of this power:

> [S]uddenly there came a sound from heaven as of a rushing mighty wind, and it filled all the house where they were sitting. And there appeared unto them cloven tongues like as of fire, and it sat upon each of them. And they were all filled with the Holy Ghost, and began to speak with other tongues, as the Spirit gave them utterance. (Acts 2:2–4)

Like many other acts of providence, the descent of the Spirit comes suddenly and with a transforming effect on individuals. The miraculous experience visibly divides the first group of Christians from the rest of the worshipers at Jerusalem and unites them, one to another, as a community of altered perception and self-expression. It is ironic (though very appropriate) that what sets them apart from others is the gift of "tongues." Their means of communicating with other people is also, paradoxically, the sign of their distinctness and distance from other people.

In mentioning transformation, changed perspectives, distinction and unification, irony and paradox, I am of course simply enumerating some elements of the New Testament's DNA, already present in this picture of the church before the Testament. The Christian church will always be depicted as an agency of transformation, but it will always be surrounded by ironies and paradoxes, by forces that work both to unite and to distinguish. The basic character of the church is paradoxical. It is both divine and human, formed by God but composed of individual human beings. It is one thing, and it is endlessly diverse. The church is the fundamental Christian institution, and Christians have never believed that they could do without it; but its paradoxical nature, as defined in these first chapters of Acts, has always made it difficult to conceptualize completely. That is a major reason why Christians have fought with each other so frequently about its structure, membership, leadership, customs—almost everything connected with the institution that is meant to unite them.

On one issue there is agreement: the church is one. Although modern Christianity is associated with many "churches," these are more accurately called "denominations"; and although they may argue among themselves about the church's defining features, all of them agree that the true church, wherever it may be found, is a single entity. But this means that tension will always exist between the idea of the one church, to which every Christian belongs, and Christianity's emphasis on the importance of the individuals who make up that church. People enter the church as individuals, and they bear responsibility for their own moral decisions, once they are inside it. No one in the New Testament ever suggests that it is right to do something simply because other people in the church think it is right. Yet according to the New Testament, God ordained the church as an institution that inseparably unites believers with himself and one another.

Clearly, the church presents complex intellectual and emotional challenges. The New Testament addresses them in a number of ways. One is the use of literary images, verbal pictures of what the church ought to be. Paul sees it as an organic unity like the human body: "Now ye are the body of Christ, and members in particular" (1 Corinthians 12:27). Peter, standing in the shadow of the temple at Jerusalem, uses an architectural metaphor, calling Jesus "the head of the corner," the cornerstone of a new and unified structure (Acts 4:11–12, applying Psalm 118:22). The New Testament, which never goes long without a story, also guides Christians' understanding of the church by providing stories of the church's history—chief among them, the book of Acts. These stories show what the church should be by describing its progressive acquisition of the characteristics it needed for its existence and survival.

Necessary Characteristics

Every institution must have a means of differentiating itself from others. This is the immediate and persistent problem in Acts. The process of differentiation begins with the miraculous gifts of

the Spirit bestowed at Pentecost, but much else needs to happen before the church stands fully apart as an institution. The
church originally manifests itself in the midst of a Jewish festi-
val, in the capital of the Jewish world. All its members are Jews.
Luke describes the post-Pentecost believers in Christ as still
"continuing daily with one accord in the temple" (Acts 2:46). But
as they look more and more to their own leaders, and as they
encounter antagonism from other people—"the priests, and the
captain of the temple, and the Sadducees" (religious teachers
who did not believe in the possibility of a resurrection)—they
develop a deeper sense of their own identity (Acts 4:1). Stephen,
a young official of the church, is accused of saying that Jesus
will destroy the temple and "the customs"; he replies with a
speech that many devout Jews regard as blasphemous, and he
is stoned to death (Acts 6:13–8:2). Then the first conversions of
non-Jews occur (Acts 10). Here is the crucial moment. The
church cannot live simultaneously both inside and outside the
institutions of Israel. Whatever similarities tend to unite the two
groups, it must now live outside. In telling this story, Acts follows the New Testament pattern of reversing ordinary expectations. Jews and gentiles, whose customs make them appear too
different to associate with one another, much less act as
"brethren," can now be seen as members of one family, united
by the new Christian belief.

A second institutional requirement, however, leads to certain
kinds of distinctions among the believers themselves. Every
institution of any size must be differentiated internally as well as
externally. It can function effectively only by assigning different
roles to different members. In Acts, the process of internal differentiation begins with the church's appointment of deacons to
manage its daily business so that people who have gifts for handling more spiritually important matters can give their full attention to those things. We hear of special roles for apostles,
prophets, and teachers (Acts 6:1–6, 13:1).

Third, every institution must have the ability to provide for
its expansion in space and its continuance in time. Acts soon
notices the presence of young people in the church, a second
generation that includes John Mark, writer of the second gospel,
and the four daughters of Philip, all of them prophets—evidence
that teaching is going on and the church will continue in time
(Acts 12:12, 13:5, 21:8–9). While every Christian is authorized to

preach the gospel, the expansion of the church is facilitated by another stage of differentiation, the authority given certain people to act as missionaries (Acts 13:1–5).

Fourth, every institution needs signs of its identity, visible means of determining whether people are inside or outside it. Acts describes the Pentecostal gifts of the Spirit as the first visible signs of the church. But they do not solve all the problems connected with symbols of identification, particularly symbols that the earliest Christians inherited from their Jewish past: dietary codes, dress codes, religious rituals, circumcision. While many Jewish Christians continue to adhere to the Old Testament law and to worship at the temple, the church grows away from the law and its symbols. The defining moment in this respect is the so-called Council of Jerusalem, described in detail at Acts 15, where the leaders of the church affirm the idea that Christians are not required to follow the law. Henceforth, the visible marks of God's institution, from the Christian point of view, will be the gifts of the Spirit and the customs that Jesus himself authorized—baptism and the celebration of communion.

The Council episode points up a fifth institutional requirement. Every institution that is internally differentiated and extended in space and time requires a means of ensuring its coherence and integrity. In practice, this means that someone must have authority to make decisions that will keep it together. The pattern one sees in Acts is that of a community showing deference to people (such as Peter and the other early disciples) who were closely associated with its Founder, and to other people (Paul is the supreme example) who are especially gifted in spreading its message. Nothing compels members of the church to accept any of these people's judgments, and there is evidence that church leaders could and did differ among themselves (Galatians 2). There is also evidence of schisms and scandals in the church (1 Corinthians 5:1, Revelation 2:14–15). But there is no reason to infer, as some scholars have, that what we see in first-century Christianity is various loose associations of believers separated from one another by local customs, traditions, and ideas. The prevailing impression is that of local churches that are conscious of belonging to a greater whole and are responsive to the counsel of the leading apostles, the "sent-forth ones" whose travels and correspondence, and the disciples whom they make and send forth, keep Christians throughout the Roman empire in touch with one another.

The Spirit and the Word

Thus far, I have presented a picture of the church that any student of social institutions might sketch. It is abstract, general, logical. Any Christian, however, would also regard it as very partial and external. It gives insufficient weight to two factors that, separately and in conjunction with each other, are more important to the church's self-perception than any of those just listed: the Spirit and the word. According to Acts, it was the Holy Spirit that inspired the church's external and internal differentiation and guided the appointment of missionaries and other leaders (Acts 6:3, 11:12–17, 13:2, 15:28). The Spirit provided the gifts of tongues and healing and the other gifts that assisted the church's most distinctive occupation, the preaching of the gospel. The Spirit and the word acted together. The Pentecostal outpouring of the Spirit was followed by a speech in which Peter explained the strange event, a speech that made liberal use of the written words of the Old Testament. What is happening, he says, is

> that which was spoken by the prophet Joel: "And it shall come to pass in the last days, saith God, I will pour out of my Spirit upon all flesh: and your sons and your daughters shall prophesy, and your young men shall see visions, and your old men shall dream dreams." (Acts 2:15–17, citing Joel 2:28)

By arguing that the outpouring of the Spirit fulfills God's purpose as prophesied in scripture, Peter gives the church something that all institutions need, even though it may be missed by a purely "institutional" analysis. Every institution needs a history, a story that explains its origin and justifies its existence. Some institutions justify themselves by a story that emphasizes their radical break with the past. The Christian church justified itself by repeating stories already considered sacred, applying their meanings to itself, then continuing the sequence of stories in its own way. From the beginning, the church was a literary event, explaining itself with the literary methods of repetition and transformation, and asserting the paradox that it is both old and new, both united with the past and divided from it by the continuous operations of God's providence.

That's one way of looking at the church, as a paradox in action. Another way is suggested by the ever-recurrent Christian idea of history as a providential journey, guided by the Spirit and interpreted by the word. This idea emerges strongly in the New Testament accounts of the apostles' means of making decisions. Paul says that he conferred with the other apostles to confirm that he had not "run" in the wrong course, and that he was directed by "revelation" how to run. When other leaders of the church "walked not uprightly according to the truth of the gospel," he argued it out with them, using gospel words and his own words to get them back on the path (Galatians 2:2, 14).

In Acts' story of the Council of Jerusalem, the Spirit is understood as offering evidence for Christian belief, but right words are still needed to explain the Spirit's interventions and place them in proper perspective. When the Council is considering whether gentile Christians should be told to obey Old Testament laws, there is "much disputing" and much reasoning and citing of evidence, both from missionary experience among the gentiles and from Old Testament prophecy. Peter rises to his feet and reminds the group that the Spirit was freely given to gentiles at their conversion, and there was "no difference between us and them." Paul and others get up to speak. Then, after the decision is made not to insist on obedience to the law, the Council sends messengers to explain its actions "with many words." It also sends out letters—words designed to refute those who "troubled" the gentiles "with words" (Acts 15:1–33). For good or ill, literary "words" are fundamental to the early church; and virtually all succeeding branches of the church have been as argumentative as the church in Acts.

Perhaps the most significant thing that appears in Acts but is missing from a purely institutional account of the church is the significance of words in giving people a reason to become Christians in the first place. The gifts of the Spirit could not be understood outside the context of the basic story of Christianity, the account of events that invite belief in Christ. This story, embodied in the *kerygma*, the "proclamation" or "preaching," is a matter of words that can be spoken or written down. It began in New Testament times, and it has been repeated ever since. The story can be introduced or concluded in many ways; its parts can be amplified, illustrated, dramatized, argued about, and interpreted for the benefit of particular people; or they can be concentrated into the terms of the old spiritual:

> If you can't preach like Peter,
> If you can't pray like Paul,
> Just tell the love of Jesus
> And say he died for all.

The *kerygma* is flexible enough to be placed before any audience.[3] It is the word that draws people to the church, and makes them remember why they came. One way of looking at the book of Acts is to see it as the story of the *kerygma* as it is repeated and adapted to the needs of successive audiences.

We hear it first in Peter's speech on the day of Pentecost. In three verses (Acts 2:22–24) he recalls the life and death of "Jesus of Nazareth, a man approved of God among you by miracles and wonders and signs," and he announces Jesus's resurrection. That is the essential story. To recommend it to an audience familiar with the Hebrew Scriptures, Peter surrounds it with quotations from the prophets of Israel, interpreting these passages as references to Jesus and his disciples. Calling his listeners "men and brethren," he adopts a confidential tone: "Let me speak freely unto you . . . " (Acts 2:29). He assures them that although they did not accept Jesus when he was among them, God's "promise" to provide a messiah is still meant for them ("unto you" [Acts 2:39]).

The primary purpose of the *kerygma* is conversion, and Peter's words are cleverly chosen to start the process, then mirror and reinforce it. The words themselves are transformative. He begins his speech by addressing his audience as if from a distance ("Ye men of Judaea"), referring to them as people who allowed the messiah to be crucified (Acts 2:14, 23)—a grievous charge, especially given the fact that crucifixion was the custom, not of the Jews, but of the heathen Romans.[4] He is aligning his listeners with paganism. Then, gradually, he changes the picture, calling them "men and brethren" and promising them the same "gift of the Holy Ghost" that he and his friends have received (Acts 2:29, 38). His story takes the audience on a journey from one group-identification to another, eventually making it seem very natural for the "men of Judaea" to unite with him and look back at the group in which they started as an "unto-ward generation" from which it is time to "save" themselves. And so they "received his word [and] were baptized" (Acts 2:40–41).

The *kerygma*, however brief, reproduces the DNA of Christianity: it is the old, old story of God's providence, repeated in ironically new forms, working through reversals, divisions, and unifications to transform the world as seen by the individual members of its audience. It keeps the same basic elements but adopts a different rhetorical form when Peter preaches to Cornelius, the Roman soldier who becomes the first gentile con-vert. This time Peter makes only one, summary reference to the Hebrew Scriptures—"to him [Jesus] give all the prophets wit-ness." He tells the story of Jesus's ministry, crucifixion, and res-urrection without mentioning the concept of the messiah, beyond the simple word "Christ," the Greek translation of that title. Still more importantly, he begins by emphasizing the idea that people of "every nation" can be acceptable to God, who "is no respecter of persons," and concludes by declaring that "remis-sion of sins" is for "whosoever" believes in Jesus (Acts 10:34–43).

This version of the *kerygma* has none of the tension and dynamism of Peter's address at Pentecost. It needs none. Cornelius is already sympathetic; he has been waiting for Peter to arrive. In effect, his conversion has already taken place. The *kerygma* comes as a confirmation of God's love for everyone, a consoling repetition of the "word which God sent unto the chil-dren of Israel, preaching peace by Jesus Christ (he is Lord of all)" (Acts 10:36). It easily unites what once had seemed eter-nally divided, and, more subtly, divides what once had seemed eternally united within itself—each of the ancient ethnic groups, secure in its own traditions, insensitive to the idea of a provi-dence that can transform the loyalties of individuals. If one misses the implicit irony, one need only look at the framing story, which concerns Peter's commission to preach to gentiles (Acts 10:9–24, 11:1–17). This story shows that before Peter set out to transform other people, his own attitudes had to be trans-formed by a vision that radically revised his customary ideas about his relationship to the "unclean" world around him.

Paul's use of the *kerygma* adds interesting variations (Acts 13:16–47). Preaching in the synagogue at Antioch, he embeds his account of Jesus in a long review of the history of Israel, showing God's providence throughout and celebrating Jesus's resurrection as the unexpected fulfillment of "the promise which was made unto the fathers." He adds his equally unexpected concept of the gospel as something that transcends the laws once given to Israel: the good news is that people can now be freed from sin who could never have gotten free by trying to follow the ancient law. By Jesus, he says, "all that believe are justified from all things [all sins], from which ye could not be justified by the law of Moses." Taking advantage of the fact that he is talking to people who are physically far removed from Jerusalem, he refers to the Jews who were present at the death of Jesus as "*they* that dwell at Jerusalem, and *their* rulers, because *they* knew him not . . . and though *they* found no cause of death in him, yet desired *they* Pilate that he should be slain." He thus ingratiates himself with his immediate audience, uniting himself with them and dividing them conceptually and emotionally from the leadership in the religious capital. It is only when opposition arises from some within the Jewish community in Antioch that he draws a distinction between that community and himself: "Seeing *ye* . . . judge *yourselves* unworthy of everlasting life, lo, *we* turn to the gentiles."

"What Will This Babbler Say?"

When Paul reaches Athens (Acts 17:15–34), however, he faces a tougher audience than he initially encountered in the Jews of Antioch, and certainly a much tougher audience than the one that Peter encountered when he met with the gentiles of Cornelius's household. Paul is no honored guest of the Greeks. Neither is he speaking to people who share his belief in providence and his respect for the Hebrew Scriptures. His audience is "certain philosophers of the Epicureans and of the Stoicks," who base their ideas on rational deduction, not on the story of God's special dealings with a particular group of people. He cannot expect to be taken seriously in his role as a learned man of Israel. His listeners are thinking, "What will this babbler say?" They are as cold an audience as any speaker ever found.

Recognizing himself as an outsider, Paul decides to speak as one, and to project the most attractive image of himself that an outsider can, that of a humble tourist, more interested in dis-

cussing his hosts' accomplishments than those of his own people. He says that he has been walking through the city, observing its religious customs, and he has been struck by the fact that
the Athenians are "extraordinarily religious."[5] They have even
erected an altar to "THE UNKNOWN GOD." Seizing this opportunity to agree with them, he says that he has come to talk about
that God. This is the kind of approach that Socrates, the philosophic idol of the Athenians, had perfected four hundred years
before: begin at the periphery of your topic, then move to the
center; begin by talking innocuously about yourself, then seize
on the controversial issues and have your way with them.

But now, having reached the subject of religion, Paul is at a
difficult transition point. He has come to preach a religion
revealed by God's miraculous interventions in human history.
His audience, however, is likely to feel nothing but contempt for
religious ideas that do not originate in processes of human reasoning. They expect philosophical deduction; he has come with
a story about incredible events in a distant and, to them, an
intellectually uncouth part of the world. There is no Gospel
According to the Philosophers. As Paul reminded the church at
Corinth, "the world by [its] wisdom knew not God" until people
like him appeared to "preach Jesus Christ, and him crucified"—
a doctrine that usually impressed the philosophic Greeks as
mere "foolishness" (1 Corinthians 1:21–23, 2:2). Yet he believed
that even these haughty thinkers had some access to the "invisible things" of God. Reason could deduce the creator's "eternal
power and Godhead" from the visible face of creation (Romans
1:19–20). That idea gave him a way to continue his presentation
of the *kerygma* at Athens.

Instead of setting the stage with an account of God's relations
with Israel, he starts with a historical event for which reason
itself can vouch—the divine creation of the world. He speaks of
a God who "made the world and all things therein" and who
"made of one blood [in some manuscripts, simply 'one'] *all*
nations of men." This puts the philosophers themselves into the
story. After that, they can travel, by an easy process of deduction, to the idea that the creator of all things visible must himself be invisible, and that he must have a concern for his
creation, providentially "determin[ing] the times" and the geo-
graphical "bounds" of historical events, and inviting his children
to "seek" him, "if haply they might feel after him, and find him."

Leading his audience in this way, Paul presents a concrete, physical image of what he and the Athenians are doing at that very moment—looking for the invisible God, seeking him with the invisible "feel" of thought.

Having expanded his story so as to include both his audience and himself, Paul solidifies the effect, quoting the Greek poet Aratus, who represents the story of the universe as the story of the god Zeus and his family: "For we are also his offspring." This homely image of the closeness of the divine and the human helps explain the difficult, indeed paradoxical, image that Paul places next to it, when he says that "*in* [God] we live, and move, and have our being." The expression combines some of the words of the poet Epimenides with the gospel idea of the communion of Christ and his disciples, who in Paul's thought, as in his Master's, are "in" God and Jesus (John 17:21, 1 Thessalonians 1:1, 2:14). Again Paul's story embraces both monotheists and polytheists, Christians and pagans.

But Paul isn't just telling a story; he is arguing, and he argues by honest rules. He doesn't want to make his message seem so easy that his audience will misunderstand it. There is a time to divide as well as a time to unify, and this is the time to change course and do the former. He draws a firm distinction between the remainder of his own story and the stories presented in pagan art and poetry. The God who created the world, he says, is not like the conceptions of Greek art; he is not "like unto gold, or silver, or stone, graven by art and man's device." And the story of his relationship with humanity is moving on from the days of humanity's religious ignorance, which God once benevolently overlooked or "winked at." Now God challenges humanity to knowledge and repentance. Paul will not flatter his listeners: if they are to remain in the story, they must change. Once more, the *kerygma*, which aims at conversion, transforms its own terms. Having begun with a creator who made the world and watched to see how his children might do in it, Paul comes to the end of the story, in which God suddenly takes the action he has long prepared:

> [H]e hath appointed a day, in the which he will judge the world in righteousness by that man whom he hath ordained, whereof he hath given assurance unto all men, in that he hath raised him from the dead.

Paul has saved the heart of the *kerygma,* the message of Christ's resurrection, until the climax. He has been working toward this moment all along, outlining the whole of human history in order to reach its culmination—just as God in his providence outlined or "appointed" the events of history in order to reach the conclusion that Paul now describes. His speech moves from common ground to a startling new claim, from ideas that everyone can grasp by philosophic reasoning to conclusions reachable only by God's unique revelation of himself in history. His speech is a bold literary effort, with implications so challenging that some of his audience stop listening and begin to "mock" at him. But "others said, We will hear thee again of this matter."

Choices

That is the most important thing—not that the *kerygma* can be presented in various ways to various audiences, but that it provides the opportunity for various types of individuals to accept or reject it. "And some believed the things which were spoken, and some believed not"—that is the keynote of Acts (Acts 28:24). Acts is the story of the church, but the story of the church is always the story of individuals and individual choices, choices that either divide people from the church or unite them to it. The narrative of the church in transformation, as it spreads from Jews to gentiles and achieves its own internal structure, always recurs to the story of individuals confronting the word that might transform them. It is a gallery of characters, caught in moments of dramatic conflict.

We see the great scholar Gamaliel, arguing with the other leaders of Israel's religious establishment, urging them to let the Christian movement alone: "If it be of God, ye cannot overthrow it" (Acts 5:39). We see the high priest and the council forgetting Gamaliel's advice and, roused to fury against the Christian preacher Stephen, casting him out of the city to be murdered (Acts 7:57–58). In a striking contrast of character, we see a minister of state from Ethiopia talking with the disciple Philip as they travel, then pointing to a stream beside their way and asking, "What doth hinder me to be baptized?" (Acts 8:36). We see hesitaters and equivocators too. There is the Roman governor Felix, who listens while Paul "reason[s]" with him, then "tremble[s], and answer[s], Go thy way for this time; when

I have a convenient season, I will call for thee." That season never comes. Then there is King Agrippa, to whom Paul speaks with urgency, thinking that he has nearly won him over: "Believest thou the prophets? I know that thou believest." But Agrippa answers, "Almost thou persuadest me to be a Christian" (Acts 24:25, 26:27–28).[6] Almost is not enough. But the drama is still there, in the moment of the soul's deciding . . . not to decide.

Whatever the decision, Acts takes its tone and color from its steady pressure toward spiritual transformation of the individual. Episodes of physical transformation maintain the emphasis—sudden events in the outer world that reflect the urgency of events in the inner world. Some of them involve miraculous healing, as in the incident at the Beautiful Gate. Some involve miraculous liberation: Peter, jailed by King Herod, is lying in chains when he sees a light shining in his cell and feels an angel smacking him on the side. "Arise up quickly," the angel says. "And his chains fell off" (Acts 12:7). Other transformations move in the opposite direction, offering dramatic signs of spiritual sickness: Herod, allowing himself to be acclaimed as a god, is immediately "eaten of worms"; Ananias and Sapphira, Christians on the outside but godless on the inside, are judged and executed in quick succession. "Behold," Peter says to Sapphira, "the feet of them which have buried thy husband are at the door, and shall carry thee out. Then fell she down . . . " (Acts 12:21–23, 5:1–10).

The Ironies of Transformation

Often, however, transformation takes a more intricately ironic form. Saul, the future apostle Paul, finds that out while he is traveling to Damascus, intent on continuing the persecution of the Christian church that began with the stoning of Stephen, in which he participated. He is pursuing a journey away from Christ, not knowing that the road leads directly back to Him. Suddenly, just at noon, Jesus appears in a glory brighter than the sun. Paul falls to earth, blinded, struck into darkness by the inconceivable light. But when Jesus speaks, he uses the earthy form of irony known as sarcasm: "I am Jesus whom thou persecutest . . . it is hard for thee to kick against the pricks" (Acts 9:4–5, 26:14).

In modern English this might be rendered, "You're only

hurting yourself when you insist on getting out of line." "Pricks" or goads are the sticks people use to make draught animals move as they ought to. Animals don't like to be poked with those sticks, but if they kick against them, they'll just get goaded some more. That's what Jesus is doing to Saul: goading him on his way. He is also turning Saul inside out—with a literary symbol. On the outside, Saul is a great leader and scholar, and he obviously regards himself as great; but on the inside he is a rebellious animal that needs someone else to steer it. Saul gets the sense of Jesus's irony, and learns from it. He turns his own life inside out, expressing his change of heart by transforming his journey to persecute Christians into many journeys to spread Christianity.

By the time he gets to Damascus, his priorities have been completely changed; and the inner reversal is immediately marked by outwardly visible reversals. He spends three days in darkness, like the darkness of Jesus's tomb; then his sight is miraculously restored by one of those Christians whom he had meant to persecute. He is baptized, accepting the visible sign of membership in the church and receiving its spiritual sign as well; he is "filled with the Holy Ghost": "And straightway he preached Christ [here, more accurately, 'Jesus'] in the synagogues, that he is the Son of God" (Acts 9:8–20).

He now has both the Spirit and the word. Another way of putting this is to say that he has many words, and the words he uses have all been transformed, even the words that symbolize his own identity. First known as Saul, the name of a king of Israel, he now calls himself Paul, the Latin word for "small."[7] It's an ostentatiously humble gesture—paradoxical, ironic, but an appropriate literary symbol of the change that Jesus wrought when he converted him with the aid of an ironic metaphor.

The story of Paul's conversion shows the range of effects of which the book of Acts is capable, at its best. It is a sober study in institutional history, yet it crystallizes the stages of that history as mysterious moments of reconciliation between God and the inner self, confirmed by argument, warmed by irony and humor, and lit by sharp flashes of dramatic action. Its model of the church, a model on which every later interpretation of the church has relied, is that of an institution composed of individuals united by the transforming power of one great, endlessly applicable and diversifiable story. Indeed, Acts represents the development of the church as if it were a great work of literary art as well as a great spiritual event. But that is what it is. The church, as Acts describes it, is the Spirit's finest literary product.

6
Paul the Thinker

One of the many ironies in the Christian story is the fact that Paul, Jesus's most influential follower, never met him in the flesh. Another is that Paul, the last apostle to be chosen, was very likely the first Christian writer whose work has come down to us. When the written gospels began to appear, Paul's career as an author had ended or was nearing its end.

That doesn't mean there is any truth in the Victorian idea that Paul was the true "inventor of Christianity."[1] As Paul frequently testifies, the gospel existed before he started preaching it. He knew the people who preached it; both he and Luke describe his meetings with them. His versions of the *kerygma* are the same as theirs in essence. He was, however, quite capable of criticizing them when he thought they failed to draw the right conclusions from gospel principles, or had lapsed from observing them. His writing shows the freshness of the earliest period of Christian writing, combined with a maturity of reflection that one might assume, if one did not know better, must come from a later age.

This tension between youthful enthusiasm and mature deliberation is one of many fruitful oppositions in Paul's writing. He is the most "progressive" intellectual among the New Testament writers, the one who is always looking for the next idea, the next argument, the next response to a plausible counterargument. He is also the best grounded in the learning of the past, pagan as well as Jewish. As we have seen, he can quote familiarly from the Greek poets; and he readily finds support for Christian ideas in Greek philosophical thought (Acts 17:28, Romans 1:19–20). A native of Tarsus, one of the eastern Mediterranean's important commercial centers ("no mean city," as he calls it), he knew the ways of Greek and Roman culture (Acts 21:39). He was a citizen of Rome from birth—an indication that he came from a wealthy or socially prominent family—but he was also proud of his origin as "an Hebrew of the Hebrews," a student of the famous Gamaliel (Acts 22:3, 25–28; Philippians 3:3–5). At a time when people looked up passages in scripture by unrolling thirty-foot scrolls and hunting through columns of text in which no division appeared between words, let alone between chapters and verses, Paul moved confidently through his arguments, citing from memory any passage that he thought was helpful.[2]

The Writer and His Audience

Paul's remarkable conversion experience added another stimulating tension to his thought. It compelled him to explore the intellectual implications of an overwhelming emotional event and construct accounts of them that he, as Christ's representative, could recommend to others. His conversion from adversary to advocate gave him a treasury of experience, and his missionary adventures added immensely to the wealth:

> Thrice was I beaten with rods, once was I stoned, thrice I suffered shipwreck, a night and a day I have been in the deep; in journeyings often, in perils of waters, in perils of robbers, in perils by mine own countrymen, in perils by the heathen, in perils in the city, in perils in the wilderness, in perils in the sea, in perils among false brethren; in weariness and painfulness, in watchings often, in hunger and thirst, in fastings often, in cold and nakedness. Besides those things that are without, that which cometh upon me daily, the care of all the churches. (2 Corinthians 11:25–28)

Notice that Paul puts the inner, psychological challenge—"the care of all the churches"—in the place of final emphasis. His letters to the Christian congregations are some of the most self-revealing documents we have from the ancient world—backed by his experience, enriched by his intellect and sensibility, enlivened by his volatile style, and inspired by his strong emotions about the people to whom he writes.

The emotions, to be sure, were not always pleasant. Although modern Christians often picture Paul's first readers as waiting eagerly to hear from him, that would not have been true in every case, considering some of the things we find in his letters:

> [I]t hath been declared unto me of you, my brethren, by them which are of the house of Chloe, that there are contentions among you. (1 Corinthians 1:11)

> What shall I say to you? shall I praise you in this? I praise you not. (1 Corinthians 11:22)

> O foolish Galatians, who hath bewitched you, that ye should not obey the truth . . . ? (Galatians 3:1)

Paul knew that his letters could "terrify" (2 Corinthians 10:9). Presumably there were very mixed feelings in early Christian congregations when a messenger showed up with a scroll from Paul. Chloe and her household must have been the target of many angry looks when someone rose to read the apostle's first epistle to the church at Corinth.

Whatever else Paul's epistles may be, they are not complacent advertisements for the church. They are rigorous examinations of the failings of its local branches, and of the weaknesses of all its members, including himself. That is one aspect of Paul's correspondence. Another can be found in his great hymn to love in the thirteenth chapter of 1 Corinthians, and its many echoes elsewhere in his work. His epistles represent his fellow Christians as his "brethren" and "children," and these are not just formal terms: he is willing to reveal himself to this family with startling intimacy. After his blistering criticism of the "foolish" and "bewitched" Galatians, his mood shifts, and he opens his heart to them:

> Brethren, I beseech you, be as I am; for I am as ye are: ye have not injured me at all. Ye know how through infirmity of the flesh I preached the gospel unto you at the first, and my temptation which was in my flesh ye despised not, nor rejected; but received me as an angel of God, even as Christ Jesus. (Galatians 4:12–14)

We do not know what "infirmity" and "temptation" plagued him (the Galatians knew), but his love is manifest. It transforms the symbols of relationship ("brethren," "children") into realities: these people whom he so passionately addresses as silly, igno- rant, foolish fellow sinners do somehow begin to seem like a family.

For a preacher or writer, the ultimate act of intimacy may be the revelation of the methods by which he works such transfor- mations in other people's minds. Paul has the courage to allow the Corinthians a backstage view of the means he used to pro- ject his identity, so as to produce their own conversion:

> [U]nto the Jews I became as a Jew, that I might gain the Jews; to them that are under the law, as under the law, that I might gain them that are under the law; to them that are without law, as with- out law . . . that I might gain them that are without law. To the weak became I as weak, that I might gain the weak: I am made all things to all men, that I might by all means save some. And this I do for the gospel's sake, that I might be partaker thereof with you. (1 Corinthians 9:20–23)

Few relationships survive such anger as Paul's, or such demanding displays of affection; fewer still survive such con- fessions as the one I just quoted. That confession might eas- ily be interpreted, by people who did not meet the test of true familial relationship, as a revelation of hypocrisy, of Paul's having merely pretended to be various things until he "gained" enough converts. The fact that his relationship to the churches did survive is evidence of the literary artistry with which he communicated his complex feelings about his con- flict-laden family. Actually, the family would not exist without the artistry, which was Paul's only way of solving, at long dis- tance, the problems that threatened the religious unity of the church.

Some of those problems were reported to him; others he had experienced; yet others he assumed were present or soon would be. They were of two basic kinds: intellectual (disagree- ments or misunderstandings about Christian teaching), and prac- tical (difficulties in applying Christian teaching, or the simple neglect to apply it). All his letters address both kinds of issues,[3] but we can separate them for purposes of analysis. In this chap- ter I will be concerned with his literary means of dealing with intellectual problems.

Grace Versus Works

Paul was the most complicated of the early Christian thinkers and one of the most complicated stylists in world literature. Yet he recognized the simplicity of the central Christian message and emphasized the simplicity with which it could be believed and preached. At the beginning of his first letter to the Corinthians he points out that "not many wise men" were called to be Christians: "God hath chosen the foolish things of the world to confound the wise." He says that when he came to Corinth he was "determined not to know anything" except "Jesus Christ, and him crucified" (1 Corinthians 1:26–27, 2:2). Later, he proves that he can tell the whole gospel story in a *kerygma* that is an ideal of simplicity (1 Corinthians 15:1–10).

In his epistle to the Ephesians, he puts the difficult concept of the church into just four memorable verses. He begins with the source and nature of its unity:

> There is one body, and one Spirit, even as ye are called in one hope of your calling; one Lord, one faith, one baptism, one God and Father of all, who is above all, and through all, and in you all.

Then he states the source and nature of the church's diversity:

> But unto every one of us is given grace according to the measure of the gift of Christ. (Ephesians 4:4–7)

All partake of the same grace, the same favor of God; but each receives the gift of grace as it is "measured" by Christ. Individuality is in tension with unity, but both, ironically, come from the same place. They exist together, and they can exist comfortably together, if you let them: don't worry about the irony; learn from it.

No one ever explained the doctrine of the church in a briefer, simpler series of ideas. It is as if Paul were carefully unpacking it, one idea at a time. Typically, however, he is a packer rather than an unpacker, concentrating as much of his message as possible into every phrase he writes. That is why he is so challenging to read. It is not unusual to find every segment of the DNA of Christianity in a very short passage of his work, with the full range of distinctively Christian literary devices working to enforce the full range of distinctively Christian ideas. One such passage appears at the start of his epistle to the Galatians, where, in a brief page or two, he shows the connections among all these ideas.

His chief concern in this letter is the teaching that will always be most closely associated with his name: the distinction between "grace" and "works," and the priority of the first to the second. In simple terms, Paul teaches that people are "saved" and "reconciled" with God because God gives them his undeserved favor (grace), not because they have earned salvation by doing something good (works). Often the doctrine is stated in another way, as the doctrine of "faith rather than works": people are saved not by how they behave but by how they believe. They hear what God says, they believe and trust in him, and he gives them grace. But again, they do not earn their relationship with God by any works they do, and it is grace that makes it possible for them to believe in the first place. Grace sent God's Son to earth, to suffer death on behalf of humanity; grace provided the gospel, the good news about the Son; and grace enables believers' hearts to respond to that good news. State the idea in any way you want; it is still, as Paul would say, a doctrine of grace: "by grace are ye saved through faith; and that not of yourselves: it is the gift of God" (Ephesians 2:8).

In one way, the doctrine is simply a commonsensical deduction from the idea of providence. There would be no reconciliation between God and humanity if God had not sought humanity and, in the person of Jesus, offered a sacrifice in humanity's behalf. Faith is the individual's claim to involvement in that story, but the story was written by God, not humanity. Nothing that human beings could ever do would *compel* God's justice to write them into the story, as if in payment for services rendered. Consider also the cry of the would-be disciple in the gospel of Mark: "Lord, I believe; help thou mine unbelief" (Mark 9:24). God's providence is so amazing that his help is needed if one is to trust it and accept it and claim it for one's own.

In other ways, however, the Pauline doctrine is very far removed from our ordinary habits of thought. If we are interested in goodness at all—and the New Testament authors always are—we will tend to think that God rewards good actions. It seems paradoxical that people who spend their lives doing bad things may be saved, because God extends his grace to them, whereas people who spend their lives doing good things may not be saved, because they lack that invisible inner something, that faith, that comes by grace. Paul's doctrine is a clear example of Christianity's tendency to turn things inside out and upside down, reversing normal understandings of the world.

The difficulty of teaching the doctrine of grace can actually increase when one tries to convey it to people who are already members of the Christian church. The church preaches righteousness, so how can it be that righteousness is insufficient for salvation? How can it be that church membership—incontestably a good work in itself—is insufficient? And what, in that case, is the point of calling oneself a Christian? For Paul, there is a further difficulty. Jewish Christians (such as he was) came to Christianity with the belief that it was the fulfillment of the law once given to Israel. The law, like the coming of Christ, was a visible manifestation of God's providence in history. In his epistle to the Romans, Paul himself speaks of "the righteousness of the law" being "fulfilled in us" (Romans 8:4). Then how can one say that doing righteous works isn't crucial to salvation?

This should not be mistaken for an abstract philosophical problem. The inner drama of "grace" had a direct relationship to the outer drama of the early Christian congregation, where people continued to wonder whether obeying all or part of the Old Testament laws was a qualification for membership. And consider the logic of the situation: if one cannot earn salvation by obeying the laws of the Old Testament, which (as Paul says) were "ordained by angels in the hand of a mediator [Moses]," then why should one bother to obey *any* laws (Galatians 3:19)?

Setting Things Straight

When Paul wrote to the Galatians, he was thinking about all these problems. True, the leaders of the church as a whole had decided, at the Council of Jerusalem, that non-Jewish Christians should not consider themselves bound by Old Testament laws. But that didn't end the argument. If it had, Paul wouldn't have had to recur to it, not just once but repeatedly. There were, apparently, many people in the early Christian congregations who continued to argue on the other side, and argue persuasively. Paul replied to them in many ways and on many occasions, but the epistle to the Galatians is his most intensely focused account of the problem and for that reason, perhaps, his most powerful. All of Pauline Christianity is concentrated in the opening of Galatians. Here he is determined to set matters straight, intellectually, historically, and in every other way.

He comes out swinging. He starts with an account of his own authority to deal with the matter, and a declaration of which side of the argument he is going to champion, the side of grace:

> Paul, an apostle, (not of men, neither by man, but by Jesus Christ, and God the Father, who raised him from the dead) . . . grace be to you and peace from God the Father, and from our Lord Jesus Christ, who gave himself for our sins, that he might deliver us from this present evil world, according to the will of God and our Father. . . . (Galatians 1:1, 3–4)

This is no mere formal salutation; neither is it a mere assertion of one man's authority (although such an assertion can be helpful in dealing with a disputed issue). It immediately removes us from the world of "men's" opinions and puts us in the world of providence, a world quite different from our ordinary conceptions. It is a world in which a man can die and be raised from the dead, a world in which the Son of God can come to earth and give his life, not to reward humanity's goodness but to pay the penalty for its sins. That was grace, the giving of something more than the deserved. And what was its source? The source of "grace" and "peace" was God, not any works of humanity.

Paul's basic theology is packed into his opening sentence. Then, next to his statements about God, he places statements about his own experience, using each kind of statement to support the other. His original audience knew, just as we know, that he became an apostle because of a sudden conversion from his life as a persecutor of the church. The facts were notorious, but Paul insists on bringing them up again. They are his evidence that God, in the person of Jesus, really did intervene in history, and that providence really does act by grace, not in response to works. He was made an apostle by undeserved favor, not his own good deeds. He was the last person on earth whom "men" would ever have made an apostle. His works were too bad. "Ye have heard," he says, "how that beyond measure I persecuted the church of God, and wasted it" (Galatians 1:13). It is colossally ironic that Paul should have been appointed an apostle, but that is the way God does his work—"his strange work," as a prophet once called it (Isaiah 28:21).

Paul's relationship to the gospel and to the church is also something different from what one might expect:

> I certify you, brethren, that the gospel which was preached of me is not after man. For I neither received it of man, neither was I taught it, but by the revelation of Jesus Christ. (Galatians 1:11–12)

This passage demonstrates that God acts not only ironically but also paradoxically: Paul's conversion simultaneously united him with the church and (in a sense) divided him from it. He became one of the "brethren," but he did not depend on their teaching for evidence that the gospel was true. His evidence of Christ's resurrection, Christ's nature, and Christ's way of dealing with humanity came from a personal revelation. To emphasize the fact that his conversion and appointment as an apostle originated with God, not man, he says that he spent years pointedly absenting himself from the apostles at Jerusalem, the "pillars" of the church whom he sarcastically calls "these who seemed to be somewhat"—adding, "whatsoever they were, it maketh no matter to me: God accepteth no man's person"; that is, respects no reputation or external characteristics (Galatians 1:17–19; 2:6, 9).

Seemingly without effort, Paul has introduced a very complex concept of the church. The church, for him, is a unity, but it is a unity of individuals whose unique personal experience is vital to its development (see 1 Corinthians 12). Nevertheless, each of these individuals is drawn and gifted by God's grace, not by personal accomplishments. The church, the appointment of its leaders, the status of everyone within it—all are revelations of providential design. Life is a journey directed by God, who shows his providence by separating human beings from one another in order to unite them with himself, transforming them into images of his grace:

> But when it pleased God, who separated me [or, set me apart] from my mother's womb, and called me by his grace, to reveal his Son in me, that I might preach him among the heathen; immediately I conferred not with flesh and blood: neither went I up to Jerusalem to them which were apostles before me . . . (Galatians 1:15–17)

Paul is developing his story about the strange ways in which grace operates, and about the authority, not just of one apostle, but of grace itself. Grace is not something that can be fully explained; it is given when God "please[s]," revealing itself in God's actions in the world. But where it appears, it is indisputable. No philosophic thought is needed to give it authority; it brings its own authority with it.

That is what happened when Paul finally did go up to Jerusalem to make sure that he and the other leaders of the church were united in the same ideas. The reason, he explains, is that certain "false brethren" were arguing that Christians needed to do the good works of Old Testament law and submit to the symbol of religious unity enjoined by that law—circumcision (Galatians 2:4). By making the distinction between true and false brethren, Paul expands and clarifies his concept of the church. He had indicated that the church exists in a tension between unity and diversity. Now he shows what happens when the tension is broken and the paradoxical unity of believers no longer exists. Obviously, when unity is shattered, people feel entitled to think up their own doctrines. But true diversity also vanishes, because the same people go about demanding that others be restricted, brought back into obedience to law. These are the ideas that Paul packs into his dramatic portrait of the "false brethren" as men who crept in "privily to spy out our liberty which we have in Christ Jesus, that they might bring us into bondage" (Galatians 2:4). It is to counter the influence of such people that he is writing his letter to the Galatians. It was to counter the same influence that he went up to Jerusalem.

His meeting with the other apostles ended well, because they accepted the line of argument he is now urging on the Galatians: the Christian faith is historical; it is based on evidence of God's intervention in history through the sacrificial death and resurrection of Jesus Christ, the same Christ who visibly intervened by converting Paul and giving him success in preaching the gospel to the gentiles, not demanding their subjection to law. Good works had nothing to do with it; it was all the story of grace. The other apostles, Paul says, interpreted the story correctly. They saw that God was "mighty in me toward the Gentiles," and, seeing that, they also "perceived the grace that was given unto me." So they told him to keep doing what he was doing, preaching a gospel of grace (Galatians 2:8–9). They also urged him, human beings that they were, to keep sending contributions back for "the poor" in Jerusalem, where they themselves were living.[4]

Seven Stories

Most scholars believe that the meetings Paul describes at the beginning of Galatians were the same meetings described in the Council of Jerusalem section of Acts (Acts 15). Others believe there were two such conferences. In any event, Paul is happy to tell the Galatians about the victory of grace. Although he is reasoning as a theologian, he grounds his ideas on the course of human events. In the first two and a half chapters of Galatians, he tells at least seven stories:

1. The story of God's grace as shown in Jesus's life, death, and resurrection; this is the *kerygma* at its most concise (Galatians 1:1–5).

2. The story of Paul's own conversion by grace and God's gracious provision for him from the "womb" onward (Galatians 1:1, 13–16).

3. The story of Paul's conference with the apostles in Jerusalem over disputes pertaining to the grace-versus-works issue (Galatians 2:1–10), disputes that were resolved by the other apostles' knowledge of another story—

4. The story of Paul's successful missionary work among the gentiles, who were converted by grace without any demand for obedience to law (Galatians 2:7–8).

5. The story of a subsequent quarrel at Antioch between Paul and the apostle Peter, who, he says, "feared" the "false brethren" and outwardly conformed to the law, thereby suggesting that people could be "justified by the works of the law" (Galatians 2:11–17). This story illustrates Paul's conviction that a character is never bigger than the story he's in. The Christian story is written by God, not men, no matter what their outward standing in the church may be; again, "God accepteth no man's person" (2:6).

6. The story of the Galatians' unaccountable failure to remember that they themselves were converted by grace (3:1–5). And finally—

7. The story of the Old Testament patriarch Abraham. This is
   the pivot of Paul's argument, because it shows that grace has
   always been primary, that God was working by grace long
   before the giving of the law and its commandments to good
   works (Galatians 3:6–9).

Both Paul and the "false brethren" understand Christianity's
character as a historical religion based on the stories of God's
dealings with his people. The "false brethren" emphasize the
fact that God gave his people a law and expected them to follow it. Paul denies that this law is eternally binding, and makes
his own appeal to history. The law came to Israel, but where did
Israel itself come from? It came from a promise that God gave
to Israel's progenitor, Abraham: "I will make of thee a great
nation . . . and in thee shall all families of the earth be blessed"
(Genesis 12:2–3, cited in Galatians 3:7). Now, why did God give
that promise? Was it because Abraham obeyed the law? Of
course not; the law did not exist. Both it and the nation to which
God gave it were the *results* of his promise. And why was the
promise given to Abraham? Was it because of Abraham's good
works? No, there was no such external cause. The process was
internal. Abraham received the promise because he "believed,"
because he had faith; and by God's grace this belief "was
accounted to him for righteousness" (Galatians 3:6, citing
Genesis 15:6). Anyone who reads the book of Genesis knows
that Abraham was a very imperfect man; yet he was "justified,"
he had "righteousness" in God's eyes, as an effect of God's
undeserved favor. He was in the same position as the Christians
of Paul's day. God has not changed; what we receive, we
receive by grace.

The Argument Moves Forward

Having gone back in history to the time before the law, Paul
now starts working forward toward the present. He reaches the
era at which Israel accepted the law from the hand of Moses.
How, at that point, was the law's relationship to humanity
understood? Well, a curse was declared on anyone who "con-
tinueth not in *all* things which are written in the book of the
law" (Galatians 3:10, citing Deuteronomy 27:26). But no one has
ever been able to continue in "all things" perfectly. Everyone

who tries to follow the law will be pronounced guilty, cursed by the terms of its own contract. If anyone wants to be counted righteous, to be reconciled with God, it cannot happen by works of the law. There is only one alternative: it must happen by God's grace, just as it happened to "faithful Abraham" (Galatians 3:9–12).

Paul's peerless knowledge of scripture has brought the story of Abraham and Israel to life as a parallel to the story of the contemporary church and its individual members. Anyone who appreciated the literary parallel would want to see the contemporary story work out in the same way as Abraham's story, with contemporary Christians trusting God's grace and being "blessed with faithful Abraham" (Galatians 3:9). This is where literary and spiritual discernment work together. But like any other good author, Paul knows that even after he has done enough to support his argument, some readers may still have problems making it their own. He needs to respond to plausible objections, and he can't wait for his audience to come up with them—he isn't in Galatia to reply. He must bring them up himself, make them part of his own work, and dispose of them immediately. Of all the New Testament authors, Paul has the most sensitive perception of the counterarguments lurking ahead of Christian arguments, and he takes the most aggressive means of dealing with them.

That is one reason why his style is so volatile, why "he keeps jumping back and forth," as readers sometimes say; he is eager to respond to counterarguments at any stage of his own argument. He knows that even discerning readers may be thinking, "Yes, yes, but if I can't be saved by works of the law, then why did God provide a law in the first place?" Or, "You're contending that providence has never changed, that it has always operated through grace, not works. But you're also saying that it *has* changed, that God once gave a law but has now annulled it. This is a paradox. Why should it be embraced?"

These are good questions. Paul anticipates them with his own: "Wherefore then serveth the law?" he asks—in other words, what was it good for? "The law," he answers, "was our schoolmaster, to bring us unto Christ, that we might be justified by faith" (Galatians 3:19, 24). What he is literally saying is that the law taught us that we are sinners who cannot live up to law's demands; we can be "justified" only by faith in God's grace. That is what the existence of the unfulfillable law tells us. Paul makes the argument more memorable by using symbolic terms. He pictures law as a "schoolmaster"—in the context of the ancient world, a slave who served as a guardian for children. No one thinks that teachers and guardians are unnecessary, yet no one thinks that being taught and guarded is the purpose and end of a child's existence. At some point, the guardians will leave. They were just one part of a continuing process, and no one would say that a parent's plan for his child had "changed" simply because he hired a teacher and then retired him. God's providence has not "changed" because God makes different provisions at different times.

Paul's choice of symbols offers a new perspective on workings of providence that might otherwise seem too paradoxical to credit. He makes the course of history look like the most natural and unstoppably normal of human events, the growth of children to adulthood. Finally the freedom of adulthood arrives, and with it the full sense of what it means to have a loving parent:

> But when the fulness of the time was come, God sent forth his Son, made of a woman, made under the law, to redeem them that were under the law, that we might receive the adoption of sons. And because ye are sons, God hath sent forth the Spirit into your hearts, crying, Abba, Father. Wherefore thou art no more a servant, but a son; and if a son, then an heir of God through Christ. (Galatians 4:1–7)

The image of Christians as children of God can be extended. In the words of an early twentieth-century hymn, "Who serves my Father as a son / Is surely kin to me."[5] The song repeats Paul's conclusions: if we "are all the children of God by faith in Christ Jesus," then "there is neither Jew nor Greek, there is neither bond nor free, there is neither male nor female: for ye are all one in Christ Jesus" (Galatians 3:26, 28). This is another apparent Pauline paradox, a unification of two ideas that seem antithetical—individualism and universalism. All Christians are the same, no matter what their gender or national origin or former religion may be, because they all have the same parent: God's family is universal. Yet both symbol and doctrine argue for the importance of individualism as well. Faith is an internal and therefore individual quality; grace is a gift bestowed on indi-

viduals. When children become adults, they are no longer in the
position of "servants," forced to obey; they're on their own, free
to make individual decisions. Paul advises his readers, "Stand
fast therefore in the liberty wherewith Christ hath made us free"
(Galatians 5:1).

However paradoxical the combination of individualism and
universalism may seem (and Paul never shrinks from the literary
use of paradox), each of the two ideas is simple and strong, simple enough to be understood by everyone, strong enough to
influence Christianity through all future ages. Their simplicity
should not lead us to ignore the fact that Paul has hewn them
out of some very tough material, with the use of some very complicated literary tools. He has mobilized the concepts of God as
providence acting in history, of God's design to bring humanity
out of division and into unity, of God's direct revelation of his
will to individuals and his conversion of their lives to his service
as disciples of Christ, and of God's unexpected way of reversing things, so that the inner evidence of the spirit becomes more
important than the outer evidence of obedience, even to his
own law—so that even the sinner Saul, transformed into the
great apostle Paul, can cry out "Abba, Father." And (to continue
enumerating the elements of the New Testament DNA that are
at work here) Paul has developed his argument with a complex
interplay of typically Christian literary devices: the unification of
things that appear to be dissimilar (Jews and Greeks, males and
females, the present age and the age of the patriarchs); the distinction of things that appear to be similar, whether apostles
(Paul versus the other "pillars") or means of relationship to God
(faith versus works); the irony and paradox involved in arguing
that things as apparently dissimilar as unity and diversity are in
some sense one; the vigorous use of symbols ("guardians" and
"parents" and "children"); the prophetic demand that the "children" develop a new, more mature perspective on their relationship to the Father.

But that is not the end of Paul's argument. One image begets
another image; one story, still another story. The pattern of
repeated ideas moves forward, into a new characterization of his
relationship to the Galatians. That relationship has sometimes
appeared tenuous, to say the least ("O foolish Galatians"). But
now, he hopes, the Galatians understand another relationship,
the connection between their own lives and the great story of

faith and grace, and they can therefore be viewed in a different light. Teaching them, Paul has transformed them. Once they were backward children, with barely enough discernment, one would think, to get through his letter. Now they appear as the ideal disciples that he wants them to become. Revisiting his story of Christians growing into adulthood, and his story of himself as separated to God from his mother's womb, he calls the Galatians "my little children, of whom I travail in birth again until Christ be formed in you" (Galatians 4:19). What once seemed so different is now the same: Paul, the uniquely authoritative intellectual, and the Galatians, the backward members of a provincial church, can now be regarded as dear members of the same nuclear family. Even Paul is transformed. The thundering apostle has become a loving mother, "travail[ing] in birth" to bring forth his children.

Paul's argument has been a journey from outside to inside, from concern with a visible law and a stubborn local church to a new and more generous state of mind and emotion. The argument corresponds to his vision of the Christian life as a progress from "flesh" to "spirit" and "bondage" to "liberty," the stern opposition within each pair of concepts emphasizing how much progress is made in traveling from one emphasis to the other (Galatians 4:22–5:1). The journey that began with the distinction between "grace" and "works" has been challenging, but unless you know how challenging it can be, you may not understand the necessity of grace to enable you to complete it. That is why, as Paul comes to the end of his argument, he uses the image of a journey, which is so much a part of the New Testament DNA, to represent the way in which grace operates. The Christian life, he suggests, is always manifested in action, in doing something (not merely being something), and in getting somewhere; thus, "If we live in the Spirit, let us also walk [or proceed] in the Spirit" (Galatians 5:25). He wouldn't need to incite people to walk on in the Spirit if it were a perfectly easy thing to do. Yet Christians do not just walk in the Spirit; they are "led of the Spirit," kindly directed by a power that touches their lives from within and, indeed, becomes their life (Galatians 5:18). That is the power of grace.

Walking in the spirit doesn't mean wandering down every possible road. A disciple of Christ will want to walk in the way Christ walked. So there is nothing wrong, Paul says, with practicing the basic virtues taught by Old Testament law (Galatians 5:13–14, 19–23). But one wants to practice them because one is inspired by grace, not because one hopes to earn salvation by one's good works.

Discipleship is a simple idea, despite the elaborate arguments that lie behind it. Yet to put the idea into practice, to use it to get someplace, not simply as an individual but also as a member of a Christian congregation, brings up a host of problems— problems that Paul as a leader of the church was forced to address.

7
Paul the Leader

In the last book of the Bible, which was probably written toward the end of the first century, the members of a local Christian church are accused of having lost their "first love" for Christ, without being aware that anything is missing. They are advised to "remember . . . and do the first works" (Revelation 2:4–5). A generation earlier, Paul had asked the Galatians why they had forgotten how they felt when they first heard the gospel. At the time, it made such a deep impression on them that they felt as if Jesus were being crucified before their eyes. Their belief was so strong that they were willing to endure opposition to their faith. But now he needed to ask them, was it all "in vain?" (Galatians 3:1, 4). Go back a generation further, to the time when Jesus discovered that his disciples had no sooner witnessed his miracles than they had forgotten their significance. "Having eyes," he asked, "see ye not? and having ears, hear ye not? and do ye not remember?" (Mark 8:18).

In Christianity, there are always two kinds of journey: the journey forward and the journey back. Right from the beginning, those two story patterns appear. The forward journey starts with the challenge to change one's life and the willingness to follow Christ into new terrain. The backward journey starts with the challenge to remember the past and (ironically) to *recover* the good *news* in the innocence with which one first heard and believed it. The richness and scope of Christian literature have been vastly increased by the New Testament's encouragement to journey through history backward as well as forward—each tendency regarded as progressive, in its way, and providential.

"Primitivism" is the name frequently applied to the journey backward. Every denomination in Christendom has periodically tried to recover the external features and the internal feelings of the "primitive" church, although the quest for them can be daunting. Roger Williams, who founded Rhode Island as a sanctuary for devout Bible readers like himself, declined to associate with any religious body, believing that the only true church was the primitive church, but it was impossible to know exactly what it was like.[1] Our only evidence of the primitive church is literary. The book of Acts describes the origin and development of the church, and establishes the idea of what the church should be, but it is not overly concerned with the church's daily operations. Paul's letters provide much more information, but there is a problem connected with the literary form in which the information is presented. A letter writer seldom sets out to tell you what you already know, and what you already know includes the basic facts about your life. Paul had no reason, given the type of literature he was writing, to provide detailed descriptions of how a Christian congregation functioned, how its meetings were organized, who was in charge of its various activities, and so on. And here is another complication: Paul's most specific accounts of the church are written in response to problems, and one has the sense that he preferred not to respond to minor problems. He wrote about difficulties that he had to notice.

Forms of Wisdom, Forms of Folly

When we read his discussions of these matters, we should not imagine that every Christian congregation was burdened with the lurid sins or embarrassed by the ridiculous mistakes he mentions. Probably we should imagine him going about his business, preaching and teaching; then, one day, he receives complaints from "the house of Chloe" or some other source, and stays up all night preparing a letter to address the problems brought to his attention (1 Corinthians 1:11). His letters have that kind of immediacy. It is a remarkable thing: Paul's writing carries the assurance that comes from a profound understanding of essential Christian ideas—their nature, their implications, their connections with one another—yet it communicates the passion of a real person, responding urgently to troublesome developments.

Scholars sometimes speak of "the apostle's tendency to digress."[2] Instead, they should be commenting on his spontaneity. We find this spontaneity at the start of his first epistle to the Corinthians, where the issue is the "contentions" reported in the local church. Some people at Corinth claim to be followers of Cephas (Peter), others of Paul's friend Apollos, others of Paul himself—and that is precisely what Paul has always wanted to prevent. The church is one. It belongs to Jesus, not to Paul or Peter or Apollos. Its members were baptized in the name of Christ, not of Paul or any of the others. Paul goes so far as to say, "I thank God that I baptized none of you, but Crispus and Gaius; lest any should say that I had baptized in mine own name." Then he pauses and recalls some others—"And I baptized also the household of Stephanas"; then pauses again and reflects, "Besides, I know not whether I baptized any other." But despite these "digressions," he knows where he is going. His point is, "Christ sent me not to baptize, but to preach the gospel" (1 Corinthians 1:11–17). The gospel, and agreement on the gospel, and walking in accordance with the gospel—these are the important things, the things his letter is about. He will address them all, and address them conclusively. Along the way, however, he can vary what he says, come up with new ideas, return to earlier points and say something more about them. His letter is not a treatise but a response, in many forms, to the central problem of Christian unity.

It is good to read each of Paul's letters twice: once to catch the flow of his thoughts and follow their unexpected movements; a second time to make sure that one grasps the pattern of the whole and sees the individual ideas in context. In the first chapter of 1 Corinthians, Paul finds many interesting ways of maintaining a single argument: that Christianity is a journey with Christ, not with some *wise* human leader (even Paul himself) who might be understood as representing an independent variant of the church. Christianity is not the product of human wisdom. It is something more "foolish," as he says in at least six ways (A–F):

Christ sent me not to baptize, but to preach the gospel: (A) not with *wisdom* of words, lest the cross of Christ should be made of none effect. (B) For the preaching of the cross is to them that perish *foolishness*; but unto us which are saved it is the power of God. (C)

For it is written, I will destroy the *wisdom* of the wise, and will bring to nothing the *understanding* of the prudent. (D) Where is the *wise*? where is the scribe? where is the disputer of this world? (E) Hath not God made *foolish* the *wisdom* of this world? (F) For after that in the *wisdom* of God the world by *wisdom* knew not God, it pleased God by the *foolishness* of preaching to save them that believe. (1 Corinthians 1:17–21)

The paradox of the *kerygma* is that "Christ the power of God, and the wisdom of God" is preached by weak and foolish mortals (1 Corinthians 1:23–25). No one could miss that point. But finding its connection with Paul's other points requires sensitivity to the dynamic quality of his writing. One might ask, for instance, how it is that, four chapters after his critique of human leadership, we find him saying, "I beseech you, be ye followers of me," and threatening to come to Corinth "with a rod" instead of "the spirit of meekness" (1 Corinthians 4:16, 21)? This is a forceful statement of another essential Christian idea, the demand for discipleship. But how does it fit with the first chapter? The answer can't be found by comparing isolated verses. It can be discovered only when one first follows Paul's arguments as each leads spontaneously to the next, linked by the kind of associations that one finds in a vigorous conversation, and then steps back to look at the pattern that the arguments create.

The link between Paul's demand that the Corinthians be Christ's disciples, not his, and his request ("I beseech you") for them to become his own "followers" is the idea that he can show them how to empty themselves and follow Christ "foolishly" and unreservedly. "Who then is Paul, and who is Apollos[?]" he asks in Chapter 3. Nothing "but ministers by whom ye believed, even as the Lord gave to every man." Later in Chapter 3 he repeats his contention that "the wisdom of this world is foolishness with God," and in Chapter 4 he puts the two concepts together, indicating that the distinguishing characteristic of Christ's true ministers is that "we are fools for Christ's sake" (1 Corinthians 3:5, 19; 4:10). The basic idea of Chapter 1 has not changed; Paul has simply amplified it in a number of ways: follow Jesus, not just me; empty yourself of your personal "wisdom"; then you will be qualified to lead others as Jesus is leading you.

Stepping back a little farther, one can see that this way of portraying leadership is precisely appropriate to Paul's purpose in writing to the Corinthians. He has been notified of divisions in the congregation, and he is determined to end them. To do this, he needs to assert his authority as a teacher, but he also needs to let the Corinthians know that authority comes from being "foolish" enough to follow the gospel, not from setting oneself up as an all-wise master. That is where the Corinthians have made their mistake. They think of themselves as "wise," and it is obvious that so many wise brethren can hardly manage to live under the same roof.

Paul has evidence that the Corinthians, in their wisdom, have created enough divisive issues to shatter any congregation. Not only have they fallen into a variety of sects giving homage to a variety of human leaders, but they actually find ways of "glorying in" their brethren's immoral lives (1 Corinthians 5:1–6). Meanwhile, they are busy suing one another (Chapter 6), bickering about dietary customs (Chapter 8), and grudging ministers of the gospel their financial support (Chapter 9). Speaking of eating and drinking, when they gather for communion, "one is hungry, and another is drunken," and they push one another aside to get at the food. "What?" Paul has to ask them, "have ye not houses to eat and to drink in?" (1 Corinthians 11:20–22).

Their meetings are a spectacle, and not a spectacle that other people would like to see. In fact, anyone who wandered in from the street would conclude that they were "mad." They all jump up at once, demanding to speak; then they talk in unknown tongues, not caring if anyone can understand them. They childishly imagine that this makes them important.

> How is it then, brethren? when ye come together, every one of you hath a psalm, hath a doctrine, hath a tongue, hath a revelation, hath an interpretation.

Please! Paul says. Remember that "God is not the author of confusion, but of peace." Do you think that God's word came to "you only?" "Let all things be done decently and in order" (1 Corinthians 14:2–40). No wonder Paul has such difficulty keeping his temper. The Corinthians even need to be reminded that worship should be conducted "decently." If you think of Paul as a stern taskmaster, consider the problems he had to deal with.

And there was a problem even worse than those I've mentioned. Paul had discovered that some people in the Corinthian congregation weren't Christians at all. Some of them claimed that "there is no resurrection of the dead." It's amazing, Paul thought. Don't they know that Christianity, as a historical religion, is based on a belief in Christ's resurrection? Hasn't it occurred to them that there's no point in saying you're a Christian unless you hold that belief? If Christ wasn't resurrected, "then is our preaching vain, and your faith is also vain" (1 Corinthians 15:12–14). Clearly, there are "heresies" among them, including heresies that some of the Corinthians don't recognize as anything out of the ordinary (1 Corinthians 11:19). So much for their "wisdom."

Transformations of Perspective

Paul's response to most of the problems in the Corinthian church is as direct and commonsensical as his response to the no-resurrection idea. Considering the Corinthians' dispute about whether to eat meat that originated as sacrifices to pagan idols, he observes that there is nothing intrinsically wrong with eating it; after all, "we know that an idol is nothing in the world." Yet he advises them to avoid troubling weak consciences by letting themselves be seen sitting down to dinner right "in the idol's temple" (1 Corinthians 8). He argues that ministers of the gospel are entitled to be financially assisted by the congregation; after all, they work for the congregation. Yet he himself, very shrewdly, refuses to accept anything, knowing that it would be held against him and could "hinder the gospel of Christ" (1 Corinthians 9:1–15). He urges the church to allow only a few people to speak in each meeting; if they are moved to speak in tongues, they should speak to themselves alone, or pray for the gift of interpretation (1 Corinthians 14:13, 27–31).[3] As for communion: eat before you go to church (1 Corinthians 11:34)!

Sound, specific advice—but Paul knows that people don't take advice unless they want to take it, and the only way to get them to is to change their perspective. That is why he begins his discussion of the chaos in the Corinthians' religious services, where people are competing to display their spiritual gifts, with an attempt to get his readers to see themselves from a different point of view (1 Corinthians 12–13).

They see themselves as individuals, and so they are; but they also need to see themselves as members of one church. As in Galatians—as in Acts, for that matter—most of the difficulties of the church stem from the tension between unity and individuality, each of which is necessary for the church's existence. For Paul as an author, the challenge is to project a clear image of a complex church. Ideally, the image should go beyond Peter's concept of a building with Christ as its cornerstone (Acts 4:11).[4] That is a good symbol of permanence and harmony, but it doesn't offer guidance for people who wonder about their individual roles in an institution in which, as Paul says, people are given "diversities of gifts" (1 Corinthians 12:4). The image that Paul prefers—one of the most famous in Christian literature—is the image of the church as a human body:

> Now ye are the body of Christ, and members in particular. And God hath set some in the church, first apostles, secondarily prophets, thirdly teachers, after that miracles, then gifts of healings, helps, governments, diversities of tongues. (1 Corinthians 12:27–28)

The symbol of the body adds flesh and blood and human organic form to Jesus's teaching that he is "in" his disciples, and they "in" him. He and all his individual disciples are united with one another in the way in which a body is united. The parts are different, but they are all useful and necessary:

> If the whole body were an eye, where were the hearing? If the whole were hearing, where were the smelling? But now hath God set the members every one of them in the body, as it hath pleased him. (1 Corinthians 12:17–18)

All are necessary, and—even more importantly, so far as the fractious Corinthians are concerned—no one who benefits from this providential arrangement has the right to compete for dominance with the others:

> [T]he eye cannot say unto the hand, I have no need of thee; nor again the head to the feet, I have no need of you. Nay, much more those members of the body, which seem to be more feeble, are necessary. (1 Corinthians 12:21–22)

If the Corinthians kept this literary symbolism in mind, it would transform their perspective; they would start to care for all parts of the body of Christ, not just themselves. Some literary images describe transformation; others are capable of producing it. This is a productive, transformative image.

Transformations of perspective happen on the insides of people; they are specific to individuals (as well as being manifestations of the New Testament DNA). It makes sense, then, that Paul should follow his discussion of the church as the body of Christ—which is still an image based on an external view—with his magnificent psalm of love, the quality he calls the "greatest" of the Spirit's gifts to the church (1 Corinthians 13). If anything is internal, spontaneous, and a property of the individual, it is love.

What he says about the significance of love (translated as "charity" in the King James version) agrees with the preference he always gives to grace over works. The possession of love, like the possession of grace, is an internal manifestation of the Spirit, and as such is very different from the visible and external accomplishments on which some in the church pride themselves. Their perspective is normal and ordinary, but Paul insists on reversing it. Again we see the New Testament DNA, returning priorities to the internal, the individual, the seemingly humble and "weak things" of this life (1 Corinthians 1:27). Paul uses himself, the Christian figure of authority, as an illustration of this reversal:

> [T]hough I speak with the tongues of men and of angels, and have not charity, I am become as sounding brass, or a tinkling cymbal. . . . And though I bestow all my goods to feed the poor, and though I give my body to be burned, and have not charity, it profiteth me nothing. (1 Corinthians 13:1, 3)

Faith, hope, and love—all of them internal qualities—are the three greatest gifts (1 Corinthians 13:13). But love, which Paul calls "the greatest of these," is the quality of the self that also tends most strongly to unite it with others. Love bridges the gap between inside and outside, individualism and Christian unity. It shows individuals how to behave—even without direct advice from a worried apostle—toward the other members of "the body," and toward God. It is a human quality, but it leads past the point where human qualities fail. Paul affirms the paradox: love "never faileth" (1 Corinthians 13:8).

While writing of love, he adds two guiding symbols of the Christian life: the image of growing and the image of knowing. First, growing:

> When I was a child, I spake as a child, I understood as a child, I thought as a child: but when I became a man, I put away childish things. (1 Corinthians 13:11)

Growing up was a perfect symbol for Paul's argument in Galatians, and it is a perfect symbol for his present argument about the individual's proper relationship with the church. It specifies something that unites the individual with "the body." What is true of one individual is true of every other: we grow up individually, but we all grow up. The image of growth puts the image of the body into motion. Christianity is about change, conversion, becoming something, getting somewhere. "Growth" combines those ideas. Paul's image not merely suggests but describes what happens as individuals change and progress, and therefore as the church does too.

Yet Christian growth is more than a natural process. Choice and intellect are involved. Christian growth is spiritual, not physical; it is a growth in judgment, perception, knowledge of God and of oneself. That is the basis for Paul's next symbol of the Christian life, the picture of a growth in knowledge:

> For now we see through a glass, darkly; but then face to face: now I know in part; but then shall I know even as also I am known. (1 Corinthians 13:12)

It is one of the most remarkable transformations in Christian literature, this change from the principal subject of Paul's letter, the Corinthians' failure to grasp and follow the gospel message in their public life, to the intensely private moment in which the self knows and is known by its Maker. But the private moment provides a perspective from which public conflicts can be viewed. If one is growing in love and is seeking knowledge of God, one will be able to understand the gospel story, which is an account of spiritual growth and transformation, and apply its message to the problems of the church.

By one of those unexpected reversals that we have now learned to expect from Christian literature, Paul's story of what happens on the inside becomes a guide to what should happen on the outside, as he continues, after his great chapter about love, to give the Corinthians detailed advice about how to conduct themselves "decently and in order" (1 Corinthians 14). What is the point, he asks, of teaching and singing and prophesying all at once, competing with one another? No one will grow in knowledge that way. And no one will grow in love. It seems a simple idea, but the Corinthians had obviously not grasped it before. Now they can hardly fail to do so; but once again, Paul's leadership depends on his literary methods. Only by successfully reversing perspectives could he enable the Corinthians to imitate his understanding of the gospel message.

The Two Selves

Institutional problems, from Paul's point of view, can be solved by a proper self-perception. The idea verges on paradox. But his second epistle to the Corinthians shows that his work as a leader of the church is never far removed from his work as an investigator of the individual self.

This second epistle was apparently written to confirm the ideas that Paul presented in 1 Corinthians about the right perspective to have on oneself as a member of the body of Christ. It is full of tender acknowledgments of his personal relationship to the Corinthians. He, the great writer of epistles, calls the brethren in Corinth an "epistle" written in the heart, a letter that is all he needs for "commendation" of his ministry (2 Corinthians 3:1-2). He expresses concern about an earlier letter, possibly 1 Corinthians,[5] that evidently provoked much soul-searching among them. He testifies that he wrote that letter in "anguish of heart," not to cause them grief but to let them "know the love" that he has "more abundantly" toward them. (2 Corinthians 2:4–5). But he continues to worry about their habit of thinking that they are wise and everyone else is foolish. This is something that he still wants to change.

One of the many ways in which his message is continuous with the gospel is his awareness that when you penetrate people's social exterior and reach the interior region of the self, there is still more work to do, because there are more "selves" inside than one. The gospel stories picture people coming to themselves, or struggling between a self that believes and a self that does not (Luke 15:17, Mark 9:24). Paul pursues the issue, expanding the gallery of pictures and transforming the basic distinctions among selves into a way of thinking about the self that has almost the status of formal doctrine. The essential idea, which can be called the doctrine of the two selves, shows itself throughout Christian literature. It is an important manifestation of the emphasis on distinction and division, conversion and transformation, that is part of the New Testament DNA.

Sometimes, many more than two selves appear. Writers who have a reason, as Christian writers do, to look at the self from more than one perspective may continue the process of analysis and discover one distinction after another among "selves." Of course, people wouldn't bother to look so closely at the self if they didn't regard it as important. It's because individualism is central to the Christian way of thinking that Christian writers tend to turn on the self and tear it into its separate components.

The moment of conversion is the crucial juncture in the individual Christian's history. That is where the central drama takes place, and that is where the presence of at least two antagonistic selves can be detected, the self that responds to God's grace and the self that prefers not to respond. Paul sometimes pictures the outcome of the conflict as a complete transformation, the replacement of one self with the other: "If any man be in Christ, he is a new creature: old things are passed away; behold, all things are become new" (2 Corinthians 5:17). Thus he echoes the gospel theme: in Jesus's words, the soul is "born again" (John 3:3). And from a theological perspective, this is exactly what happens: conversion is the transformation of a self that was alienated from God into a self that is reconciled with him as a child to its father.

From another point of view, however, one can see a continuing war within the self. Paul pictures it as a war between "flesh" and "spirit," with "flesh" representing the outward person, the one who responds to the temptations and attachments of "this world," and "spirit" representing the inward person, invisible to the world, who is touched by God's own Spirit. Writing to the Romans, he pictures the self that responds to God as more central than the self represented by the "flesh." The first self is "the mind," "the inward man"; the second is "my members," outward things that grotesquely manifest a will of their own, a will so strong that he cries, "O wretched man that I am! who shall deliver me from the body of this death?" Ironically, "the good that I would [do] I do not: but the evil which I would not, that I do." He would like to resolve the irony by saying that it is not "I" that does evil; it is the "sin that dwelleth in me." But the sin is still, just as he says, "*in* me" (Romans 7:15–25).

Paul's perspective on the self provides insight into the church's problems. The church consists of individuals who are "saved" or "born again" yet continue to sin in the normal round of daily life. Their double selfhood naturally produces conflicting ways of seeing the world and their position in it. While Paul is struggling to transform their perspective, reversing the normal relationships of inner and outer, higher and lower, so that his fellow believers can focus on invisible and spiritual things instead of the outward concerns that most people assume are more important, something inside the Corinthians keeps struggling to transform their perspective in the opposite direction. Ironically, something *inside* them keeps making them "look on things after the *outward* appearance" (2 Corinthians 10:7).

This is the reason why the Corinthians believe they are wise enough to criticize Paul's leadership and think they can see the contradictions in him. They are looking at the outside of things: "For his letters, say they, are weighty and powerful; but his bodily presence is weak, and his speech contemptible." They are blind to the contradictions in other preachers, because those people are better at "commend[ing] themselves" by their external appearance (2 Corinthians 10:10–12). "False apostles" are therefore accepted as true apostles, and "another Jesus," "another spirit," and "another gospel" are received as if they were the true and original ones. Everything is reversed, everything is transformed into its opposite, as if by a Satanic miracle that mimics God's ability to convert and transform.

Multiple Ironies

"And no marvel," Paul says, "for Satan himself is transformed into an angel of light. Therefore it is no great thing if his ministers also be transformed as the ministers of righteousness" (2 Corinthians 11:4, 13–15). The Satanic world is something like a literary parody of God's world. If God has ministers, so has

Satan; if God transforms, so does Satan; if Christ has disciples in
the church, so, emphatically, does Satan. The difference is that
Satan's disciples lack the self-knowledge necessary to recognize
his use of irony. They think that they're looking at things
straightforwardly, understanding the inside by a quick glance at
the outside. They don't know that they're seeing everything in
reverse; they don't know that they're the butt of Satan's joke.

Paul addresses the Satanic ironies with one of his own great
passages of irony. He sarcastically assumes that the Corinthians'
perspective on themselves is correct, since it gives them such a
miraculous ability not to notice anything that might shake their
self-confidence:

> For ye suffer [tolerate] fools gladly, seeing ye yourselves are wise.
> For ye suffer, if a man bring you into bondage, if a man devour
> you, if a man take of you, if a man exalt himself, if a man smite
> you on the face. (2 Corinthians 11:19–20)

Obviously it is right to "glory after the flesh": so "many" people
are doing it, and doing it so confidently (2 Corinthians 11:18).
Anyone who doesn't do it must be a fool. That's the way the
Corinthians think, confusing the "fleshly" self with the spiritual
one.

Paul decides that he also will "glory"—and in the process set
things to rights, one irony canceling out another. If the
Corinthians' favorite preachers keep turning Christianity upside
down, recommending themselves by external appearances and
accomplishments, so will he. He is "fool" enough to do it—at a
length even greater than that of the verses I quoted in the last
chapter:

> [W]hereinsoever any is bold (I speak foolishly), I am bold also. Are
> they Hebrews? so am I. Are they Israelites? so am I. Are they the
> seed of Abraham? so am I. Are they ministers of Christ? (I speak as
> a fool) I am more; in labours more abundant, in stripes above mea-
> sure, in prisons more frequent, in deaths oft. . . . Thrice was I
> beaten with rods, once was I stoned, thrice I suffered shipwreck, a
> night and a day I have been in the deep; in journeyings often, in
> perils of waters, in perils of robbers, in perils by mine own coun-
> trymen, in perils by the heathen, in perils in the city, in perils in
> the wilderness, in perils in the sea, in perils [note well!] among false
> brethren; in weariness and painfulness, in watchings often, in

hunger and thirst, in fastings often, in cold and nakedness. (2
Corinthians 11:21–27)

Paul was a lover of lists. Some of his best literary effects result
from long lists of parallels. This is one of them. The mighty catalogue of external, "fleshly" experiences should be enough to
flatten any objector to his authority. But his thesis is that spiritual authority is *not* "commended" merely by such things.
Spiritual authority is a matter of the spirit, a matter of events
touching the inner self. So, at the end of his list, the point of
emphasis, he turns to spiritual qualities:

> Beside those things that are without, that which cometh upon me
> daily, the care of all the churches. Who is weak, and I am not
> weak? Who is offended, and I burn not? The God and Father of our
> Lord Jesus Christ, which is blessed for evermore, knoweth that I lie
> not. (2 Corinthians 11:28–31)

The inner self, the self that the Corinthians have such trouble seeing, is the self that has the power of love and "care"—a
power that, ironically, can have the strongest external effects.
You may not be able to see them all, but God "knoweth" it is
true. And if you think that Christ's apostle is weak and contemptible, this is how he is weak and contemptible.

Paul, the great rhetorician, knows that here is a place to pause
and let the Corinthians feel as guilty as they deserve to feel. The
pause is effected by two verses of anticlimax (2 Corinthians
11:32–33) in which he briefly returns to the list of his external
adventures, adding a curious episode in which he escaped from
enemies by being lowered in a basket from a city wall. The outward Paul is someone about whom many curious, even seemingly ridiculous, stories might be told. The inward Paul . . . that
is another matter. The odd picture of the distinguished theologian dangling in a basket emphasizes how different the inside
can be from the outside, and the importance of distinguishing
these two ironically opposed aspects of human identity.

Paul takes another view of the problem of the self in the next
passage, which he introduces by an extraordinary effect of
irony. First he swears off his recent career of boasting about
himself: "It is not expedient for me doubtless to glory." He indicates that he is changing the topic: "I will come to visions and

revelations of the Lord." But this turns out to be the start of another story of his own relationship to Christ:

> I knew a man in Christ above fourteen years ago (whether in the body, I cannot tell; or whether out of the body, I cannot tell: God knoweth), such an one caught up to the third heaven. And I knew such a man (whether in the body, or out of the body, I cannot tell: God knoweth), how that he was caught up into paradise, and heard unspeakable words, which it is not lawful for a man to utter. Of such an one will I glory: yet of myself I will not glory, but in mine infirmities. (2 Corinthians 12:1–5)

The context, which is a discussion of Paul's rightful authority as Christ's apostle, clearly identifies the "man in Christ" as Paul himself. So we see him in two different ways, as the "man in Christ," the recipient of a heavenly vision, and as the "real," everyday Paul, who does not know and "cannot tell" all the pertinent facts about God's relationship with him in his capacity as a "man in Christ." This is the double self again, but the terms have changed. It isn't the good versus the bad self, nor is it strictly the "fleshly" self versus the spiritual self. It is Paul himself, all of him, looking at Paul himself, all of him, caught up to God at a specially important conjunction of his story with the story of God.

Once more, Paul's emphasis on the contrast between various versions of the self makes good literary sense. The Corinthians looked at the everyday Paul and judged him with a measure of contempt. Some of them had trouble telling him apart from any number of false apostles. But notice the dramatic transformation when one sees him, as it were, from God's perspective, "caught up" to glory. Obviously, "God knoweth" what you don't—and won't, in your supposed wisdom, until the time when you see God, not "through a glass, darkly," but "face to face." He knows more than even Paul knows about Paul, the "man in Christ."

There is an interesting bit of literary commentary in Paul's account of his experience. By presenting himself in the way he does, he recognizes a fact that every writer knows: stories look different from the perspective of authors than they do from the perspective of their characters, even when authors are characters in the stories that they themselves write. When you try to tell a story about yourself, you may discover how little you understand and can communicate about your experience, even of what is most intimately present to you. Paul's reticence about becoming too specific ("I cannot tell: God knoweth") concedes this point. Even a writer of his ability can be baffled by the attempt to "tell" (or "know") it all. This literary realization is closely connected to a theological one. It is the same realization that comes from reading the gospel narratives, which say *what* happened but ordinarily do not try to explain *how* such things could happen: the writers of words see a lot less than the Author of events.

This is where the doctrine of the two selves becomes especially relevant to Paul's concern with the well-being of the church he is trying to lead. Given the fact that there is more than one possible perspective on the self, and that there is a great deal we do not know, even about our own selves, we should always be alert to the possibility that the stories we tell about ourselves may not be complete, or even true. As far as the Corinthians are concerned, they are "wise" and Paul is "foolish." That's their story, a story in which they cast themselves as heroes. This particular story isn't just incomplete; it's wrong. But wrong stories can be corrected. Paul is trying to correct the Corinthians' story, by telling it in another way.

Everyone knows that we can often learn otherwise inaccessible truths about ourselves from a story that is supposed to be about someone else. Jesus's parables are based on that assumption. Paul uses it also. For the benefit of the Corinthians, he applies to himself the moral of the story that he has just told, the story of his "visions." The Lord must have known, he says, that he would try to make himself the hero of that story, although that would have been the wrong thing to do. It wouldn't have been a case of Paul's fleshly self coming too much to the fore, but it might have been a case in which the intensity of his spiritual life tempted him to think that he was entirely spiritual. His visions might have prompted him to start telling the same kind of boastful stories about himself that the Corinthians have been telling about themselves. In this world, even good things can turn to bad. The Lord therefore made sure that Paul remained aware that his fleshly self still existed:

> And lest I should be exalted above measure through the abundance of the revelations, there was given to me a thorn in the flesh, the messenger of Satan to buffet me. (2 Corinthians 12:7)

No one knows the nature of this famous "thorn in the flesh." It may have been some bodily impairment or some besetting weakness. Whatever it was, it operated as the kind of control that every author needs: it kept Paul's story within "measure." It also kept him alert to the importance of his own doctrine of grace. When he asked the Lord to remove the "thorn," the Lord, by revelation, refused, saying, "My grace is sufficient for thee." From this Paul learned that he should "glory" in his weaknesses, because they were occasions of grace. The paradox is that he came to take "pleasure in infirmities . . . for when I am weak, then am I strong" (2 Corinthians 12:9–10).

The Spiral Structure

There is a final irony: in a sense, the Corinthians were right after all. They thought that Paul was a flawed character, and he is. But that shouldn't surprise anyone. In a complicated and interesting way, it brings us back to the simple truth, that no Christians are perfectly wise, perfectly holy. If they were, they wouldn't need any leaders, or letters from them, either; and they wouldn't need God's grace. But they're not perfect, and the best kind of leadership is the intellectual (and literary) guidance that reminds them of the reality.

While enforcing this lesson, Paul has led his readers on a journey through the world of early Christianity, from conflicts among individuals to conflicts within individuals to the mysterious revelations of God himself. T.S. Eliot concludes *Four Quartets*, his series of meditations on Christianity, by describing such a spiraling investigation of the world and depicting it as a journey that every Christian needs to take. He represents it as both a return to the beginning and an advance to a loftier perspective:

> We shall not cease from exploration
> And the end of all our exploring
> Will be to arrive where we started
> And know the place for the first time.[6]

We saw spiral structures in the gospels of Luke and John. Now we see a spiral structure used to address the problems that arise after people have accepted the gospel. It was problems in the church that launched the intellectual journey of Paul's letters to the Corinthians. He responded by tracing the outward defects of the institution back to the original, inward infirmities of its members. He admitted his own infirmities. He expressed his hope that he would not be humbled further by discovering that his message hadn't inspired his readers to take the same intellectual journey that he took (2 Corinthians 12:20). But they can't do it, he believes, unless they are willing to imitate his own processes of self-examination and follow them to the end, which is the willingness to confront one's relationship with Christ and see whether one still depends on him as one did at first—depending, in one's weakness, on "the power of God"

> Examine yourselves, whether ye be in the faith; prove your own selves. Know ye not your own selves, how that Jesus Christ is in you . . .? (2 Corinthians 13:4–5)

You can't get more basic, more "primitive," than this backward look at the Founder of Christianity and his existential connection to the individual believer. And you cannot get more sophisticated, more "advanced," than the means Paul uses to bend the reader's course back to the Jesus who reveals himself "in you."

For all their fiery emotion, Paul's letters are models of the reflective, intellectual approach to the church's problems. But there is yet another literary approach to be considered, the one taken by the book I quoted in the first paragraph of this chapter—the final book of the New Testament, the Revelation. Paul had "visions and revelations of the Lord," but here is a whole volume of them, a vast symbolic drama about the conflicts within the church, the church's conflicts with the outside world, and much, much more. It is the last, irreplaceable part of the New Testament's contribution to Christian literature.

8
The Art of Revelation

The New Testament's final book is one of the most controversial in the Bible. We know that early Christian authorities attributed the Revelation or Apocalypse (the terms are interchangeable) to the apostle John, the "beloved disciple." The author says that the visions from which the book resulted came to him on Patmos, an island off the west coast of Turkey, where he had been exiled because of "the testimony of Jesus Christ" (Revelation 1:9). During the last decade of the first century there was a persecution of Christians by the Roman empire, and some second-century Christians believed that the Revelation was written then. That would place its authorship in John's extreme old age. But there had been another persecution, thirty years before, and the book could have been written at that time.

Modern scholars observe that the Greek style of Revelation is very different from that of the gospel of John and the three epistles attributed to him, and notice that Revelation itself attributes its writing to "John" but does not identify him as "the disciple whom Jesus loved" or the author of any other works. Nevertheless, some of the theological ideas and terminology of Revelation have parallels in the other Johannine books. Like John 1:1, the Revelation calls Jesus the "Word of God," not in the sense of a mere preacher of righteousness but in that of a cosmic Lord; and it identifies Jesus with the Father as "the first and the last," the "Alpha and Omega" (Revelation 19:13, 1:17, 22:13). A popular way of harmonizing the evidence is to suggest that Revelation was the product, not of John the apostle, but of an associate who bore the same common name. Another conjecture is that the apostle's visions and revelations were committed to writing by one of his followers.

The larger issue is the meaning of Revelation, most of which is composed of prophetic narratives, projected with a variety of symbols—animals, cities, precious metals, stars and clouds and jewels and blood, and numbers, many, many numbers. Because the book opens with the declaration that it is "the Revelation of Jesus Christ, which God gave unto him, to shew unto his servants things which must shortly come to pass," Christians have understandably attempted to discover precisely what events the symbols predict. Also understandably, their interpretations have varied greatly and bewilderingly from one another.

Some things are certain. What the book predicts in the near term is the destruction of Rome, the persecutor of the early Christians. "Rome" is never named, but on this point the symbolism is transparent. Revelation's portrait of a woman whose name is "MYSTERY: BABYLON THE GREAT" does not present a mystery that is hard to solve. Just put the parts of the vision together. First, the mystery woman is politically powerful, having "committed fornication" with the "kings of the earth" and made "the inhabitants of the earth . . . drunk with the wine of her fornication." Second, she herself is drunk "with the blood of the martyrs of Jesus." Finally, she, like the city of Rome, sits on seven hills or "mountains" (Revelation 17:1–9). When one arrives at this point, one hears a barely suppressed whisper: "It's Rome!" This is the city that God will utterly destroy (Revelation 18:8).

But the prophecy of the fall of Rome is part of a broader prophecy, Revelation's great pageant of predictions of the end-time, when human history will be concluded by the providence and might of God. It is the long-term meanings of Revelation that interpreters argue about. What exactly will happen in the end-time? And "when," as Jesus's disciples asked about his own end-time prophecies, "shall these things be?" (Matthew 24:3).

When we ask these questions, we enter an apocalyptic tradition that goes back farther than the New Testament. In the Old Testament book of Daniel, to which the New Testament Revelation frequently alludes, the prophet says, "I heard, but I understood not: then said I, O my Lord, what shall be the end of these things?" The answer is, "Go thy way, Daniel, for the words are closed up and sealed till the time of the end" (Daniel

12:8–9). It's quite possible for a prophet to speak without under-standing all the implications of what he says. It is even more possible for a literary critic to miss the implications of the text he is reading. But my job in this book is not to set forth the final meanings of prophecy; it is to provide, if I can, a sense of prophecy's literary framing and literary effects.

Uncovering the Present

One effect is the alluring glimpse of a mysterious future. Another, often neglected, is just the opposite: a clear view of what exists right now. It is always helpful to remember that "apocalypse" (ἀποκάλυψις) means "uncovering," and that for Judeo-Christian prophetic literature the significance of the pre-sent is usually just as important to uncover as the significance of the future.[1]

For whose benefit does the present need to be uncovered? John answers the question by addressing his book to the "ser-vants" of God. Throughout the New Testament, as we have seen, God's servants show a disconcerting tendency to drift away from their jobs. That is why Jesus, when he was still in this world, told his servant Peter three times what his work should be (John 21:15–17). That is why Paul's letters are full of exhortations, exclamations, and rhetorical questions ("Know ye not . . . ?" "Do ye not know . . . ?") about things that his brothers and sisters should remember but may have forgotten (1 Corinthians 3:16, 6:2). Only rarely in the Bible are prophets sent to people who frankly do not believe; it is the alleged believers who need the prophetic message. The crucial thing about this message is its literary force. Something has to be done to wake people up. So prophets become "apocalyptic." Apocalypse is prophecy raised to a pitch of intensity that only the cosmic backdrop of the "end-time" can give it. Yet the prophecy still relates to the here and now as well as to the future, be it far or near.

That may help us understand why the book of Revelation begins, not with elaborate prophecies of the world's end, but with the appearance of Christ to one of his disciples, on one of the lesser islands of the Mediterranean, in the midst of an ordi-nary "Lord's day." Jesus manifests himself to John as "the first and the last" and as the "Son of man" who has "the keys of hell and of death"; yet he says to the Revelator, as to his friend, "Fear not" (Revelation 1:9–18). The encounter continues with Jesus's command for a batch of letters (those very mundane objects) to be sent to seven Christian churches in the vicinity. The letters inform them (four out of seven of them, at any rate, and perhaps a fifth) that they are badly mistaken in their belief that they are, at the moment, serving Christ.

Five out of seven is about the right number to emphasize that the church is mainly composed of Christians who are no longer authentically Christian, and to indicate for the benefit of future ministers of the gospel the constant need for revival within the church. The issue raised by Jesus in the Revelation is the same that was raised by Jesus in the gospels. His listeners were usually devout people, or thought they were, but there was a difference between the inner self and the outer. The Jesus of the Revelation tells John to write to the church at Laodicea:

> Because thou sayest, I am rich, and increased with goods, and have need of nothing; and knowest not that thou art wretched, and miserable, and poor, and blind, and naked: I counsel thee to buy of me gold tried in the fire, that thou mayest be rich; and white raiment, that thou mayest be clothed, and that the shame of thy nakedness do not appear; and anoint thine eyes with eyesalve, that thou mayest see. As many as I love, I rebuke and chasten: be zealous therefore, and repent. (Revelation 3:17–19)

At issue, once again, is the problem of the two selves, a problem represented here as a conflict between the rich and attractive "outsides" of the Christian personality and the poor and miserable "insides." A related issue is the problem of moral perception, the failure to see what exists inside oneself. That is why a prophetic uncovering is necessary. Revelation uses multiple ironies to demonstrate how serious the deficiency is. It shows that the "best" people are actually poor and wretched—and blind, too, because they can't even see that they are poor and wretched. It is like one of those dreams in which you imagine that you walk out of the house not only naked but also strangely oblivious to the fact that you are—except that in this case, it's not a dream. To discover that they are naked, the Laodiceans have to be stripped naked again, by Christ's uncovering of their condition. Another, more hopeful irony is that after they are stripped, they can be dressed in the fine clothes that they originally thought they were wearing, the "white raiment" of the disciples of Christ. In order to be clothed, they must be stripped; in order to "buy" the true gold of the gospel, they must see that they are too poor to buy anything except the gospel, which is free to all.

These ironies, like so many others in the New Testament, are transformative; to grasp them, Revelation suggests, is to change one's life. Their climax is the same miracle of transformation that John the gospel writer offered as proof of Jesus's divinity, the recovery of sight by the blind: "Anoint thine eyes . . . that thou mayest see" (compare John 9:6). That commandment summarizes the moral and psychological message that runs throughout the New Testament: repent, be changed, be healed. In this sense, the verses I just cited (Revelation 3:17–19) are the New Testament in microcosm, and Revelation in microcosm as well, despite the fact that they contain no prophetic prediction, any more than the one that William Blake had in mind when he said that a prophet's job is to warn you that "if you go on So the result is So."[2]

One of the most ironic things about Revelation is the way in which its ironies and paradoxes work together with its plain statements of fact. Jesus may be stating a paradox when he says, "As many as I love, I rebuke and chasten," but the paradox is as easy to understand as the little picture of an unexpected visit that immediately follows it:

> Behold, I stand at the door, and knock; if any man [Greek: *tis*, "any-one"] hear my voice, and open the door, I will come in to him, and will sup with him, and he with me. (Revelation 3:19–20)

If this is prophecy, a story about what is going to happen, it is a very homely and accessible story. Revelation offers many stories like this. They are remarkable for their concreteness, their reliance on images from everyday life, and their boldness in representing the story of God and the story of humanity as one united story, in which the divine is always ready to cross the path of the human. "Supping" is a purely human action, yet there is Christ, standing at the door, ready to come and share. This Christ brings up none of the problems that vex the abstract philosopher: time versus eternity, human choice versus overruling providence . . . In Revelation, the relationship between God and humanity is full of surprises, ironies, and paradoxes, but so is any relationship between friends—isn't it?

Yet immediately after Jesus promises to sup with anyone who invites him in, he makes a promise in another key:

> To him that overcometh will I grant to sit with me in my throne, even as I also overcame, and am set down with my Father in his throne. (Revelation 3:21)

In Revelation, there is only a single step from this world to the world of eternity. At one moment, the relationship between Jesus and his disciples is that of two friends dining together at twilight in a little house in an obscure part of the Roman empire. In the next moment, the scene shifts, and we are standing by the throne of God.

This is an extraordinary literary effect. Some of its success depends on the framework that other books of the Bible have already established. If one is familiar with the ways in which Jesus is presented in the theological passages of the gospel of John and the epistles of Paul, and the ways in which God's magisterial providence is described in both the Old and the New Testaments, one need not pause and wonder at the sight of Jesus sitting with the Father on his throne, preparing to rule the nations "with a rod of iron," and welcoming his disciples home to share his kingdom with him (Revelation 3:21, 2:26–27). Knowing the framework, one can appreciate the drama and the visual effects, not worrying about the lack of detailed explanation or patient narrative development. Revelation is about making the blind to *see*, not about explaining everything that is seen.

The Perspective of Eternity

That means, however, that people who look for ordinary story connections will have a frustrating time reading it. There is, indeed, a single overarching story, leading from the temporary victory of God's enemies, the persecutors of the church, to the eternal victory of his friends. Inside that great story, hundreds of smaller stories are packed, each revealing some part of it, viewed in some particular way. But the stories are not arranged in a single sequential order. They are presented in three series of "uncoverings"—the opening of seven seals, the sounding of

seven trumpets, the pouring of seven vials. Each sequence liber-
ates a torrent of stories and images. That does not mean that at
each stage the big story advances. It stops, it jumps forward, it
retreats. Even climactic events repeat themselves. At Revelation
6:13–14, the stars fall and the heavens depart; at Revelation 8:12
a third of the stars, which had "previously" fallen, are cast into
darkness. The destruction of Babylon is proclaimed both at
Revelation 14:8 and at Revelation 18:1–4 (where Christians who
remain in Babylon are advised to "come out of her," as if she had
not already fallen). The birth of Jesus is narrated not at the beginning of events but in the midst of them (Chapter 12), after many
of his actions have already been described.

In a way, Revelation imitates the manner in which events in
time are viewed from God's perspective in eternity—as
unbound by the order of time. Omniscience can view events in
any "sequence" it wishes. And that is the perspective that
Revelation implies. As soon as the letters to the churches have
been dictated to John, a trumpetlike voice calls him to "come up
hither" and see things from the heavenly point of view
(Revelation 4:1). This is the start of the real "action" of
Revelation—an emphatic change from the earthly to the heavenly perspective. Then, in one of the book's many stories of the
world as seen from above, John reports:

> I saw another angel fly in the midst of heaven, having the ever-
> lasting gospel to preach unto them that dwell on the earth, and to
> every nation, and kindred, and tongue, and people. (Revelation
> 14:6)

One thinks of a gospel as a specific book or a specific
announcement of the "good news" by the church. But this is
"the everlasting gospel," the gospel that existed before the
church was organized or any gospel books were written, and
endures even after the church has had time to lose its "first love"
(Revelation 2:4). The reference to "the everlasting gospel"
assumes a continuity between the first preaching of the gospel
and Revelation's own preaching. More important, it asserts that
the "news" always remains "new," because it is eternal. That is
a paradox; but again, from the standpoint of eternity, all gospel
stories can appear as if they happened "at once," free of fleshly
restrictions.

Like the gospels themselves, Revelation insists on the paradox of eternity manifesting itself at a particular place and time. Of course, the eternal and invisible can be represented to us only by symbols derived from the world of time, the things of earth. Revelation is filled with *things,* and although most of these things are symbols, their firm connection to this earth helps greatly in interpreting their meanings. No one imagines that there is any furniture in eternity, but when we hear that "a throne was set in heaven," we know what is meant, even before the "four beasts"[3] exclaim around the throne, "Holy, holy, holy, Lord God Almighty, which was, and is, and is to come" (Revelation 4:2, 8). The throne is a concrete representation of something that would otherwise be virtually unimaginable— God's eternal dominion.

The meaning of many apocalyptic symbols is less immediately apparent, but their familiar associations often provide a way of understanding them. One of Revelation's most provocative symbols appears in Jesus's promise that "to him that overcometh" he will give "a white stone, and in the stone a new name written, which no man knoweth saving he that receiveth it" (Revelation 2:17). The specifics are odd—therefore arresting. Why is it a stone? Why is it white? Why is there a new name written on it? At least part of the answer is implicit in the ordinary associations of these things. A stone is hard and definite; white is a traditional symbol of purity and innocence. One recalls the sudden innocence of the new birth, Christian conversion (John 3:3), and the moral firmness that Christians are supposed to exhibit thereafter. A new name is an appropriate symbol of the Christian's new life, invisible and mysterious, a matter of the inner self. "Your life," Paul says, "is hid with Christ in God" (Colossians 3:3). The curious "white stone" shows some qualities of the hidden life, although it does not try to explain it. To do so would negate the inherent mysteriousness of the Christian self: "no man knoweth saving he that receiveth it."

Revelation's symbolism ranges from the easy to the deeply obscure. But the literary appeal of the book does not depend on everybody's ability to interpret every one of its symbols in detail. If it did, Revelation would never have exerted the enormous influence on Christian ideas and literature that it has. Revelation shows the power of the literary DNA that we have seen in the other books of the New Testament and that we have already encountered in our first look at Revelation itself: the providential story of God's convergence with humanity; radical distinctions, transformations, reversals, and changes of perspective; strong dependence on irony and paradox; the use of symbols to evoke the invisible and the mysterious . . . As for the literary impact of the symbols in Revelation, that often depends more on their resonance and suggestiveness than on specific knowledge of what they represent.

In Chapter 18, for instance, there is a symbolic account of the end of "Babylon" in which "the kings of the earth" and "the merchants of the earth" and "a mighty angel" react to her downfall. One can speculate about exactly what these observers represent, exactly what ideas about politics, economics, and theology they may imply; but the chapter's immense vitality comes from its brilliantly suggestive procession of literary images. Like Paul, the author of Revelation loves lists, and this chapter contains some of the finest examples of the art:

> And the merchants of the earth shall weep and mourn over her; for no man buyeth their merchandise any more: the merchandise of gold, and silver, and precious stones, and of pearls, and fine linen, and purple, and silk, and scarlet, and all thyine wood, and all manner vessels of ivory, and all manner vessels of most precious wood, and of brass, and iron, and marble, and cinnamon, and odours, and ointments, and frankincense, and wine, and oil, and fine flour, and wheat, and beasts, and sheep, and horses, and chariots, and slaves, and souls of men. (Revelation 18:11–13)

One element of the New Testament DNA is repetition, and Revelation is a very repetitious book. Yet it makes even its redundancy effective. It describes Babylon as "the hold of every foul spirit, and a cage of every unclean and hateful bird" (Revelation 18:2). One would think that foul spirits were enough; why add birds to them? And why make the birds not only "unclean" but "hateful"? (Have you ever heard of a "hateful" bird?) No, that imagery is redundant, but it has its effect. Nothing could be more *conclusive* than this sequence of dreadful images. But the "merchants of the earth" passage is different. It is a profound social satire, deriving its power from the ease with which the reader sinks into its redundancies and starts to enjoy them.

Here are all the good things of this world, all the things that appeal to eye, ear, taste, smell, and touch. There is nothing easier than to get lost in the seductive, seemingly endless array of pleasures, just as one might have gotten lost in the luxuries of Rome itself. And that, evidently, is what Revelation intends. Get lost in it—until you reach the phrase that is cunningly reserved for last: "and souls of men." That is a test line. Are you still seduced by the pleasures of "Babylon"? Do you approve of slavery? Oh, no! But don't you understand that slavery was where the list was heading from the start? To narcotize oneself with "merchandise" is to sell one's own soul to it, and probably not to worry much about selling other people's souls as well. That is the mentality of the normal citizen of Rome. But if the list has woken you up, you have passed the test. The passage is a beautifully contrived rehearsal, and reversal, of this world's values.

In discussing Revelation's beautiful contrivances, I may seem to neglect the fact that it is a series of visions, which one might expect to be received and expressed quite "spontaneously." No one, however, can claim to understand just how vision translated itself into Revelation's literary forms and devices. Later Christian poetry sheds light on the ways in which intense experience can arrange itself in complexly logical ways, with subtle and clever literary effects.[4] Every student of Revelation recognizes its wealth of allusions to Old Testament prophecy, something that is very important to its literary character; and this repetition of Old Testament material has a conscious aim. It asserts that there is one great plan lying beneath both the old and the new revelations; it testifies to the continuity of God's purposes. Now, whether the Old Testament allusions came fully formed at the moment of vision or were elaborated during the process of composition, they are learned and complex literary constructions. Anyone who compares the vision of God's glory in Revelation 4 with the visions to which it alludes in Isaiah 6 and Ezekiel 1 will see the features that Revelation maintains and adapts, and will feel how purposefully it argues for the harmony of all the visions and revelations we find in scripture. But when one has appreciated effects like that, one has only begun to discover the literary intelligence at work in Revelation.

Visionary Art

Notice what happens in the visionary story of "the two witnesses" in the book's eleventh chapter. The story begins and ends at "the temple of God"—a framing device that provides the story with a sense of completeness and integrity. It suggests the possibility that we can read this episode and receive a capsule version of Revelation as a whole, the story of this world as viewed from the perspective of "the temple of God" in eternity. The framing device implies that the story develops around a sacred enclosure that the evils of the world cannot penetrate. That is an important implication, because the story is about events that might threaten one's faith in providence if one were not assured that providence had limited their effects. The Revelator is told, indeed, that the *outside* of the temple is given up to the "gentiles," who are allowed to tread down the holy city that surrounds it. But that is not the end of the story. The gentiles operate within a strict temporal frame: they have only "forty and two months" to do their worst.

As usual in Revelation, vision expresses itself in images of real things. The visionary temple recalls the temple that stood in Jerusalem until it was destroyed by the Roman army in A.D. 70. If Revelation was written before that date, the vision communicates a straightforward sense of reality. But assuming, as most scholars do, that it was written later, then it communicates an additional impression. It indicates that what the temple represented is still in existence, transcending the destruction of the literal building. There is still a sacred enclosure, a sanctuary that protects the sacred from the profane, the people of God from the people of the world, the Godly inside of reality from the Satanic outside of it. The sanctuary may be invisible, or visible only to the visionary eye, but nothing can match its strength.

Christian stories normally emphasize the contrast between insides and outsides. An effective way of doing so, as we have seen in the gospels and epistles, is to shift perspective from one to the other. That is what happens when the Revelator is given a measuring rod and told to "measure the temple of God, and the altar, and them that worship therein." To take measurements is to study what can be seen on the surface. One can do that with holy objects such as temples and altars and worshipers, although one knows that there is no holiness in the measurements themselves. The process seems a bit absurd. But there is no point in even bothering to measure something that is completely outside the sacred enclosure: "measure it not." The outside "is given unto the [spiritual] Gentiles," and they make no pretense of holiness. There is nothing about them but a materialist point of view.

What is worth measuring is the length of time that will be permitted them. When the Revelator announces that the gentiles will have their way for "forty and two months" or (to say the same thing in other words) "a thousand two hundred and threescore days," he shows that their regime does not partake of eternity. There is a providence that maintains the limits of their time. It is bad that the gentiles will prevail for three and a half years, but it is good that there are boundaries to their rule. No one needs to be fooled by their apparent success; God has appointed "two witnesses" to reveal the truth about it. Though in "sackcloth," the emblem of mourning, these witnesses have "power" to "prophesy" during the time allotted to the gentiles. So history can be viewed from two perspectives. Seen from the worldly outside, it looks like the triumph of evil. Seen from the spiritual inside, as the Revelator and the two witnesses see it, it is only a moment of evil, guarded by the power of God.

The witnesses are servants of God and, in a way, fixtures of his temple: "these are the two olive trees, and the two candlesticks standing before the God of the earth." Initially, this seems like another view from an external perspective, one that makes them appear like little more than pieces of temple furniture. But look again. The two witnesses are alive, like trees; and like olive trees, they are rich in value. They act, and their acts are more than mere movements of celestial clockwork. They are the individual and volatile parts of God's cosmic purpose. They act "as often as they *will*." Their foes undoubtedly regard them as distressingly unpredictable. People who think they can harm the two witnesses find that suddenly "fire proceedeth out of their mouth, and devoureth their enemies." They also have the power to repeat the miracles of Elijah and the plagues of Egypt, preventing rain and turning water into blood; their story thus incorporates, in yet another way, the Old Testament in the New (1 Kings 17:1, Exodus 7:19–20). The presence of these dynamically human witnesses emphasizes the idea that God's story, as the Bible tells it, is always the story of humanity as well.

Why are there two of them? The historical applications have been endlessly debated. The literary meaning is less difficult to find. God has more servants than one on this earth, but he doesn't have a throng of them, either. Two is a number of loneliness, but not of complete isolation. Later in the eleventh chapter we hear, as we do in Old Testament prophecy (Isaiah 9), about a "remnant" of potentially faithful people—not everyone, but more than one.

The witnesses are fully human; their adversaries are less than human, at least in their behavior. One of Revelation's ways of showing the spiritual condition of God's enemies is to picture them as animals, sometimes even as animals worshiping another animal ("the image of the beast" [Revelation 13:15]), in an insane procession heading downward to what Revelation 11 calls "the bottomless pit." The two witnesses are slain by a "beast" from that pit. And there, from a purely external, materialist point of view, their story should end. We see them now as "dead bodies" lying in the street. (In Revelation, "witness" and "martyr" are represented by the same word [*martus*].) Their enemies leave the bodies to rot, thus emphasizing their assumption that there is nothing sacred, nothing spiritual in this world. As in virtually all the conflicts of the New Testament, this is not just a contest between forces but a contest between perspectives, between rival ways of assessing the world. One set of eyes looks for the inner, the invisible, the symbolic connection with the unseen God. The other set of eyes finds only the outer, the visible, the literal, the fleshly and the deathly.

The two witnesses are literally dead. Their enemies therefore give themselves up to the pleasures of the flesh, celebrating and even (sarcastic touch) "send[ing] gifts one to another," as if they had done something worthy of congratulations. They do not perceive God's strange ways with time, space, and matter. The world is filled with God's meanings, if they could only see them. But they don't. They miss the connection between the three and a half years that limit the gentiles' ability to tyrannize over God's city and the three and a half "days" during which the witnesses lie dead, which are simply the years in microcosm. Nor do they see, because they are unfamiliar with Bible story, the curious similarity between those three and a half years and the three and a half "times" that pass until the end of evil, as indicated by Daniel 7:25–27 and 12:6–7, or notice the nice literary adjustment that fits the three and a half days to the three days that Jesus spent in the tomb. Each of those periods of time marks an *apparent* victory for the powers of darkness. But because the gentiles cannot interpret literary symbols, they do not see that their city is doomed. It would be pointless to tell them that they are living in "the great city, which spiritually is called Sodom and Egypt, where also our Lord was crucified." Those terms would be meaningless to them.

But don't the two witnesses die in Jerusalem, where God's temple was located? Yes, that's literally true, if the literal is still relevant at this point. And Jerusalem was literally the place where Jesus was crucified. "Spiritually," however, every place where Jesus and his witnesses have been persecuted is a place like Sodom and Egypt, where God's people suffered in Old Testament times, and where God ultimately avenged their sufferings. What about Rome? For the Revelator, the city that is "spiritually" Sodom and Egypt is also "the great city": Rome, of course. It was, after all, the Romans who crucified Christ. It's a matter of perspective. From the eternal point of view, every place and time is visible at once and identified by its internal, spiritual qualities. Jerusalem and Egypt, Sodom and Rome—all, from that perspective, are the same. And because all history is driven by eternal, spiritual forces, we can expect to see the same kind of events play out repeatedly in the same kind of ways.

Uniting and Dividing

This repetition is all the more likely if one sees history, as Revelation does, as a struggle between the same two emphatically distinguished forces. New Testament literature is full of sharp distinctions; Revelation has, perhaps, the sharpest. Virtually all its stories are dramatic episodes in the titanic battle between light and darkness. Many of them repeat, in outline, the story of Christ's life, death, and resurrection. Good shows itself, is apparently overwhelmed by evil, then rises again, victorious. That outline appears in Revelation's account of Jesus's birth (Chapter 12), in its story of his church (Chapter 6:9–17), and, naturally, in its story of the two witnesses. If their enemies had been better interpreters of historical symbolism, they would have seen this coming. Just as Jesus's crucifixion led to his resurrection, so the two witnesses, after lying dead, like

Christ, suddenly stand on their feet, and, like Christ, ascend to heaven "in a cloud."[5]

A story about distinctions and divisions now becomes (as prompted by the usual New Testament DNA) a story about unification—the unification of beings who from the world's point of view might appear quite different. The two witnesses ascend on the command to "come up hither," the same command that the Revelator himself had heard (Revelation 4:1). The story and the story-teller are coming together. All of us, in fact, "come up hither": the perspective effortlessly shifts to heaven (which was never as distant as it seemed), and we hear the Church Triumphant sing the victory of the Almighty God, "which art, and wast, and art to come." The living and the "dead" are gathered together in eternity.

We have seen God's victory—in miniature, in the story of the two witnesses and their strife with an angry world. Now we hear it told again: first, in the story of God's rebuke to the spiritual Sodom and Egypt—"and the same hour was there a great earthquake,[6] and the tenth part of the city fell"—and second, in the prophetic chorus of the saints in glory:

> And the nations were angry, and thy wrath is come, and the time of the dead, that they should be judged, and that thou shouldest give reward unto thy servants the prophets, and to the saints, and them that fear thy name, small and great; and shouldest destroy them which destroy the earth.

The story within Chapter 11 has now been completely transformed. Its perspective has changed from earth to heaven, from the present to the future and the eternal, from the particular conflict to the universal triumph. A lesser artist would have stopped the story there. But as frequently happens in New Testament narrative (recall the story of the Prodigal Son, and the story of the resurrection itself), the apparent climax is not the end. A sequel (like the story of the second brother, or the breakfast scene in the last chapter of John) is needed to secure the effect. In its final movement, the story of the two witnesses returns to the temple, which at the beginning was seen and assessed from the outside. Now it is shown from the inside, in one of the many revelations that make up the book of Revelation:

And the temple of God was opened in heaven, and there was seen in his temple the ark of his testament: and there were lightnings, and voices, and thunderings, and an earthquake, and great hail.

For hundreds of years, the ark of the covenant (or "testament") had been missing from the literal temple in Jerusalem. The temple itself was destroyed in A.D. 70. With the opening of the symbolic temple in Revelation, it is as if we had returned, once more, to Old Testament days. It's one more instance of the incorporation of the Old Testament in the New. It is also visual confirmation of the fact that the eternal God will let nothing of his own be lost in time—not his place of worship, not his testament, and certainly not his witnesses.

Now that readers have been prophetically reassured about the certainty of God's providence—and now that they have been reminded of prophecy's own power to bend time to its will—they should have no difficulty with the next chapter of Revelation, which goes back to tell the story of Jesus, starting with his birth. The visual, sonic, and tactile effects of Chapter 11 (lightning, thunder, earthquake) have prepared for the great events to come; or, if one is thinking literally, for understanding the great events that have already happened. Chapter 12 reveals that the birth of Jesus, which to external and literal sight appeared so peaceful, was enveloped in the same violent spiritual conflict that we see throughout the Apocalypse: "There was war in heaven" (Revelation 12:7).

Conflict continues on earth, where "the dragon . . . that old serpent, called the Devil, and Satan," wars against "the remnant" who "have the testimony of Jesus Christ" (Revelation 12:9, 17). Interpretations of the conflict as told in the stories of Revelation 12–16 are themselves exceptionally conflicted, whether they are focused on the near-term, first-century applications of the symbols, or on their end-time meanings. Who is the beast with a man's number, 666 (Revelation 13:18)? Was it the emperor Nero?[7] Was it some twentieth-century dictator? Is it an antichrist who is still to come? What is "the place called in the Hebrew tongue Armageddon" (Revelation 16:16)? Is it a literal location? Is it the pass near Megiddo in Israel? Or is it a spiritual place like "Sodom and Egypt"? Will the battle itself be literal or spiritual? Who or what, exactly, are the first beast, the second beast, and the image of the beast (Revelation 13)? What is the "mark" implanted on those licensed by the second beast (Revelation 13:16–17)?

The answers to these questions are not for my book to hazard. But a number of things can be said about the literary method of these chapters of Revelation. Readily recognizable, beneath the mysterious symbolism, are familiar elements of the New Testament DNA: repetition, reversal, distinction, unification. On earth, the dragon and his disciples, all of them beasts like him, unite to conduct their war; in heaven, Jesus's disciples, "they which follow the Lamb whithersoever he goeth," unite to sing before the throne (Revelation 14:3–4). The two sides are similar in discipleship, though very different in what they do as disciples. The wretched worshipers of the image of the beast are marked on their foreheads; the blessed worshipers of the true God have the "Father's name written in their foreheads" (Revelation 13:16–17, 14:1). There are malevolent "beasts" on earth, and there are benevolent "beasts" in heaven (Revelation 14:3). There is a false prophet on earth; there are true prophets in heaven, predicting the end of all things false. The important thing is to distinguish the false from the true, the things of earth from the things of heaven, no matter how similar they may seem. The earthly "marks" are clearly visible, but the heavenly name is, well, heavenly; it can be seen only in vision and symbol. Yet by an ironic reversal of normal expectations, the invisible becomes the most important thing.

Willingly or not, all who fail to see what is going on in God's world are drawn into the dragon's world and marked with his brand. Meanwhile, all who have "gotten the victory over the beast, and over his image, and over his mark" are gathered beside the sea of glass, singing the Song of Moses and the Lamb—all, from first to last, included in the story, continuous from the Old Testament to the New, of him who is both first and last (Revelation 15:2–4). Few people on earth can see the heavenly chorus looking down on them, or the heavenly arsenals preparing to launch "the seven last plagues" on Satan's disciples (Revelation 15:1). But the reader sees and, seeing, is symbolically gathered in.

Chapter 11, with its microcosmic view of the cosmic struggle, prepared for these succeeding chapters of conflict and redemption. It also prepared for the much later scene in which the eternal and the spiritual fully replace the temporal and the literal. In that scene, "Babylon" has at last been destroyed; even the old Jerusalem has vanished. Now comes the supreme moment of unification: the "new Jerusalem," "the holy city," "come[s] down from God out of heaven, prepared as a bride adorned for her husband" (Revelation 21:2).

In Chapter 11, attention was focused first on the temple of God, walled against its enemies, and then on the temple of God that "was opened in heaven." In Chapters 14, 15, and 16 there was a temple in heaven from which announcements were made and commands were given. But now there is no need for a temple as a sacred enclosure. The distinction between sacred and profane has been abolished; all is sacred. Even the gates and walls of the city are adornments of art, not means of warfare or defense:

> And the twelve gates were twelve pearls; every several gate was of one pearl: and the street of the city [a city street, but utterly different from the dirty street of the place called Sodom and Egypt, where the bodies of the two witnesses once lay] was pure gold, as it were transparent glass. And I saw no temple therein: for the Lord God Almighty and the Lamb are the temple of it. And the city had no need of the sun, neither of the moon, to shine in it: for the glory of God did lighten it, and the Lamb is the light thereof. (Revelation 21:21–23)

It is as if the religious scaffolding had fallen away, leaving only the object of religious devotion, God himself. In this literary effect, however, we can still discern the influence of the New Testament's own scaffolding, its literary patterns: the representation of history as a providentially-directed journey or progress, leading from natural to supernatural by means of radical changes in perspective; the revelation of inner meanings by the use of symbolic narrative; the emphasis on simultaneous processes of uniting (all is now Jerusalem) and dividing (Jerusalem is now *without* both its temple and its enemies); the vision of a reversed and transformed cosmos, in which everything that was material is now spiritual and everything that was humble has now been exalted. These themes and devices bring us finally to the culmination of the New Testament, the moment when literary device and spontaneous vision reach their simultaneous fulfillment.

But while it is the end of the New Testament, it is far from the end of Christian literature.

Part II

The Patterns Renewed

9
Early and Late

As Paul told the church at Corinth, some true stories are highly improbable, and the Christian story is one of the most improbable of all (1 Corinthians 1:21–25). Two thousand years ago, a small group of people in a backwater of the Roman Empire formed the belief that a crucified carpenter was the Son of God. This belief, which originated among devout Jews, famous for their isolationism, gradually established itself in the sophisticated urban centers of the Mediterranean world, including Rome itself. Persecution failed to stop it. Even intellectualism failed to stop it. It attracted some of the most ambitious thinkers of the time, who after squabbling among themselves succeeded in systematizing its theology. In the fourth century, it attracted the sponsorship of the imperial house and became the empire's official religion.

This is improbable enough, but consider what happened next. The empire of the West collapsed, leaving the Christian church as the only coherent and universal institution in vast areas of Europe. Parts of the former Empire were reconquered for paganism by invading tribes, such as the Angles and Saxons who occupied the region we know as England (Angle Land). But the church sent missionaries to the western and northern lands and eventually converted or reconverted them. During the next millennium Christendom engaged in war after war, both spiritual and literal—with its would-be successor, Islam, with ever-recurring waves of pagan invaders, and with itself, in conflicts between western or "catholic" and eastern or "orthodox" Christians, between officials of the church and officials of secular states, and finally between "reformed" and "unreformed" varieties of western Christianity. And Christendom emerged from these ugly conflicts as the mightiest and most influential civilization the world had ever known.

A preposterous story, but true. One might expect, among all these adventures and vicissitudes, that Christianity itself would have changed its nature. Much did change, in the customs and governance of various branches of the church, and in the church's relationship to state and society. But there was one thing that did not change: the New Testament. Interpretations changed, again and again, producing strifes and schisms that continue to this day. But the DNA of Christianity remained, embedded too deeply in the New Testament to vanish or be removed. Whenever people interested themselves in repeating the New Testament story, the literary features of Christianity, its characteristic emphases and devices, were able to return to life.

This meant that Christian literature would have its own continuity, and that the continuity would not need to come from the imitation of one latter-day writer by another. Many conscious imitations took place, but the New Testament always existed as a common source of repetition and independent variation. Period styles and local customs could vary wildly, new concerns could arise and express themselves forcefully in new literary texts; but the underlying patterns would remain.

This chapter is about two works of English literature, originating in radically different worlds inhabited by radically different people, and written in radically different literary genres. Neither influenced the other. On the surface there is nothing to unite these works, except that they are both written in English— although the English of one of them is so far removed from the modern language that it needs to be read in translation. Their similarities, however, are deep and strong, and they reveal much about the continuity of Christian literature.

The first work is *The Dream of the Rood*, one of the earliest surviving poems in the English (at that time the Anglo-Saxon or Old English) language. It was composed by an anonymous tribal poet around A.D. 700, presumably to be recited orally. Its earliest surviving representations are words carved on a tall stone cross set up in the English countryside. The *Rood* poem recounts, with seeming directness, the history of Christ's death and resurrection; it is an overtly devotional work.

The second work is "The Gardener" (1926), a short story by Rudyard Kipling (1865–1936), one of the founders of modern literature. It appears, at first glance, to have nothing devotional about it. Quite the contrary: it appears to represent Christianity as irrelevant to the modern world. Its author could not be called a Christian, in any strictly doctrinal sense. He was born in India, when the British empire was reaching the acme of its power, and he became the foremost literary exponent of British imperialism. He dreamed of a world empire in which all religious cultures would find a home. His novel *Kim* (1901) weaves together strands of Christianity, Hinduism, Buddhism, Islam, and nineteenth-century rationalism, none of them predominating, to show that all high spiritual conceptions are compatible with one another.

But "God is no respecter of persons," as Peter said (Acts 10:34), and neither is literature. No matter what beliefs an author holds as a personal philosophy—and those beliefs may change or remain obscure, even to the author—it is hard for anyone to get free from New Testament ideas and literary devices, once one has started to tell the Christian story. And the Christian story is what one finds, at last, that "The Gardener" is telling. Both *The Dream of the Rood* and "The Gardener" are distinguished expressions of the DNA of Christianity.

Finding the Cross

It is easy, though misleading, to say that the earlier work takes a more straightforward view of its subject than the later one. The narration of the *Rood* poem (See below, Texts, pp. 325–28) is certainly straightforward. The narrator has a dream in which the "rood" or cross of Christ appears and relates the story of the crucifixion, then commands the dreamer "to speak this sight to other men," so that they will revere the cross and bear it on their breasts until the day of judgment,

> for through the Rood shall each soul reach
> its way to life with heaven's Lord.[1]

But this summary of the poem does not include its most memorable features, one of which is its complex unification of New Testament and Anglo-Saxon ideas. Here Jesus is not a

Galilean rabbi but a "geong hæleth" ("yeong haleth"), a young warrior or "hero" like Beowulf in the Anglo-Saxon epic. This Christ climbs boldly onto the cross; and after his death, he "rest[s] awhile" on the ground, as if briefly recovering from combat. The practice of war and the ideal of the warrior were vital elements of Anglo-Saxon society. When Anglo-Saxons thought of a leader, they thought of a warrior chieftain. Jesus was a leader; therefore, he must have been something like that.

The idea seems strange, but it is not entirely foreign to the New Testament. The poet could have found support for it in Revelation's picture of the heavenly Jesus as a warrior king (Revelation 19). More support might be found in the New Testament's emphasis on the division between the godly and the ungodly, and the need for the former to struggle against the latter. Paul likens Christians to soldiers and the Christian journey to an athletic competition (Ephesians 6:10–17, 1 Corinthians 9:24). The *Rood* poem's concluding passage shows Jesus returning victorious from a campaign to liberate souls in hell. This episode— the so-called harrowing of hell—is a story that developed in the church after the New Testament period; it does not appear in the New Testament itself. Yet it strengthens the portrait of Jesus as a warrior hero, bearing out the conception, both of the *Rood* poet and of the New Testament, that Christ's journey, and all Christian journeys, are occasions of dramatic conflict.

The *Rood* poem reflects an understanding of two principles that are basic to Christian writing:

> Because Christian literature is the literature of discipleship, it must faithfully repeat the essential Christian story.

> Because Christian literature is the literature of discipleship, it must adapt itself to the understanding of those whom it would make disciples.

Those two considerations may seem a paradoxical pair, but every good preacher knows that each requires the other. The key text is Paul's frank description of his own preaching methods: "Unto the Jews I became as a Jew, that I might gain the Jews; to them that are under the law, as under the law, that I might gain them that are under the law . . . I am made all things to all men, that I might by all means save some. And this I do for the gospel's sake" (1 Corinthians 9:20–23). Paul, who insisted at all times on keeping the gospel pure (otherwise there would be no point in preaching it), also suggested that its preaching should be adaptable (otherwise it would not be understood). We have seen the ways in which the *kerygma* was adapted to its audience by such distinguished preachers as Peter and Paul himself.

Clearly, the *Rood* poet felt licensed to recommend the Christian story to Anglo-Saxon warriors by adapting its details to their understanding. In his poem, even the personified Cross has the characteristics of an Anglo-Saxon warrior. It is loyal to "the mighty King" and would, if the King had wished, have "felled" all his "foe[s]." With Christ it shares the grim intimacy of warriors facing death: "I trembled when the warrior . . . embraced me." Ironically, it is love—the Rood's love for Christ, Christ's love for the world—that emerges most strongly from this warrior's story, just as it does from the gospels and the Pauline epistles. So the poet, if challenged, could maintain that he was doing what the New Testament itself does, and in general terms he would be right. A good author provides insights into the Christian story that allow its meanings to gather significance far outside the original context. This is and must be the motivating assumption of Christian creative literature in all times and places.

But a more important, though less obvious, feature of the *Rood* poem is its refusal to go all the way with the process of adaptation to contemporary life—in this case, the life of the Anglo-Saxon warrior class in the eighth century after Christ. Warrior society was deeply skeptical about personal independence. It was a society in which all needed to work together, fight together, think together, or risk perishing at the hands of the enemies waiting just over the hill. In *Beowulf,* which is roughly contemporary with the *Rood* poem, advice is repeatedly given: watch your heart; don't let it stray beyond the circle of your friends and relations. If it does, the result can only be exile or defeat.[2] But New Testament Christianity emphasizes the individual perspective, the ability to be transformed in ways in which your friends and relations are not. So, strangely for an Anglo-Saxon, the speaker of the *Rood* poem sets himself at a distance from society. While all other "speechbearers" (the Old English term for "human beings") enjoy a dreamless sleep, the revelation of the Cross comes to him alone. The Cross addresses him as a "beloved warrior," but he is not like other warriors. He prays all "alone"; his "bliss" is to seek "the victory beam [the cross] / more often than any others"; he spends his time longing for the day when God will gather him "to the banquet of heaven."

The Cross directs him, as Jesus directed John the Revelator, to announce his vision to other people (Revelation 1:1), yet the thrust of the announcement is highly personal. At the Last Judgment, the Cross declares, the Lord will ask

> where in that multitude the man may be
> who for the Savior's name would suffer death
> bitter as he on the beam sustained.
>
> They will fear, and few will think
> how they will come to answer Christ.
> But no moment of fear need any man feel
> who on his breast bears the best of signs.

The poem offers the most literal interpretation possible of Jesus's admonition, "Whosoever doth not bear his cross, and come after me, cannot be my disciple," and it carries much of the force of Jesus's preceding sentence, in which he says that his followers must be willing to surrender their closest relationships for his sake (Luke 14:26–27). In the *Rood* poem, as in the gospel, the imitation of Christ is an individual and often an alienating choice. One of the most eloquent passages in the poem is its description of Christ lying in the tomb after everyone else has gone away: "reste he thær mæte weorode"—"he stayed there alone."[3]

The impression of lonely but triumphant individuality is reinforced by the Rood's history of itself. Certainly the importance of the Cross could have been emphasized without giving it a personality, but a cross that thinks and feels like a human being can offer an unusually intimate account of discipleship. In the story that the *Rood* poet tells, the Cross was originally just one tree among many; then it was singled out to be the companion of Christ's passion. Like Christ, it endured the journey to Golgotha, and there it shared his wounds. The nails that pierced him pierced the Cross as well, but like the warrior Christ, the warrior Cross "stood fast" and accomplished the providential purpose. Then, like Christ, the Cross was buried, and like Christ, "the light of the world" (John 8:12), it was raised in glory, transformed from an object of hatred into a beacon shining across the world.

A similar transformation awaits the poem's visionary dreamer. Outwardly obscure and lonely, lacking "strong friends," he knows from the dream that is given to him alone that he is an heir to the irony of the Cross: he will follow the crucified Christ on his journey from exile on earth to his "homeland" above, the heavenly kingdom where the disciple will be united with his Lord and with the saints in glory. And so will you, the dreamer says, if you make his vision your own: "through the Rood shall each soul reach / its way to life." You also can participate in the enormous reversal.

The *Rood* poem is thus a fourfold repetition of the Christian story: in the life of Christ, the life of the Cross, the life of the dreamer, and (potentially) the life of the hearer. Each version of the story describes a transformation of life and aims at a transformation of the hearer's life. It is important to consider, once more, the original audience of the *Rood* poem. By the time it was composed, the Anglo-Saxons had become Christians. It assumes a Christian audience. Yet the Christian story still needed to be repeated or "revealed" in a dramatic form—as, for instance, a literary "dream" or "vision"—so that these people could discover, as if for the first time, their own part in its pattern. To reconstruct the pattern, the poet reproduced the literary patterns of the New Testament. It is interesting that, while Christian literature always uses symbols, the *Rood* poem takes them seriously enough to turn the symbol of the cross into its spokesman and central character. But as a glance at Figure 5 (p. 23, above) will show, even my brief discussion of the poem has identified the presence within it of virtually every other element of the New Testament DNA, from the presentation of the godly life as a providential journey and progress to the emphasis on discipleship, the insistence on transformation, and the literary use of repetition and reversal.

Finding the Christ

"The Gardener" (See below, Texts, pp. 351–360)[4] is also a work of rediscovery, and it too is a history of the cross, of transformation, of discipleship, and of revelation—although it is anything but a dream, and it has none of the overtly "inspiring" features of the *Rood* poem. Kipling, recipient of the seventh Nobel Prize in Literature, was renowned for his realistic depictions of modern life. In "The Gardener," life does indeed seem "real" in the plainest meanings of the term: normal, typical, predictable, and sadly remote from any ideal. But this is the "reality" that the story prepares to reverse.

The protagonist, Helen Turrell, is a 35-year-old Englishwoman. Her brother, it seems, has died in India, and she has adopted his son. The child was apparently born out of wedlock, but Helen, who is known for her honesty, believes that "scandals are only increased by hushing them up"; so she makes no secret of the fact that he has had some difficult family connections. Nevertheless, Michael is "as accepted" by their small community "as Helen had always been." More important, he is dearly loved by Helen, whom he calls, in their private moments, "Mummy." Then the First World War begins, and Michael is killed, as millions of other young men were killed, in the brutally predictable process of modern fighting. Helen feels as if she herself were the victim of the mechanical forces of industrial production:

> Once, on one of Michael's leaves, he had taken her over a munition factory, where she saw the progress of a shell from blank-iron to the all but finished article. It struck her at the time that the wretched thing was never left alone for a single second; and "I'm being manufactured into a bereaved next-of-kin", she told herself.

The war ends with a British victory, but Helen feels nothing. Then she receives an official notice of the location of Michael's grave—a new military cemetery in Belgium. When she travels there, she discovers that people who are used to dealing with the bereaved have a peculiarly apt phrase for such visits. They call it finding "your grave." But finding it is not easy. Wandering in the "merciless sea" of black wooden crosses, Helen becomes "hopelessly" lost. She wonders "by what guidance she should ever come to her own." Then a man—"evidently a gardener, for he was firming a young plant in the soft earth"—guides her to the cross under which Michael is buried.

That is the story. It contains no direct indication that it has anything to do with religion. There are no explicit references to Christ, and only two mentions of God, both of which appear as stock phrases in conversation. The local church is mentioned, but the effect is to emphasize its lack of relevance to Helen's life. When Michael is reported missing, the priest tries to console her, and fails: "The Rector, of course, preached hope"—a predictable and meaningless generality—"and prophesied word, very soon, from a prison camp." His prophecy goes conspicuously unfulfilled. There is no "word" with any religious content, no "hope" arising from faith in God. It is true that the little poem with which Kipling introduced the story offers an allusion to God's angel "roll[ing] the stone away" from a grave that is tearfully watched. Yet in the context of a "realistic" modern story, this allusion to the empty tomb (Matthew 28:1–2, Mark 16:1–6, Luke 24:1–5) can easily be taken as a simple symbolic expression of how strongly Helen felt when she came at last to Michael's grave. Most readers forget the poem before they have gone very far in the story. A later reference to Easter season as the time of Helen's journey is buried among incidental details.

One must read to the story's final sentence before one realizes that a naturalistic interpretation is impossible, and this realization comes only to people who know enough about the New Testament to identify the biblical allusion in that sentence. After visiting the grave, Helen turns "for a last look" and sees "in the distance" the man who guided her, "bending over his young plants." Then she goes away, "supposing him to be the gardener." Those final words are a quotation from the twentieth chapter of the gospel of John, where Mary Magdalen, Jesus's disciple, visits his tomb and finds it empty:

> She turned herself back, and saw Jesus standing, and knew not that it was Jesus. Jesus saith unto her, Woman, why weepest thou? whom seekest thou? She, supposing him to be the gardener, saith unto him, Sir, if thou have borne him hence, tell me where thou hast laid him . . . (John 20:14–15)

Helen "supposes" the man she meets "to be the gardener" in the same way that Mary Magdalen did.

Here is evidence that beneath the surface of this realistic story, and perhaps of this real and natural world, providence is

at work. Do you recognize it? Can you read the signs of its presence? Mary Magdalen had difficulty doing that; Helen Turrell
apparently finds it impossible, although she gets the benefit of
its presence anyway, as a gift of grace. But the story isn't just a
test of Helen's understanding; it is a test of the reader's, too. Do
you look for God only in explicit and dramatic revelations?
Perhaps revelations take place more subtly. Perhaps they
require you to interpret the symbolism of "normal" events more
carefully than you do.

Once aware of this possibility, the reader may want to go
back to the beginning, as Christian literature frequently encourages us to do, and experience the story again, looking for more
meanings than those that appear on its placid, seemingly obvious surface. When you start noticing subtle signals, you see that
the "man" whom Helen encounters and, like Mary Magdalen,
mistakes for a gardener, has several other characteristics of the
Jesus of the gospels. He is a nurturer of life; he cares how
"young plants" grow. He is also a transformer of life; he is working to change the cemetery's hellish landscape of "naked black
crosses" into a garden that reflects the Creator's love. In
Kipling's story, as in the gospels, he is a providential guide who
feels and responds to the hidden movements of a stranger's
heart. When the gardener asks Helen, "Who are you looking
for?", she responds, just as she has responded "many thousands
of times in her life," "Lieutenant Michael Turrell—my nephew."
But the gardener says, "Come with me . . . and I will show you
where your son lies." He knows that Michael is much more
important to her than a "nephew."

But what exactly is her relationship to Michael? Naive readers—and almost everyone is naive, on a first reading of this
story—usually do not notice the transformation of "nephew" to
"son." If they notice it, they usually think, "Oh, but of course
Helen *acted* as his mother." That is what she led us to believe.
But the gardener knows the inside of the story, an inside that
readers can see for themselves only after they surrender the typically modern assumption that nothing exists except what meets
the eye.

Reread "The Gardener's" first two pages. How plausible is
Helen's story about her relationship with Michael? According to
her, he was born in India just after his father died in an accident.
A nurse took the child to France, where Helen happened to be

recuperating from a "threat" of illness. The nurse, the last witness to the child's parentage, was then dismissed as incompetent. Helen came home, after a long and visibly taxing absence, with an infant who closely resembled her—a child who, as Kipling tells us, pleased her very much when he began to treat her as if she were his mother. The more one considers this story, the stranger it seems. Michael's presence can be explained much more easily if one assumes another history: Michael is Helen's child, born out of wedlock, and she has made up an elaborate counter-history to render life less difficult for both of them. It is odd, is it not, that Helen's own word is the only evidence for her story? She freely admits that there is a "scandal" connected with Michael's birth. But the best liar is the person who seems to be admitting some scandalous truth, while covering up a more scandalous one.

Sin and Discipleship

No one should be surprised to find that a nice person like Helen is a sinner, "for all have sinned, and come short of the glory of God" (Romans 3:23). The only people who may be surprised are those who are operating with modern naturalist premises and do not recognize the existence of a standard of perfection higher than being a responsible member of society. If one looks only at the surface story in "The Gardener," the story that Helen tells, there is nothing wrong, nothing worthy of forgiveness, in what she did. But it is only when one looks beneath the storytelling surface that one detects the supernatural implications of her meeting with the gardener. Then, looking beneath the surface, one also detects her pattern of lies. They are lies in a good cause, but they are lies nonetheless. "The Gardener" is a work of literature in which deep patterns are more important than surface plot. Perhaps, the story suggests, the world itself is like that. We may make up our own plots, but in the end they will yield to the history that providence writes; and the distinctions between good and evil, as they appear from that author's point of view, will assert themselves as well.

In any event, now that we are aware of things going on beneath the surface, we can consider the possibility that Helen's story has more connections with Christianity than her final meeting with the Gardener. There is, for instance, her name. "Turrell" doesn't return any symbolic echoes, but "Helen" does. Helena is one of the better known saints in the calendar. She was the mother of Constantine, the Roman emperor who made Christianity the state religion. She traveled to Jerusalem, looking for relics of Christian history, and—so it is said—she rediscovered the cross of Christ. Helen Turrell is also looking for a cross, the cross on Michael's grave; and in finding it she also finds, at the end of her journey, the visible evidence of Christ on earth. By associating Helen with Helena, Kipling subtly emphasizes the idea that her story is not just about death and mourning in the natural world but about the discovery of indications of a life beyond the apparently unyielding surface of the natural and the predictable. Helen, like her sainted namesake, finds her cross; but she also, without quite knowing it, discovers Christ.

Helen's more obvious symbolic identification is with Mary Magdalen, who encountered the "gardener" on Easter morning. What else does the Bible say about her? She was one of the people whom Jesus miraculously healed. He expelled "seven devils" from her, working a spiritual transformation. Afterward, she followed him as a disciple; she stood at the foot of the cross; she came to the tomb; she met the risen Christ (Luke 8:1–2, John 19:25, 20:1–18). More than that, scripture does not say for certain.[5] In later story and art, Mary often appears as a "fallen woman," a prostitute who after her conversion spends her life in penitence. The obvious connection with Helen Turrell is the idea of sexual "fallenness." But this association would not mean much to "The Gardener"—Helen is clearly not a "prostitute"—if Kipling had not pursued the question of what makes someone "fallen" in a deeper, more spiritual sense.

Suppose that Helen violated the sexual code, and lied about it. That, to Kipling, is not the end of the story. Men and women are not, after all, just "manufactured" objects, creatures of their experience. Their "progress," unlike that of the shell that Helen saw being made, is always individual. To show this, he uses the typically Christian device of distinction-between-similars, as Jesus did in the story of the Prodigal Son. That story turns on the distinction between the son who recognizes that he is a sinner and the son who does not. Kipling too adds a second character to his story, a character who is similar to Helen in several respects—a certain Mrs. Scarsworth, who has also undertaken a pilgrimage to the cemetery in Belgium, has also been scarred by life, and has also sinned. Driven by a desire to confess, she blurts out her story to Helen. She is there to visit the grave of a secret lover, a man to whom she was never married.

> "But why do you tell me?" Helen asked desperately.
> "Because I'm *so* tired of lying. Tired of lying—always lying—year in and year out. When I don't tell lies I've got to act 'em and I've got to think 'em, always. *You* don't know what that means."

But Helen does know. She lied throughout Michael's life. She is still lying about her relationship to him.

Mrs. Scarsworth's next statements help, in a curious way, to put all this in a Christian perspective:

> "Do you understand? It doesn't matter about *me*. I was never truthful, even as a girl. But it isn't worthy of *him*. So—so I—I had to tell you. I can't keep it up any longer."

"I was never truthful, even as a girl." Mrs. Scarsworth doesn't mention theology, but she presents the evidence for an important New Testament teaching. Helen isn't innocent; Mrs. Scarsworth isn't innocent, either; and it shouldn't surprise anyone to discover that she wasn't innocent as a child. She is simply being honest about what everyone can see: children are sinners, just as adults are. We are all sinners. At least this is what Christian authors have maintained, from Paul to Augustine to Jonathan Swift.[6] It's the doctrine of original sin: as Paul says, "*all* have sinned," because all are born sinners, born imperfect and unable not to act imperfectly.

But in normal, conventionally Christian society, to admit that one is a sinner is so remarkable a thing as to invite a number of misinterpretations. The first is that one's sin must be very terrible, or one would never feel impelled to admit it. The second is that one's reaction to sin must be greatly exaggerated, or one would not "fixate" on it. The third is that, however serious one's sin may be, nothing can be done about it except, perhaps, to "unburden" oneself by confessing. Kipling responds to each of these misinterpretations.

First, he emphasizes the fact that sins may be "small." There are many sins worse than that to which Mrs. Scarsworth confesses. He could have made her a truly scandalous sinner, but he didn't. The same can be said of Helen, who, if she sinned, has done the best she could to bring good out of bad. The only way she saw to do that was to commit the additional sin of lying to prevent society from ostracizing her—together, of course, with her son. Lies of this kind are not a "terrible" sin. But they are a sin. Even Mrs. Scarsworth knows that.

Second, Kipling takes up the question of whether conscientious reactions to sin must be exaggerated. The crucial issue is the effect of sin on the inner person, and here he makes a telling distinction between Helen and Mrs. Scarsworth. To be sure, Helen is a reserved personality, and we see Mrs. Scarsworth for only a page or two, so the revelation of their inner selves is performed, for the most part, symbolically—but how much more do we actually see of the selves we meet in "real" life and believe that we understand? Like the New Testament authors, Kipling gives us specific events that symbolize the inner condition of his characters; and his point is that sin is as likely to be underemphasized as overemphasized. We can tell that Helen's lies are motivated by a desire to protect her son, but what motivates Mrs. Scarsworth's moment of honesty? The more she explains her motives, the worse they seem. Her choice of words—"so *tired* of lying," "I *can't* keep it up"—suggests that even her honesty is a yielding to temptation, while her hectoring approach and complete lack of empathy with her audience—"Do you understand?"; "*You* don't know what that means"—belie her statement that "it doesn't matter about *me*."

Third, Kipling dramatizes the problem of confession. From a Christian point of view, confession is pointless if it is merely a way of writing "The End" to a bad story. A real confession is not just a revelation but a request for help and a plea for transformation. One confesses in order to be reconciled with God or one's fellow human beings. That is why one confesses *to* someone. But here is what happens after Mrs. Scarsworth confesses to Helen:

> Helen reached forward, caught [Mrs. Scarsworth's hands], bowed her head over them, and murmured: "Oh, my dear! My dear!" Mrs. Scarsworth stepped back, her face all mottled.

"My God!" said she. "Is *that* how you take it?"

Helen could not speak, the woman went out; but it was a long while before Helen was able to sleep.

Helen has the kind of heart that tries to help; Mrs. Scarsworth has the kind of heart that not only rejects help but refuses to comprehend the desire to give it—"My God! Is *that* how you take it?" Her mottled face suggests that she is now enraged. What could have enraged her? The only possibility is that she is angered by Helen's unforced giving of sympathy and concern, which is the human analogue of God's grace. Mrs. Scarsworth recognizes and cares very much about what the world calls morality, but she is immune to the inner life of the spirit. Her reference to "God" is empty of meaning, as empty as the story's only other explicit reference to the deity, her earlier, lying statement, "*I* haven't lost any one [in the war], thank God." When Helen extends Christlike charity to Mrs. Scarsworth, she is spurned.

Jesus said to his disciples, "[H]e that despiseth you despiseth me" (Luke 10:16). At the cemetery, the Gardener reaches out to Helen, as Helen reached out to Mrs. Scarsworth, and gives her guidance. But we have no such story about Mrs. Scarsworth, who, from a normal human point of view, appears very much like Helen. God has a different point of view. "The one shall be taken," Jesus said of two women who seemed very similar, "and the other left" (Luke 17:35).

Something Has Changed

Helen's journey has not, after all, been the hapless "progress of a shell"; nor, at the end of the story, does she think of herself any longer as a mechanical object, passive and dead to feeling. If—returning to the story's poetic introduction—Kipling's poem expresses Helen's feelings, then at the tomb she finds real progress: a new insight into the spiritual life, and a new emotional connection. The fact that in the story itself she "turn[s] for a *last* look" at the cemetery suggests that her journey has given her a measure of peace and a measure of distance from the horror of Michael's death. The fact that she does not object ("Oh, I said that he was my nephew") when the Gardener tells her that he will show her where her "son" is buried strongly suggests that she feels Christ's "infinite compassion" penetrating the false front of stoicism that she has used as a shelter from other people's emotions, and her own. Something has changed about Helen.

True, we do not see the radical change that the dreamer in the *Rood* poem reports about himself. He was consciously concerned with the "hidden man" (1 Peter 3:4), viewed as the man to whom God reveals himself in the secrecy of dreams. In "The Gardener," the revelation seems to register someplace deeper than the conscious or even the dreaming mind. The *Rood* poem adapted the Christian message to a culture that honored the warrior. "The Gardener" recommends itself to another, more skeptical and "realistic" age, an age that respects the psychologist more than the soldier, the saint, or the prophet. The dreamer of the *Rood* poem understands his dreams; they do not exist in an unconscious that is hidden from awareness. Helen is different. She feels the effect of Jesus's presence, but she does not fully understand it, still "supposing him to be the gardener." It is up to the external interpreter, the author-psychologist, to explain what has happened, by repeating that word "supposing." Helen supposes; the author knows.

Just as there is nothing more common than dreams in medieval literature, so there is nothing more common than the author-psychologist in modern literature. And like many other modern writers, Kipling goes farther, expecting that attentive readers will also act as psychologists, interpreting the symbols of inner experience and finding out for themselves what literary characters are like beneath the surface—finding out more than the characters know themselves. Thus, in a curious way, the ancient assumption of Christian literature, that what matters is the individual self and its mysterious connection with God, is re-emphasized for the benefit of a modern world. It is important to know that Kipling, like Helen Turrell, lost a beloved son in the terrors of the First World War. As an author-psychologist, Kipling is recreating, then interpreting, his own bewildered experience. This is as good an example of the double self as one is ever likely to find among modern authors. Yet in Kipling's echo of the word "supposing" there is no double meaning. Whatever Helen "supposes," she has actually encountered Christ.

In Christian literature, as in modern psychological analysis, the purpose of interpreting the self is to produce a change. The idea is relevant both to the *Rood* poem and to "The Gardener." Each work tells the history of an isolated, outwardly insignificant person in whose experience something exceptional is revealed by a mysterious providence. In each case, the revelation suggests that the world in which we live is not simply a world of time and space, bound by the rules of physical nature and afflicted by the predictable cruelties of our own sinful nature. It is, instead, a world of time penetrated by eternity, a world in which a compassionate God unites himself with suffering human beings. In one story, and probably in the other, the revelation changes the perspective from which the protagonist regards the world; but in both stories, the revelation works toward transforming the reader's perspective.

"Are you sure you know your grave?" Helen is asked, in the unintentionally symbolic language of a functionary in Belgium; "it makes such a difference." "Yes, thank you," she replies. At the moment, she does not understand, and probably the reader does not understand, either—not having arrived at the end of the journey—that she is fulfilling Jesus's command, the same command that inspired the *Rood* poem:

> If any man will come after me, let him deny himself, and take up his cross daily, and follow me. For whosoever will save his life shall lose it: but whosoever will lose his life for my sake, the same shall save it. (Luke 9:23)

Finding one's final self means denying one's ordinary self; saving one's real life means transcending one's ordinary life. For Kipling, who would never see his son again, there may have been a special significance in Jesus's statement about taking up the cross. It converts a "daily" round of suffering into a journey with the significance of discipleship. *The Dream of the Rood* was intended to produce a revival of religious feeling and perhaps an initial conversion on the part of "Christians" who had never felt the power of the Christian story. The more one looks at "The Gardener," the more one sees the transformation message in it too.

Revival, or conversion? It is a complicated question, especially when one considers the subtleties of Kipling's development of Helen's character and the subtleties of his own approach to religious belief. Yet the question may be more complicated for psychology and theology than it is for literature. From a literary point of view, revival and conversion often amount to the same thing—a transformation of perspective, and (ironically) a return to the old story, with the means of making it new again. That is the process I want to examine next.

10

Revive Us Again

No sooner had Christianity started than it needed to be revived. The history of the church can be seen as a continual history of loss and restoration. In the words of William Blake, the earthly church is "continually building & continually decaying desolate!"[1] Paul's letters make many exasperated demands for recovery: "Remember ye not, that, when I was yet with you, I told you these things?" (2 Thessalonians 2:5). This kind of concern runs throughout the New Testament.

The church of the Middle Ages was frequently disturbed by movements of reform and revival. Sometimes it shook them off; sometimes it incorporated them in the form of new monastic or popular institutions. Then came the greatest of all revivals, the Protestant Reformation of the sixteenth century. Protestant denominations that trace their identity to the great Reformation could hardly avoid institutionalizing the spirit of reform and revival. Revival was regularly anticipated and demanded. It is not an accident that a popular hymn of American evangelicalism is "Revive Us *Again*."[2]

As I discussed in Chapter 7, one of the ironies of Christianity is that the church is expected to move forward and backward at the same time. Its forward course, its course toward renewal, is a repetition, guided by memory, of its "first works" (Revelation 2:5). The same can be said about the journeys of individual Christians, for whom progress is, in some sense, a recovery of the ancient past. After the first century, no personal memories of the "first works" remained among Christians. Their journey must thereafter be guided by the literary reflections of those works, as they appear in the New Testament. Christian history, individual and institutional, can be seen as the continual loss and recovery of the New Testament story, as the New Testament tells it.

"I Taught Nothing but the Word of God"

The origins of literature in modern English coincided with the Protestant Reformation. The two most strongly marked features of that movement, wherever it appeared, were the desire to restore the "primitive" church and the desire for broader knowledge of the New Testament, virtually the only direct source of information on that church. John Tyndale, whose translation of the New Testament was the first to be printed in English (1526), told a "learned man," "If God spare my life ere many years, I will cause a boy that driveth the plough, shall know more of the Scripture than thou dost."[3] Tyndale was hunted down and judicially murdered in 1536. By that time, however, Henry VIII, King of England, had followed the lead of many princes on the Continent and had separated the church in his country from the authority of the Pope and the Roman Catholic church. Henry at first had no intention of licensing full-scale religious reforms, or Bible translation, either; but the course of reformation could not be controlled, and a translation was soon being issued with his permission. Doctrinal revisions accompanied it.

Bloody quarrels for possession of the state church continued for many years, with Protestants persecuting Catholics, and sometimes other Protestants, under the reigns of Henry and his son Edward VI, and Catholics persecuting Protestants under the reign of Henry's daughter "Bloody" Queen Mary. A refugee from the Marian persecutions, John Foxe (1516–1587), collected stories about martyred Protestants and published them (in Latin) on the Continent. After Queen Elizabeth, a Protestant, acceded to the throne, he returned and published (in English) his *Acts and Monuments*, better known as the *Book of Martyrs* (1563). One of the most popular works in the English language, it discovered models of Christian conduct in the stories of Reformation heroes, who in turn had based their conduct on New Testament stories.

For the English-speaking world, Foxe's book was a powerful link between the primitive church, as represented in the New

Testament, and the modern church, which (as Protestants tended to think) could be based directly on a literary model, omitting the precedent of the historically evolving institutions of Roman Catholicism. In time, the Catholic church in English-speaking countries would adopt many features of the primitive church as seen by Protestant reformers and revivalists, including a large degree of participation by lay people and a de-emphasis on such extratestamental ideas as purgatory and the monarchical authority of the pope.

When one looks at Foxe's book, in most of its printings, one notices that the margins are full of references to the Bible verses to which his stories allude. These texts are re-enacted in the stories and used in argument by his reformers and martyrs. To mention one example, Foxe's account of the persecution of Protestants in Scotland features the story of Master George Wisehart, a scholar tried and executed for heresy by Roman Catholics. The largest part of the story consists of Wisehart's arguments in defense of his ideas, arguments in which the New Testament is the principal feature. The ninth charge against him is that he maintained "that every lay man is a Priest, and such lyke," and "that the Pope hath no more power, then any other man." Wisehart replies:

> "My lords! I taught nothing but the word of God. I remember that I have read in some places in S. John and S. Peter, of the whych one sayth: he hath made us kinges and priestes. The other sayth: he hath made us a kingly Priesthode. Wherefore I have affirmed that any man being cunning [skillful] in the word of God and the true fayth of Jesu Christ, hath hys power given him of God, and not by the power or violence of men, but by the vertue of the word of God, the which word is called the power of God, as witnesseth S. Paul evidently enough. And again, I say that any unlearned man, not exercised in the word of God, nor yet constant in his fayth, whatsoever estate or order he be of [including the priesthood], I say he hath no power to binde or loose, seeing hee wanteth [lacks] the instrument, by the which he bindeth or looseth, that is to say, the woord of God."
>
> After that he had sayd these wordes, all the Bishops laughed and mocked him.[4]

The notes in Foxe's text refer the reader to Wisehart's sources in Revelation 1 and 5, 1 Peter 2, and Romans 1.

According to Foxe, the bishops who oppose Wisehart resent his attempt to reverse the normal order of authority, which proceeds from outside and above (the visible church and its officials) to inside and below (the "cunning" of individual Christians who can read the New Testament for themselves). What they object to isn't just independent Bible reading. They object to people's giving themselves prominent parts in the New Testament story, making themselves the "kings and priests" whom they find in the text. This, in their view, is an illegitimate self-transformation of individuals who remain unlearned or simply foolish—commonplace after all. But lest anyone think that Wisehart is coming up with a new idea when he talks about the written "word of God," Foxe prefaces his account of Wisehart's defense with quotations from a sermon given by a member of the bishops' own party, a sermon about heresy and its detection. Heresy is to be known, the preacher says, "by the undoubted touchstone: that is, the true, sincere, and undefiled worde of God." So on the issue of biblical authority, Catholics and Protestants appear to agree. But their agreement, as Foxe tries to show, is only on the surface. Distinctions must be made between people who know the New Testament story, as if from the outside, and people who insist that they themselves have a role in it.

Foxe never lets one forget that Wisehart is enacting roles authorized by the New Testament. As a disciple of Christ, he repeats Christ's experience. Christ is tempted by Satan in the wilderness; later, he is tempted by Peter, who urges him to escape martyrdom. Jesus replies, "Get thee behind me, Satan" (Matthew 4, 16:23). Similarly, Wisehart, on his way to execution, is tempted by two human "fiendes," who urge him to give up his beliefs, "to whom he answered meekly, 'Cease, tempte me not.'" On the cross, Jesus prays for his enemies: "Father, forgive them, for they know not what they do." The disciple Stephen imitates Jesus during his own martyrdom: "Lord, lay not this sin to their charge" (Luke 23:34, Acts 7:60).[5] Wisehart, preparing to be hanged and burned, says (in a slightly qualified, scholarly way), "I beseche Christ to forgeve them that have condemned me to death this day ignorauntly." The words of Jesus on the cross are, "Father, into thy hands I commend my spirit" (Luke 23:46). The words of Master Wisehart are, "Father of heaven I commende my spirite into thy holy handes."

When, in the book of Acts, Philip encounters the Ethiopian minister of state and converts him to belief in Christ, his text is the prophecy of Isaiah: "He is brought as a lamb to the slaughter" (Acts 8:32, Isaiah 53:7). Writing to the church at Rome, Paul quotes the Psalms: "Yea, for thy sake are we killed . . . we are counted as sheep for the slaughter" (Romans 8:36, Psalm 44:22). In Revelation, Jesus is "the lamb that was slain" (Revelation 5:12). Foxe extends the long series of literary re-enactments of this theme, describing Wisehart's execution as "this innocent Lambes slaughter." Like the New Testament writers, Foxe binds his narrative to as many parts of scripture as he can, weaving the repetitions together into the same story. Despite Wisehart's arguments that the Bible is the unique and sufficient authority for the Christian life, it is very likely that many Protestants regarded the *Book of Martyrs*, which like the Bible was officially distributed for use in churches, as a second book of Acts. Its arguments for Protestant Christianity had a powerful effect, but its repetition of Bible story was probably much more powerful. And when Bible story is repeated, so is its reproductive DNA, incorporating in new generations of Christian experience the insistence on discipleship, the emphasis on radical distinctions, the reversal of inner and outer, higher and lower, the transformation of the commonplace, the dependence on symbol, and all the New Testament's other fundamental ways of seeing and doing.

In Foxe's book, the literary effects are sometimes unforgettably strong. The heroes of the episode just before Wisehart's are a group of martyred Scottish Protestants who present a movingly literal repetition of the primitive church.[6] One imagines, indeed, that the people in this story of Perth in the year 1543— William Anderson, James Hunter, James Raveleson, James Founleson, Hellen Stirke, and the well-named Robert Lambe— were exactly the type of people who might have been attracted to the church of the first century and would have had the courage and individualism to stick with it, no matter what. Hellen Stirke in particular showed that she could find a place for herself in the New Testament story without losing the sense of herself as a real individual. In an interesting variant on the doctrine of the two selves, she represents herself as both a small and a great person: the smallness is inherent; the greatness comes from God, the author of all stories, big and small:

The woman Hellen Stirke was accused, for that in her chyldbed [delivery of a child] she was not accustomed to call upon the name of the virgin Mary[,] beyng exhorted thereto by her neyghbours, but onely upon God for Jesus Christes sake, and because she sayd in lyke maner, that if she her selfe had beene in the time of the virgine Mary, God myght have looked to her humility and base estate, as he dyd to the Virgyns, in makyng her the mother of Christ, thereby meaning, that there was no merites in the virgyn, whych procured her that honor, to be made the mother of Christ, and to be preferred before other women, but Gods onely free mercye exalted her to that estate.

The account of the little congregation of Perth closes with the symbolic immediacy of Revelation 3:20—"If any man hear my voice, and open the door, I will come in to him, and will sup with him, and he with me"—and the ironic reversal of Luke 12:37: "Blessed are those servants, whom the lord when he cometh shall find watching . . . he shall gird himself, and make them to sit down to meat, and will come forth and serve them." Hellen Stirke tells her husband that the day of their execution "ought to be most joyfull to us both, because wee must have joy for ever. Therefore I will not byd you good night, for we shall sodaynly meete with joy in the kyngdome of heaven." Her friends agree that they will "sup together in the kyngdome of heaven that night." So they die "constantly in the Lord," as if there were nothing simpler than to believe that eternity is waiting just on the other side of the door.

The Word in Popular Culture

Now let us change earthly times and places and look at some later expressions of religious revival that have influenced the popular culture of English-speaking people—expressions that, like Foxe's book, have often exerted almost as much influence as the Bible itself, but are sometimes harder to analyze and appreciate.

Just outside the tiny town of Rome, Pennsylvania (named for the city of Rome, because it lies near the same latitude) there is a cemetery, surrounded by farmland. At its center is a tall stone monument, erected by contributions from people on both sides of the Atlantic, and consecrated to the memory of Philip P. Bliss (1838–1876). Bliss does not lie beneath the monument. His charred remains are somewhere in the communal grave of eighty anonymous victims of a disaster that occurred at Ashtabula, Ohio, on December 29th, 1876. A railroad bridge gave way, and the train on which Bliss and his wife were traveling plunged into a deep ravine. Many passengers drowned; many others perished in the flames that consumed the wooden carriages. Bliss escaped from the wreck but went back to help his wife. Both perished, and their bodies could not afterwards be identified. Nevertheless, the inscription on the monument declares of Bliss (and of all faithful Christians): "Their Names Shall Live."

It might have been more accurate to say, "Their Stories Shall Live." Bliss's name endures among a tiny group of scholars, but his versions of New Testament story remain on the tongues of millions. Bliss was a writer of gospel music, songs that were sung in the great revival campaigns of the nineteenth century and that continue to be sung in Protestant churches, a permanent witness to America's revival roots.

The "televangelism" and "new church" revivals of the 1980s and 1990s; the revivals of religious feeling in mainstream American churches in the 1950s; the crusades of Billy Sunday and Aimee Semple McPherson in the 1920s; revivals of the pentecostal spirit in the Azusa Street meetings in Los Angeles in 1906 and in the holiness movement of the century before; Dwight Moody's international campaigns of the 1870s and 1880s; the Adventist movement, focusing on expectations of Christ's second coming, that blossomed in America in the 1840s; the Great Awakening of the eighteenth century in seaboard America and its more radical successor in the West, the Second Great Awakening at the turn of the nineteenth century; the Methodist agitation that began in England in the 1730s and spread rapidly to America; the ferment of English puritanism in the early seventeenth century and the migration of religious "pilgrims" to New England in 1620—the line of Protestant revivals reaches back to the beginnings of English culture in America, and the line is virtually unbroken. America, which has been called the world's most religious nation, formed its character in an atmosphere never wholly clear of revivalist cloud and lightning.

Most major revivals of Christian experience have been supported or inspired by Christian intellectuals. The Reformation bore the stamp of thinkers as distinguished as Erasmus, Luther, and Calvin. John Milton was a leading figure in English puritanism. Methodism began with the work of John and Charles Wesley. Jonathan Edwards was a leader of the Great Awakening. The fundamentalist movement was supported by the learning of J. Gresham Machen, the eminent scholar and essayist. Contemporary evangelical movements derive constant inspiration from the writing of C.S. Lewis. But whatever else it may be, revivalism is always a movement in the popular culture, involving people whose names may not have "lived" in intellectual history but whose responses to the New Testament have given unexpected richness and intensity to its relations with modern culture.

I say "unexpected" because every revival returns to the New Testament, but no revival ever reads it in exactly the same way. The changes may be merely "stylistic," but style is never unimportant when one responds to a literary work. No one who has heard Bliss's conversion hymn "Almost Persuaded"—once enormously popular, still holding its own in evangelical congregations—can forget this response to the passage in Acts where the double-minded King Agrippa listens to Paul's preaching and says, "Almost thou persuadest me to be a Christian" (Acts 26:28). Bliss, adapting his message to a modern, nominally Christian, self-consciously respectable audience, takes a hint from Governor Felix's earlier remark to Paul—"when I have a convenient season, I will call for thee"—and creates the ironic picture of an unsaved soul politely demurring to the Holy Spirit's summons:

> Go, Spirit, go Thy way;
> Some more convenient day
> On Thee I'll call.[7]

Unlike Felix and Agrippa, modern "Christians" know all about the Spirit; but that doesn't keep them from treating him like an unwanted business caller who can be cordially put off till some other time.

In the culture of Christian revival, almost anything of popular interest can work as an approach to Bible story. Bliss was attending a religious meeting in 1870 when he heard a Civil War veteran telling the history of the battle of Altoona Pass, where Union troops found themselves surrounded and were preparing to surrender. Then they saw, at the top of a distant mountain, a

signal from General Sherman: "Hold the fort; I am coming."
Sherman's soldiers came, and the Union won the battle. At his
meeting the next day, Bliss went to the blackboard and chalked
up the words of "Hold the Fort," which became one of the best
known songs in America:

> See the mighty host advancing, Satan leading on;
> Mighty ones around us falling, courage almost gone!
> "Hold the fort, for I am coming," Jesus signals still;
> Wave the answer back to heaven, "By Thy grace we will."

Bliss, we are told, thought the song was far from his best, and
he was right; but it ended up on his monument at Rome, which
identifies him as "Author of 'Hold the Fort' And Other Gospel
Songs."[8] The song was a successful adaptation, for the audience
of its time, of the apocalyptic idea on which all revival movements depend: the concept of the true church, surrounded by
its enemies (even in a "Christian" world), and reliant solely on
God's grace for survival.

It is sometimes easier to specify how Milton achieves his
effects than to specify how a popular song writer achieves his
own. Perhaps, in Bliss's song about the crucifixion and resurrection, it is simply his tune, lively yet solemn, that gives a special emphasis to the ideas; or perhaps it is the song's ironically
joyful turn on the familiar idea of Jesus as "a man of sorrows,
and acquainted with grief":

> "Man of sorrows," what a name
> For the Son of God who came,
> Ruined sinners to reclaim!
> Hallelujah! What a Saviour![9]

Whatever the source of their power may be, you cannot talk
about hymns strictly as literature or music (just as you cannot
talk about the Bible strictly as literature). You have to see them
as hymns, as works whose purpose is to revive and reproduce
the New Testament story, the story of the church and the story
of all the individuals who are part of it. But who is really part of
the church? That is an important question, especially for evangelical hymn-writing, which is an art intended to inspire the
conversion and transformation of people who are used to being

"in church" but are not really "members" in any sense that Paul would recognize (1 Corinthians 12:12–31). Waking those people up requires considerable literary skill.

Renewals of the Light

Since the time of Isaac Watts (1674–1748), the "father of English hymnody," English and American hymns have responded to the need for individual conversion with highly individual expressions of religious feeling. Watts, a young evangelical Christian, tired of the churches' habit of singing either Old Testament psalms, rendered in English translations of feeble spirit and anonymous tone, or recent compositions that were even worse. He began writing songs that joined New Testament ideas with personal emotions and reflections. His songs led worshipers to re-experience "the old, old story," as seen from a personal point of view. His example has been followed ever since.

Like many other things about Christianity, hymn writing is distinctly paradoxical. A hymn needs to divide and unite at the same time. It needs to express an individual perspective that can nevertheless be adopted by the church as a whole; yet it also needs to produce the kind of intensified experience that separates the authentic Christians in the congregation from the merely nominal ones. All this must done by repeating, in a new way, the literary patterns of an ancient text.

Anyone who knows popular Christianity in the English-speaking world knows that the Bible is its most important means of conveying its message, and that songs are the second most important. The ministers in *Elmer Gantry*, Sinclair Lewis's encyclopedic satire of American Christianity, regret that people cannot remember the sermons they hear, but it's obvious that they all remember the songs. Daniel Webster is reported to have gone to church but missed the sermon because he was reading the hymn book and worrying about the changes made in one of his favorite songs.[10] Christian songs, unlike Christian sermons, often survive for centuries. They are set to new tunes, translated into new languages, contracted and expanded and adapted to the needs of new audiences. There are songs that took generations to complete; there are songs that were inspired by other songs or written about other songs.[11] Through centuries of revival, and centuries of popular music, the DNA of Christianity passes from one author and religious group to another.

Here is a characteristic story about the persistence of that DNA. Frances Jane (Fanny) Crosby (1820–1915) was the nineteenth century's most popular and prolific hymn writer. But until she was thirty years old, "the queen of gospel song" had never been converted. She was brought up a Christian; she believed in Christianity; yet for a long time she failed to experience the radical change inside the self that New Testament conversion is supposed to represent. She did not feel that her path had crossed the path of providence, in the way in which New Testament story and the stories of the great hymns indicated that it should. In 1850 she visited the Broadway Tabernacle in New York, where revival services were held. Her biographer describes the scene:

> Twice she got down on her knees and the frenzied elders all but crushed her skull, laying hands upon her head and roaring prayers for her conversion, and twice the hours went by without her "getting happy." Finally, on November 20, Fanny, now torn with frustration and anxiety, was led for a third time to the altar. This time she was frantic. "It seemed to me that the light must come then or never." She was there alone that night, for no other candidates had presented themselves. For hours the deacons and elders prayed but nothing happened. The congregation began to sing Isaac Watts's "grand old consecration hymn," "Alas, and Did My Savior Bleed." Finally, at the fifth and last verse—"Here, Lord, I give myself away. 'Tis all that I can do"—it happened. Suddenly Fanny felt "my very soul was flooded with celestial light." She leaped to her feet, shouting, "Hallelujah! Hallelujah!"[12]

Revivals look to the experience of the early church; they also look to the experience of earlier revivals. The connection is literary. It is provided by the DNA of the New Testament and succeeding works of Christian literature, such as Isaac Watts's hymns. And it is transformative. The extent of the transformation is poignantly indicated by Crosby's account of her conversion: "My very soul was flooded with celestial light." She didn't have to mention, because everyone knew it, that she had been literally blind since she was six weeks old, when a wandering "doctor" treated her eyes with a poultice that destroyed her sight. For the same reason, she didn't have to mention the fact that her conversion repeated the experience of the blind people whom Jesus healed. Everyone familiar with the New Testament knew the stories she was re-enacting. Neither did she have to emphasize the idea, deeply inscribed in the New Testament DNA, that the inner self and the inner light are more important than any literal sight of the external world. When she saw the "light," she was repeating the literary experience of nineteen hundred years. Once again, the metaphor of light was transforming itself into the reality of light.

Described in that way, the event seems miraculous; and it is certain that Crosby saw herself, and all other Christians, as re-enacting the miracles described in the New Testament. The fact that conversion could happen to anyone, at any time, provided a logical basis for writing about the experience that "I" have had, then offering it for repetition by the rest of the church. With that in mind, we can see Crosby's blindness as she saw it—an attribute that connected her with New Testament story and could also be used as a symbol for anyone else's experience as a prospective follower of Christ. In her song "Blind Bartimeus" (with an affecting tune by Philip Phillips, known as "the Singing Pilgrim"), the blind man from Mark, Chapter 10, calls to Jesus as he approaches on his way to Jerusalem:

> Son of David! hear my cry;
> Saviour, do not pass me by;
> Touch these eyelids veiled in night,
> Turn their darkness into light.[13] (Texts, p. 348)

Then the miracle of enlightenment occurs:

> Glorious vision! heavenly ray!
> All my gloom has passed away.
> Now my joyful eye doth see,
> And my soul still clings to thee.

Bartimeus's experience is individual and particular, yet any Christian could sing those words.

The expression "do not pass me by" had already appeared in Crosby's "Pass Me Not" (Texts, pp. 347–48), one of America's most widely known religious songs, and today second in popularity, among her own works, only to "Blessed Assurance."

Crosby was speaking at a religious meeting in a New York City prison when she, in her blindness, heard one of the prisoners cry out, "Good Lord! Do not pass me by!" She assimilated the real-life episode to the type of gospel narrative represented by the Blind Bartimeus incident and the synoptics' account of the healing of Jairus's daughter (see page 52, above), stories of Jesus journeying onward amid crowds of people reaching out to him from literal or spiritual darkness.

> Pass me not, O gentle Saviour,
> Hear my humble cry;
> While on others Thou art smiling,
> Do not pass me by.[14]

Within a few days, Crosby heard the hymn sung in services at the prison where she had received her inspiration. Many of the inmates were converted, and Crosby, we are told, "was so moved" that she fainted and "had to be carried out."[15]

As a woman who was literally blind, Crosby had long experience wondering what was going on around her, asking herself whether the people whose presence she dimly sensed outside would simply pass her by, paying no heed to her, or actually engage her in their lives. Like a prisoner, she longed to change mere existence into action. She saw special significance in the New Testament stories of people whose lives were transformed when they became Christ's followers and began to journey with him (as Bartimeus did, in the literal as well as the symbolic sense). And like Paul, she had no trouble joining New Testament with Old Testament stories, and combining those with stories of individual and private experience, seeing them all as episodes in a single great history of liberation. Her own journey was essentially the same, she thought, as that of God's children in the Old Testament, when he guided them out of captivity in Egypt. In those days, God gave manna from heaven and water from the rock, and the only difference from the experience that Christians now have is that Christians can appreciate the symbolism; they know that both the manna and the rock are Christ, and that the effect of interpreting the symbols rightly is inward transformation as well as outward blessing:

> All the way my Saviour leads me;
> Cheers each winding path I tread;

Gives me grace for every trial,
Feeds me with the living bread;
Tho' my weary steps may falter,
And my soul a-thirst may be,
Gushing from the Rock before me,
Lo! a spring of joy I see.[16]

By directly appropriating the stories and pictures of the pre-Christian past, Crosby shows that God's providence isn't "past" at all. And if you follow the parallels she establishes between ancient Israel's experience and her own, you will see that she regards life as a constant escape from imprisonment in "Egypt" and a constant journey "all the way" to the promised land. You will also see that she is doing what another important hymn writer had done a century before—using symbolism to reverse a certain common idea of God. People often assume that God is distant and unyielding, ruling the world by a providence that is unconcerned with human beings and their individual experience. That, William Cowper asserts, is merely how he seems from the stubbornly distant viewpoint of our fleshly sight:

Judge not the Lord by feeble sense,
But trust him for his grace;
Behind a frowning providence,
He hides a smiling face. (Texts, pp. 344–45)[17]

For Crosby, as for Cowper, the inwardness of providence is joy; it is the "smiling face" of God. God shows a human face to human beings; he is prepared to journey *with* the friends who "trust" him, the friends he "leads."

The Grand and the Immediate

To create surprising insights or simple, lyrical effects, it is enough to mention one or two important Bible incidents or images, as Crosby usually does in her hymns. But biblical resources will easily support larger, more theatrical effects, effects that even humble congregations can understand and join in producing, so long as they know the Bible basics. One of the most impressive hymns of the Protestant church is "Glorious Things of Thee Are Spoken" (Texts, pp. 343–44), written in 1779 by the Reverend John Newton (1725–1807), a convert to Christianity who produced many revivals of faith among his generation. After "Amazing Grace," "Glorious Things" is the most famous of his many hymns. Especially in its most familiar setting—the tune "Austria," by Franz Joseph Haydn—it shows that common Christian ideas can be rendered in any emotional register, including the grandest and most solemn.

The language of "Amazing Grace" (Texts, pp. 342–43) is generally intimate and personal:

> Through many dangers, toils, and snares,
> I have already come;
> 'Tis grace has brought me safe thus far,
> And grace will lead me home.

In the last verse, which the twenty-first century never sings, the curtains part and the story of the individual journey and conversion is seen against its background in cosmic history and transformation:

> The earth shall soon dissolve like snow,
> The sun forbear to shine;
> But God, who call'd me here below,
> Will be for ever mine.[18]

The emphasis of the song, however, is on God's providential leading of the individual to conversion.

"Glorious Things" has a different emphasis. Its purpose is not to celebrate the transformation that attends conversion but to produce a transformation of attitude about the life that follows conversion, specifically the life that Christians lead in association with the church. The local church can seem a very shabby thing to the people who attend it. As a clergyman, Newton was well aware of this, and anxious to provide a more dramatically interesting perspective than the one that routine churchgoers usually have. His song pictures "Zion," the church, both as the holy city envisioned in Revelation and as the congregation of Israel in the liberation account of the Old Testament—the assembly of God's people, journeying across the desert of this world, fed by God's miraculous food, the manna, and guided by God's presence in the symbols of fire and cloud. If you raise your eyes from the

church's daily failures and the attacks of its "foes," you will find
that the church is moving forward with God, along with every
individual in it:

> Round each habitation hov'ring,
> See the cloud and fire appear!
> For a glory and a cov'ring
> Showing that the Lord is near;
> Thus deriving from their banner
> Light by night and shade by day;
> Safe they feed upon the Manna
> Which he gives them when they pray.[19]

The idea that the Lord is actually "near" each humble
Christian "habitation" provides the same sense of immediacy
that one receives from Foxe's treatment of Master Wisehart,
Hellen Stirke, and their friends. Ultimately, this is Luke 12:37
and Revelation 3:20, again repeated. What Newton adds is the
grand historical and theological stage-set, fully invested with
symbols of power:

> Glorious things of thee are spoken,
> Zion, city of our God!
> He, whose word cannot be broken,
> Form'd thee for his own abode:
> On the rock of ages founded,
> What can shake thy sure repose;
> With salvation's walls surrounded,
> Thou mayst smile at all thy foes.

The most striking effects, however, sometimes result from the
most immediate images. A powerful example comes from
another hymn by Cowper (1731–1800), Newton's collaborator
on the *Olney Hymns*, a frequent literary resource of evangelical
Christianity. Cowper's best known hymn, written a few years
before his collaboration with Newton, begins with a startling,
though doctrinally orthodox, picture of Christ's constant availability as a remedy for sin:

> There is a fountain fill'd with blood
> Drawn from Emmanuel's veins:

And sinners plung'd beneath that flood,
Lose all their guilty stains. (Texts, pp. 345–46)[20]

The lines are a direct statement of traditional Christian teaching: Jesus's sacrifice is always potent, always accessible, always *there*; and sinners are always invited to wash "their robes, and ma[k]e them white in the blood of the Lamb" (Revelation 7:14). Jesus's words about eating his flesh and drinking his blood were too vivid for many of his disciples (John 6:53–60); similarly, Cowper's hymn has proven too vivid for many Christian congregations. It is still popular, however, with people for whom the conversion experience, the dramatic and disturbing *sight* of Jesus's relationship to the soul, is the core of religious life. That is the sight set forth in Cowper's eighteenth-century hymn, even as, by Paul's preaching, Christ was "evidently set forth, crucified among" the first-century Christians (Galatians 3:1).

The Nominal and the Real

In the context of Christian revival and conversion, people are meant to be disturbed. The purpose of revival literature is to focus on their failures and internal divisions, revealing both their sins and their blindness toward them—the blindness of people who, in most instances, call themselves Christians. Every soul must *see* the conflicts inside itself and *believe* in their providential remedy. But self-examination can be a tricky process, as Crosby indicates in the second verse of "Pass Me Not":

Let me at a throne of mercy
Find a sweet relief;
Kneeling there in deep contrition,
Help mine unbelief.

She is quoting the crucial text of conversion psychology, Mark 9:23–27, where Jesus tells the man who seeks a miracle of healing that "all things are possible to him that believeth"—to which the man replies, "Lord, I believe; help thou mine unbelief."

Seeing his honesty about his divided mind, Jesus immediately performs the miracle. The moral for modern, uncompleted Christians, is to realize that the self is more complicated than they thought. They must admit that there is something inside them that does not really believe in God. Until the self that wants to believe understands its internal divisions and asks for "help," no transformation will occur. The function of revival literature is to insist—rudely if necessary—that ordinary, nominal Christians notice such unpleasant facts. Perhaps that is why this literature, though often enormously popular, tends to be produced by unusual and eccentric people. It is these people who can offer new perspectives on the "normal" inhabitants of Christendom.

William Cowper was subject to periodic attacks of insanity. His friend John Newton was a slave trader and *de facto* atheist, before attaining a dramatic conversion to Christ and, eventually, to abolitionism. Fanny Crosby waited over three decades after her conversion to join a church, then did so for unknown reasons. Isaac Watts went to visit friends for a week and spent thirty-six years with them; too ill, most of the time, to practice the Christian ministry that was his profession, he nevertheless published profusely, writing works on logic, theology, and other subjects, in addition to hymns and other poems.[21] Dwight Moody, the most successful of late nineteenth-century evangelists, complained that his audiences consisted of people who seemed far too respectable, "chronic attenders of religious meetings, who crowd everybody else out. . . . Why, they look as if they had been running to religious meetings for the past twenty years." Go out and find some people who don't come here automatically, he told his hosts, echoing many a remark by Jesus, who was, after all, not wholly in tune with the religious congregations of his own day.[22]

Sometimes, however, religious individualism takes a tragic form. Robert Robinson (1735–1790), a working-class boy who became a Methodist minister, was the author of one of the most moving evangelical hymns, "Come, Thou Fount of Every Blessing" (Texts, p. 342). It is the story of the Prodigal Son, altered so as to emphasize the sinner's continued self-division. Jesus, like the father in the parable, goes forth seeking the soul, trying to bring it home; but the soul isn't seeking Jesus; it prefers to stray:

Jesus sought me when a stranger,
Wandering from the fold of God;
He, to save my soul from danger,
Interpos'd his precious blood.

So the speaker is rescued. But the next dramatic revelation is that even after the speaker has "come to himself," like the Prodigal, he still wants to be lost—or at least one part of him does:

> Prone to wander, Lord, I feel it;
> Prone to leave the God I love . . .

He prays for God's grace to restrain him, to act as a "fetter" on his heart so that he cannot wander again, no matter how much he wants to. The song, composed when Robinson was twenty-three, offers prophetic insight into his own, apparently worsening, self-divisions. Years later, it is said, he was traveling on a stagecoach when he met a woman who was singing "Come, Thou Fount." "Madam," he told her, "I am the unhappy man who wrote that hymn many years ago; and I would give a thousand worlds, if I had them, if I could feel as I felt then."[23]

Of course, there would be no need for revival if the Christian journey simply stopped at some convenient point. And conversion is far from the end of the road. There are always opportunities to lose one's way. Isaac Watts, whose hymn "Alas, and Did My Savior Bleed?" moved Crosby to conversion, wrote another perennially popular song, asking a series of pointed questions about whether Christians are still on the right path:

> Am I a soldier of the cross,
> A follower of the Lamb?
> And shall I fear to own his cause,
> Or blush to speak his name? (Texts, p. 341)[24]

It must always be remembered that revivals occur in places where people *think* they are Christians. Otherwise, there would be nothing to revive. The speaker in Watts's poem may be an unconverted nominal Christian. More likely, he is a real Christian in need of revival and recovery. Looking into himself, as the New Testament urges him to do, he realizes that being a Christian in a "Christian" community causes him fear and embarrassment: he "blush[es] to speak" Christ's name. If he is able to accept that wound to his self-esteem, he may be on the way to a larger healing. But questions persist. What exactly does he expect the Christian journey to be like? The only way he can learn about the road ahead is to recall the experience of those who have taken it before him. To learn what his own story will be, he needs to consider the stories of other people, instead of trusting his self-serving imagination:

> Must I be carried to the skies,
> On flowery beds of ease;
> While others fought to win the prize,
> And sail'd thro' bloody seas?

Like most Christian literature—like the Christian journey itself—this poem partakes of both past and present. The idea of fighting to win the prize assimilates several of Paul's comments (for instance, 1 Corinthians 9:24–26, Philippians 3:14). The image of the bloody seas comes from the bloody maritime battles of Watts's own time, with some hints from Revelation 8:8–9, 14:20, 16:3–6, and Foxe's *Book of Martyrs*. The images work together, each intensifying the contrast with the ludicrous picture of a soul that wants to be wafted to heaven in a bed strewn with flowers. That luxurious furniture has no precedent in Christian literature, unless it is in Revelation 3:17, where the nominal Christians say, "I am rich, and increased with goods . . . ." If one part of the self still thinks that the Christian journey "must" be luxurious, then as Paul says, "now it is high time to awake" (Romans 13:11). Watts puts it in this way, with inspiration from 1 Timothy 6:12 and Revelation 5:10: "Sure I must fight, if I would reign."

"While We Try to Preach the Word"

Revival, as I have said, is a very literary event. This is true even in circumstances that approximate those of the primitive church. One of the most eloquent works of revival literature is a "simple" song that was current in backwoods America during the early nineteenth century. The song is called "Brethren, We Have Met to Worship" (by reference to its first line) or "Holy Manna" (by reference to its last) (Texts, pp. 346–47).[25] It touches all the literary bases of Christianity, without leaving them "literary" in any unfavorable meaning of that term—remote, over-refined, inaccessible to ordinary people. There's nothing more immediate than the song's reminder of Jesus's words about divisions within families (Matthew 10:34–36), seen here as a motive for trying harder to "see" and reach the unsaved:

Brethren, see poor sinners round you,
Trembling on the brink of wo[e];
Death is coming, hell is moving;
Can you bear to let them go?
See our fathers—see our mothers,
And our children sinking down . . .

The song's chief access to the New Testament, however, is the Pentecost story in Acts. The verses depict Christian experience as a constant attempt to reenact that story, which was itself a reenactment of the Old Testament stories of God's provision for his people. The providence that gathered the church by word and Spirit was the same providence that gave God's people manna in the wilderness. Whenever Christ's disciples come together, the cycle of Bible stories comes to life again, with all their transformative effects:

Brethren, we have met to worship
And adore the Lord our God;
Will you pray with all your power
While we try to preach the word[?]
All is vain, unless the Spirit
Of the Holy One come down;
Brethren, pray, and holy manna
Will be shower'd all around.

Like Paul, the obscure author of this song views the church as an organic unity, a body in which every member has an indispensable function (1 Corinthians 12). The song dramatizes the individuality of the people who sing it, casting them as different kinds of characters in the New Testament story. We see the leaders who "try to preach the word"; the people whose prayers are needed for the preaching to do its job; the unfledged converts who are like the "trembling jailer" from Acts 16:25–34, the "mourners" from Matthew 5:4, the "weeping Mary" from Luke 7:37–50. All the genres of the New Testament contribute to the song, including apocalypse, which provides the prophecy that "our God" will at last make "all things new" (Revelation 21:5).

When that happens, according to Revelation, the church will be seen as "the holy city," the glorious New Jerusalem (Revelation 21:2). The song uses a homelier image, but an equally interesting one. It turns to Luke 12:37, where Jesus says that when the master returns and finds his servants waiting faithfully for him, he will enact the ultimate reversal of the higher and the lower: "he shall gird himself, and make them to sit down to meat, and will come forth and serve them." In the words of the song,

> Then he'll call us home to heaven,
> At his table we'll sit down.
> Christ will gird himself and serve us
> With sweet manna all around.

This is a memorable effect, not just because the song follows the New Testament story by dramatically reversing the relationship between the Master and his followers, but because, in doing so, it presents the magnificence of heaven with the persuasive straightforwardness of a family dinner. It does not simply *allude to* the New Testament idea of innocence restored by reconciliation with God; in its innocent and homely way it *embodies* the idea.

Needless to say, the Christian church hasn't always conformed to this straightforward ideal of unity, or allowed itself to be transformed by a return to its New Testament roots. It has often been characterized not only by diversity but also by animosity; it has allowed the external features of church organization to attain more importance than the essential features represented by the New Testament's DNA. Yet even times of deadly conflict within the church have been marked by great literary achievement—as the next chapter will show.

11
The Christian Life

In the seventeenth century two different, though equally Christian, approaches to life and literature flourished in England. One of them was associated with the learned priesthood of the state-supported church, the Anglican Church or Church of England ("Anglican" means "English"). The other was associated with popular preachers at odds with the established church. These preachers and their followers differed widely among themselves, but for the sake of distinct classification they are ordinarily considered "puritans." Like the reformers of the preceding century, they hoped to purify the church and return it to something approaching its "primitive" condition. Among their descendants are the Christians we now call Baptists, Congregationalists, and Presbyterians.

The seventeenth century was the seedbed of these modern denominations, but none of them had an exact counterpart then. And there were "puritans" in the Anglican church, too. As always, it is easier to label people than to understand them. The Anglican church produced many simple and lucid expressions of "primitive" Christianity, while the most distinguished puritan writer was the very unprimitive poet John Milton, one of the most learned people of his time, and the wielder of one of the most complicated styles in English literature. Even the religious differences between the two parties seem much less definite when one considers how many beliefs united them. They quarreled mightily over the organization of the church, its leadership, its methods of worship, and sometimes its attitude toward such important issues as baptism and the celebration of the

Lord's supper or communion. Both parties were fraught with internal disagreements about organizational problems, the nature of Christians' acceptance of grace (whether by free will or God's absolute determination), and many other things. But about the importance of the New Testament and the meaning of its central story, Jesus's life, death, and resurrection, there was almost universal agreement.

The differences between puritans and Anglicans received a bloody emphasis in the civil wars that broke out in England in the 1640s between supporters of the king and supporters of Parliament. The king was the champion of the Anglican Church; the parliamentary forces were dominated by puritans. Eventually, the parliamentary army led by Oliver Cromwell vanquished the forces of church and king. The king was executed, and the puritans exchanged monarchy for a "commonwealth" under Cromwell's military dictatorship. The situation reversed itself in 1660 when, after Cromwell's death, the monarchy was restored, along with the Anglican state church.

That is the political story. The religious story is best summarized by T.S. Eliot, a modern poet to whom the similarities between the enemies appeared more important than their differences. He saw in their disputes a paradox that is characteristic of all disputes among believers—they were divided by the intensity of their adherence to the faith they shared. No one fights as hard as they did over issues that don't matter deeply to the participants. If their Christianity had been less serious, their divisions would never have become so murderous.

From Eliot's perspective, the two groups were opposing sides of the same movement. And now

> These men, and those who opposed them
> And those whom they opposed
> Accept the constitution of silence
> And are folded in a single party.[1]

The partisans of both sides have perished; they are literally silent. Yet Eliot maintains that something still speaks from their conflict, however sinful it may have been. The enemies perished as martyrs to contending beliefs, but in so doing they left a heritage that transcends all contentions. And as always, the means by which Christians transcend the past is literary. The seventeenth-century Christians bequeathed a literary legacy, "a symbol . . . perfected in death." Dying, they passed on to future generations the story of their devotion to a faith approved by suffering.

So the blind poet Milton, discarded in disgrace when the monarchy revived, and King Charles, executed by the party that Milton served, are characters in the same story, after all—closely related characters. Their story follows the routine pattern of Christian literature: what seems similar (such as the versions of Christianity that they derived from the same Testament) turns out to be different; what seems different (such as their reenactments of New Testament roles) turns out to be similar. "He that shall endure unto the end," said Jesus, "the same shall be saved" (Mark 13:13). We read, therefore, on the same page of history "of a king at nightfall" and

> Of three men, and more, on the scaffold
> And a few who died forgotten
> In other places, here and abroad,
> And of one [Milton] who died blind and quiet.

All Christians are sinners, saved by grace, ill-sorted individuals gathered by the Spirit into a story they did not devise themselves. Remembering that, Eliot sees Milton and Charles and all the rest of them as one might see any group of Christians—as

> people, not wholly commendable,
> Of no immediate kin or kindness,
> But some of peculiar genius,
> All touched by a common genius,
> United in the strife which divided them.

Regarded in this way, their lives are "renewed, transfigured, in another pattern" from the visible pattern of their combats with the weapons that Paul terms "carnal" (2 Corinthians 10:4). The inside story triumphs over the outside. What appears on the inside is two seemingly opposite things that paradoxically work together, like the elements of the church's organic unity in 1 Corinthians 12. One is the distinct individual, the "peculiar genius." The other is the "common genius," the one Spirit that revives and transforms all.

That is Eliot's view, and it is a good introduction to the two broad tendencies within seventeenth-century Christian literature, each of which, in its own way, strove to "transfigure" Christians' perceptions of their religion: puritan plainness and Anglican "metaphysics."

The Drama of Intellect

That last word needs to be explained. "Metaphysics" is the branch of intellectual inquiry that deals with the ultimate questions: what is the nature of being, of time and eternity, of the universe as a whole? As a literary term, "metaphysical" was invented in the eighteenth century by a critic who was trying to find a word for the highly intellectual methods of the Anglican poets of the early seventeenth century.[2] The Anglican church prided itself on its educated clergy and its primacy in the English universities and the English governing class. Religious literature in the Anglican tradition naturally tried to judge itself by rigorous intellectual standards. It often became as complicated and as "cosmic" as any metaphysical argument in philosophy. It deployed all the elements of the New Testament DNA, but it had a special taste for those that create intellectual drama—such elements as irony, paradox, reversal, and transformation. In addition, a leading characteristic of the "metaphysical poets" is a particularly complex use of symbols and a tendency to put the greatest possible distance between a symbol and its literal meaning.

They attempted in this way to increase the intellectual challenge, drama, and intensity of their works. A fine expression of the tendency is "I am a little world made cunningly" (Texts, p. 329), one of the *Holy Sonnets* of John Donne.[3] Donne (1572–1631) was an adventurer, court official, and later priest of the Church of England. He was a complex personality who well understood the scope, tensions, and contradictions of the self. He begins the sonnet by describing himself as "a little world," a microcosm or model of the planet, with all the complexities of the outer world built into the inner one. Having introduced the world as a symbol of the soul, he tells the history of the soul's religious experience as if it existed on the same scale as the history of a world. He invites astronomers who have found new planets to pour the water from their seas upon him, so he can "drowne [his] world" with "weeping" for his sins. His repentance will be like the flood of Noah's day.

This is all a spectacular reversal of normal priorities: the individual soul now seems as large as the earth, and even more important. As Paul teaches, however, none of the soul's works will avail with God; they cannot put an end to sin, any more than Noah's flood could put an end to it. You cannot save your soul by any action you perform, even if it is action on a cosmic or "metaphysical" scale. Only God's grace can save the soul. Knowing this, the poet exclaims, "But oh it must be burnt"—an allusion to Revelation's image of the lake of fire and to the picture of the end of the world in the second epistle of Peter (Revelation 20:10–15, 2 Peter 3:10).

"Oh it must be burnt": that is a plain statement. But for a metaphysical poet, there's no reason to leave it that way; it needs to be accompanied by a clever irony that will bring in other ideas. So Donne confesses that his soul has *already* been burnt by "the fire / Of lust and envie," thus unexpectedly joining Peter and John's images with Paul's comment about burning with lust (1 Corinthians 7:9). And why not, since anything in the Christian cosmos can be used to symbolize events in the microcosm, the individual self? The poet's cleverness is justified by reference to the cunning that God himself displayed when he joined flesh and spirit ("Elements, and an Angelike [angelic] spright") to produce this little world.

But there are other references to fire in the New Testament, and these can be exploited too, even those that are of an opposing character. The fires of lust and the fires that will end this world are images of destruction, quite different from the Holy Spirit's descent at Pentecost to begin the construction of Christ's "house," the church; but Donne seizes the Pentecostal image to dramatize the conclusion of his poem. He begs God to manifest his grace in the same way in which it was manifested in the New Testament, in the transforming fire of the Holy Spirit:

[B]urne me ô Lord, with a fiery zeale
Of thee and thy house, which doth in eating heale.[4]

The final reversal ("eating" revealed as "healing") is a paradox: as God mysteriously united flesh and spirit to build the self's "little world," so he unites destruction (the "eating" or devouring of a fire) with healing (the miraculous gift of the Spirit) to revive and restore that world.

The idea of holy *sonnets* is itself paradoxical. These particular poems are narratives of religious crisis,[5] but the sonnet is not, by nature, a narrative form. It is too short and too closely structured. One has to force a story into it. And the normal subject of this genre of poetry is romantic love. It is the kind of poetry that "burns" in a nonreligious way. By turning it toward religious narrative, converting fleshly or "carnal" feeling into the account of a spiritual journey, Donne again shows the transformative power of Christianity.

Given the important place that irony and paradox hold in the New Testament DNA, there are, in principle, no limits to the spiritual use of "carnal" images. In another *Holy Sonnet*, Donne begins with an allusion to Revelation 3:20 ("I stand at the door, and knock") and to the doctrine of the trinity: "Batter my heart, three person'd God" (Texts, p. 329). But he ends with an invitation for God to "ravish" him. To "ravish" is to seize by force, and it is generally used in a sexual context. This is a very peculiar love poem, and Donne means it to be. He means to startle and therefore to challenge the reader, to make the reader see the experience of conversion or religious revival in a new and more powerful way. Every time there is a choice of images, Donne selects the strongest possibility. His Jesus doesn't just "knock" at the door; he "batter[s]" it down. Where Revelation promises that Jesus will "come in to" the Christian's house and "sup with him"—a comfortable, familiar activity—Donne demands that Jesus "bend [his] force" to "break" the Christian and "make [him] new."

This, again, is basic Pauline theology, the theology of God's grace and power exerted on behalf of those who cannot help themselves—who are, indeed, in their fleshly selves, doing their best to resist his grace. But Christians often fail to experience the full implications of this familiar idea. So Donne expresses it with the most violent imagery he can find. Sexual violence is the ultimate carnality. If Donne can take that image and use it for Christian purposes, he will provide a stunning example of transformation. He does so by joining the image with one exactly opposed to it in its moral associations: the New Testament's image of sanctified marriage, the metaphor of Christians as the bride of Christ (Matthew 25:1–13; John 3:28–29; Revelation 21:2,

9–10). The story, as he tells it, is that of a marriage that ought to happen but cannot, until Christ takes action. "[D]early I love you," the soul says to Christ, "and would be lov'd faine, / But am betroth'd unto your enemie." Sin is the enemy; it is sin that resists the marriage, and sin is inside the soul. Liberation must come from the outside, and it is not an easy process; it is violently paradoxical. The poet asks Christ to "divorce" him from his sins; to "untie" him, "breake that knot," and yet to take him captive:

> Take me to you, imprison me, for I
> Except you enthrall mee, never shall be free,
> Nor ever chaste, except you ravish me.

After the initial shock and disgust of "ravish," the careful reader notices the quiet word "chaste." Chastity, purity, innocence is the aim of all this violence; the overwhelming power of grace is the means of attaining it.

The general idea of metaphysical poetry is that less is not more; more is more. So, in another section of "Batter my heart," Donne adds something to his story of marriage and divorce—a contrasting story of politics and military violence. He pictures the soul as a "towne" that should be ruled by God's "Viceroy," "Reason." But reason, as Paul suggests when he discusses "wisdom" in 1 Corinthians, Chapter 1, is far from perfect. In Donne's words, it proves either "weake or untrue." In either case, it is "captiv'd" by sin. The city of the soul is similarly "captiv'd." As you would expect, given the doctrine of the two selves, there are contending parties in this town. The better party "labour[s] to admit" God's liberating forces, but cannot do so; meanwhile, reason dithers, or traitorously attempts to keep God out. Once again, the conflict can be resolved only by grace, which can batter open the gates of any town.

And once again, only careful readers will see what is happening. Only they will work their way through the poem's imagery of towns and battles and public officials—all of which seems so external, so much a part of this world—and find the New Testament story inside. Like many other works of Christian literature, the poem is both a revelation of truths about the human condition and a test of the reader's ability to understand that revelation. "He that hath ears to hear," Jesus said when he spoke a parable, "let him hear" (Luke 8:8). The New Testament DNA can be detected only if you want to detect it. That, in modern language, appears to be Donne's assumption. To "hear" Donne's poems, one must exercise the intellect; the various strands of Christian story can be brought together only by conscientious thought. His emphasis on intellect gives his warning about "reason" a double strength. Reason is God's viceroy; but it can still lose track of the stories that it ought to follow. It is quite capable of occupying itself entirely with the outsides of things, to the neglect of spiritual meanings, even meanings that ought to be obvious. The right use of reason requires the intervention of God's grace.

The Intervention of Grace

This, among many other things, is the subject of George Herbert's "The Collar" (Texts, p. 330), one of the most memorable examples of metaphysical poetry. Herbert (1593–1633), like Donne, was an Anglican priest. He lived at a time when priests of the state church often regarded their occupation as a job like any other job, simply a way of supporting oneself in a gentlemanly trade. But Herbert, the son of a prominent family, saw the priesthood as a religious calling, not a business interest. His parish was a humble village; its house of worship was built by Herbert himself, a true disciple of the carpenter from Nazareth. But his literary way of repeating the New Testament story was usually not so simple and direct. He preferred to tell it in a manner that emphasized dramatic conflicts and required the reader to uncover hidden meanings. "The Collar" is a narrative poem, but like many other narratives inspired by the New Testament (recall Kipling's "The Gardener"), it cannot be grasped just by following the plot from beginning to end. Its meanings emerge only when one looks at it a second time and notices the patterns that lie beneath the surface, waiting to be discovered by a conscientious reader.

Even the significance of the poem's title cannot be taken for granted, but we have to start somewhere, and we can do so by giving "collar" its normal meaning, for the present. A collar is something that restrains or constrains; specifically, something that constrains a working animal or a slave. "The Collar" presents itself as the history of a person who has been caught, collared, and constrained to work against his will. Now he is rebelling.

> I struck the board, and cry'd, No more;
>   I will abroad.
> What? shall I ever sigh and pine?[6]

The first thing to notice is that this is a person who is talking very vigorously to himself, as if there were someone else in the room who needed to be argued out of an opposing view. Remember that. Remember also that he strikes "the board," the table, in front of him. Of course, it's a normal thing to do when you're angry and you want to leave, to go "abroad." And it follows naturally that the speaker should complain that his table offers nothing good to eat or drink. There used to be "corn," he says, "[b]efore my tears did drown it"; there used to be "wine. / Before my sighs did dry it." Now, the only thing left is a "thorn," to let out "bloud." Remember these things, too.

As the speaker continues talking about his poverty and misery, it seems increasingly appropriate that he is talking to himself, because that is where the blame lies. His "cage," he acknowledges, was created by his own "fears," which haunt him like a "deaths head." But because his fears and tears are psychic symptoms, creatures of the self, perhaps they can be dispelled by action he himself can take, action as direct as his brisk reminder to himself that "there is fruit, / And thou hast hands." That would be a simple and rational way of dealing with the problem. It's the way recommended by every modern self-help manual: reflect on yourself, recognize your fears and inhibitions, take personal responsibility for your errors, do something to change your life. You can get what you want if you stop preventing yourself from getting it.

This wisdom was known to the seventeenth century, too. But are you sure it's enough? In Herbert's poem, the more convinced the speaker becomes that it's up to him to free himself from his psychic "collar" by summoning his own will power, the more irrational he appears:

> . . . I rav'd and grew more fierce and wild
>   At every word . . .

That doesn't look promising. Neither, when you think about it, does his striking the table, back in the first line.

So, while the speaker tells the story of his self-analysis, the reader is invited to tell another story about the same thing, a story offering different judgments from the ones the speaker argues himself into. Apparently, his is not a story that will explain itself completely. It requires a more reliable perspective than he can provide. And suddenly, such a perspective is offered. Suddenly, the raving speaker hears another voice, a voice much calmer and more authoritative than his own:

> Me thoughts I heard one calling *Child*:
>   And I repli'd, *My Lord*.

The speaker has heard the voice of God.

If metaphysical poetry defines itself as a continual reaching for cosmic effects, this is the most metaphysical of moments. But ironically, it has nothing to do with remote, intellectually difficult symbolism. It is completely straightforward—the most straightforward passage in the poem, and one of the most straightforward in all of Christian literature. Thus, with the intervention of God, the poem ends. Now one is free to go back and reread it.

The final phrase ("My Lord") leaves no doubt about the proper interpretation of the rest of the poem. The phrase is an echo of Thomas's confession of faith: "My Lord and my God" (John 20:28). We know, therefore, that the speaker's rebellion has not been simply against himself or whatever conditions he thinks are keeping him confined; his rebellion has been against God. And we know, for the first time, exactly what kind of poem we're reading: it is another repetition of the Prodigal Son, another story about a person "coming to himself." This is probably not what we assumed when we first overheard the speaker talking as if to someone else. His habit of doing so made his self-divisions clear enough, but it appeared that he was trying to remedy them by rejecting an overbearing Master. Now he is coming to himself in an opposite way. He is acknowledging a loving Father.

There is obviously more to the story than we could see at first. Once alert to the possibility of hidden significance, we can uncover new meaning in the "board," the "corn," the "wine," the "tears," the "sighs," and the bloody "thorn." There is a pattern among these things that is not accidental. It is borrowed directly from the New Testament. The central ritual of the Christian church, the communion service, is a meal of wine and bread, and the bread is usually made from wheat or "corn." Obviously, tears and sighs can ruin a literal meal, but they can also ruin a spiritual communion. A person who is frustrated because he believes he is being kept from other enjoyments will disparage the bread and wine served on Christ's "board" or altar. He may even strike the board, complaining that Christianity is a very restrictive thing.

Of course, tears and sighs are conventional signs of repentance. But the question is, repentance from what? Herbert's speaker is not like the speaker in Donne's poems, a man laboring to achieve full Christian repentance and willing to be "burnt" or "ravished" in order to reach that goal. Until the last line of "The Collar," Herbert's speaker is repenting of Christianity itself, repenting because it keeps him from pleasure. He looks at the altar and sees the bread and wine set out on it as *merely* symbolic, empty of substance. He forgets the New Testament stories that explain these things. He disregards Jesus's word that "my flesh is meat indeed, and my blood is drink indeed" (John 6:55). Seeing that physical sustenance is available elsewhere ("there is fruit, / And thou hast hands"), he ignores the ready availability of spiritual food: "that which was from the beginning, which we have heard, which we have seen with our eyes, which we have looked upon, and our hands have handled, of the Word of life" (1 John 1:1).[7] He is right (ironically) about one thing: he himself is the cause of his deprivation. His own sighs have dried the wine; his own tears have drowned the corn. He has missed the joy of Christianity and found only its "thorn"—an ironic verification of the New Testament idea that inward attitudes are more important than outward conditions (Mark 7:15). In his self-pity, he pictures himself, not Jesus, the wearer of the crown of thorns, as the suffering victim.

The reader sees that now. At this point, the reader knows much more about the speaker than the speaker appeared to know. His surface story of suffering and denial concealed the real story, which was that of a Christian's flight from a religion he didn't really comprehend. In the dramatic reversal of the last two lines, however, the poem's narrative of deconversion becomes a narrative of reconversion—not because the speaker works things out for himself, but because Christ steps in to resolve his conflicts. The speaker talks about getting free, but only God's grace can free him. Only grace can make the transformation happen. It does so simply by reminding him that he is a child and God is his father. If that is true, then he was never a slave or captive, whatever he thought. He was the child of a loving parent, a parent who was willing to seek him as the father in the parable of the Prodigal Son sought his child.

Herbert's poem gains more meaning when one recalls that its author was a priest. He was used to standing before a board with wine and corn upon it, and he was presumably used to the self-conflicts that accompany the surrender of worldly pleasures to the duties of the priesthood—conflicts mirrored in the poem's sense of a person constantly arguing with himself. Even a priest can fail to reach a stable understanding of his relationship with God, until grace intervenes and provides the interpretive key. We will see this idea again, in modern stories in which religious people forget the biblical clues to self-understanding amid the daily, official business of religion. We will also find the idea that even the simple things in life can reverse their apparent meanings and reveal God's story beneath the details of mundane existence. "Collar" is a simple word, a word that naturally implies restriction of some kind.[8] But speak the word aloud, and you discover how readily "collar" can become "caller": "Me thoughts I heard one *calling* Child." A caller like this is more welcome than a collar, but the two words have the same referent. The Lord is both the soul's restraining collar and the soul's gracious caller.

Which meaning do you see as primary? It depends on your perspective, on how you view the service of Christ. Remember Paul's experience on the road to Damascus, when Jesus advised him to stop "kick[ing] against the pricks" (Acts 26:14). Jesus constrained Paul to work as if he were a collared animal, yet he simultaneously welcomed him as one of God's adopted "sons" (Galatians 4:5). As in the New Testament story of Paul's conversion, so in Herbert's account of a priest's transformation: Jesus intervenes in the life of a self-righteously religious man who is trying to escape from him, and turns him into another path. Also re-enacted in "The Collar" (or "Caller") are the call of Jesus to his first disciples, his call to Lazarus at the tomb, and his call at the door of the heart in Revelation (Mark 1:17, John 11:43, Revelation 3:20). For Herbert himself, the call came, not in an audible voice, but in echoes from the New Testament. What happens at the poem's climax is the Christian's sudden recognition that the familiar words of the Bible are actually calling to him.

One of the major functions of Christian literature is to defamiliarize the familiar, to provide a fresh perspective on what one thought one understood. Herbert does that by challenging the reader to see New Testament patterns concealed inside ordinary thoughts and everyday affairs, even commonplace sins and rebellions against God. That, in general, is Donne's strategy too. Although his religious poetry has a wider range of reference than Herbert's, and is much less strictly dependent on the New Testament than "The Collar," it too involves the investigation of personal problems, such as the perceived inability to be fully converted, in the light of Bible stories and images, and other learned targets of allusion. But there was another approach to Christian literature, the approach often taken by seventeenth-century puritans.

The Power of Plainness

John Bunyan, the finest representative of puritan plainness, sees everyday life from the opposite direction. He is aware, as Herbert is, that in a nominally Christian society the New Testament itself has become familiar and ordinary. He is also aware that it is not regarded as vivid and pressing in the way in which many ordinary and familiar things are. But his response is to translate the Christian story back into the terms of everyday life, turning "Bible writing" into "real writing," accounts of ancient history into "real" and immediate experience. This, in its own way, is a startling thing to do. He does not start with a contemporary stage-set and challenge his readers to discover what drama is being played on it. He starts with characters named Christian and Faithful and shows what happens to them in a contemporary world that is mistakenly supposed to be Christian and faithful—and that is challenging enough.

Bunyan (1628–1688) was a "dissenting" preacher who refused to conform to the practices of the state church, the church in which Donne and Herbert served. For this strange eccentricity, he was imprisoned for many years. His great work, *Pilgrim's Progress* (1675–1679; Texts, pp. 331–340), begins in this way:

> As I walk'd through the Wilderness of this World, I lighted on a certain place, where was a Denn: And I laid me down in that place to sleep: And as I slept I dreamed a Dream.[9]

The "dream" is the story of *Pilgrim's Progress*; the "den" is the jail where the author was held; the whole is a repetition of the Apocalypse, the vision given to another follower of Christ while he, too, was being punished for preaching "the word of God" (Revelation 1:9).

Like Revelation, *Pilgrim's Progress* is a story told in symbols, although generally speaking, Bunyan's symbols are much easier to interpret than those in Revelation. To cite one of hundreds of instances: during the first parts of Bunyan's story, Christian, the "pilgrim" who is on a journey to paradise, carries a heavy burden on his back, a burden that leaves him only when he reaches the cross of Christ. The "burden" is an obvious symbol of sin. If you doubt it, Bunyan's marginal references will lead you to the biblical source of his symbolism, Psalm 38:4. All this would be predictable and boring, if that were all there is to it.

But it's not. Bunyan assumes that Christian symbols are more than just a conceptual alphabet to be learned by rote. They point at reality. So why not treat them as if they *were* reality? And that is what he does. There is a big difference between hearing someone say, "Oh, I am a sinner; I am burdened by sin," and watching while someone droops under the burden he is trying to carry, fearing that it is about to "sink" him, and actually sinks and "tumble[s]" in the swamp "alone" (pp. 12–13). Bunyan is entirely on the side of the second way of telling a New Testament story.

Few passages in literature are as powerful as the opening scene of *Pilgrim's Progress*. It doesn't tell us about the Bible; it places us in the reality of the Bible:

> As I walk'd through the Wilderness of this World . . .

For Christians, this world *is* what the Bible suggests that it is: a "wilderness" (John 1:23, Revelation 12:6, 14).

I dreamed a Dream . . .

Of course that's what happened; you can expect it to happen in
the Bible's world: "Your young men shall see visions, and your
old men shall dream dreams" (Acts 2:17). It's a repetition of the
New Testament, which in this case is also a repetition of the Old
Testament (Joel 2:28). But it is presented as simply as if it were
happening before your eyes.

> [A]nd behold I saw a man cloathed with Rags, standing in a certain
> place, with his face from his own House, a Book in his hand, and
> a great burden upon his Back. I looked, and saw him open the
> Book, and read therein; and as he read, he wept and trembled: and
> not being able longer to contain, he brake out with a lamentable
> cry; saying, What shall I do? (p. 1)

One thinks of Revelation 3:17 and Luke 15:14–17, but one soon
stops looking for precise New Testament references; one is now
fully inside the story of self-division and conversion as it is told
throughout "the Book."

There is nothing "theological" about this narrative; it has the
spareness and rapidity of a story that must be told, a story full
of conflict and urgency—in short, a "real" story, the kind of story
in which people must *do* something. But ironically, that is the
gospel method, too. The gospels have exactly this concreteness
and immediacy of presentation, and they also insist that action
must be taken. That is why they were written. Further, they omit
everything that is not . . . the gospel. They place you immediately in the center of the action—which is where Bunyan places
you—and the DNA of the New Testament is present in every
part of them, just as it is in *Pilgrim's Progress*. Almost all of it
appears right away, in the first edition's title page:[10]

The
Pilgrim's Progress
From
This World,
To
That which is to come:
Delivered under the Similitude of a
DREAM

Wherein is Discovered,
The manner of his setting out,
His Dangerous Journey; And safe
Arrival at the Desired Countrey

It would be tedious to list every trace of DNA in those twelve lines, but a few brief identifications will show how much of it Bunyan can pack into a few words. Of course, the slighting reference to "this world" is significant: here is the traditional Christian emphasis on the priority of the inner reality to the outer appearance. "This world," by implication, is not the final one; there is a larger scheme of things than anything we literally see, right now. The deeper reality can be communicated by story, prophetic "dream" or vision, and symbolism ("similitude"); that is the New Testament method. The central narrative, in each case, is one in which people are urged to journey from "this world," the world of time, toward a sharply distinguished world, "the desired country," the world of eternity. The story is embodied in the adventures of recognizably real characters, such as the pilgrim, a person of irreducible individuality whose course nevertheless reveals or "discovers" what the "progress" of any "pilgrim" may be like. The story turns on a striking reversal: the "dangerous journey" becomes a "safe arrival"—which is good evidence of the providential nature of the "progress." Anyone familiar with the gospels will recognize the parallel with Christ's dangerous journey and safe arrival; Bunyan's work is one more version of the perennially repeated history of discipleship. No overt paradox or irony appears on the title page, but its ordinary, unemphatic tone suggests the irony that runs through the work as a whole—the irony involved in presenting the stupendous revelations of Christianity as if they were the normal business of an ordinary day.

"The Nearest Way"

For Bunyan, undoubtedly, they were both; but his literary strategy is to show the Christian story playing itself out as much as possible in "normal" circumstances. Nothing can be more straightforward, more ironically unemphatic, than the way in which he describes the execution of Faithful, Christian's friend, by the normal people of this world. The description seems almost off-hand:

> They therefore brought him out, to do with him according to their Law; and first they Scourged him, then they Buffeted him, then they Lanced his flesh with Knives; after that they Stoned him with Stones, then prickt him with their Swords; and last of all they burned him to Ashes at the Stake. Thus came Faithful to his end. Now, I saw that there stood behind the multitude a Chariot and a couple of Horses, waiting for Faithful, who (so soon as his Adversaries had dispatchèd him) was taken up into it, and straitway was carried up through the Clouds, with sound of Trumpet, the nearest way to the Cœlestial Gate. (p. 165).

Bunyan takes his cue from the shocking directness of gospel narrative: "And it was the third hour, and they crucified him . . ." (Mark 15:25). He does everything he can to accentuate that style. The breezy "therefore," like the biblical "and," suggests how easy it is for monstrous people to do monstrous things. "Now" is a remarkably casual transition from the natural to the supernatural, and the equally casual "nearest way" drives home the point: the two worlds are closer than you thought. "Nearest" means "quickest." The way from this world to eternity is quick indeed: it takes no *time* at all. The supernatural chariot and horses[11] are like the chariots and horses of this world, only a million times better. This immediate, unheralded penetration of time by eternity is a brilliant literary effect. Now, whenever you hear of a "multitude" of ordinary human beings gathered together to kill some innocent person, you will be able to visualize the forces of God, standing just behind them, "waiting." Bunyan has changed your point of view.

Another transformation of perspective happens when one realizes that "this world," which is so "dangerous" to Christian and his friends, is a nominally Christian world. It is, by and large, the world of England as Bunyan knew it, the England in which he was persecuted by other "Christians," even as Jesus was persecuted by other religious leaders. What Bunyan's title page does not say, but every reader knew, is that the purpose of his work is to revive Christianity among his fellow citizens of Christendom. Revival, for him, is not a matter of complex argument. It is a matter of showing what New Testament Christianity is—and who its enemies are—as sharply and clearly and urgently as he can.

His plot moves as rapidly as his sentences. Christian's religious crisis occurs on the first page, as soon as he actually begins to read the gospel that all Christians supposedly "know." Immediately he faces the challenge of "this world": his family and friends close in on him, trying to keep him from the separation and distinctness that Christian self-awareness demands. Bunyan does not portray these people as overtly evil; that would be too easy, from a literary point of view, and it would do nothing to develop his audience's ability to distinguish godly conduct from mere "good" conduct. When Christian's friends witness his spiritual distress, they are concerned, sympathetic, helpful (at least at first). The bad thing about them is their helpfulness. It shows that matters of the spirit, such as his religious crisis, are irrelevant to them. They are living in what our own contemporaries call a "post-Christian" world, a world that seeks only naturalistic explanations for anything that causes trouble:

> At this his Relations they were sore amazed; not for that they believed, that what he said to them was true, but because they thought, that some frenzy distemper had got into his head. (p. 2)

They see Christian's belief as a psychological symptom.

The irony is that although he has started on a journey to something better than this world, he still suffers terribly, while his friends and family, who have no notion of anything better than their own petty, mediocre lives, are perfectly contented. Respecting only the outside of things, they have no concern for his inner life or individual feelings. When his eccentricity continues longer than one night, they punish him in the ways in which helpful friends are so expert:

> They also thought to drive away his distemper by harsh and surly carriages [behavior] to him: Sometimes they would deride, sometimes they would chide, and sometimes they would quite neglect him. (p. 3)

At this point, Christian has no friend except "Evangelist," the gospel itself (εὐαγγέλιον—"euangelion," "evangel"—is the Greek word for "good news"); and Evangelist recommends that he become still more individualistic: "Then he gave him a Parchment-Roll, and there was written within, Fly from the wrath to come"—which means that he must fly from everyone he knows, for the sake of his soul:

> So I saw in my Dream, that the Man began to run; now he had not run far from his own door, but his Wife and Children perceiving it, began to cry after him to return: but the Man put his fingers in his Ears, and ran on, crying, Life, Life, Eternal Life: so he looked not behind him, but fled towards the middle of the Plain. (p. 5)

This is one of Christian literature's most uncompromising pictures of the individual's relationship to the world, and certainly one of the most vivid. Bunyan will use any device he can to make his story compellingly realistic. He will even make his hero "put his fingers in his ears," if that's what it takes to show how determined he is not to listen to the advice of this world, and if that's what it takes to show how childish, how absurd the practice of Christianity must look from a conventionally "realistic" point of view (1 Corinthians 1:18–29). Imagine a grown man running about with his fingers in his ears! But what's at stake is "Life, Life, Eternal Life."

Bunyan contrasts this scene of strife and alienation with a vision of worldly success and harmony, the vision one sees when Christian and his friend Faithful enter the consummately worldly town of Vanity Fair (pp. 88-97). This section of *Pilgrim's Progress* is a masterpiece of sarcasm, inspired by Revelation's sarcastic treatment of "the great city, which spiritually is called Sodom and Egypt" (Revelation 11:8). Christian and Faithful are the "two witnesses" of Revelation, Chapter 11, and the city they visit is a display case loaded with the kind of desirable things one finds in the great list at Revelation 18:11–13. It offers, as Bunyan puts it:

> Houses, Lands, Trades, Places, Honors, Preferments, Titles, Countries, Kingdoms, Lusts, Pleasures, and Delights of all sorts, as Whores, Bawds, Wives, Husbands, Children, Masters, Servants, Lives, Blood, Bodies, Souls, Silver, Gold, Pearls, Precious Stones, and what not? (p. 149)

"And what not"—*et cetera*! While immersing us in the allurements of Vanity Fair, Bunyan also allows us to see them as they look from an ironic distance, to recognize that they are, after all, just "vanity." One can tire of worldly goods. After a while, they can even look ridiculous.

Bunyan's treatment of Vanity Fair as essentially comic shows how useful comedy can be in providing the transformation of perspective that is crucial to Christian literature. Comedy arises from the sudden perception that what one is used to regarding as important, serious, and therefore intimidating is actually not worthy of one's concern.[12] The Bible makes good use of comic effects. The adventures of the Old Testament prophet Jonah show how silly even a spokesman for God can be when he decides that he knows better than God; if you are intimidated by professionally religious people, this is your chance to see them in a different light. The book of Revelation has many darkly funny moments. One's respect for "the kings of the earth" lessens a good deal when one sees that they are led by "spirits" that look "like frogs" (Revelation 16:13–14). Then there are the inhabitants of "the great city," Revelation's Vanity Fair, whose persecution of God's two witnesses makes the inhabitants themselves seem something less than smart and sophisticated. They bustle about, having parties and "send[ing] gifts one to another," until the uncanny moment when they hear a voice saying, "Come up hither," and they see their enemies start to life, stand on their feet, and soar to heaven "in a cloud" (Revelation 11:7–12). So much for the celebration! It's a serious scene, but it's comic too.

The same can be said of the Vanity Fair episode, in which Christian and Faithful are put on trial for the bizarre crime of refusing to buy any of the goods displayed in the Fair. When one thinks about it, one realizes that this was also the complaint against Jesus: he wasn't buying any. He insisted on the idea of a kingdom that is no part of "this world" (John 18:36). The consequences for him were serious; he, as Revelation says, was crucified in "the great city . . . called Sodom and Egypt." The consequences are serious for Bunyan's characters too. Although Christian escapes (so that the plot can go forward) Faithful is condemned and executed at Vanity Fair. But the farther you move your point of view from the things of "this world," the more you see how foolish the Fair really is.

Its judicial proceedings are especially ridiculous. What can you say about a presiding judge named Lord Hategood, and a jury whose names are Mr. Blind-man, Mr. No-good, Mr. Malice, Mr. Love-lust, Mr. Live-loose, Mr. Heady, Mr. High-mind, Mr. Enmity, Mr. Lyar, Mr. Cruelty, Mr. Hate-light, and Mr. Implacable? These people seem even funnier when you realize that they haven't a clue about what their names mean. Their failure to sense their own absurdity is the final touch. We don't just look down on them; we see inside them and discover the contemptible self-righteousness that they cannot see themselves. In a deep sense, one cannot take them seriously.

As in the Two Witnesses episode of Revelation, one has the satisfaction of seeing one's verdict approved by heaven; for immediately after the judicial forces of Vanity Fair have their way and execute Faithful for his imagined crime, we are given the glorious sight of the victim being carried "straitway . . . up through the Clouds, with sound of Trumpet." Very few passages of literature evoke so intensely, and harmonize so well, the dirge of mourning, the song of triumph, and the shout of laughter. This literary paradox, this combination of seemingly contradictory effects, is as shocking and inspiring as anything in the metaphysical poets. But the larger paradox, so well illustrated by seventeenth-century Christian literature in both its forms, is the paradox of the Christian life itself. That life is complicated enough to be intellectually challenging on many levels, yet simple enough to be repeated in endless combinations, to be at home in every time and place, and in the most opposite literary modes.

In Donne, Herbert, and Bunyan, we see brilliantly individual adaptations of denominational styles. Yet Christian life and thought are capable of much more radically individual expressions.

12

A Tradition
of Individualism

Whether the individual self is pictured as a rebel against "this world" or as "a little world" that summarizes the larger one, an awareness of the importance of the individual is an essential strand in the fabric of Christian literature. From the beginning, Christian literature has been enriched by the very individual gifts of such writers as Luke, John, and Paul; and individualism has always been a part of the New Testament's DNA. While the individualist spirit of the modern West is often very different from the spirit of Christianity, the two are not unrelated. The Christian focus on the struggles of the individual soul, seeking the way to God, provided a precedent for much that would follow in the world's intellectual life.

The modern expectation that all good literature will be individual, even eccentric, began in the mid-eighteenth century. You can see what happened when you look at the eighteenth-century transformation of the word "original," which within a few years changed its common implication from "foolish" or "stupid" to "fresh," "authentic," "suggestive of genius." Responding to the surge of literary interest in people's unique experience of life, John Newton, the preacher and hymn writer, emphasized the idea that Christian belief and Christian expression proceed from an "experimental" knowledge of "inward feelings."[1] Since the eighteenth century, many of the most effective defenses of Christianity have come from literary individualists, people whose unique perspectives have enabled them to see resources in the Christian story that other people would have missed.

This chapter is devoted to William Blake and Emily Dickinson, two authors deservedly famous for their originality. They are, in fact, two of the most eccentric authors in English literature. Their eccentricity was productive. One of them, Dickinson, had an uneasy, uncommitted, skeptical relationship to Christianity during most of her life; yet she left unforgettable expressions of Christian ideas. The other, Blake, journeyed from skepticism to something very close to orthodoxy—a remarkable intellectual adventure—while maintaining his astonishing ability to transform ancient ideas into fresh poetic images.

Prophetic Independence

Blake (1757–1827) was an English painter and engraver, the writer, illustrator, printer, publisher, and marketer of his own poems. Authorial individualism can go no farther. His religion was equally independent. Baptism in the Church of England was his last institutional connection with any church. His religious inspiration was the Bible, certain writings of Christian mysticism, the works of Milton and such evangelical Christians as Isaac Watts and John and Charles Wesley, founders of Methodism, and his own visions. "Visions" was a word he took literally—too literally, indeed, to communicate exactly how his visions happened. He regarded them as a commonplace of life, unnecessary to explain.[2] It's impossible to say just what they were. Certainly they were not the ghostly "visions" that spiritualists or occultists claim to see. At the least, they were a way of seeing things with unusual intensity and insight into their symbolic potential. At the most, they were immediate perceptions of God's influence on his life. But his visions were largely inspired by the Bible, and when he reproduced them in his poetry and art, they often adapted themselves ingeniously to biblical stories and ideas.

One of those ideas was the conception of prophecy. Blake considered himself a prophet, and he named a number of his narrative poems "prophecies." That does not mean that he gave them the same status that he gave the Bible. In one of his notes he says that "Every Honest man is a Prophet,"[3] but his continual recourse to the Bible as a model and inspiration indicates its privileged position in his mind. His response to it varied as his ideas developed. During his thirties, he was impatient with orthodox interpretations and wrote a manifesto, *The Marriage of Heaven and Hell*, satirizing ordinary Christian ideas about self-restraint, moderation, and the sinful nature of "the flesh." He disparaged "Priesthood" and extolled the individualism of the Bible prophets, who, he suggested, found God by means of their visionary "imagination." He thus gave a special turn to the biblical theme of *seeing* the truth and correctly interpreting literary *images*.[4] Even in poems written at roughly similar times, however, he was capable of emphasizing quite different aspects of Christianity.

His first artistically mature collection of poetry, *Songs of Innocence*, gives an individual treatment to the familiar world of New Testament symbols. *Innocence* is full of apparently ordinary beings whom his artistic vision forms into New Testament patterns. Early in the book, one encounters a poem about a shepherd and learns that his sheep "are in peace, / For they know when their Shepherd is nigh." Blake does not say who the Shepherd is. Then one finds a poem about a child and a lamb. The child asks the lamb, "who made thee[?]", and as Paul and Jesus often do, he answers his own question:

> Little Lamb I'll tell thee,
> Little Lamb I'll tell thee!
> He is called by thy name,
> For he calls himself a Lamb:
> He is meek & he is mild,
> He became a little child:
> I a child & thou a lamb,
> We are called by his name.
> Little Lamb God bless thee.
> Little Lamb God bless thee.[5]

Now one knows exactly whom the "Shepherd" represents. One also knows that the lamb, the shepherd, and the child are united in a circle of symbols of which Christ is the center, each of them revealing an aspect of his divinity and his harmony with creation.

Like the New Testament, *Innocence* emphasizes the union of God and humanity (Christ the child), Jesus's role as mediator and exemplar (Christ the Lamb of God), and the role of God-given symbols as our guide to the inner meaning of our experience (Christ the shepherd). Underneath its simple surface, *Innocence* is a providential world. It is not a world like Eden, where nothing (initially) went wrong; it is a world where things are always going wrong, but God is always there to interpret them, transform them, and make them right. In a pair of the *Innocence* poems, "The Little Boy Lost" and "The Little Boy Found," a child loses sight of his father while they are journeying through the dark. Finding himself alone, the child begins "to cry, but God ever nigh, / Appear[s] like his father in white." Providence assumes the role that the human father lost or abandoned, and leads the boy to safety.[6] The providence that manifests itself on a universal scale in the Bible manifests itself on a human and domestic scale in *Innocence*.

In one of the more complicated parables of providence in the *Songs of Innocence*, a child is "sold" by his father into miserable servitude as a chimney sweeper. He cries when his head "[t]hat curl'd like a lambs back, was shaved" in preparation for his horrible job. But "that very night," God, the great Shepherd, seeks his lamblike child. He sends a vision in which the chimney sweepers are resurrected (freed from their "coffins of black"), transfigured (they "shine in the Sun"), and caught up to heaven (they "rise upon clouds"). Then an angel ("who had a bright key," like the keys in John's visions [Revelation 1:18, 3:7, 9:1, 20:1]) tells the child that he will "have God for his father & never want [lack] joy."[7] If you use Blake's symbols as keys to inner meanings, you will see that the child has repeated, with appropriate variations, the experience of Christ, who had God for his father and was transfigured, entombed, resurrected, and caught up to heaven. The *Songs of Innocence* are expressions of all those elements of the New Testament DNA that have to do with providence, transformation, the convergence of time with eternity, and the repetition of Christ's experience by his disciples.

But not the whole experience. What is omitted in *Innocence*, as in the skeptical *Marriage of Heaven and Hell*, is the central episode of the Christian story, the experience of the cross. There is suffering in *Innocence*, a suffering with which providence sympathizes and provides miraculous remedies; but suffering is not in itself redemptive. Each of these early works of Blake includes the apocalypse or prophetic uncovering of reality that appears at the end of the New Testament, but not the crucifixion that stands at its heart. In *The Marriage*, indeed, Blake takes the Christian story in a new direction, psychologizing it and individualizing it in radical ways. He represents "heaven" and "hell" as states of mind, one a condition of order and conventional virtue, the other a condition of energy and rebellion. Both, he asserts, are "necessary to Human existence," which will be seen and known as paradise once the apocalypse or uncovering happens within the visionary's individual mind. If you understand what Blake is saying about vision, he cheekily insists, then today you will be in Eden:

> For the cherub with his flaming sword is hereby commanded to leave his guard at the tree of life, and when he does, the whole creation will be consumed, and appear infinite. and holy whereas it now appears finite & corrupt.[8]

Individualism and Orthodoxy

Blake's idea of apocalyptic glory comes from the New Testament; his idea of humanity's ability to save itself has a number of analogues in the writings of his contemporaries, "deists" who deduced their idea of God from contemplation of the natural world and looked to the human mind as the source of progress. From the start, however, Blake was even more critical of deist "natural religion" than he was of traditional Christianity. "Nature," for him, seemed wholly opposed to "vision." He thought that nature is what appears to exist, on the outside, while vision shows what really exists, on the inside.

The distinction between nature and vision was one of the things that led him to revise his critique of Christianity, which makes its own strong distinction between the inside and the outside of things. In notes written two decades after *The Marriage*, he comments, "Many persons.such as Paine and Voltaire [both deists] with some of the Ancient Greeks say we will not Converse concerning Good & Evil we will live in Paradise & Liberty[.] You may do so in Spirit but not in the Mortal Body as you pretend . . ."[9] Blake's ideas went through long and complex revisions.[10] The crucial factor was probably a series of visions that he experienced around 1800, visions that gave him a new interest in Jesus as the savior and a new emphasis on the crucifixion as the central episode in a providential history of redemption and transformation.

Before that period, Blake had seen Jesus as a figure whom he could associate with a variety of conceptions, often distinguishing traditional ideas about Christ from his own ideal of him as a prophetic and imaginative rebel. After that period, he continued to associate Christ with the imagination, which was the crucial human quality so far as Blake was concerned, but he now saw him as both a person and, in a full sense, God. Blake had come to this orthodox Christian view by looking more deeply into his ideas about God and his interpretations of the Bible. He used New Testament imagery to represent the evolution of his ideas, symbolizing it both as a journey and as a process of prophetic uncovering, a removing of all that is not Christ, in imitation of Christ's putting off the "natural body," "the body of this death," on the cross (1 Corinthians 15:44, Romans 7:24).[11] Blake's vision left the earthly Eden at the start of the Old Testament, moved beyond the stories that he himself had formerly told about the Bible, and united itself with the hymns sung in heavenly Eden at the end of the New Testament:

Then sang the Sons of Eden round the Lamb of God & said
Glory Glory Glory to the holy Lamb of God
Who now beginneth to put off the dark Satanic body[.]
Now we behold redemption Now we know that life Eternal
Depends alone upon the Universal hand[.][12]

Blake's doctrines are specifically Pauline, and he develops specifically Pauline ways of using such elements of the New Testament DNA as distinction, unification, transformation, and reversal of priorities. His primary interest is in the distinction between the spiritual and the natural or "fleshly," the priority of the gospel of grace to the veneration of works and "law," and the transformative nature of the disciple's journey and identification with Christ. In a prologue written for a sequence of engravings, *The Gates of Paradise*, he identifies the "gates" not as good behavior, an absence of error and an abundance of good works, but as a Christlike willingness to forgive the sin that is bound to happen. Then, providing his own interpretation of the fact that the ten commandments given to Israel at Mount Sinai were enclosed in the ark of the covenant, under a cover that was called the "mercy seat," he says that God wrote the law, "then Wept!"—

And the Dead Corpse from Sinais heat
Buried beneath his Mercy Seat[.]
O Christians Christians! tell me Why
You rear it on your Altars high.[13]

In Blake's time, many churches mounted the ten commandments above the altar, where one might have expected to find
the cross. As he saw it, God in Christ had exalted grace over
law, but the churches seemed intent on reversing the relationship. That looked like a deconversion from true Christianity, like
one more sign of what Blake had always suspected:
Christendom and Christianity are utterly distinct.

Soon after he published *Songs of Innocence*, Blake supple-
mented it with another series of poems, *Songs of Experience*,
several of which attack nominal Christians and the nominally
Christian church for maintaining a system of law-built tyranny,
despising and repressing the individual soul. *Experience* draws
attention to the sheer ugliness of European life—its sickening
extremes of poverty, its degraded views of sex, its gross
infringements of freedom—all of which raised questions about
the responsibility of the church for the evils of a Christian country. Those are the kinds of questions that prophets are traditionally supposed to raise. After Blake's conversion, his
conscious identification of himself with traditional Christian doctrine, he continued to publish these (and other) attacks on the
church, but he added a new poem to *Experience*, a poem that
allows for a more complex view of the issue.

The poem is called "To Tirzah." In the Old Testament, Tirzah
was the capital of a kingdom that sponsored a rival form of worship to that carried on at the temple of God in Jerusalem (1
Kings 14–16). Blake saw in the opposition between Tirzah and
Jerusalem the same type of distinction that Revelation makes
between Jerusalem, the true church, and her antithesis, Babylon
the harlot, a false religion that is saturated with materiality, with
the love of riches and political power. As a visionary, Blake also
associated Tirzah or Babylon with the destructive emotions that
block the soul from spiritual perception. He calls her the
"Mother of my Mortal part," who

With cruelty didst mould my heart
And with false self-decieving [sic] tears,
Didst bind my Nostrils Eyes & Ears.[14]

The moral of "To Tirzah" is plain Pauline teaching: "stand fast . . . in the liberty wherewith Christ hath made us free, and be not entangled again with the yoke of bondage" (Galatians 5:1). That would be true individualism. As Blake's concluding couplet puts it:

> The Death of Jesus set me free,
> Then what have I to do with thee?

His illustration to the poem is still more interesting. It shows a group of people gathered around a corpselike figure. One of these mourners is an old, old man—never a good sign in a Blake illustration; it is a symbolic contrast with his ideal of joy and freedom, and with Jesus's command to be born again. The old man is anointing the dead body. This is a seeming act of piety, a good work, surely, the kind of work that Jesus's disciples were prepared to perform after his body was laid in the tomb (Luke 23:55–24:1). But good works are not Christianity, and pious people are not necessarily the body of Christ. To help readers make the difficult distinction, Blake engraves on the old man's garments a reference to Paul's theology: "It is Raised a Spiritual Body." He is quoting the apostle's account of the resurrection: "It is sown a natural body; it is raised a spiritual body" (1 Corinthians 15:44).

That passage concentrates the whole meaning of Blake's religious philosophy. Christianity is a matter of the spirit, not the flesh; not a corpselike following of law or custom, which amounts to the worship of death, but the joy of resurrection. Joy frees the individual and unites the (true) church, releasing its members from the delusions of the fleshly Tirzah. The angel at the empty tomb asked Jesus's disciples, "Why seek ye the living among the dead? He is not here, but is risen" (Luke 24:5–6). Blake asks the same question, and makes the same proclamation. To the student of literature, his use of the Bible has an additional importance. It suggests that even the most radical religious individualism can keep coming back to the New Testament for conclusive expressions of itself.

Skeptical Questions

For Emily Dickinson (1830–1886), as for William Blake, Christianity had everything to do with the individual spirit and individual interpretation of the New Testament, and practically nothing to do with institutional traditions or arrangements. Her work with Christian ideas was inspired by her own continuing resort to the Bible, especially to the gospels and the Pauline epistles. Like Blake, she offered, in her most challenging interpretations, a distinctive combination of originality and orthodoxy.

It is ironic that Dickinson, who is (rightly) regarded as one of the greatest exemplars of the American national literature, is also known for her withdrawal from the world around her. A member of a prosperous and well connected Massachusetts family, she gradually abandoned all direct contact even with the village in which she lived, restricting her movements to her own house. She followed a mysterious path of self-alienation. Her approximately eighteen hundred poems, only a handful of which were published in her lifetime, seem to have been written largely for her own appreciation. She may have been ambitious of posthumous fame, but whatever interest she had in publication during her lifetime was outweighed by her refusal to give her work the easy and conventional form that would recommend it to the public. In her work, as in Blake's, everything had to be the way the artist wanted it. Exotic imagery, expressive punctuation, peculiar allusions, unusual conjunctions of ideas—all were products of her individual imagination, and she refused to part with them.

Yet her intellectual engagement with the world never ceased. Not every poet is an intellectual, but Dickinson was. She read widely in the liberal arts, she knew and appreciated science, and she had a viselike grip on the Bible and the main themes of Christian thought. Her poems, which are written in the meters of Protestant hymns, frequently recur to Bible stories and sayings, and they are strongly marked by the New Testament's formative devices—paradox and irony, transformation of perspective, the repetition of sacred stories in contemporary terms, the revelation of spiritual meanings in ordinary things, and use of the symbolic journey as the framework for a progression of religious ideas.

It is, however, notoriously difficult to determine exactly how close she stood to Christian belief at any given period of her life. Her poetry and letters include many expressions of religious skepticism and outright embitterment toward religion.[15] In a time and place repeatedly swept by revival movements, she stood her ground, declining to be converted, while probing her soul to discover the reasons. Sometimes her poetry affirms Christian ideas; sometimes it rejects them, or revises them into unorthodox forms; and sometimes it uses Christian ideas and literary devices primarily as means of psychological exploration, revelation of the self to the self. Yet that has always been one purpose of Christian literature. Christian theology would not be Christian theology if it were deprived of its interest in the conflicts and adventures of the individual soul.

And there is no question that Dickinson took theology seriously. Her poetry contains some of literature's most powerful and engaging formations of theological ideas. As the New Testament itself bears witness, literary power often originates in the adoption of a fresh perspective. From a strictly literary point of view, Dickinson's alienation from the ordinary world—the pleasant town, the respectable social circle, the nice New England church—could not have been more helpful.

What does she see when she looks at the Christian church? Sometimes she sees a smug and mindless conformity to the world, a conformity that might be disturbing if it wasn't so obvious and easy to reject. She is capable of reacting to it with a cheerful deism:

> Some keep the Sabbath going to Church —
> I keep it, staying at Home —
> With a Bobolink for a Chorister —
> And an Orchard, for a Dome[.][16]

This is not Christianity but "natural religion." The poem offers no history of God's involvement with humanity, no story except the easy, gradual journey of a worshiper who is going "to Heaven," not "at last," but "all along." Dickinson is expressing the attitude that Isaac Watts satirized when he asked, "Must I be carried to the skies, / On flowery beds of ease?" He would agree with Dickinson on one issue: nature's church is much less demanding than the Christian church. In the church of nature, as she says,

> God preaches, a noted Clergyman —
> And the sermon is never long.

But one of her agreements with Watts is less predictable. In the hymn I just quoted, "Am I a Soldier of the Cross?", he asks the Pauline question, "Is this vile world a friend to grace, / To help me on to God?" His answer is clearly No. That is Dickinson's answer, too—if one defines "world" as "social world," the world of which the church often seems too much a part. In that world, teaching comes not from God but from one or another "noted [human] clergyman." The phrase perfectly imitates the pompous style of ecclesiastical self-advertisement. No inspiration can be expected from people who accept their worldly roles so dully and happily, no matter how long their sermons are.

The cheerful tone of "Some keep the Sabbath" is balanced, at the other end of the tonal scale, by the grim sarcasm of "Safe in their Alabaster Chambers," a poem that Dickinson was writing and revising at about the same time (poem 124, 1859–1862). The "Chambers" are the tombs of Christians, "the meek members of the Resurrection," who are waiting for something that never seems to come:

> Light laughs the breeze
> In her Castle above them —
> Babbles the Bee in a stolid Ear,
> Pipe the sweet Birds in ignorant cadence —
> Ah, what sagacity perished here!

Were these Christians truly "sagacious"? No evidence appears that they were any brighter than the people whom Paul sarcastically addressed as "wise" (2 Corinthians 11:19). Perhaps they were as stolidly imperceptive before their deaths as after. But notice the difference between nature in this poem and nature in "Some keep the Sabbath." Now nature has nothing to teach. It laughs, babbles, pipes, but remains as "ignorant" as the ignorant Christians. And when Dickinson revised "Safe in their Alabaster Chambers" she made nature still less a source of human significance. She pictured humanity as isolated even from the warmth of the birds and bees. She imagined all human events proceeding "Soundless as Dots / On a Disc of Snow." The universe is blank, unfeeling, incapable of instructing us in anything.

"Creator—Was It You?"

About a year later, however, Dickinson returned to the problem of the blank and "soundless" cosmos and addressed it in a specifically Christian way (poem 525, "My period had come for prayer," *circa* 1863). Now the journey has challenge and significance; it is a successful search for a personal God. As one might expect from the precedents for this search in the New Testament and in such Christian literature as *Pilgrim's Progress* (with which every child of New England was familiar), it is the journey of an eccentric individual. The speaker is alone when she begins to inquire about God. And she no longer assumes that God can be known as spontaneously and familiarly as the orchards and the bobolinks. She assumes, as the New Testament does, that there is always something mysterious about God. She returns to nature imagery, but with an intentionally strange, disorienting shift of perspective. She pictures a God who "grows above" the horizon, so that those who would approach this "Curious Friend" must step "upon the North" to see him. A God who "grows" like a plant, a God who can be seen only when one journeys to the north celestial pole—that is a "curious" friend indeed.

Of course, Dickinson isn't speculating that God actually resembles a plant. The point of her literally unvisualizable imagery is that God cannot be conceptualized with the aid of the things around us, the nature that we literally see. She is striking free from nature, from ordinary religious understandings, and from ordinary acts of prayer. The poem begins with the realization that ordinary Christianity is not nearly strange enough to accomplish its purpose:

My period had come for Prayer —
No other Art — would do —
My Tactics missed a rudiment —
Creator — Was it you?

Prayer as "tactics"? That doesn't sound right. That sounds as if prayer were being reduced to a professional practice, the system of a religious denomination or a person who sees Christianity as mere routine. And it isn't right. It's nowhere near the DNA of New Testament Christianity. No wonder it "missed a rudiment." Like the prayers of the people whom Jesus reproved for their religious formalism, it has everything in it except the Creator (Luke 20:46–47).

The Creator must be found, but where? The deists discovered proof of his existence in the order of nature, the order of the stars and planets to which Dickinson's astronomical imagery refers: "And so I stepped upon the North." But now she reaches a more distinctively Christian view. She suggests that a God who was simply the First Cause of the physical world, possessing none of the strangely distinguishing qualities that we find in human beings, could never be discovered, never be recognized. He would be hidden in the pattern of his own creation. He might be a "cause," but he could never be a "friend."

Looking for an image that can represent the problem plainly, she finds it in the contemporary American story of exploration in the wild lands of the West. Translate the deist account of humanity's search for God into the story of Americans' journey into the wilderness, and you will see the inadequacy of deism. Taking a symbolic journey across the frontier, Dickinson locates no "natural" evidence of God's individual personality:

> His House was not — no sign had He —
> By Chimney — nor by Door —
> Could I infer his Residence —

Imagine yourself traveling west, trying to find some evidence of human habitation—a settler's house, the signpost of an inn, a door, a chimney . . . You find nothing but the endless empty plain, "Vast Prairies of Air / Unbroken by a Settler." In that "Infinitude," there is no "Face" to "look on." That, put in American terms, is the search for the God of nature. There is plenty of evidence out there, an "infinitude" of evidence that God exists, but it provides no indication of his personhood; it does not reveal his "Face."

But this is the problem that the gospel story is intended to solve:

> Philip saith unto him, Lord, shew us the Father . . . Jesus saith unto him, he that hath seen me hath seen the Father. (John 14:8–9)

As Paul puts it, "the world by [its] wisdom knew not God," until the personal manifestation of God in Christ, "for in him dwelleth all the fulness of the Godhead bodily" (1 Corinthians 1:21, Colossians 2:9). Jesus showed the "face" of God.[17] In the New Testament, people seek God, but God is also seeking them. He enters the story; he reveals himself in a way that humans can understand. Now imagine that you are crossing the infinite, silent prairie, looking for someone, and suddenly you find that the person you are looking for has also been looking for you.

That is not the normal course of nature; it is the manifestation of a God who is simultaneously more personal and more cosmic than nature. And that is the God whom Dickinson finds:

The Silence condescended —
Creation stopped — for Me —

Only persons "condescend." Only a divine personality can work a miracle, "stop" the apparent order of the world because of his interest in encountering another personality. Humanity seeks God, and God seeks humanity. Where the two stories cross, conversion can take place:

But awed beyond my errand —
I worshipped — did not "pray" —

There is an irony in this transformation of the speaker's point of view, here at the poem's end. She has made miraculous progress; she has found God, despite all the apparent odds against her. Yet the end of the poem—like the Christian journey itself—looks backward to the beginning. It confirms the introductory suspicion that there is something inadequate about routine approaches to God, conventional "prayer." Real worship means going beyond such busy "errands," into the simplicity of knowing that God is as real as the worshiper, and as personally involved in the journey. Recall that according to the gospel of John, Thomas's first act of worship after his conversion from a career of doubt was the simple, awed expression, "My Lord and my God" (John 20:28).

Weighing the Arguments

Dickinson wrote a number of gospel poems cast as journeys from doubt to trust. One is the touching poem in which she says that while "We do not know" what death may be, "Christ's acquaintance with Him" may "Justify Him — though." We can trust Christ as the guide who is "no stranger" to Death, and follow where he leads across the seemingly endless prairie:

> His sure foot preceding —
> Tender Pioneer —
> Base must be the Coward
> Dare not venture — now — (poem 727, 1863)

More typical are poems in which Dickinson combines ideas from the gospels with ideas from the Pauline epistles. In one of these poems—eight lines that are a masterpiece of brevity—she starts with the question that some Christians at Corinth asked about the resurrection: "And with what body do they come?" (1 Corinthians 15:35). Paul was annoyed by the over-specific inquiry, because it implied that if we do not know everything about how God does things, he must not be doing them. Dickinson takes the skeptical question and reverses it, emphasizing the grounds of faith that are implied by its very terms:

> Then they *do* come, Rejoice!
> What Door — what Hour — Run — run — My Soul!
> Illuminate the House! (poem 1537, 1880)

As always, she rejoices when theological ideas can be incarnated in human stories, with "real" images of human life: "'Body!' Then real — a Face — and Eyes . . ." But while she is running ahead, visualizing the resurrection, she is also running back, reporting the history of the idea: first the Corinthians' question ("'And with what Body do they come'?"), then the assumption from which the question arose ("Then they *do* come"), then the prior teaching of Paul, which elicited the question, and finally the first announcement of the gospel by Paul's master, Christ, which she repeats as if she were watching the arrival of an exciting stranger at the local inn:

Paul knew the Man that knew the News —
He passed through Bethlehem —

Good news, indeed—and still able to be announced as "news," despite its long journey to the modern world.

This is a brilliantly concise crystallization of the *kerygma*, as derived from Luke and Paul. Another poem, also a response to skepticism, restores the original order, starting with the gospel and letting it lead to Paul. The poem begins with Dickinson's version of the command to preach the news: "'Go tell it' — What a Message" (poem 1584, *circa* 1882). The words express the general sense of a number of Bible passages, especially the "great commission" at Matthew 28:19–20. They come closest to the words of the resurrected Jesus at Matthew 28:10, in the King James version: "Go tell my brethren that they go into Galilee, and there shall they see me." If Dickinson is thinking of that verse, it continues her habitual emphasis on *seeing* the evidence of God. As for such people as Peter and John, who witnessed the first announcement of the good news, they responded, as she says, "simply — we — obeyed." No skepticism there.

But what did they obey? she asks. Was it "a Lure — a Longing?" Was the Christian movement merely a psychological phenomenon after all? If one accepts the modern assumption that everything must be explained in accordance with natural processes, with no room for genuine human response to supernatural events, then that's what it must have been—a psychological "lure" or delusion. Dickinson, the master-analyst of her own psychology, is too skeptical merely to embrace that skeptical (or is it a dogmatic?) assumption, despite the fact that it provides an easy and "natural" explanation of some very strange events. She is thinking instead in Pauline terms. To her, "nature" suggests "law," a law or dogma that can be respected but must be transcended.

She herself will not be bound even by conventional and "natural" language. She answers the skeptical question in as individual a way as she possibly can:

Oh Nature — none of this —
To Law — said Sweet Thermopylae
I give my dying Kiss —

Thermopylae is the mountain pass where, in 480 B.C., during the Persian Wars, Spartan soldiers sacrificed their lives for the freedom of Greece. It's an exotic image, un-Christian in origin; but like Paul addressing the men of Athens, Dickinson demonstrates the freedom to recommend Christian ideas in any way she finds effective, including the use of pagan sources. And the Pauline ironies and paradoxes are firmly in place: respect for "Law," yet desire to be free from it; association of "law" with the rebelliousness of one's natural "members," which ought to be repressed ("Oh Nature — none of this"); willingness to "die" to one's former life in order to live free from this "law" of "death" (Galatians 2:19–21, 3:19, 5:1; Romans 6:3, 7:20–8:15).

To Dickinson, the New Testament is finally about grace and freedom, the grace by which God suggests his presence, the freedom with which a would-be believer responds to his suggestions. Grace and freedom are both necessary parts of what it means for God to be sought and found, in an encounter that is not a matter of philosophy or physics but of a relationship between two very individual personalities. That is what she emphasizes in her version of Revelation 3:20 — "I stand at the door, and knock." She pictures Jesus not as a guest prepared to batter down the door if it remains unopened but as one who "raps" quietly, waiting patiently before pounding "at the Knocker." When he "retires — / Chilled — or weary," he still provides "ample time" for the soul to seek him "[u]pon the steps" (poem 263, "Just so — Christ raps," *circa* 1861). "[U]ntil then," the poem concludes, "Heart! I am knocking — low at thee."

Who is knocking at the heart? Jesus—probably. But it may also be the poet herself, constantly weighing gospel claims against her native skepticism. Perhaps it makes little difference. From Dickinson's perspective, the crucial thing is what happens inside "the lady's soul"—provided that it is not just a "longing" but a real event, an event that involves the individual as an active participant in the things of God. Jesus knocks persistently; yet he allows the lady to answer for herself. And that is not far from Revelation's teaching: "*If* any man hear my voice, and open the door, I will come in to him . . ." (Revelation 3:20).

It's not entirely clear that Dickinson opened the door, and kept it open.[18] As Paul says, "God knoweth" about that. Nevertheless, the poetry of this supreme individualist represents Christian belief, the problem of believing, and the problem of remaining skeptical, as vividly as anything in American literary history. And, as I will show, not only did Dickinson dramatize New Testament ideas; she caught a glimpse of New Testament glory.

13
The Glory Part

Several of Dickinson's poems demonstrate the importance of the book of Revelation to the continuity of Christian literature. One of them is the poem just discussed, in which the gospel idea of God as the seeker of souls and the Pauline emphasis on the conflicts of the soul find a culminating literary expression, the image of Christ knocking on the door and the soul deciding whether to let him in. That is the homely, domestic, psychological part of Revelation's message. But there is another part, which is still more influential on the progression of Christian ideas. That is the glory part.

The Irreplaceable Finale

Imagine the New Testament without its final book, the book that some Christians—including even Martin Luther—have found difficult to accept because it is so different from the other texts in the canon. True, it is an apocalypse, and there is only one book representing that genre in the New Testament. But without that one book, Christian literature would have the beginning of the story of Christianity, the gospel accounts of Jesus's birth, ministry, death, and resurrection, and the middle of the story, Acts and the epistles' accounts of the development of the church and its teachings; but it would not have the end of the story, the fulfillment of God's plans for the church and the world. The story would break off, roughly where Acts breaks off. Further, Christian literature would be lacking virtually all its concrete images of the supernatural world, of the ascended Christ and his hosts and of Satan and his dupes, not to mention its pictures of Christ's final triumph and Satan's final defeat and history's inexorable movement toward them. It would be lacking the final glory. This helps to explain why it is difficult to find a substantial body of subsequent Christian literature that does not draw implicitly or explicitly on Revelation. Indeed, Christians often cherish ideas that they think are derived from the gospels or epistles but that are actually derived from Revelation.

The "glory part" of the New Testament impressed even so skeptical, so apparently unapocalyptic, a writer as Dickinson, as she shows in her poem 353 (*circa* 1862), "I'm ceded —I've stopped being Their's."[1] This is a poem of extreme individualism, which takes its support from several parts of the New Testament—gospel, epistle, and apocalypse. Jesus in the gospel demands that the soul be born again (John 3:3). Paul in his epistles speaks of the "new creature," born of grace (Galatians 6:15). And Revelation promises true Christians a wonderful "new name . . . which no man knoweth saving he that receiveth it" (Revelation 2:17). Dickinson brings the concepts of the new birth, the new being, and the new name—all ideas with individualist implications—into judgment against the ceremonies of the church itself.

The majority of Christian denominations practice infant baptism, the ceremony in which a child is given its "Christian name" and is thereby recognized as a person under the Church's care. Dickinson takes the idea of the new birth much farther. She questions the idea that any community can name and thus, in a way, own an individual. "I'm ceded," she announces, deeded to someone other than the name-imposing community:

> I've stopped being Their's —
> The name They dropped [u]pon my face
> With water, in the country church
> Is finished using, now . . .

Like the radical Protestants of the Reformation period, she is trying to separate the original meaning of baptism, which signified the transformation of an individual person out of "death" and into the life of Christ (Romans 6:1–11), from the social meanings and customs that gathered around it as generation after generation of infants had water "dropped upon" their faces.

238 *Chapter 13 The Glory Part*

The occasion of the poem is a change that has happened inside herself. She says that she was

> Baptized, before, without the choice,
> But this time, consciously, Of Grace . . .

To be baptized "of grace" is to leave childish things behind— "my Dolls, / My childhood, and the string of spools / I've finished threading " (compare 1 Corinthians 13:11)—and hurry to the culmination of one's personal history. The partial life, the partial light, of "childhood" is replaced by the full illumination of the soul that has been called by God—as the full moon grows from a lesser phase:

> Called to my Full —The Crescent dropped —
> Existence's whole Arc, filled up,
> With one small Diadem . . .

Isaiah prophesied, "Thou shalt also be a crown of glory in the hand of the Lord, and a royal diadem in the hand of thy God" (Isaiah 62:3). Revelation picks up the Old Testament theme and associates it with images of the saints in heaven, who sit with Christ on his Father's throne, wearing "crowns of gold" (Revelation 3:21, 4:4). In the letters to the churches, Jesus urges the saints on earth to resist the forces of the outside world, just as Dickinson is resisting: "[H]old that fast which thou hast, that no man take thy crown" (Revelation 3:11).

The poet does not repeat the new name that she received at her new birth. That special word remains as mysterious as it does in Revelation. But she flaunts its promise of glory, picturing herself as a newborn child who is also an imperious monarch,

> With Will to choose,
> Or to reject,
> And I choose, just a Crown —

The off-hand manner ("*just* a Crown") shows that the "crown" is a symbol of something more glorious, her relationship with God—the paradoxical relationship that leaves her, as she says, "Crowned" yet "Crowing" like a baby on her "Father's breast." If she is a "Queen," she is "a half unconscious Queen": ironically, growing up means returning to childhood. Although this is the familiar Christian idea of the believer as a child of God and of the journey forward as a journey back, a repetition of the past, it is something that the soul can only "half" understand. Yet one knows that a crown is a glorious thing. You can ask a lot of questions about the nature of glory, but you can never mistake its presence.

The Idea of Progress

Contemporary Christians are sometimes much less comfortable with the idea of glory than Dickinson was. They suspect that glory is something brazen instead of bold, and that they would be childish instead of childlike if they indulged a taste for it. But American churches have never been able to resist the glory part of the New Testament—for two reasons.

First, one of the most powerful currents in American thought is the idea that America is the land of progress, spiritual as well as material, and that all progress is providential and will come to a triumphant end. The puritan immigrants to New England were certain that God, not the vagaries of seventeenth-century politics and commerce, had led them to their new home in the American wilderness. They were not mere explorers; they were pilgrims. The Great Seal of the United States represents the eye of God shining in the desert, the wilderness of this world; written above it is *Annuit Coeptis*, "He Has Favored Our Undertakings"; written below it is *Novus Ordo Seclorum*, "A New Order of the Ages." For people who see history in this way, the book of Revelation, which describes the progress of God's people toward the final fulfillment of his plan, is a natural source of thoughts and images, whose end is glory.

Second, the great revival movements that have marked the country's history have accustomed Americans to view the soul as a scene of violent divisions and glorious transformations. Revelation's stories and pictures provide decisive means of visualizing this kind of drama and the happy results expected from it. And if individual souls can emerge from the violence of spiritual warfare and find themselves in the city of God, so, perhaps, can a nation of individual souls. The religious revivals of the past two centuries have often featured apocalyptic forecasts of the end-time of history, inspired by the book of Revelation. Any tumultuous political event can easily awaken a feeling among Americans that God is about to intervene in a climactic way and turn the nation's journey upward, toward the Throne. Campaigning for president in 1912, Theodore Roosevelt proclaimed, "We stand at Armageddon, and we battle for the Lord" (compare Revelation 16:16).[2] Some people laughed; many people applauded; but everybody understood what he meant.

The pervasive influence of the book of Revelation, the kind of influence that is so common that few Americans pause to notice it, is exemplified by Katharine Lee Bates's universally popular hymn "America the Beautiful" (composed 1893–1913).[3] The song was inspired by a vision of the American heartland, seen from Pike's Peak, a 14,000-foot mountain; but the vision as expressed in the lyrics and approved by popular acceptance is more about history than geography. The history begins with the "stern, impassioned stress" of puritan feet, continues through the "liberating strife" of the Civil War, and concludes with a prophecy of earthly cities built like the New Jerusalem, their form revealed in

> patriot dream
> That sees, beyond the years,
> Thine alabaster cities gleam
> Undimmed by human tears!

Every stanza contains an invocation to providence, asking that history be brought to its perfect climax:

> Till all success be nobleness,
> And ev'ry gain divine.

This is apocalypse in a relatively mild form. It has several basic literary features of New Testament apocalypse (providential history, prophecy, transformation, even the emphasis on the inner qualities of soul that make external events meaningful), but the emotional demands are much less urgent. At the other end of the spectrum is America's other great popular hymn, Julia Ward Howe's "Battle Hymn of the Republic" (1862). The verses—sung to a tune first used in revival meetings, then fitted to verses in praise of John Brown, the mar-

tyred abolitionist—were written in circumstances that recall the
providential inspiration of John the Revelator. Howe was interested by the suggestion that she write a replacement for "John
Brown's Body"; but then, she says, "a word was given me to
say," as by the power of God:

> I went to bed that night as usual, and slept, according to my wont,
> quite soundly. I awoke in the gray of the morning twilight; and as
> I lay waiting for the dawn, the long lines of the desired poem
> began to twine themselves in my mind. Having thought out all the
> stanzas, I said to myself, "I must get up and write these verses
> down, lest I fall asleep again and forget them." So, with a sudden
> effort, I sprang out of bed, and found in the dimness an old stump
> of a pen which I remembered to have used the day before. I
> scrawled the verses almost without looking at the paper.[4]

Like the vision of the Revelator, Howe's inspiration was both
miraculously spontaneous and miraculously well organized.
Like Revelation, the product was a prophecy, a review of history, and a repetition of its own historical and literary precedents. Like Revelation, the song retells the story of Christ's birth:
"In the beauty of the lilies Christ was born across the sea." Like
Revelation, it adapts the gospel message to contemporary circumstances: "I have read a fiery gospel writ in burnished rows
of steel." And like Revelation, it foretells the future: "Let the
Hero, born of woman, crush the serpent with his heel." The
hero born of woman, the crushing of the serpent, the grapes of
wrath, the terrible swift sword, the trumpet call, the judgment
seat—all are repetitions of the biblical Apocalypse (Revelation
8:2, 12:1–10, 14:18–20, 19:15, 20:4; see also Genesis 3:14–15).
They put nineteenth-century political events in an end-time
frame of reference, making them seem part of the final things.

But to put it in that way omits something important, something that Howe meant not to omit. She was well aware that
prophecy is not just supposed to predict the future; it is also
supposed to uncover the significance of the present. This purpose is apparent throughout her poem. If you don't understand
that the Civil War is a climactic fight for Christian liberty, the
song will show you that it is. It may even inspire you to join the
fight. The most poignant verse is the one that speaks of modern
individuals' transformation and unification with "the Hero, born
of woman":

In the beauty of the lilies Christ was born across the sea,
With a glory in his bosom that transfigures you and me . . .

Howe recognizes that the story of Christ can seem very remote.
It is something that happened "across the sea." Yet for her it is
still the everlasting gospel, and she wants it to be seen as
perennially fresh, as fresh as "the beauty of the lilies." She
wants her retelling of the story to convert its hearers, return
them to Christlike innocence, "transfigure" them as Christ was
transfigured before his disciples, and make them do what he
once did: "As he died to make men holy, let us die to make
men free."

Howe's expert joining of theological terms ("transfigures"[5])
with the terms of everyday life ("you and me") recalls the book
of Revelation, which forges the same unity between the abstruse
and the homely. Apocalypse, these works suggest, isn't over
there or back then or far away in the future. Apocalypse is here
and now. It happens when any Christian uncovers the real
meaning of events, is transformed or "transfigured" by the discovery, and recovers in his or her own experience the glory of
the Master: "Mine eyes have seen the glory of the coming of the
Lord . . ."

The Irresistible Temptation

Apocalyptic glory has traditionally constituted a temptation even
to anti-Christian writers. *Go Tell It on the Mountain* (1953) is
James Baldwin's classic account of a boy at odds with the
African American church. It is a chronicle of unanswered
prayers, moral hypocrisy, and fruitless religious inspiration. Yet,
as ordinarily happens with anti-Christian literature, the story is
shaped by the New Testament DNA—in this case especially by
the New Testament emphasis on conversion and transformation,
the providential journey, and the moment of revelation in which
time encounters eternity and the individual soul encounters the
glory of God.

The church members in Baldwin's novel have embarked on
journeys toward the place where, they believe, God will "wipe
all tears from [their] eyes."[6] The protagonist views them skepti-
cally, often scornfully. Yet there is a reason why his name is
"John": in the climax of the book, he himself is led to an apoc-

alyptic vision. Suddenly, the skeptic is visited by the Spirit, and the last scene of Revelation, quoted at the novel's beginning, is finally re-enacted: "The Spirit and the bride say, Come" (Revelation 22:17). Writhing on the dusty floor of a tiny Pentecostal church, he sees "the Lord." All is reversed. He looks at the apparently wretched and insignificant members of the congregation and sees them transformed, as the first-century Christians were transformed by the vision of John, into living symbols of the Church Triumphant. Like the saints in Revelation, they have followed Christ as his disciples, repeating his experience even to the shedding of "blood" (Revelation 6:10); like them, they are now singing and rejoicing; like them, they are a host that "overcometh . . . even as [he] also overcame" (Revelation 3:21) and arrived at his "homeland," as the *Dream of the Rood* calls it—the city of God:

> [T]hey moved on the bloody road forever, with no continuing city, but seeking one to come: a city out of time, not made with hands, but eternal in the heavens. No power could hold this army back, no water disperse them, no fire consume them. One day they would compel the earth to heave upward, and surrender the waiting dead.[7]

As in Revelation, the vision incorporates a wealth of images and narratives from earlier works; the brief passage I just quoted refers not just to the "city" imagery of Revelation but also to ideas derived from Hebrews 13:14, 2 Corinthians 5:1, and Revelation 20:13. And as in Christian literature, so in Baldwin's critique of Christianity: the past is not merely repeated (as if all experience were exactly the same); it is repeated in such a way as to provide an individual perspective on the present and the future. Baldwin's protagonist (like Baldwin himself) proves unable to resist the attraction of the Christian story, but he uses the perspective it gives him in his own way, a way that may possibly be misconstrued by others. He tells a friend, "[N]o matter what happens to me, where I go, what folks say about me, no matter what *any*body says, you remember—please remember— I was saved. I was *there*."[8]

The friend sees John's conversion in terms of Revelation images, rejoicing that God has given his disciple a "*new* name" (Revelation 2:17, 3:12). Remembering the New Testament's picture of the Christian life as a journey, he says, "Run on, little brother."[9] We are not told what that name might be; neither are we told where the protagonist's run will take him. Given the autobiographical nature of this novel and John's suggestion that he will be severely criticized by the church folk for the direction he chooses, it seems likely that he has been saved in order to prophesy both for and against his people's religious experience. One thing is clear: his vision of glory will enable him to "run" in a very individual way.

Again, this is no surprise. The book of Revelation is a story of the church, but it is told from an individual point of view: "I John, who also am your brother, and companion in tribulation . . ." (Revelation 1:9). A brother, or "little brother," is someone like you, but he is not precisely *you*. If he is chosen to be a prophet, he will probably turn out to be noticeably different from you. James Baldwin showed himself a very opinionated and quarrelsome companion of his people "in tribulation." But this is well within the scope of apocalyptic writing, especially in individualist America.

"He Saw King Jesus"

A remarkable instance of the personal and the social uses of Revelation is Vachel Lindsay's poem *General William Booth Enters into Heaven* (1913; Texts, pp. 349–350), perhaps the first really popular work of "avant garde" American poetry. Lindsay (1879–1931), born in Springfield, Illinois, was the archetypal poet of the American Midwest. He saw its failings and felt them keenly, but he cherished a utopian view of its future. Although he drifted away from the evangelical Protestantism of his parents, he frequently returned in thought to primitive Christianity as an example of spiritual pursuit. The metaphor of the Christian journey was intimately real to him. He tramped the roads of America like an itinerant preacher, exchanging poems for meals and places to sleep, and disseminating what he called "the gospel of beauty." He sometimes slept in Salvation Army shelters.

At that time, the Salvation Army was exactly what its name implies—a militantly revivalist organization. Its founder, General William Booth, sought the conversion of people on whom normal churches had given up: the addicted, the criminal, the profoundly poor. The sight of his converts was as astonishing to the churches as the sight of the early Christians had been to established religious groups in the first century. When the Salvationists showed up in a city center, singing and shouting, many Christian communities blanched with embarrassment and tried to usher Booth's army out of town. It didn't work. The Salvationists kept coming. Lindsay greatly admired the Army's union of warm social concern and stubborn individualism. When General Booth died in 1912, Lindsay celebrated his life with a dramatic account of his arrival in glory, *General William Booth Enters into Heaven.*[10]

Any literary work that tries to show what goes on in heaven is probably an apocalypse. Lindsay's poem resembles the New Testament Apocalypse in more specific ways as well. One of them is its torrent of pictures drawn directly from Revelation: saints and trumpets and spotless raiment, God's world as "new," Jesus as "King," "the blood of the Lamb" as the means to glory— all familiar apocalyptic images. Of course, any set of pictures tends to lose its impact, once it has become familiar. Lindsay solves the problem by returning to the process that created the pictures in the first place. Revelation transforms earthly sights into heavenly spectacles: clothing into robes, dirty pavement into streets of gold, the people in the local church into the saints in glory. Lindsay's poem does the same thing, but to make the apocalyptic imagery fresh again, it includes pictures drawn from modern American life (Booth was British, but you would never learn that from the poem). Heaven is not a palace but a "courthouse square," the kind of place you see in any Midwestern town; the heavenly music is provided by drums and banjos, as well as an "angel choir"; and the biblical "King of Kings" (Revelation 17:14) becomes "King Jesus," which is the kind of title you see in newspaper headlines ("King Edward Honors Ten in Ritual of Court").

Then there is the raffish horde of converts that accompanies Booth to heaven. Lindsay's realistic way of representing these people may come as a shock to Christians who attend beautiful churches filled with well-dressed people; if so, he intends the effect. The poem offers his version of the letters to the churches in Revelation, letters that reveal the spiritual poverty of self-satisfied Christians. The converts Booth takes with him to the other world are lepers, drunks, drug addicts, street prostitutes ("drabs from the alleyways"); in general, "vermin-eaten saints with

mouldy breath, / Unwashed legions with the ways of Death."
But they, not normal churchgoers, are the Christian story's main
cast of characters, so far as Lindsay is concerned. His realistic
picture of the "saints" keeps his poem honest. Even he admits
that there is something ugly about this version of Christianity.
The "lasses"—the women—of the Salvation Army are "tranced,
fanatical." They don't just "sing"; they "shriek." Well, Revelation
is not a *pretty* book, despite the saints and angels and the
pearly gates of the New Jerusalem. Glory and prettiness are two
different things. Christian literature is a system of unexpected
distinctions, strange convergences, and ironic reversals; as Jesus
said, the last shall be first (Mark 10:31). Accordingly, Booth's
followers make "noise," not music; they "shout Salvation!",
rather than singing carols; and in spite of it all, they join the
saints in glory.

But we should consider another quality of Revelation, the
greatest book of glory: it is generous; it invites the reader to see
what is happening from more than one point of view. It never
denies that there is such a thing as outward beauty; it does
insist that one should look beneath the surface, to see whether
there is inward beauty as well. When everything has been
uncovered and comes to light, everyone will be able to assess
it all. Lindsay shows that happening. The citizens of heaven see
Booth and his people approaching, and they put things in
proper perspective: "The Saints smiled gravely and they said:
'He's come.'" They are serious ("grave"), as saints should be,
but they also smile, as anyone would, at the oddities of the
Salvationists. "He's come": no need to state who "he" is; Booth's
entry is anticipated. Despite his strangeness (or because of it),
he is part of God's plan. We too may smile at his "unwashed
legions," but despite the fact that they are "queer to see," the
speaker of the poem shouts "Hallelujah!", and there is good reason to join him.

One important similarity between Lindsay's poem and
Revelation is that each proceeds in its special way, even while
proclaiming its dependence on literature from the past. Just as
Revelation alludes to Old Testament apocalypse and prophecy,
reviving and reapplying its ideas and methods, so Lindsay's
poem depends both on Revelation and on an earlier work of
American literature in the apocalyptic tradition, "Are You
Washed in the Blood of the Lamb?" (1878), a hymn with words

and music by a fellow Midwesterner, Elisha Hoffman. This is the hymn I mentioned in Chapter 1. It was so popular that Lindsay needed to do no more, in the heading of *General William Booth*, than say that his poem should "be sung to the tune of *The Blood of the Lamb*"; everyone would recognize the allusion. Like the New Testament apocalypse, Hoffman's song presents both a vision of the saints in glory and a challenge to self-examination for would-be saints who are still on earth:

Are you washed in the blood,
In the soul-cleansing blood of the Lamb?
Are your garments spotless? Are they white as snow?
Are you washed in the blood of the Lamb?[11]

Lindsay, who chanted his poem to a rough approximation of Hoffman's music, uses the phrase "Are you washed in the blood of the Lamb?" eight times in the work.

The distinctive thing about Hoffman's song is that it asks that personally targeted question: "Are *you* washed in the blood of the Lamb?" The book of Revelation never does this directly, although it does picture Jesus's followers as washing their robes in the blood of the Lamb, and it raises doubts about whether many in its first-century audience are authentic followers (Revelation 7:14, 12:11; Revelation 2:1–3:22). Hoffman puts the issue more pointedly. He was a revivalist calling for individual repentance in a highly individualistic age and nation. That, of course, is what Lindsay does too, more subtly but more powerfully than Hoffman. Seven times he encloses "Are you washed . . . ?" in quotation marks or parentheses, as if it were nothing but a refrain, nothing but a recurrent reference to Hoffman's song; then suddenly, in the last line of the poem, he drops the parenthetical marks of repetition and asks the question in his own voice, to *you*: "Are you washed in the blood of the Lamb?" That makes it embarrassingly personal, as embarrassingly personal as the ministry of General Booth, or his Master.

The method followed in most of Revelation, like the method followed by Jesus in his parables, is to teach the audience about itself by telling stories about other people. Jesus's conversations, however, often come with directly personal stings in their tails. Accosted by self-righteous questioners who evidently want to know why God permits people to suffer, Jesus gives them some good advice about themselves: "[E]xcept ye repent, ye shall all likewise perish" (Luke 13:1–5). Lindsay's poem is like that. It saves its explicitness about its readers for the climax. When they get there they find, probably to their surprise, that the poem's real subject is them, not Booth or his poor unwashed followers.

This is another example (compare "The Gardener," "The Collar," and the parable of the Prodigal Son) of a conclusion that transforms the rest of a work. When one rereads the poem with the ending in mind, one sees that the final transformation has been prepared by a series of earlier transformations. The most obvious—Booth's conversion of the people who follow him to heaven—happened before the poem started. Lindsay might have left it at that. He might have shown Booth mounting to heaven with his hands folded piously, heading a host of glowing converts. But then no one would *see* the transformation. Instead, Lindsay starts by picturing Booth's army as a disreputable throng of street people, until Jesus intervenes, quietly changing them into "sages and sibyls . . . and athletes clean."

Booth himself is transformed. At the beginning of the poem, he is still exactly who he was on earth. He marches "boldly" into heaven,

>   and he look[s] the chief
> Eagle countenance in sharp relief,
> Beard a-flying, air of high command
> Unabated in that holy land.

This is, perhaps, as close as a resurrected saint can come to sinning. Booth carries on as usual, despite his approach to the presence of God; and there is more than a hint of spiritual pride. It is probably significant, symbolically, that Booth doesn't notice the moment when his followers are transformed, when their "blind eyes [are] opened on a new, sweet world." He remains blind, as literally blind as he was on his deathbed, until Jesus miraculously heals him also.

That is the outward transformation. There is an inward one as well. In preparation for the change of direction, in the last line, from an "outward" concern with others to an "inward" concern with one's own spiritual condition, Lindsay starts changing the perspective at the beginning of the final sequence, making our view of Booth progressively more intimate and personal. First we see him "halted by the curb for prayer." This is an external perspective; we view him from the outside. Next we are told what he sees: "He saw his Master thro' the flag-filled air." The external is becoming internal; we see Booth looking, then we see more clearly through his eyes: "Christ came gently with a robe and crown / For Booth the soldier." Because Booth sees Christ, we know he is no longer blind, in the literal and outward sense of that word. Yet we also know that he is being transformed spiritually. He remains "Booth the soldier," but he is surrendering his leadership to a higher power. Jesus is now the leader and provider. The shouting dies, the crowd is kneeling, the view contracts to Christ alone . . . Now Booth himself falls "a-weeping" at Jesus's feet. The reader has been led, by example, from pride to humility, from the physical "outside" of events to the spiritual "inside," and with these reversals accomplished is ready for the final, personal question: "Are you washed in the blood of the Lamb?"

So the loud, public poem becomes the quiet, private, introspective one, as increasingly introspective as the passage in Revelation that encourages its recipients to look within and see whether they have lost their "first love" for God (Revelation 2:2–4). There is no plainer, quieter language in American poetry than the last three lines of Lindsay's poem—three short sentences, which include only three polysyllables—but it is hard to find language more powerful. It is as simple and stately as a courthouse square.

> He saw King Jesus. They were face to face,
> And he knelt a-weeping in that holy place.
> Are you washed in the blood of the Lamb?

If one listens carefully, one hears an echo not only of Revelation but also of that intimate, introspective passage where Paul, urging his readers to transform themselves and "put away childish things," speaks of the last stage of spiritual progress, the Christian's final encounter with Christ:

For now we see through a glass, darkly; but then face to face: now I know in part; but then shall I know even as also I am known. (1 Corinthians 13:11–12)

Lindsay has shown, with apocalyptic flamboyance and then with apocalyptic calm, what that final vision might be like. That is glory.

14
Scornful Wonder

During the past three hundred years, there has been a vast rebellion against Christianity in the nations of the West. The rebellion, which began in the intellectual and literary classes, has naturally had its effect on English and American literature.[1] The fact that Christianity has survived and often flourished can be explained in many ways, but one part of the explanation is the ability of Christian literature to respond to the assault.

Opposing Forces

Before looking at the responses, we need to look at the attacks, and at their own involvements with literature. We can distinguish two general types of criticism of Christianity, one arising from social and political developments, the other from scientific ideas and assumptions.

Until the foundation of the United States, no national government appears to have existed without some form of official religious establishment. Even in America, individual states maintained established churches as late as 1833. It is clear that this practice resulted in the politicization of Christianity; it is less clear that it resulted in the Christianization of government. In any event, both Protestant and Catholic churches were blamed for the abuses of the governments with which they were connected. Eighteenth-century intellectuals, exponents of the "Enlightenment"—such writers as Voltaire, Gibbon, Paine, and

Jefferson—made the politicized church a major target of satire and invective.

Following the two great revolutions of the eighteenth century, the American and the French, official politicization of the church went into a long decline, a decline from which it has not recovered anywhere in Christendom. But the intellectual attacks did not cease. As a result of a third great revolution, the capitalist revolution of the nineteenth century, society adopted quite a different shape from any previously known. Wealth and social mobility enormously increased; mortality declined; women achieved an independent social status; eventually a sexual revolution challenged accepted interpretations of biblical rules. Perhaps most importantly, the expectation of material progress that began with the astonishing material improvements of the nineteenth century made everything old appear old-fashioned, irrelevant. Few things in Western culture seemed more old-fashioned than the ideas of the Bible. At least many intellectuals thought so, and many ordinary people as well. They were the audience for social and political critiques of Christianity.

The scientific critique came first from the physical, then from the biological sciences, and finally from the aspiring science of biblical criticism. At the beginning of the eighteenth century, physical science basked in the enormous prestige it had acquired from its ability to discover experimentally confirmable laws of nature. Such laws were considered proof of God's existence, for how can law exist without a lawgiver? Some scientifically minded people, indeed, regarded them as the best, or even the only, evidence of God. The evidence of the Bible, which like any history is an account of events that happened only once, was incapable of experimental verification. Why, then, worship the God of the New Testament rather than the God of nature?

On this premise, the Christianity of many eighteenth-century intellectuals turned to deism, which usually consisted of a belief in God as manifested in natural law, not in scripture, tradition, or miraculous interventions in human history. Deism is "natural religion," as opposed to "revealed religion." It took a variety of forms, but it ordinarily assumed a God who is both omnipotent and benevolent, a God who, like the Christian God, desires his creatures to imitate his benevolence. Everything in the Bible that went beyond such fundamental moral teachings was likely to be rejected. The Jesus of the deists was a good man and a teacher of good works, nothing more.

The next stage in the criticism of Christianity was inspired by nineteenth-century biology. On the basis of Darwin's theory of undirected evolution, it was possible to conclude that the existence of God is unnecessary to explain the development of life. The evolutionary hypothesis generally carried with it three related assumptions: all development is gradual, similar things develop in similar ways, and supernatural influences can never be admitted as explanations of natural or historical events.

Such assumptions were soon applied, not just to the natural sciences, but also to the humanities and to the study of Bible texts and religious practices. By the mid-nineteenth century, they had helped to produce a large and very influential school of biblical study directed mainly to understanding, in a "scientific" way, the origin and development of scripture. This study was called by some of its adherents the Higher Criticism. (The Lower Criticism was close analysis of Bible manuscripts, with special concern for the accurate transmission of the text.) Higher Critics tended to view the various parts of the New Testament as gradually evolving reflections of different attitudes prevailing in different Christian communities, with very uncertain relationships to any true story of Jesus or his disciples. To say that the biblical "Mark" wrote the second gospel or that authentic teachings of "John" are embodied in the fourth gospel was regarded by some critics as painfully naive. The idea that one can identify first-hand observations or even significant historical truth in any of the gospels was sometimes dismissed as prescientific. The gospels were often seen as manuals of instruction in what various local churches believed, as the kind of work that is subject to negotiation and gradual revision, not as literature guided by the desire of individual authors for accuracy or literary integrity.

Many anthropologists and historians regarded the points of contact between Christian ideas and those of other religious traditions as obvious evidence that they had evolved from similar sources. Sir James G. Frazer, the most prominent writer on this theme, suggested that religion in general is descended from prehistoric fertility rituals. Vegetation dies in autumn and revives in spring; prehistoric ritual embodied this observation in the concept of a "dying god." Jesus was a "dying god." Christianity,

Frazer implied, must therefore owe the crucial idea of Jesus's death and resurrection to pagan sources.[2]

Such anthropological speculations were just that, speculations; as were many of the Higher Critics' speculations about Bible texts. Their theories were vast and varied. Some were of permanent interest; others encountered strong opposing evidence and had to be discarded. Many of the Higher Critics were convinced, for example, that the gospel of John, with its "advanced" theology, must be a product of lengthy evolution. Unfortunately for that assumption, the manuscript evidence to which I referred in Chapter 4 was discovered, indicating that the gospel was published by the end of the first century, as church tradition had taught. Some Higher Critical theories have disappeared for lack of proof, or plausibility; some (the theories based most closely on objective literary study) have been patiently revised into basic tools of research; still others have vanished, at least for the time being, because new generations of scholars have become interested in other things.

A detailed account of the Higher Criticism is beyond the scope of this book. Its influence, however, is unquestionable. Most contemporary academic study of the Bible descends from it. Purged of its naive scientism, it produced a greater appreciation, among both believers and nonbelievers, of the New Testament's intricacy and wealth of suggestion. Yet as a nonreligious way of thinking about religion and religious documents, it contributed to the division between Christian and secular thinking that characterizes modern intellectual life. Even in the nineteenth century, it produced divisions among Christians themselves, divisions that led to further criticism of Christianity as contentious and self-embittered. That was Samuel Stone's concern when he wrote his hymn, "The Church's One Foundation" (1866),[3] which responds to a battle in the English church in South Africa between traditionalists and followers of the Higher Criticism. The hymn celebrates the church as a single, divinely unified organization, while conceding that the church doesn't always look that way:

Though with a scornful wonder
Men see her sore opprest,
By schisms rent asunder,
By heresies distrest . . .

This is a strikingly candid observation for a hymn to make. Hymns, after all, are intended to express a community's universal and ideal experience. That the observation was made at all is an indication of how serious the problem of modern "schisms" was, even in 1866.

By 1896, when the American novelist Harold Frederic published his antichristian satire *The Damnation of Theron Ware*, the assumptions and speculations of the Higher Criticism no longer needed to be defended in many intellectual circles. To make his point about the backwardness of Christianity, Frederic needed only to have the intelligent people in his novel casually mention, as if it were a proven fact, that Bible characters have been wiped out of existence by "modern research." Frederic's intellectuals consider it perfectly plausible that the ancestry of "this Christ-myth of ours" can be traced to

> the ancient Chaldean Meridug, or Merodach. He was the young god who interceded continually between the angry, omnipotent Ea, his father, and the humble and unhappy Damkina, or Earth, who was his mother. . . . [T]his Merodach or Marmaduke is, so far as we can see now, the original prototype of our "divine intermediary" idea.[4]

I doubt that Marmaduke still figures prominently in any explanations of Christianity, but the retelling of his story does illustrate a tendency that the Higher Critics shared with the Bible itself. Like the Bible writers, they expressed their ideas about religion in historical narratives, with all the concern for origins and genealogies that one sees in such Bible passages as Genesis 1 and Luke 3. Meanwhile, the attempt to expose the "mythological" nature of Christianity encouraged several generations of creative writers, whether scholars or novelists, to mythologize it in their own ways. The standard by which Christianity was either approved or condemned became more literary than theological or "scientific"—a somewhat ironic development, considering the nonchalant literary treatment often given the New Testament itself. The life of Christ was viewed as a charming story, as in Ernest Renan's popular and influential *Life of Jesus* (1863), or as a quarry of symbols for other stories.

Novelists might now be considered more cogent interpreters of Christianity than priests and ministers, who were routinely condemned for their inability to transform historic teachings into stories relevant to modern life. Some authors urged them to leave the old stories alone and find new ones. In Sinclair Lewis's *Elmer Gantry*, the dean of a seminary tells himself that he would have led a better life if he had done something more useful, something more scientific. Just think: he might have become "a great chemist"![5] Other authors advised the clergy to preach only the nicest parts of the Bible. According to the Rev. Gail Hightower, William Faulkner's renegade minister in *Light in August*, the problem with the church is that "the professionals . . . have removed the bells from its steeples," maintaining their authority while omitting the joy and forgiveness of the New Testament at its best.[6] There's more to be said about Faulkner's novel, as I will suggest in the next chapter. But this much is clear: according to Faulkner, clergymen just don't know what a good story is.

Founding Fathers

One of the most interesting places to turn, if one wants to see literary standards at work on judgments of Christianity, is the correspondence of John Adams and Thomas Jefferson, the most distinguished correspondence in American literature. Religion is a very frequent topic. Both men were deists—Adams of an idiosyncratic type—but neither was willing to surrender the name of "Christian." They thought that the title was merited because they accepted Jesus's moral ideas as "the most sublime and benevolent" ever taught. Jefferson, indeed, considered mainstream clergymen insufficiently Christian and referred slightingly to the "soi-disant [self-styled] Christian world."[7]

Their objection to mainstream Christianity, and to its New Testament foundation, was in the broad sense literary. Jesus's teachings, Jefferson argued (with Adams's acquiescence), were not "committed to Writing by himself, but by the most unlettered of Men, by memory, long after they had heard them from him, when much was forgotten, much misunderstood, and presented in very paradoxical Shapes."[8] Compared with Adams and Jefferson, of course, virtually everyone else was "unlettered"; but they assumed that truth was most likely to be conveyed by cultivated literary people. Their rejection of "paradox" ("the Word was with God, and the Word was God" [John 1:1]) was consistent with the Enlightenment's literary emphasis on clarity and scientific precision.

Other literary issues were in play as well. Jefferson constructed his own version of the gospels by taking a Bible and cutting out everything he did not regard as the original, truly Christian material. He thus enacted in his own way the recurrent drama of Christians returning to their origins, determined to discover the primitive religion within the Bible text. Cutting texts apart and putting them together as he saw fit, he also adopted, and carried to a remarkable extreme, the Christian practice of finding distinctions among similar things and unities among dissimilar ones. But how did he distinguish what should be rejected from what should be retained? His idea was that the real Jesus could "easily" be "distinguished" amid the "rubbish" of the gospel writers by "the stamp of [Jesus'] eloquence and fine imagination,"[9] the kind of imagination that emerged in his stories. For Jefferson, as for the early Christians, a good story was of great value—although his idea of such a story was that it must be purely "natural," with no taint of theological paradox.

To Jefferson and Adams, the best stories would be about intelligent persons like themselves. Jesus was obviously such a person, although the gospel writers had often represented him inaccurately. But what of God? Like traditional Christians, Adams and Jefferson conceived of God as a personality. The story of Jesus could be converted into the story of a very good man; but what stories could be told about the God of the deists, a God who remained hidden behind natural phenomena? As Emily Dickinson suggested, he might be difficult to distinguish from the phenomena themselves. Here Adams—who, contrary to popular stereotypes, was an even better writer than Jefferson, more individual, more imaginative, and much more colorful—had something unexpected to say. For him, the deists' lack of appreciation for a really good story was a sign that something had gone philosophically wrong with deism itself.

The key document is his letter to Jefferson of March 2, 1816. "I cannot be serious!" he begins. "I am about to write You, the most frivolous letter, you ever read." That is Adams's ironic way of introducing his serious intellectual business, which is an insider's critique of the Enlightenment, as represented in its major figures, "Voltaire, Dalembert, Buffon[,] Diderot, Rousseau . . ., " people whom he charges with having been "totally destitute" of

"Common Sense." Why? Because, as he sees it, they didn't believe in God. Some of them may have pretended to believe, or presumed that they believed. But they attributed nothing to God that they didn't attribute also to nature; there was no difference between their "God" and simple, storyless "Fate"—mere happenings, without a connecting personal intention. But "Who, and what is this Fate?" If Fate created the natural phenomena of which the Enlightenment made so much, he would have to be nothing less than the all-providing, all-contriving God of the Christian story:

> He must be a sensible Fellow. He must be a Master of Science. He must be Master of spherical Trigonometry and Great Circle sailing. He must calculate Eclipses in his head by Intuition. He must be Master of the Science of Infinitesimal "Le Science des infiniment petits." He must involve and extract all the Roots by Intuition and be familiar with all possible or imaginable Sections of the Cone. He must be a Master of Arts Mechanical and imitative. He must have more Eloquence than Demosthenes, more Wit than Swift or Volltaire, more humour than Butler or Trumbull. And what is more comfortable than all the rest, he must be good natured, for this is upon the whole a good World. There is ten times as much pleasure as pain in it.
>
> Why then should We abhor the Word God, and fall in Love with the Word Fate? We know there exists Energy and Intellect enough to produce such a World as this, which is a sublime and beautiful one, and a very benevolent one, notwithstanding all our snarling, and a happy one, if it is not made otherwise by our own fault.[10]

For Adams, the story-teller, it's personality that counts—the personality of an author ("I cannot be serious!") and the personality of God, the author of nature. It was no impersonal "fate" that was "sensible" enough to create all the things we know to exist, all the things that Adams's jocund imagination uses to show the vivid color and strange variety of this world, from "Le Science des infiniment petits" to "all possible or *imaginable* Sections of the Cone." While rebelling against the paradoxes of Christianity, Adams emphasizes one of Christianity's major sources of paradox, the curious relationship between the mortal and the immortal—in this case, between men like him, gifted with wit and humor and the free will to use them, and the genius of a providential God whom he imagines as the universal Writer, always telling wonderful, entertaining stories.

Assimilations of Christianity

Adams's wit strikes some damaging blows against the deist attitudes that he in general accepted. Basically, however, he assimilates the Christian story to the kind of story he is good at telling. Assimilation of one kind or another has been very common in the literary history of the past 250 years. It has been used to debase the Christian story; it has also been used to transform it into something that authors like better. In the eighteenth century, deists usually presented Jesus as the hero of a moral tale that, they believed, was an improvement on the gospel. Their successors, the romantic poets of the early nineteenth century, did the same, in their own ways.

One of them, Percy Bysshe Shelley (1792–1822), was the first significant author in the English language to profess himself an atheist. Not only did he profess that faith; he was expelled from Oxford University for writing a pamphlet (with his friend Thomas Jefferson Hogg) entitled "The *Necessity* of Atheism." Yet when Shelley wanted to recount the intellectual history of the world, he found that he could not leave Jesus out. As an apostle of individual freedom, Shelley knew that Jesus had an important role in the history of liberty and individualism. Shelley put him into the narrative, but he assimilated him to the liberating figure in Greek mythology, Prometheus: Jesus was a "Promethean conqueror" whose moral ideas illumined the world.[11] Drawing on a good story from the book of Acts, the episode in which Paul addresses the Athenians, Shelley calls Jesus a "power from the unknown God" (Acts 17:23). It's a clever literary move. To Shelley, the "unknown God" remains unknown, because he is nonexistent; but the idea of a mysterious Power is still dramatic and challenging. Mystery and paradox (as in Shelley's idea of the Power from Nowhere) are dismissed on the level of theology but return on the level of psychology. There remains a psychological power in the unknown and "nonexistent."

In later literature, references to Christianity are often meant to ensure the opposite effect, to deprive the Christian story of force and dignity. A.E. Housman (1859–1936) was a very late romantic poet and a man with a much greater animus against Christianity than Shelley had. Known for his evocations of backward, rural areas where a modern intellectual might expect Christianity to retain its strongest hold, Housman nevertheless works to neutralize its influence. In "Bredon Hill," one of the most memorable poems in his lyric sequence *A Shropshire Lad* (1896), he begins by reducing the church to a building with a bell, marking time.[12] A young woman lies with her lover on Bredon Hill, hearing but resisting the "happy noise" of distant bells. She is happier staying as she is:

> The bells would ring to call her
>   In valleys miles away:
> "Come all to church, good people;
>   Good people, come and pray."
> But here my love would stay.

When her resistance finally ceases and she does go to church, it is a sad conversion. She goes ominously "alone," and only "one bell" tolls:

> Groom there was none to see,
> The mourners followed after,
>   And so to church went she.

The church is the place of death, not love; it is the end of the inevitable journey to extinction. Realizing this, and hearing the bells still calling all "good people" to church, the speaker can only say,

> Oh, noisy bells, be dumb;
> I hear you, I will come.

The poem accepts the Christian idea of the journey as the pattern of human life, but reverses its course. With the aid of the church, the journeyer arrives not at glory but at dust and silence. Yet this kind of irony—the discovery that what the "good people" of this world respect is as false and hollow as a noisy bell, and as indifferent to love—is native to Christianity itself (compare 1 Corinthians 13:1).

And Housman cannot resist assimilating the story of Christ. He makes it central to another memorable poem, "The Carpenter's Son."[13] Again, however, he appropriates the form of Christian narrative, while ironically reversing it so as to insist on the hopelessness of a world that is, from his point of view, merely fated and "natural." The poem offers a parodic, naturalized version of Jesus, who is now simply and unmiraculously the son of the village carpenter. Like a seventeenth-century painter putting his own contemporaries into his depictions of New Testament scenes, Housman casts the Carpenter's Son as an ordinary English boy facing execution in the ordinary English way—hanging—for some nameless but presumably ordinary crime against society. This is not a setting into which the supernatural will ever intrude. The Carpenter's Son is going to be hanged, that's all, hanged between two other wretches, and it makes no difference that "the midmost hangs for love." The relationship of "love" to the rest of the story is never specified; all that matters is that the three suffer the same bad "luck." The best that the Carpenter's Son can do is advise his friends to be "shrewder" than he was. "See my neck," he says, "and save your own."

It goes without saying that Housman's world offers no prospect of a resurrection, despite the fact that his poem is largely constituted by the DNA of Christianity. Christian literature takes normal values and reverses them. It shows that the insides of things are more important than their seemingly formidable outsides; it makes individual crises of values the turning points of the human story, yet it sees the events of its characters' lives as repetitions of earlier conversions and transformations exemplified in literature. Housman starts with a world in which Christianity is the outward and accepted face of culture and values. He then devises stories in which individuals are inspired by the supremely Christian value of love and uses these stories to reveal the hollowness of "love," together with the hollowness of the church and the moral and social codes that are built on it. Such stories cannot be understood apart from the New Testament's stories of love triumphant. In both "Bredon Hill" and "The Carpenter's Son," the implicit idea is, "I wish there actually were something to the Christian story." Neither poem makes emotional sense on any other assumption; the effect depends on one's regret that Christian love and goodness and the Christian prospect of immortality are false promises, based on false premises. So, in Housman's version of the gospel, the Carpenter's Son turns against his own religion of "love," in the same way in which (it could be argued) the original Carpenter's Son turned against the religion in which he was schooled. What the modern figure seems to convert from is the heroic love and individualism of the ancient figure, which he replaces with the sadly inadequate individualism of "save your own." Thus is the Christian story transformed and reversed—yet without it, Housman would have no story.

Much the same can be said of D.H. Lawrence (1885–1930) in his anti-Christian assimilation of the Christian story, his short novel *The Man Who Died* (1929). More polemical, and infinitely more optimistic, than Housman's work, it is directly descended from the hopeful myth-making of the Higher Critics and early anthropologists, people who ordinarily conceived of themselves as light-bearers, not bringers of despair. "The man who died" is Jesus, and the irony is not, as in the New Testament, that he was more than man, but that he was simply man, all along. This is a another thoroughgoing naturalization of biblical history. Lawrence represents Jesus as surviving his crucifixion ("They took me down too soon, so I came back to life"),[14] then attempting to discover, without the aid of faith or scripture, what the meaning of life really is. He finds it in natural joys and insights, the pleasures of the body and the wisdom of pagan religions, which Lawrence depicts as pathways to the discovery of man's rightful place in this natural world.

Yet throughout the novel, Lawrence is overwhelmingly indebted to Christian habits of storytelling. Most obviously, he is writing with the same purpose as the New Testament writers— so that the reader "might believe" (John 20:31). Readers will know the truth, and the truth will set them free (John 8:32). Like the New Testament accounts of Christ, Lawrence's story offers many more than one reversal, irony, and paradox: the man who died did not die; his suffering was the road to a more abundant life; spiritual progress comes from making the clamor of the outside world yield to the vitality of the "inner man"; that vitality can be attained by emptying oneself and becoming, in the Bible phrase, "a new creature," free of earlier religious ideas . . . (2 Corinthians 5:17).[15] The journey device of Christian literature reappears in the protagonist's travels from familiar surroundings in Judaea, the shrine of the One and the Supernatural, to the temple of a goddess of Egypt, the shrine of Nature with her many wiles, the ancient enemy of God's people. This is a parody, on the intellectual level, of the journey that the Christ child took to Egypt and of the journey that Paul took to Damascus, though with opposite results: the Christ child did not stay in Egypt, but returned to Israel; and Paul was converted to Christianity, while the Jesus of Lawrence's story is converted away from it (Matthew 2:13-21, Acts 9).

Of course, if Lawrence actually had a completely naturalized view of the world, one would not expect him to make this sharp distinction between "Judaea" and "Egypt," or between the person Jesus was and the person he becomes. There might be an evolution of attitudes, but we would not anticipate a sudden intellectual reversal. Change would happen by accident or "luck," by the process one sees in any number of modern works that depict Christianity as something that one gradually moves away from, perhaps not knowing why, or retains out of simple inertia, obscurely understanding that Christianity is not the point of one's life story. These are neither Christian nor anti-Christian works; they are non-Christian works. But literature that is centrally concerned with Christianity tends to be polarized by ideas of truth and falsehood, derived from Christianity itself. Literary works that stand at the antichristian end of the spectrum tend to mirror the demands for total conversion that are made by their opposites at the Christian end. Certainly Lawrence, whose methods have been likened to those of a puritan preacher, is not just parodying Christian narrative; he is putting its devices seriously to work. Even his attitude toward the function of words is similar to that of the New Testament, in which the word is the means of proclaiming the unique importance of a certain historical experience. True, his Jesus rebels against words of this kind:

> The Word is but the midge that bites at evening. Man is tormented with words like midges, and they follow him right into the tomb. But beyond the tomb they cannot go. Now I have passed the place where words can bite no more and the air is clear, and there is nothing more to say . . . [16]

But that's just the beginning of a torrent of words in which he preaches, with pentecostal spirit, the new gospel of his unique, post-"resurrection" experience of Experience itself.

The Deconversion Experience

This may be a good time, however, to turn to less solemn works. The two richest expositions of anti-Christian themes in American literature are a pair of novels written a generation apart: Frederic's *Theron Ware* (1896) and Lewis's *Elmer Gantry* (1927). Both are works of satire, and a great deal more. They are compendiums of anti-Christian attitudes, and they are examples of Christianity's way of infiltrating its DNA into literary attacks upon itself.

Theron Ware was very popular on its first appearance. Since then, it has been periodically "forgotten,"[17] but it has too much vitality to be forgotten for good. It is a brilliantly perceptive portrait of modern people who are either trying to live a Christian life or trying not to live one. Theron Ware is a Methodist minister in a small town in upper New York state. The town is culturally backward, to put it mildly, and the Methodist church is one of its most backward parts. The trustees of the church object when Theron's wife attends services in a fashionable hat: the flowers in her "bunnit" show that she lacks "a meek an' humble spirit" (p. 28). Thus the trustees exemplify their own meek and humble spirit. From Frederic's perspective, the problem with the village church isn't just its obvious hypocrisy; it's the church's (futile) effort to revive the spirit of primitive Christianity. When the local Christians aren't cracking down on their brothers' and sisters' displays of individuality, they are falling into fits of religious enthusiasm, "groaning and shouting and crying . . . jumping up and down with excitement," "bellow[ing] out their praises" as if they were victims of "occult forces" (pp. 176, 232, 233).

The fact that Ware himself regards this behavior as backward is a telling argument against it, because his own standing as an intellectual is none too high. He is so ignorant that he sits down to write a book about Bible characters, only to realize, to his enormous surprise, that he has nothing to say. Seeking to improve his mind by association with the brightest people in town—a scientist, a Catholic priest, and an educated young woman—Ware discovers that none of them regards the Bible as anything but a collection of myths. Impressed by their display of intellectual authority, by a reading of Renan, and by the attractions of the lady, who is wealthy and beautiful, the minister transforms his religious ideas. He becomes a thorough nonbeliever.

His change, like that of Jesus in *The Man Who Died*, is a parody of Christian conversion. It comes "all at once," this "revelation," this "most important experience of his life" (pp. 134, 242). It is, Frederic sarcastically says, a "new birth": "the former country lout, the untutored slave groping about in the dark after silly superstitions . . . was dead," and "in his place there had been born a Poet . . . a child of light" (p. 210). Like the transformed Christians of Paul's epistles, Theron is "free" and no longer "in bondage" (Galatians 4:25–30). Truly, he walks "by faith, not by sight" (2 Corinthians 5:7). And he is even more a man of faith than Paul was: he has seen no particular evidence for his new, supposedly scientific beliefs, but he holds them, nonetheless. His faith came simply "by hearing" a new gospel, and so he was converted (Romans 10:17).

The question of whether to conceal his new ideas causes him some initial difficulty, which he overcomes with the unexpected aid of Sister Soulsby, a traveling revivalist. It is her job to inspire faith in people who have lost it. But she sees the job in a very modern way, *as* a job, a specialized calling with its own self-justifying techniques. She got started on it when she attended someone else's revival service, "just to kill time," and thought to herself, like a typical American businessman or inventor, "[w]hat tremendous improvements there were possible in the way that amateur revivalist worked up his business" (p. 180). Formerly an actress, she considers evangelism a pursuit like writing plays and performing them. It's a literary and dramatic occupation. Ware, she thinks, is offended at the hypocrisies of the church because he doesn't understand that it's a "theatre" with props and machinery: "The trouble is that you've been let in on the stage, behind the scenes, so to speak, and you're so green—if you'll pardon me—that you want to sit down and cry because the trees *are* cloth, and the moon *is* a lantern. And *I* say, Don't be such a goose!" (p. 173). He resolves to stop being one. He will continue acting as a Christian minister, continue producing Christianity's literary effects on other people, but he will do it in a purely professional manner. He needn't "believe" in what he now regards as his own stage play.

The act is successful, at least at first. People evidently cannot tell the difference between theater and reality. He himself quickly loses the ability to distinguish between his real personality and the splendid image he wants to project. He even thinks

that his spiritual exodus from the church has made him a better
man. Actually, the journey has made him a great deal worse.
Condemning the church's hypocrisy, he has turned into the
worst kind of hypocrite, the one who willingly blinds himself to
what he is. Compared with his hypocrisy, Sister Soulsby's open-
eyed play-acting seems like refreshing innocence. And he is not
content with purely theological hypocrisy. He sneaks and
snivels around town, lying and spying and plotting to seduce his
new lady friend and enjoy her wealth, meanwhile freezing his
wife out of his affections, then blaming her for the plight he has
put her in. "Thou hypocrite," Jesus said, "cast out first the beam
out of thine own eye, and then shalt thou see clearly to pull out
the mote that is in thy brother's eye" (Luke 6:42). Like Jesus's listeners, Ware cannot see his inner self; someone else has to tell
him. The revelation comes from the woman he has been trying
to seduce: "What you took to be improvement was degenera-
tion." His mind is "an unpleasant thing to contemplate" (p. 327).
She is right, and the realization crushes him.

The novel's climactic emphasis on the difference between
insides and outsides puts it on essentially Christian ground. Not
every author has regarded that difference as a moral issue. In
classical literature, it's often a virtue. The hero of the *Odyssey* is
considered a model of wisdom for assuming disguises, using
guile to get his way, and telling lying stories to his closest
friends. In any era of literature, an author can attack misconduct
without worrying much about hypocrisy: characters can be punished for their deeds, whether they hypocritically conceal them
or not. But Christianity emphasizes belief, not simply virtuous
conduct, ritual observance, or other external "works." The story
of Jesus, from his conflicts with other religions leaders in the
gospels to his admonitions directed to erring churches in the
Apocalypse, is very largely the story of his opposition to
hypocrisy among the would-be people of God. In the many
New Testament passages in which hypocrisy is at issue, the dramatic emphasis ordinarily results from the revelation to hypocrites of the truth about themselves.

And that is what happens in *Theron Ware*, the anti-Christian
novel. Frederic proves his artistic integrity by unmasking not just
the hypocrisy of the church but also the hypocrisy of such self-
righteous unbelievers as Ware, whose deconversion (though
intellectually appropriate, from the novel's point of view) is a

comedy, not the heroic drama that he thinks it is. And Frederic is clearly amused by his double transformation of the reader's perspective, which first produces contempt for the Christian believers of Octavius and then produces contempt for its leading unbeliever. So here is Christian literature's familiar method of reversal, together with its familiar shift of perspective, its familiar irony, its familiar focus on conversion and transformation, and its familiar sense of repetition: Ware is the disciple of every religious hypocrite in the Bible. Frederic relishes the similarities between the New Testament and his own story, whenever possible using the New Testament's own phrasing to point them out. And it is evident that neither Theron Ware nor the Methodist church of Octavius, New York, nor anything else in the novel would have any definite significance, in itself or in respect to its literary treatment, apart from its involvement with the New Testament story.

"AM & PM Star"

Lewis's *Elmer Gantry* is simpler in concept but more entertaining than *Theron Ware* (and *Theron Ware* is a very entertaining book). It is the most extensively researched and also the most colorful of the many anti-Christian novels written in modern America. With a wealth of realistic detail, it demonstrates what can happen when the Christian church loses its integrity by conforming to the outside world. The presentation of the *kerygma* has always been adapted to its audience, but you can tell that the process has gone too far when you hear churchmen translating New Testament ideas into poolroom slang. Jesus tells the story of the ninety and nine obedient sheep whom the shepherd leaves to find the one that is lost (Luke 15:3–7). Elmer Gantry, a Protestant evangelist, follows up on the idea by criticizing a fellow preacher for spending too much time with the good sheep, "slop[ping] all over some old dame that's probably saved already, that you, by golly, couldn't unsave with a carload of gin!" (p. 637). The "carload of gin" shows the novel's exuberance; Gantry's choice of that expression shows the bad times on which the church has fallen.

Gantry has a favorite sermon, which like almost everything else that is pious about him is plagiarized, discipleship having transformed itself into parody and theft. His source is a passage from "Orthodoxy" by Robert G. Ingersoll (1884), a nineteenth-century opponent of Christianity, whose essay wanders into the subject of love, "the Morning and the Evening Star" (p. 534). In Gantry's sermon notes, the pilfered idea appears in the short-hand sentiments of the professional preacher:

> *Love:*
> a rainbow
> AM & PM star
> from cradle to tomb
> inspires art etc. music voice of love
> slam atheists etc. who not appreciate love (p. 622)

If the problem with Christianity, according to its critics, is its failure to keep up with the modern world, Gantry is a reassuring figure: he is a truly modern "Christian."

Lewis, a friend of scientific and Higher Critical approaches to religion, has hardly any respect for Christianity's outdated doctrines and "Mithraic phrasing" (p. 526), yet he views the conformity of the Christian clergy to various slack, silly forms of modernity as even more appalling. When Gantry brags about his success as a salesman for Christ ("We had over eleven hundred present on my last Sunday evening in Zenith, and that in summer!"), his audience, an old-fashioned village preacher, replies with something less than enthusiasm. "Mr. Gantry," he asks, "why don't you believe in God?" (pp. 847–48). The target of Lewis's satire is Christianity and its clergy, yet the standard against which he measures them is the primitive preacher to whom "Christianity," as currently practiced, is just a thin disguise for atheism. The country parson is backed, in turn, by the moral and literary standards of the New Testament, all of which Gantry systematically flouts—and there is no question that Lewis is satirizing him for doing so. In attacking the hypocrisy that is one of the New Testament's favorite objects of attack, Lewis has as much difficulty as Frederic in freeing himself from Christian attitudes and Christian stories.

Elmer Gantry contains four prominent stories in which hypocrisy is a major issue: the story of Gantry himself; the story of Bruno Zechlin, his teacher at the Mizpah Theological Seminary; the story of Frank Shallard, a fellow-student at the seminary; and the story of Sharon Falconer, the evangelist who takes him as a lover.

Intellectually, Zechlin is the most interesting figure. A learned man, lost and lonely among evangelical barbarians (as Lewis depicts Zechlin's students and colleagues), he is secretly a disciple of the Higher Criticism in its most radical form. He believes that "the teachings of Jesus were contradictory and borrowed from earlier rabbis," and he has ceased to admire the teachings anyway. When a young disciple asks Zechlin whether he should stay in the church, Zechlin answers, "Maybe you should stay in it . . . to destroy it!" But Zechlin masks his ideas so that he can keep his job at Mizpah (p. 600). He is, then, a hypocrite, in one sense even more of a hypocrite than Gantry, who at least believes in the literal truth of the Christianity he preaches, but fails to practice.

Yet Lewis appears not to notice Zechlin's hypocrisy. He represents him as a kindly, almost cloyingly sweet old gentleman, an inoffensive spokesman for Lewis's own ideas about the New Testament. In fact, Lewis seems uncertain about whether he has made Zechlin sympathetic enough. To make sure, he turns back to the supposedly discredited New Testament stories, looking for the literary effect he needs. He finds it in the story of Christ's betrayal by Judas. Gantry, who knows enough about Christianity to see that Zechlin does not believe in it, betrays him to the dean, who fires him—precisely (strong ironic moment) at Easter. Zechlin dies from the effects of his academic crucifixion. He, like Christ, is a martyr to religious truth, or the truth about religion. For betraying him, Gantry receives from an anonymous source the same reward that Judas got for betraying his own Teacher— thirty silver coins (p. 604; compare Matthew 26:15). The only thing missing is Zechlin's heavenly reward, which is the one part of the Christian story that Lewis is unwilling to repeat.

This formula—Christian story, with anti-Christian moral— appears again in the subplot involving Frank Shallard, a well-meaning young preacher who loses his faith and, after years of Zechlin-like hypocrisy, goes on a lecture tour on behalf of the League for Free Science, speaking on the topic, "Are the Fundamentalists Witch Hunters?" Lewis regards this as both a heroic action and a sign of true conversion. Yet the fact that Shallard is advertised as "the Reverend Frank Shallard" and that he is "delighted to feel an audience before him again" shows that he has never really resigned his membership in the clergy class. His story is nearly identical to that of the evangelists whom Lewis satirizes for their conviction that they have a special contact with sacred truth, a truth to which they have been converted and now wish to convert others; the only difference is that Shallard's truth is anti-Christian.

The book of Revelation warns of an end-time when the elect will be imperiled by the forces of Satan; Shallard warns of an end-time when the elect—atheists and religious liberals, in this case—will be threatened with extinction by Christians: "We might live to see men burned to death for refusing to attend Protestant churches" (pp. 872–73). The credibility of his prophecy is confirmed by the effect it produces: for preaching his sermon Shallard is attacked, beaten, and blinded. To reinforce the connection with the central story of Christianity, Lewis specifies that Shallard is not only martyred but *betrayed* by hypocritical associates.

Many readers have found the Shallard narrative remarkably thin, considering the violent appeal it makes for our sympathy. The problem is that Shallard—whose name irresistibly suggests the word "shallow"—isn't enough of a person to take the principal role in a drama of Christlike martyrdom. His anti-Christian convictions are clearly insufficient to produce the transformation and strengthening of character associated with Christian conversion. Whether he is cast as a Christian hypocrite or as a sincere advocate of a new, "scientific" faith, his role is merely that of a victim. Jesus and Paul were more than victims. They spent much of their time preaching against religious hypocrisy, yet their message was more than a warning to "watch out, or the religionists will get you." Telling Shallard's story as a repetition of the New Testament emphasizes the inadequacy of the imitation—and, again, the fact that Lewis cannot manage to attack Christianity without adopting its story forms.

Opposing Selves

Among those forms is one that is especially useful in bringing out the psychological intensity of flawed characters. This is the type of story associated with the doctrine of the two selves and typified by the gospel saying, "Lord, I believe; help thou mine unbelief" (Mark 9:24). Lewis's ostensible heroes, Zechlin and Shallard, simply conclude that there's nothing much to be said in favor of Christianity after all; so they give it up. But there is a more compelling character—probably the one compelling *character*—in *Elmer Gantry*. She is Sharon Falconer, an object of Lewis's satire whose story is nevertheless enlivened and dignified by the doctrine of the two selves.

Sharon is an evangelist of highly questionable moral character. In itself, this may not be particularly interesting, from a literary point of view. But her significance is greater than that. She brings to mind an intensely ambivalent comment once made about the American evangelist Aimee Semple McPherson, a flamboyant and controversial figure and a partial model for Sister Sharon. Well, someone said, "If God continues to bless His word and save souls under those conditions, it is very *wonderful*." [18] Whatever Sharon's sins, her ministry has an uncanny power, a power that seems to restore the pentecostal tradition, to replicate the charismatic "miracles" of "the great revivals of 1800" (pp. 679–680). Lewis is certain that the power does not come from God, but he does recognize the existence of "power, power, wonder-working power" in her form of evangelical Christianity.[19] Every reader of *Elmer Gantry* feels a falling-off in the novel's own power when she leaves the story.

Technically, Sharon is a hypocrite, a person who is different on the inside from the way she makes herself appear on the outside; but her literary power is generated by another kind of division, a dramatic conflict within the self, to which the New Testament provides the key. She is not a cynical unbeliever; she is as convinced as Paul was that salvation comes by grace instead of works. Indeed, she carries this belief in grace to its "antinomian" extreme, contending that people to whom grace is given can never sin:

> "I can't sin! I am above sin! I am really and truly sanctified! Whatever I may choose to do, though it might be sin in one unsanctified, with me God will turn it to his glory. I can kiss you like this—" Quickly she touched his cheek, "yes, or passionately, terribly passionately, and it would only symbolize my complete union with Jesus! I have told you a mystery." (p. 654)[20]

She is quoting Paul ("Behold, I shew you a mystery" [1 Corinthians 15:51]) and invoking the paradox of the soul's union with Christ, the union that lies at the heart of Christian faith and discipleship. Simultaneously, she is invoking the doctrine of the two selves. "Some day," she tells Gantry,

> "I might fall in love with you. A tiny bit. If you don't rush me too much. But only physically. No one," proudly, "can touch my soul!" (p. 654)

Thus she repeats the Pauline distinction between flesh and spirit.

But the reference to pride is a warning: if this is Pauline theology, it is running off the rails. It is worship of the self rather than worship of God, and Paul was opposed to it, just as Lewis is. Sharon also senses that something is wrong with her. Trying to live up to her own self-conception, she changes everything perceptible about herself, even her name (compare Revelation 2:17). This is another, more interesting imitation of Christian conversion: "If any man be in Christ, he is a new creature: old things are passed away; behold, all things are become new" (2 Corinthians 5:17). Through the lens of Pauline theology, one sees the specific form that Sharon's self-deception takes: she is retelling the story of Christ and the disciples whom he transforms into "new creatures," but she is casting herself in both roles. One also sees the force of faith that even a heretic can summon, as Sharon strives with enormous intensity to make her conversion real, to *be* entirely that "new" person whom she aspires to be:

> "And yet I'm not a liar! I'm not! I *am* Sharon Falconer now! I've made her . . ." (p. 664)

Foolishly, Sharon tries to resolve the paradox of the soul's union with God by, in effect, becoming God, creating her own life: "I've *made* her." Yet even after the reader understands that this is what she's doing, her story continues to radiate the power of a belief that is always warring against and conquering its unbelief. She struggles to the end. Her last episode is her death by fire in the tabernacle she has built to celebrate her ministry. Instead of fleeing the flames that are enveloping the building, she grasps a cross and strides forward, expecting a miracle. When her body is discovered, her hand is still gripping the cross (pp. 705–06).

The Real Story

If the strength of *Elmer Gantry* is Sharon Falconer, the strength of Sharon Falconer is her strange re-enactment of the story of triumphant faith. Gantry himself is a weak character, little more than Lewis's means of assembling the novel's vast catalogue of ecclesiastical sins by putting them all into one person's life. His story is essentially that of Jesus, sickeningly reversed, the story of a man who keeps appearing in the situations in which Jesus appeared but who keeps doing exactly the opposite of what Jesus would do. The parody is supported by a wealth of Christian symbolism. There is, for instance, the Eastertide betrayal of Zechlin. Almost simultaneously, there is another scene of betrayal, in which Elmer is threatened with having to marry a girl he's been "fooling with," and he responds by arranging for someone else to seduce her and take her off his hands—a telling reversal of the incident of Jesus and the woman taken in adultery (pp. 613, 618–19; John 8:1–11). This particular betrayal occurs on Good Friday. Lewis's method is clear, as is his dependence on the New Testament for his ironies and reversals.

What psychological interest adheres to Gantry's story comes mainly from the possibility that at some time he may actually experience conversion. And he does, in a way, countless times; countless times he decides that he has taken a wrong course and promises to change it. This is Lewis's joke on the Christian conversion experience itself: perhaps if it were more of an experience it could be guaranteed to last a while longer. Of course, the New Testament recognizes that conversion isn't the final part of the Christian experience; there may also be such a thing as revival. How is it, Jesus demands of the churches in Revelation, that "thou hast left thy first love[?] Remember therefore from whence thou art fallen, and repent, and do the first works" (2:4–5). But Lewis is not laughing at the concept of conversion, only at the concept of conversion to Christianity. He sees conversion, the sudden change of values that is characteristic of Christian narrative, as Gantry's only chance of redemption—supposing that he can manage to be converted away from Christ.

One of the book's many conversion episodes finds Gantry "kneeling" before a beautiful view of nature and finding that

> his soul was free of all the wickedness which had daubed it—
> oratorical ambitions, emotional orgasm, dead sayings of dull seers,

dogmas, and piety. The golden winding river drew him, the sky uplifted him, and with outflung arms he prayed for deliverance from prayer. . . .

"Oh, I'm not going on with this evangelistic bunk. . . . No, by God, I'll be honest!" (pp. 660–61)

Then comes the relapse. "How could he keep away from evangelistic melodrama if he was to have Sharon? . . . *Besides!* There is a lot to all this religious stuff. We do do good" (p. 661).

So he returns to "Christianity." Both his "deconversion" and his "reconversion" bear out New Testament ideas: change must come with decisive reversal, or it will not come at all; the human mind is divided against itself, incompetent to produce its own transformation; if it is not in the same story that God is in, it cannot ultimately have a story. "O wretched man that I am!" Paul exclaimed. "Who shall deliver me from the body of this death?" (Romans 7:24). According to him, only God can do that; only God can create a "new" self. Since that never happens to Gantry, one is not surprised that his conversions never amount to anything. In delivering his account of the novel's protagonist, Lewis appears to agree with Paul about the radical nature of conversion. But he cannot, on his principles, rely on anything that looks like divine intervention as a motive for Gantry's actions, despite the fact that he also cannot think of any other way of producing fundamental change in him. So Gantry remains Gantry until the end, and one of the liveliest novels in the language deteriorates into a slowly unrolling portrait of a damned soul that does not even realize it may be damned. The real story stopped when the Christianity ran out.

15
Keeping Watch

Few Christian writers would be consoled by the observation that a great deal of anti-Christian literature bears the DNA of Christianity itself. Whether arguments against Christianity use New Testament concepts and methods or not, they have still needed to be answered. During the past three hundred years, many counterarguments have been made. Some have been technical and scholarly: learned challenges to the Higher Criticism, to the assumption that religion is irrelevant to modern life, to the theory of unguided evolution or its application to intellectual and religious history. Some responses have appealed only to sophisticated intellectual circles; others have been directed at the broadest popular audience. Some have been expressions of evangelical, others of modern liberal thought. Some have been monuments of close analysis and inspiring argument; others have simply been affirmations of faiths that were never shaken to begin with. And some have been triumphs of imaginative literature. There is space in this book to discuss only a few of the many responses that have made provocative use of New Testament ideas and methods.

The authorship of these responses is itself a provocative issue. Many of them are, predictably, defenses of Christianity by Christian authors. The faith has been defended by such talented Christian writers as Dorothy Sayers, Evelyn Waugh, Flannery O'Connor, J.R.R. Tolkien, G.K. Chesterton, and C.S. Lewis—men and women of high intellectual standing who demonstrated that the New Testament can speak fluently and forcefully to the modern condition. But other able defenses of Christianity have come from writers whose personal beliefs were by no means firmly Christian. The Victorian hymn that mentions the "scornful wonder" of the enemies of Christianity also mentions the "saints" who keep "watch" over the church to ensure its safety (Chapter 1, Figure 3). Yet the literary attraction of Christian ideas is demonstrated by the fact that even people who are far from "saints" (Kipling and Dickinson come to mind) have made distinguished use of them. The effect of those ideas is all the greater when they appear in works that freely admit the presence of contrary ideas and attitudes, and come to grips with them. If anything can demonstrate the endurance of Christianity and the continuity of Christian literature, it is the presence of New Testament ideas and methods in books by firmly "secular" authors.

Attack or Defense?

Thornton Wilder, an avant-garde author who managed also to be extremely popular, wrote two such works, each a critique of Christianity so carefully constructed as to make one doubt whether it is an attack or a defense. His novel *Heaven's My Destination* (1935) opens with a painfully naive young man leaving Bible verses on the writing desk in a hotel lobby, on the unlikely chance that passing businessmen will read them and start hungering for the word of God. George Brush travels America's heartland as the representative of a textbook publisher, but his real business is evangelism. His ministry is as simple and sincere as that of any first-century disciple of Christ. It is also ridiculous. Or is it?

George is a test of one's reaction to New Testament attitudes. An extreme individualist, he continually withdraws into himself to think and pray. His values are the reverse of those held by almost everyone he meets, "Christians" though many of them claim to be. He does good for the sake of doing good, not because it "profiteth" him anything or pleases other people (1 Corinthians 13:3); in fact, the objects of his charity are usually quite annoyed with him. He is frequently hauled into court for re-enacting New Testament stories of charity and justice, at one point ridding a community of a crooked money-changer by causing a run on his bank.[1] The faith he practices resulted from a sudden and very individual conversion. When a judge asks

him, "Your ideas aren't the same as most people's, are they?",
George assures him that he didn't "go through a difficult religious conversion in order to have the same ideas as other people have" (pp. 224–25). It's hard to argue with logic like that, as
tangential as it may seem. Gradually one realizes, along with
most of the people whom George encounters, that one would
hate to part with him, no matter how annoying he is. And no
one would want him to give up on his journey to heaven and
become just another business traveler in the Kansas City region.
That would be the end of a good story.

But the story almost ends that way. "One day," Wilder writes,
George "arose to discover, quite simply, that he had lost his
faith. It was as though in some painless way he had lost his arms
and legs" (p. 294). So much for Christianity, one thinks; Wilder
regards the whole thing as merely an accident of psychology.
Yet the loss of one's arms and legs would be a real loss; it would
be difficult for anyone not to want George to get his faith back.
And he does, in as inexplicable and miraculous a way as he lost
it. He is in the hospital, not caring whether he lives or dies,
rejecting even the ministrations of a functionary from the First
Methodist Church, when a package comes in the mail. It is a
present from a man whom he never met but who, he knows,
has been praying for him. That man has died, but he remembered George and sent him . . . a silver spoon. The dying man
knew that "it was a sort of foolish thing to give"—like
Christianity, which Paul said was a very foolish thing (1
Corinthians 1:18–31)—but he gave it anyway. Seeing the spoon,
and understanding its symbolism, George receives the ridiculous
gift of faith again. Soon he is healed and released from the hospital, and "continue[s] on his journey" (pp. 302–04). Somehow
(by God's providence?) the course of his life has been reversed
again, and so has the apparent meaning of the book. There is
something to be said for Christianity, after all—in the unity it
brings to divided people, in its transforming power, in its suggestion of a providential order in "accidental" episodes, in the
dignity it can bestow on even the most eccentric individuals,
and not least in the variety of stories it can bestow on the willing author.

A similarly ironic defense of Christianity emerges in
Wilder's earlier novel *The Bridge of San Luis Rey* (1927). It
begins with a seemingly hostile examination of the Christian

belief in providence. A bridge falls, carrying five travelers to their deaths. Why did God permit such a thing to happen? Brother Juniper, a Franciscan friar, sets out to prove that God had good reasons. Perhaps he was punishing the five victims for their wickedness; perhaps he was rewarding them for their goodness, by taking them to himself. Brother Juniper gathers all the evidence he can, on the assumption that the objective features of the victims' behavior will provide the key that explains God's providence. This hopeless effort to turn Christianity into a science gets him in trouble with the Inquisition (the novel's setting is eighteenth-century Peru), and he is executed for heresy—apparently because of his implicit subordination of divine grace to human works, to the quantifiable goodness or badness of the victims' lives.

So both "orthodox" and "heretical" Christianity are made to look ridiculous. The case against Christianity seems closed—until one finds out more about the victims and the people they know. What one discovers is that people are more than their outward works, or the manner of their deaths, or the philosophical observations that can be made about them. The crucial events in life now appear to be the sudden, mysterious opportunities given to people to change, to be converted, to turn from works of the flesh to expressions of faith, hope, and love.

This typically Christian reversal shows itself especially in the life of one of the victims, the Condesa de Montemayor. She is a rich, ugly old woman whose unrequited idolatry of her beautiful daughter drives her alternately to fits of rage and to craven, superstitious prayer. The Condesa is a brilliantly accomplished writer, but she narrows her talent to glittering displays of wit, futilely intended to impress her daughter. One day, however, she notices the example of a servant girl who loves with bravery instead of cowardice. Suddenly the Condesa understands that there is an invisible realm of grace that cannot be commanded by "works" or accomplishments. "Let me begin again," she whispers; and sits down to write to her daughter in a different style:

> It is the famous letter LVI, known to the Encyclopedists as her Second Corinthians because of its immortal paragraph about love: "Of the thousands of persons we meet in a lifetime, my child . . . "[2]

Always a disciple of love, the Condesa has now become a specifically Christian disciple of the love that Paul describes in the thirteenth chapter of 1 Corinthians. The next day, the "accident" of the bridge claims her life—her physical life. But by now, we are more interested in the fulfillment of her spiritual life, her new birth as a Christian, which has already taken place, and in the kind of love she has discovered, a love that forms a real though invisible connection between time and eternity. The ostensible subject of the book, the event that happened at the Bridge of San Luis Rey, no longer seems important in itself. What remains important, according to the novel's final sentence, is that "there is a land of the living and a land of the dead and the bridge is love, the only survival, the only meaning."

A Christian conclusion to an anti-Christian story? Not really. When one reaches the end, one realizes that every segment of the DNA of Christianity has been shaping it all along: ironic reversal and transformation, the idea of the journey (the prodigal's path that doubles back to God), distinctions and unifications (the failed human parent who discovers the perfect heavenly parent), the crucial use of symbol and paradox (the bridge of death that is also the bridge of love), the modern repetition of New Testament conversion and discipleship, the change of perspective on what is important in human life . . . "Of the thousands of persons we meet in a lifetime," some, through a crisis of faith, discover real faith. That is the story of Christians both in the New Testament and in Wilder's novel.

When one reaches the end, one may also realize that the novel as a whole is a repetition of a particular passage in the New Testament. Looking back at the Condesa and a number of other powerful characters, one sees that what Wilder does with their story recalls the Tower of Siloam episode in the gospel of Luke, the incident in which Jesus is questioned about God's providence by people who apparently assume that it must be measured by the rewards it provides for good works. They ask him about the victims of what lawyers call "acts of God," instancing the eighteen people on whom a tower in Siloam collapsed. "[T]hink ye," he replies, "that they were sinners above all men that dwelt in Jerusalem?" No, he says, but the important thing is that "*ye* repent," or "*ye* shall all likewise perish" (Luke 13:1–5). Jesus thus changes the perspective from the external to the internal. He isn't saying that a tower is bound to fall on his listeners if they don't change their way of looking at the world; he is concerned that if they don't change, their souls will perish. Wilder's novel produces the same transformation of perspective. It begins by viewing people and events from the outside, as visible evidence for or against God's providence. It ends by looking at people and their relationship with God from the inside, from the standpoint of faith and the inexplicable events of grace.

Wilder elaborates no theology. In the sad example of Brother Juniper he even discredits attempts to do so. But his novel clearly leans toward the New Testament view of things. The title of the first part of the book is "Perhaps an Accident." The title of the last part is "Perhaps an Intention." That's as far as Wilder will go, but it's a long way, given the starting point. In effect, it's a conversion.

The Christianity of the Unbelievers

Thousands of novels and poems have advocated Christianity by retelling the story of Christ or his disciples, without any serious engagement with opposing ideas. Some recommend themselves simply by adding the romance and intrigue that novel-readers usually expect. Lew Wallace's *Ben-Hur* (1880), with its three film versions (1907, 1926, 1959), is a good example of the type. Its author actually became a convert to Christianity while he was doing the research for this book, but it is very doubtful that the story as he tells it would be capable of converting or intellectually interesting anyone who was not already a Christian.[3] Other retellings of the Christian story have adopted brashly "modern" formats. Bruce Barton's *The Man Nobody Knows*, which was an enormous bestseller in 1925, is the model here. It presents Jesus as the world's greatest specialist in public relations and the marketing of a message, thus solving, to its author's satisfaction, the problem of Christianity's old-fashioned style.

Both literature and Christianity have often been better served by unbelieving writers, including some who have not made the gospel their most obvious theme. A work that subtly but strongly suggests the emotional richness of the Christian story is Ernest Hemingway's *The Old Man and the Sea* (1952). The plot—a poor fisherman does battle with a great fish, catches it, then sees it torn to pieces by sharks—initially seems quite unrelated to the New Testament, except for the fact that Jesus's first disciples were fishermen ("San Pedro was a fisherman," the old man says to himself).[4] But by the end of the book, when Santiago falls on his bed "with his arms out straight and the palms of his [wounded] hands up" (p. 134), one knows that his story is patterned on Christ's. There are outward symbols: the occupation he shares with Peter; his own name, derived from St. James, one of Jesus's other close followers; his lonely cry when the sharks come, which "is just a noise such as a man might make, involuntarily, feeling the nail go through his hands and into the wood"; the presence of his disciple, a young fisherman who mourns for him as Jesus's disciples mourned at his tomb (pp. 118, 138–140). And there is the inward reality, which is that of a man of Christlike courage and magnanimity, of "humility" that paradoxically "carrie[s] no loss of true pride" (p. 14). Santiago's story repeats the emphasis on the individual and individual psychology that is virtually inseparable from Christian stories; it also repeats their paradoxical way of reversing perspectives: the Old Man appears to be dying in the flesh, yet he remains fully alive in the spirit.

Hemingway is undoubtedly saying that Christlike qualities can display themselves in any human circumstances. It is evident, however, that the story of Christ gains less from the story of Santiago than the story of Santiago gains from Christ. Santiago, a sympathetic and beautifully realized character, gives Christian qualities a freshness and immediacy that they lack in many direct retellings of the gospel. Yet without the story of Christ rising up behind him, his story would lose much of its significance. It would not be symbolic; it would not be a parable of humanity's relationship to a realm transcending the material and temporal; it would simply be the story of a man courageously battling a big fish.

William Faulkner claimed that he preferred the Old Testament to the New, because "the New Testament is full of ideas and I don't know much about ideas. The Old Testament is full of people."[5] Still, he seems to have had enormous difficulty avoiding New Testament stories, which appear in one form or another throughout his fiction. His ultimate satire, and satirical defense, of Christianity is *Light in August* (1932). The novel tells the story of Joe Christmas, a stranger who wanders into a little Southern town whose residents are so bigoted against outsiders that they regard his surname as un-Christian, because they have never met anyone who had that name. They consider themselves Christians, but they hate and fear the very symbols of Christ. Religion in Jefferson, Mississippi, which Faulkner created in the image of his own town, Oxford, Mississippi, consists largely of Churchianity. It's not the worship of God but the worship of a white, complacent, supposedly stainless community, a community that defines itself not by its imitation of Christ but by its attempt to exclude all strangers and sinners. On a less socially respectable level, religion in this community is a crazed, pseudo-evangelical preaching of damnation, the *kerygma* of a God implacably intent on revenge for every violation of his laws, with no purpose of reconciling those who are divided from him. The two forms of "Christianity" are modern projections of the two sources of enmity to Christ that the gospels identify in "religious" people: the self-righteous conviction that *we* are not sinners, and therefore stand in no need of salvation; and the horrified fascination with sin itself, expressed in the fixation of Jesus's opponents on his supposed disregard for law: "Behold a gluttonous man, and a winebibber, a friend of publicans and sinners" (Luke 7:34).

Joe Christmas arrives in Jefferson at the Christological age (he is around thirty years old, as Jesus was when he began his ministry [Luke 3:23]) and stays for the Christological period of time (three years, the traditional length of that ministry). The people whom Faulkner gathers around him are not conventional church members but people of deeper, more eccentric religious feeling—the kind of individuals whom one pictures being attracted to Jesus. These people have dropped out, are dropping out, or have been thrown out of the visible church, yet they are capable of charity, and concern with truly spiritual matters. Unfortunately, such people cannot avert the violent conclusion of the story, in which Joe is lynched by a mob of "Christians"— thus completing Faulkner's exposé of the conventional religious community.

Summarized in this way, Joe's story seems a fairly straightforward repetition of the story of Christ. But there is a significant complication: Joe may fit Christ's story in certain ways, but he does not fit Christ's character. Clearly, Joe does not deserve to be lynched; but clearly, too, he is almost as great a sinner as anyone else in the story, and as full of confusions about his identity. He rejects the Christianity he sees—and who can blame him?—yet he cannot shake his affiliation with it, or with the complicated question of what his role in the Christian story really is. Nothing would be easier than for Faulkner to answer that question, specifying that Joe is either victim or criminal, believer or unbeliever, "Christ" figure or "antichrist." He refuses to do so. He allows Joe to remain a symbol of the difficulty of interpreting the New Testament story and of finding one's own role in it.

The more significant thing, perhaps, is that the other characters do manage to find their roles, for better or worse. The conventional Christians respond as the conventionally religious people in the gospels responded, with indifference or hatred; while the outsiders, the "primitive" Christians, do their best to respond with love. In the end, *Light in August* is a parable, not of Christ, but of the true church.[6] If it seems that in this novel Christianity sits in judgment of Christianity, that is something that has been going on since Paul sat down to write the Corinthians about their need for love. The novel leaves no doubt about the standards by which judgment should be rendered. They are not the standards of a post-Christian age; they are New Testament standards of love and reconciliation.

"Such a Belief Is Quite All Right . . ."

All the writers I have mentioned so far in this chapter, Christians or otherwise, have something to say about Christianity's continuing relevance. Curiously, however, none of them identifies the real threat to Christianity as the theory of evolution and the antireligious conclusions often drawn from it. This is far from a central issue in either the defenses of Christianity or the attacks on it in modern imaginative literature. Theron Ware, Elmer Gantry, and George Brush are satirized for their scientific ignorance, yet their stories turn not on science but on the moral and psychological issues represented in the New Testament. To be sure, the evolution controversy has produced a torrent of books during every decade of the past century and a half. Many essayistic defenses of Christianity are attacks on evolution—Phillip E. Johnson's skeptical analyses of the philosophical underpinnings of the theory are a good current example.[7] Others—*Human Destiny* (1947), by the scientist Pierre Lecomte du Noüy, is a classic instance[8]—have adapted the theory to Christian purposes, using it as a demonstration of the providence that has always guided humanity on its journey. From a literary perspective, however, biology has always remained somewhat beside the point. The New Testament story has nothing to do with it, and even the Old Testament book of Genesis, which devotes two chapters to the creation of the physical universe and the remaining forty-eight to the story of God's dealings with humanity, is hardly *about* biology. Defenses of Christianity by imaginative writers are almost always situated where the Bible situates itself, at places where the story of providence and the story of human choices come together.

To some modern defenders of Christianity, indeed, the problem with exclusively scientific explanations of the universe, the kind of explanations that are often said to be in the process of replacing Christianity, is that they aren't good stories, by any standard. John Betjeman (1906–1984), who became the British poet laureate in 1972, took up this issue in his poem "The Conversion of St. Paul" (1955).[9] Betjeman was known for his satirical verse, and this poem is a satire. Its immediate target is one Margaret Knight, a "scientific humanist" and author of *Morals Without Religion: And Other Essays*. Knight, as Betjeman says, "caused a sensation by her broadcasts on BBC radio attacking Christianity." Betjeman's reply is a retelling of the story of Christianity, which he considers a good story in every way, but especially good in what it has to say about intellectual arrogance.

He begins the story, not in Eden or even in Bethlehem, but at the moment when Christianity's greatest intellectual opponent, Saul of Tarsus, encountered convincing evidence for the truth of an idea that he thought totally absurd (Acts 9:1–20, 26:9–20).[10] Quite unexpectedly, he was "Converted! Turned the wrong way round" by his meeting with the risen Christ:

> [I]n a sudden blinding light
> Paul knew that Christ was God all right . . .

Transformation happens when the intellectual suddenly experiences the untestable, unaccountable, unmistakable intrusion of God into his own story. That event renders history a good deal more exciting than a tale of time and chance collaborating in a universe where nothing supernatural can ever be a threat. Such a universe might, hypothetically, be one in which rational beings, once evolved, could make rational arrangements for order and moral improvement, without reference to "absurd" old stories. *That* story of the universe is easy to tell; it is the story told from the "scientific humanist" perspective. Betjeman finds it a dull story, and an incoherent one, since it begins in the chaos of physical accident and ends in the smugness of man-made law. There is no dramatic conversion in this story, and not much love—only a continued certainty that smart people (like Saul of Tarsus) know all the answers. The Christian story has much more mystery, heart, and relevance to volatile human lives:

> What is conversion? Turning round
> From chaos to a love profound.
> And chaos too is an abyss
> In which the only life is this.
> Such a belief is quite all right
> If you are sure like Mrs. Knight
> And think morality will do
> For all the ills we're subject to.

Neither John Betjeman nor St. Paul thinks that "morality will do."[11] Morality provides no sense that life has a larger story, that we are going somewhere and that someone is there to meet us. Christianity tells that larger story. Despite its mysteries, it is grounded in the history of actual human experience, and it shows the importance of that experience by placing it at the center of a cosmic drama. It leads us to essentially the same conclusions reached by Saul of Tarsus:

> Injustice, cancer's cruel pain,
> All suffering that seems in vain,
> The vastness of the universe,
> Creatures like centipedes and worse—
> All part of an enormous plan
> Which mortal eyes can never scan
> And out of it came God to man.

To know about God, you don't have to know everything about "creatures like centipedes and worse." As John's gospel says, "the only begotten Son . . . he hath declared him"—made him

known (John 1:18). The universe need not be totally comprehensible in human terms, and we need not pretend that it is.
The important thing is that "out of it came God to man."

Of course, one must turn to other sources than Betjeman's
poetry if one wants to evaluate the historical evidence for
Christianity. What Betjeman has done is simply to reverse the
relationship between the Christian story and the humanist story.
Like Paul preaching to the Corinthians, he has offered the "wise"
of his generation the "foolishness" of the cross, while pointing
out that they know even less about the "vastness of the universe" than he does, since they seem not to know that they have
anything more to learn (1 Corinthians 1). Who then is foolish?
And whose story is finally more "humanist"—the planless story
of natural processes, or the story in which God seeks humanity,
and meets us "face to face" (1 Corinthians 13:12)?

Self-Corrective Christianity

Many, perhaps most, modern objections to Christianity do not
pretend to be scientific; they are frankly social and political.
Betjeman touches on them in his ridicule of people who think
that "morality"—being "a good person"—will enable us to live
without God. For many contemporary thinkers, the story of
human life is that of humanity's attempt to win moral and social
progress on its own. Christianity's emphasis on the internal, the
spiritual, and the individual strikes them as a failure to address
the relevant issues. But on this front Christianity has found many
powerful champions. The most effective of them may have been
Martin Luther King, Jr.

No one could assert that King was disengaged. But he came
to the great struggle of his life, the struggle for civil rights in
America, from the pulpit of the Baptist church. In his sermons
and essays we find all the characteristic emphases and devices
of Christian literature, used to demonstrate Christianity's continuing and unique relevance to humanity's problems. One of the
most interesting and representative of his essays is "Transformed
Nonconformist," which King published in 1963 in a book called
Strength to Love, a volume composed mainly of sermons
"rewrit[ten] . . . for the eye."[12] His text is Romans 12:2: "Be not
conformed to this world: but be ye transformed by the renewing of your mind."

The influence of New Testament individualism has never been absent from American society and American churches. King cites with approval the saying of Ralph Waldo Emerson, a Unitarian preacher who became America's most prominent exponent of individualism: "Whoso would be a man must be a non-conformist." He compares Emerson's saying with Paul's. It is easy, he knows, to forget the uncompromising nature of these injunctions against conformity. "This world" includes a great deal that people merely accept as normal and therefore right. It includes a form of Christianity that manages to live comfortably with all kinds of abuses. He is thinking, of course, about the ability of many churches to tolerate racial discrimination, although his critique is broader and deeper than that. He boldly compares the Christian clergy, of which he is one, to Pontius Pilate, who "yielded [his] convictions to the demands of the crowd" and allowed Jesus to be crucified. This is not a failure about one matter alone; it is a general failure of character.

In focusing his critique on the religious leaders of his time, King places himself directly in the prophetic tradition of Christian writing. He is not envisioning or "dreaming" the future, as he did in his most famous speech, but he is fulfilling the other part of the prophetic role, uncovering the truth about current reality. Operating in the tradition of the reformers and revivalists, he urges the return of the church to its primitive experience, "the gospel glow of the early Christians," and preaches conversion to those who think they have no need of it. The pattern of doctrinal and literary repetition is so strong that if there were nothing else in his essay, King would seem to be arguing that the church, reverting to its historic roots, should make itself even less relevant to the modern world.

But his essay is based on paradoxes and ironic reversals. Far from ignoring the world, he accepts its criticism of the church's lack of healthy engagement. And he shows that his demand for conversion is inspired not simply by nostalgia for primitive Christianity but by the challenge for modern Christians to do better in the future. That, as he reminds us, is the second part of Paul's injunction: "be ye transformed by the re*new*ing of your mind." Looking back on Christian history, he suggests that "renewal" has meant progress for the "world" as well as the church. The gospel "put an end to such barbaric evils as infanticide and bloody gladiatorial contests"; now it can put an end to racial discrimination.

Christian literature has always likened life to a journey, and the symbol is very convenient for King's purpose, because a journey can take you somewhere you haven't been before. Very well. Invoking Christianity's traditional distinction between time and eternity and its traditional, though paradoxical, account of their convergence in the Christian life, King suggests that the only remaining question is: "Will we march only to the music of time, or will we, risking criticism and abuse, march to the soul-saving music of eternity?" Against modernists who charge that Christianity fails to engage itself with the world because Christianity is by nature other-worldly, King asserts the church's traditional account of itself as an actor in both eternity and time. This is a paradoxical role, but proper so long as the church's actions are governed by Jesus's equally paradoxical command to love the enemies one finds in the world.

So the direction of King's essay is outward, toward the world, after all. But there is another reversal. King returns to the text from Romans and its emphasis on the renewal of individual minds. Christian love may renew the world, but remember: the starting-place for Paul was the renewing of oneself. By going back to the idea of a self-critical individualism, King is able to stay one step ahead of the secular reformers who attack the church for its failure to notice its own faults. He asks, in effect, What enables *you* to see yourself critically? Can't reformers be blindly self-righteous too? King knew what he was talking about; he spent his life among reformers. What Christianity offers, he observes, is the ability to turn things not just upside down but inside out. It offers the idea of "transforming" oneself, "renewing" one's own mind, so that people who want to reform the world can make sure that they do a good job of it, by first reforming themselves. This is the familiar Christian concept of the new birth, and it offers the basis for King's strategy of non-violence: "Only through an inner spiritual transformation do we gain the strength to fight vigorously the evils of the world in a humble and loving spirit." It should be noted that this paradoxical idea of a humble and loving fight actually worked in the "real world."

The Dead Sea

In a more radical sense, one that goes deeper than politics, Christianity has always been involved with paradoxical propositions, just as it has always been involved with the ideas of progress, conversion, transformation, reversal, the successful journey from one place to another. Those are essential elements of its DNA. From the Christian perspective, there is really *nothing* in this world apart from that providential journey; all else is the wasteland of time. In *The Screwtape Letters* (1942), C.S. Lewis's satiric account of modernist demons who try to deconvert a recent convert to Christianity, a leading demon reminds his colleagues that it is their job to "edge" people "away from the Light and out into the Nothing," the "nothing" consisting of time spent outside the perspective of eternity. The ideal state would be "a dreary flickering of the mind over it knows not what and knows not why, in the gratification of curiosities so feeble that the man is only half aware of them, in drumming of fingers and kicking of heels . . . Murder is no better than cards if cards can do the trick." [13]

In *Four Quartets* (1943), T.S. Eliot distinguishes the timeless moments when the soul encounters God, the moments that bring spiritual growth and change, from the time-bound moments of everyday life. That "life" is as close to "Nothing" as can be imagined, because it is filled with movements that do not matter, do not constitute a progress:

> Only a flicker
> Over the strained time-ridden faces
> Distracted from distraction by distraction
> Filled with fancies and empty of meaning
> Tumid apathy with no concentration
> Men and bits of paper, whirled by the cold wind
> That blows before and after time . . . [14]

One would probably have seen such "time-ridden faces," such "drumming of fingers and kicking of heels" in the streets of ancient Jerusalem and Rome. First-century Christianity undoubtedly appealed to people who wanted something else, who wanted to find their part in a story that was not bound by "time." The anonymity of modern society and the intricacy of its means of wasting time can make the two alternatives seem even starker: spiritual movement, or spiritual death in the coils of organized mediocrity. Are you going somewhere, or are you simply a bit of paper, "whirled by the cold wind"? Both Christian and anti-Christian writers are repelled by the second possibility. That is one reason why anti-Christian works of literature, even such self-critical stories as *The Damnation of Theron Ware*, tend to be structured, like Christian stories, as progressive journeys, travels toward truth through the reversal of normal expectations and everyday assumptions. The difference is that anti-Christian literature is often written out of disappointment with Christianity's inability to fulfill its own vision of progress.

A novel by James Wood, *The Book Against God* (2001; see p. 39, above), presents a curious picture. It is one of the few works of any length that have been written about the Christian controversy that are *not* built on the idea of a journey or progress, toward or away from Christ. The "change" that happens in this book is only a slow sinking into a morass. The protagonist, Thomas Bunting, a graduate student in philosophy, fails to complete his doctorate, fails to hold onto his wife, fails even to rise in the morning. He gives all his energy, such as it is, to notebooks full of objections to God. His father and mother hope that since he is at least thinking about religion, he is "on a path towards God and towards Christ." Actually, he is devolving toward nothingness. "You don't exist," his wife informs him, and that's very close to the truth.[15] His first name is ironically appropriate; he is always asking skeptical questions, to which he never finds an answer. He is like the people in the second epistle to Timothy: "ever learning, and never able to come to the knowledge of the truth. . . . But they shall proceed no further" (2 Timothy 3:7, 9). It is not clear where the author's religious sympathies ultimately lie; it is clear that his character's struggle against God fails to constitute intellectual progress, no matter how one might define it.

The struggle is motivated, however, by what Bunting regards as Christianity's own lack of progress in dealing with the problem of suffering and evil, a problem that twentieth-century political events did much to emphasize. The existence of suffering and evil in a world presumably governed by providence is one of the principal modern arguments against Christianity, and certainly the most effective one, emotionally.

Bunting gets to the root of the problem, in a way. He sees that suffering could not exist in a world from which God prohibited it, and that it could be prohibited only if the freedom of choice that permits humans to inflict it on one another were also prohibited. Why, he demands, didn't God create a choiceless, motionless world, a place like the Dead Sea, where conditions do not allow people to drown? This, he believes, would already be equivalent to the world described at the end of Revelation, where there is "no more death, neither sorrow, nor crying" (Revelation 21:4). In other words, faced with the choice between a story with a happy ending (the Christian story) and a story that never started (the Dead Sea story), Bunting chooses the latter.[16] That's his right. But the literary irony is that he hasn't really escaped from God; he is simply copying one of God's own literary forms, writing his own apocalypse. The philosophical irony is that he is choosing a world in which there would be no choice. If he is intended as a representative of modern secular intellectuals, then the reader is entitled to conclude that they have much less to offer, philosophically, than the Christian church.

"Whole and Sole"?

A larger consideration of skepticism appears in one of the nineteenth century's most complex literary defenses of Christianity, Robert Browning's poem *Bishop Blougram's Apology* (1855). Blougram (pronounced *Bloo*-gram) is Browning's characterization of a Roman Catholic prelate. His "apology" is not his admission of error but an exercise in Christian "apologetics," the argumentative defense of the faith. Browning himself was a liberal Protestant. He appears to have chosen a conservative Roman Catholic bishop as his "apologist" because he wanted the argument for "old-fashioned," "unreformed" Christianity to be stated as forcefully as possible. He casts the apology as a "dramatic monologue," a form of literature of which he was the greatest master. In a dramatic monologue, one character speaks at length, revealing his or her ideas and the motives behind them, so that both the ideas and the character's individuality can be fully developed. The monologue is "dramatic" because it is spoken in a situation, like a situation in a play, that calls for revelation of character and motive. The situation in this case is the Bishop's argument with a modern opponent of Christianity, a skeptical, Bunting-like intellectual.

Gigadibs (for that is the ridiculous name Browning gives this essentially satirical character) is a young journalist, interested in making his mark on the world as a purveyor of new ideas. From what the Bishop says to him, we know that Gigadibs is familiar with the Higher Criticism; with evolutionary anthropology, which assumes that humanity and its ideas developed "naturally," unassisted by revelation or divine intervention; with pragmatism, the idea that thoughts and actions should be judged by whether they "work" in practical ways; and with a kind of individualism whose ideal is thinking and doing whatever one wants, so long as one's self remains "whole and sole." Clearly, Gigadibs' "ideal of life / Is not the bishop's." Indeed, Gigadibs "despise[s]" the Bishop for serving a church that an intelligent person, such as the Bishop admittedly is, must know is spurious—as spurious as Christianity itself.[17]

The Bishop, who likes good food and drink, entertains Gigadibs agreeably on a feast day of the church, Corpus Christi, a day that celebrates the body, and therefore the sacrifice, of Christ, as commemorated in the Holy Eucharist or Lord's Supper. The irony seems plain: the Bishop is far from leading a sacrificial life. Believing that the soul can be "free a little" only after "dinner's done, / And body gets its sop," he has turned commemoration of the Eucharist into one more occasion for "dinner" (18–20). Thus Browning dramatizes a major argument of anti-Christian literature: Christianity, besides being false, hypocritically refuses to live up to its own ideals—just look at how the clergy live. The Bishop even admits, as Elmer Gantry would never do, that he himself does not "believe" (161). What more evidence could the skeptic want?

But modern skeptics may not know all there is to know about the New Testament and its concept of belief. The New Testament does not describe the believing self as "whole and sole." Its watchword is "Lord, I believe; help thou mine unbelief" (Mark 9:24). The Bishop, unlike Gigadibs, appreciates the doctrine of the two selves. When he says, "I do not believe," he adds, "If you'll accept no faith that is not fixed, / Absolute and exclusive" (161–63). He understands the meaning of Mark 9:24 and of the scene that follows, in which Jesus works a miracle on behalf of the man who did not believe "absolutely." With that understanding, the Bishop is free to ask:

> What matter though I doubt at every pore,
> Head-doubts, heart-doubts, doubts at my fingers' ends,
> Doubts in the trivial work of every day,
> Doubts at the very bases of my soul
> In the grand moments when she probes herself—
> If finally I have a life to show . . . ? (610–15)

And his life looks like a miracle. He candidly admits that his job requires "no immoderate exercise / Of intellect and learning," yet by his power as Bishop he can enact all kinds of "miracles," especially financial miracles. He can, as it were, "Bid the street's stones be bread and they are bread" (312–15). So much for the pragmatist's desire for material progress, for things that "work." "Come, come," the Bishop says, "it's best believing, if we may; / You can't but own [admit] that!" (269–270). The Bishop's faith may be imperfect, but he has "a life to show" because of it. It was faith that "reared this tree— / This broad life and whatever fruit it bears!" And faith exists in response to doubt: "The more of doubt, the stronger faith, I say, / If faith o'ercomes doubt" (603–09). In fact, it is only

> when the fight begins within himself,
> A man's worth something. God stoops o'er his head,
> Satan looks up between his feet—both tug—
> He's left, himself, i' the middle: the soul wakes
> And grows. Prolong that battle through his life!
> Never leave growing till the life to come! (693–98)

The picture of God and Satan quarrelling over the human soul may seem hopelessly unmodern, a throwback to medieval art and medieval conceptions. Blougram knows that it does, but it's a useful way of dramatizing a concept of individualism that is even older than the middle ages. It is a concept rooted in the New Testament: the soul has dignity because it is the center of a cosmic conflict, and because, thanks to the grace of God and the dynamic conflict of the two selves, it is capable of "growing" until it arrives at eternity. According to the Bishop, conditions for spiritual growth are actually more favorable in the modern age, when threats to faith are always available to provoke still more faith, than they were in "that dear middle-age these noodles praise." Those were the days when

> a traveller told you his last news,
> He saw the ark [of Noah] a-top of Ararat
> But did not climb there since 'twas getting dusk
> And robber-bands infest the mountain's foot!
> How should you feel, I ask, in such an age,
> How act? As other people felt and did;
> With soul more blank than this decanter's knob . . . . (684–690)

That wasn't individualism; it was blind credulity and conformity. But strictly modern individualism, the kind that Gigadibs cherishes as an ideal, is an attempt to enjoy the self—a self presumably "whole and sole" and unbelieving in anything but itself—without enduring the soul's internal conflicts. That attempt, if it succeeded, would relieve the story's dramatic and often painful intensity, but it wouldn't do much for the dignity of human life, which would become an endless series of minor external conflicts, petty attempts to gratify oneself to the extent that other people will allow:

> Sometimes certain fears
> Restrain you, real checks since you find them so;
> Sometimes you please yourself and nothing checks:
> And thus you graze through life . . . (887–890)

Sheep grazing without a shepherd . . . Is that life better than medieval ignorance?

In any event, the Bishop doubts that anyone, even Gigadibs, can actually live that life. He doubts that the skeptic's self is really "whole." He suspects, indeed, that denial of Christianity would not be so important to Gigadibs if he were not sometimes tempted to believe in Christianity. The lure of the Christian story cannot be completely ignored. Suppose, the Bishop says, I agree to give up my troublesome beliefs?

> And now what are we? unbelievers both,
> Calm and complete, determinately fixed
> To-day, to-morrow and forever, pray?

You'll guarantee me that? Not so, I think!
In no wise! all we've gained is, that belief,
As unbelief before, shakes us by fits,
Confounds us like its predecessor. Where's
The gain? how can we guard our unbelief,
Make it bear fruit to us? (173–181)

Just as something is always turning up to make Christians
doubt their faith, so something will always turn up to make the
"complete" atheist wonder whether there may be truth in this
idea of God:

Just when we are safest, there's a sunset-touch,
A fancy from a flower-bell, someone's death,
A chorus-ending from Euripides,—
And that's enough for fifty hopes and fears
As old and new at once as nature's self,
To rap and knock and enter in our soul,
Take hands and dance there, a fantastic ring,
Round the ancient idol, on his base again,—
The grand Perhaps! . . .
All we have gained then by our unbelief
Is a life of doubt diversified by faith,
For one of faith diversified by doubt . . . (174–190, 209–211)

The Truth at Sunrise

Of course, the modern world has its own faiths—political, philosophic, scientific. Each is a competitor to Christianity. The Bishop
asks, When these faiths are scrutinized with the same degree of
skepticism, how do they bear up? The answer is, Not very well.
Start with politics. Gigadibs, like many journalists, has lofty political ideals, but modern stories of political progress are supported
by evidence that is much less definite than the evidence for the
Christian story. What exactly, the Bishop asks, is this

vague good o' the world, for which you dare
With comfort to yourself blow millions up?
We neither of us see it! we do see
The blown-up millions—spatter of their brains
And writhing of their bowels and so forth . . . (455–59)

Now consider the stories told by the anthropologists, stories that account for moral laws by reference not to God but to the gradual evolution of human behaviors. The Bishop is thinking about the nineteenth-century equivalents of the "sociobiology" movement. Well, he asks, "Does law so analyzed coerce you much?" (812–834). How likely are you to refrain from murdering your neighbor because you've discovered that the laws against murder resulted from the course of evolution? Then consider the anti-stories told by the Higher Critics—how much inspiration can one find in them?[18] They stimulate no one: "What can I gain on the denying side? / Ice makes no conflagration." Besides, he remarks sarcastically, there's always that "hundredth chance" they "may be wrong" (580–88).

Indeed, the Higher Critics' skepticism seems remarkably naive. What would happen if they gave the same querulous treatment to the story of Blougram's life that they give to the stories of Christ, worrying over the fact that the gospels trace his origins both to Nazareth and to Bethlehem?

> You form a notion of me, we'll suppose,
> On hearsay; it's a favorable one:
> "But still" (you add), "there was no such good man,
> Because of contradiction in the facts.
> One proves, for instance, he was born in Rome,
> This Blougram; yet throughout the tales of him
> I see he figures as an Englishman."
> Well, the two things are reconcilable. (636–643)

But on such specious grounds, people reject the possibility of belief, as if they were determined to reject it from the start.

That's the real question, according to Blougram: where you start. Are you resolved to reject the Christian story, no matter what; or are you prepared to argue with yourself about it? In plain terms,

> "What think ye of Christ," friend? when all's done and said,
> Like you this Christianity or not?
> It may be false, but will you wish it true?
> Has it your vote to be so if it can? (626–29)

People whose consciences are troubled by their inability to deal with every single objection to the Christian story should remember what the end of the journey is supposed to be:

> It is the idea, the feeling and the love,
> God means mankind should strive for and show forth
> Whatever be the process to that end,—
> And not historic knowledge, logic sound,
> And metaphysical acumen, sure! (621–25)

Here "we're back on Christian ground," the Bishop says (601). He's right, at least in a literary sense. He is recurring to Paul's theme in the first chapter of 1 Corinthians: Christianity is not a philosophy originally addressed to the "wise," yet their wisdom was finally rendered "foolish" by the story they rejected as absurd. The question is whether the Bishop's modern listener, convinced of his own wisdom, really wants to consider the story that "mortified philosophy is hoarse, / And all in vain, with bidding you despise"—despise as Paul says that Christianity was originally despised, or as Gigadibs originally despised the Bishop (632–33, 13).

By now, even Gigadibs cannot despise him any longer: "Enough; you see, I need not fear contempt" (431). But does Gigadibs still despise Christianity? One advantage of the dramatic *mono*logue is that it keeps the author from having to answer such questions directly. Because the "original" audience of the monologue (Gigadibs, in this poem) isn't allowed to speak, the "next" audience, we the readers, can think for ourselves about how we would regard it. That is the virtue of ending a story without fully specifying its effect; witness the ending of the parable of the Prodigal Son, which never divulges the second son's response to the father's argument. The issue is: How will we respond to the Bishop's "foolishness of preaching" (1 Corinthians 1:21)?

As in the New Testament, it all comes down to the individual. *Bishop Blougram* presents a challenge even to sophisticated Christian readers. Many have taken the poem seriously and have grasped both its ironies and its straightforward relationships to the New Testament. Others have simply missed the point. G.K. Chesterton, himself a skilled apologist for

Christianity, interpreted the Bishop as a "snob" and a
"scoundrel," claiming that his life is a "tottering compromise"
and asserting that the poem is "one of the most grotesque in
the poet's works."[19] Chesterton forgot, as it is easy to forget,
that the Christian story is not about perfect people. Bishop
Blougram follows the path of Paul, who candidly admitted his
weaknesses—and continued preaching.

Browning, however, has complicated matters by adding a
brief, ambiguous finale in which he comments elliptically on the
effect of the Bishop's sermon (1006–1014). The Bishop has pictured the Christian life as a journey—a hike across the wilderness, a progress toward maturity, an emigrant's voyage:
"Outward-bound." As we know, the "voyage" is only a symbol;
but Christian ideas have often been taken out of the religious
context and applied in whatever way people wanted to apply
them. And that is what Gigadibs does. He is inspired by the
Bishop's stories about spiritual adventures to undertake an
adventure in the material world. He buys a lot of "settler's-
implements" and takes ship for the colonies in Australia. And
"[t]here I hope," Browning writes,

> By this time he has tested his first plough,
> And studied his last chapter of St. John.

"His last chapter of St. John"—what does that mean? Perhaps
it expresses the hope that Gigadibs will give up on the Higher
Critics' skeptical examination of the gospel of John (one of their
favorite targets).[20] But perhaps the poet hopes (and this is a better fit with the pattern of the poem) that Gigadibs will finally
read the last chapter of that gospel, the chapter in which the
risen Christ not only talks but acts, and provides for others, serving breakfast to his friends at dawn in Galilee. Didn't the Bishop
say, after dinner on Corpus Christi Day,

> I promised, if you'd watch a dinner out,
> We'd see truth dawn together?—truth that peeps
> Over the glasses' edge when dinner's done,
> And body gets its sop and holds its noise
> And leaves soul free a little. Now's the time:
> Truth's break of day! (17–21)

The Bishop cannot predict his listener's reaction to his words. Christianity presents a universal message of "truth," yet it solicits an individual response. Nevertheless, he has followed Christ's command, "Feed my sheep" (John 21:15–17). He has re-enacted the last chapter of St. John, providing both spiritual and mundane food in honor of the Body of Christ. From his table, both Gigadibs and the reader can take whatever nourishment they are willing to receive. Wait till the last chapter of the story, Browning suggests, and you can see its meaning for yourself. With patience, with due allowance for the conflicts of the human heart and the frequent incapacity of the human intellect, all the arguments will come out. Keep watch.

16
Difficult—and Easy

I began Chapter 1 by quoting Samuel Johnson, who said that the Bible is "the most difficult book in the world." In some sense, of course, we know that it isn't. People all over the world have repeated the experience of Paul's first listeners, who understood what he preached, at least well enough to become Christians. They did not need to be "wise men after the flesh" to receive his message (1 Corinthians 1: 26). Bishop Blougram was right when he said that Christianity requires no "metaphysical acumen" in its followers. Yet even the most complicated intellectual will find in the brief, verbally simple statement that "God was in Christ, reconciling the world unto himself" suggestions of ideas that are impossible to exhaust (2 Corinthians 5:19). The experience of Christianity is both "difficult" and "easy."

One way of analyzing Christian literature is to divide it into two broadly different kinds of texts, corresponding to two perspectives on Christian experience. One type of literature seems easy, natural, ordinary; the other seems formidably intellectual. The first takes up the apparently simple things of life and reveals the complexities beneath them. The second starts with complexities but looks for the simplicities of which they are made. Both ask questions that should be important to every Christian. The first asks, How do I know I am one? The second asks, What is Christianity, after all? The irony is that, like the two specialized styles of Christian writing that flourished in the seventeenth century, both of these large types of literature turn out to be "difficult" and "easy" at the same time.

This last chapter is devoted to distinguished exemplars of the two ironically related types of Christian literature. The "easy" kind is represented by the stories of J.F. Powers, the "difficult" kind by the *Four Quartets* of T.S. Eliot. If one knows both these ways of approaching Christianity, one knows a great deal about modern Christian literature.

The Surface and the Depth

Powers (1917–1999) was the most accomplished literary descendant of Sinclair Lewis. Like Lewis, he specialized in satirical stories filled with realistic American detail and exact reproductions of American patterns of thought and language. Like Lewis, he mercilessly exposed the failings of the church and clergy. A Roman Catholic layman, he wrote almost exclusively about the problems of Roman Catholic priests, and it is clear that the priests in his stories are test cases for the Catholic church as a whole, just as Elmer Gantry is a test case for the Protestant churches. In both instances, the participants usually fail the test.

In one of many drunken conversations, Father Joe, the protagonist of Powers's novel *Wheat that Springeth Green* (1988), tries to defend traditional Catholic ideas to a group of seminarians who are breathing the rebellious spirit of the 1960s. "People living normal lives can't identify with Our Lord," one of them tells him. "Or with *us*—because of the celibacy barrier."

> "That so?" said Joe. "And where you *don't* have that barrier? I mean how well do *we* identify with Our Lord? . . . And when you consider we work at it full time, unlike the laity—well, it makes you wonder, doesn't it?"

"It did me," says a young man who has left the church.[1] The results of the thought-experiment seem certain.

And there is nothing about Powers's stories that restricts his criticism to Roman Catholics. Catholic priests may have greater difficulty adapting to the modern world than Catholic laymen and Protestants in general ("because of the celibacy barrier"), but for Powers, adaptation is the problem, not the solution. If priests are guilty of over-adaptation, what of the others? All the charges that Powers—and before him, Lewis—levels at the clergy apply to both Protestants and Catholics: intellectual emptiness, time-serving, hypocrisy, treating the church as a business, and above all, the failure actually to believe.

But Powers never left the Christian church. He was so devoutly religious that he went to prison during World War II because he could not reconcile Christian beliefs with carnal warfare. In the end, his stories are vindications of those beliefs. His method is a modern application of the ancient Christian idea of the conflict between two selves.

Look at virtually any passage of Powers's stories, and you will think that the battle has already been lost. It's not that any of his protagonists is wholly bad, and knows it. Almost all of them are basically "good" people, and some have flaws that most people would call very slight. The difficulty is that they're mediocre, and they've settled for mediocrity. They are like the people in the church of Laodicea, "neither cold nor hot," or those in the church of Ephesus, who had "left [their] first love" (Revelation 3:15, 2:4). They are like the parishioners whom Father Joe sees coming to church after the sermon has been going on for some time: "'You're good people,' he called to a young couple. 'Good and late.' No response."[2]

Powers's characters sense that something is wrong, but they have trouble looking beneath their surface of religiosity to find out what it is. They either project their guilt onto other people or gaze at their own failings blankly, as if they were facts of nature. Hearing that someone has lost his faith, Joe feels "sorry to hear it, of course," and knows that something more in the way of response is "expected of him," but he doesn't want to react as if he were "rolling in the stuff himself." That counts as recognition of a conflict, but not as the serious self-examination that Paul recommended: "Examine yourselves, whether ye be in the faith" (2 Corinthians 13:5). Joe, who drinks all the time, momentarily sets a bottle "beyond his reach—not that wine, unfortified wine, was really alcoholic, not that *he* was."[3] If a conflict or a contradiction is sensed within the self, it is quickly rationalized away.

Usually it is not even recognized. Bishop Dullinger, in Powers's short story "Keystone," prides himself on his humble origins. Yet when he decides to permit a special spiritual intimacy between himself and the young rector of his cathedral, His Excellency's way of expressing it is to say, "Just call me 'Bishop.'" He has no idea how phony either his speeches or his thoughts can sound. He is a moral conservative, but he resents his right-hand man, Monsignor Holstein, for embarrassing the church with old-fashioned statements about moral issues. Commenting on a sociological study of sex, Holstein tells the local paper, "Only an old priest with years of experience in the confessional should write such a book, and he wouldn't." "This," the Bishop thinks, "though true, had looked silly in print."[4] Yes, but the Bishop's failure to see the conflicts in his own mind looks even sillier.

Powers doesn't put quotation marks around the Bishop's thoughts. He represents them as if they were transcriptions of objective reality, which is what the Bishop assumes they are. If they are absurd, Powers depends on the reader to detect the absurdity. This is where the doctrine of the two selves becomes important in a new way. If Powers's characters refuse to assume the Christian duty of self-reflection, then his readers must assume it. If readers are nice people like most of Powers's characters, they may be inclined to take the characters' thoughts at face value. But that would be accepting this world as it is, making no higher demands on it and accepting no higher challenges to oneself. At some point, the audience should begin to "come to itself," like the Prodigal, and question its own standards, even if that means picking a fight with the lax, indulgent, "nice" side of one's nature. Are you prepared to accept a mediocre faith as good enough under the circumstances? If so, perhaps you will still be startled by Father Joe's "rolling in the stuff" remark, and what it says about his internal conflicts. In that event, you may go back and reread the earlier parts of his story, examining him as you might examine yourself, and reflecting on the contradictions you may have missed in your own standards.

By now, this is a familiar process—rereading a deceptively simple work of literature to make sure that one grasps more than the surface meaning. It reflects Christianity's emphasis on the inside over the outside, and on a change of perspective. Of course, that is a psychological and literary as well as a theological mandate. We understand the elusive parts of ourselves in much the same way in which we understand an elusive literary character, by looking for external symbols of internal conflicts. The idea that emerges from Jesus's parables is that to become a good disciple of Christ, one must become a good reader of symbols. As Powers's method shows, that can be a complicated task, because the world is full of symbols for the Christian to read.

Even the simplest events have symbolic implications. One of Father Joe's colleagues preaches a dull sermon about the proverbial camel that is permitted to put its nose inside the tent and gradually follows the nose with the other parts of its anatomy, until there is nothing inside but the camel. "*How. Like. Sin. That. Is,*" the priest intones. Joe regards the sermon as a "joke," and it's hard not to agree—until one sees that the inane little story effectively symbolizes the truth of Joe's own life, and maybe of the reader's life, too: one can lose one's spiritual path without noticing what is going on.[5]

That is precisely what happens to Bishop Dullinger. In the first part of "Keystone," we see the portrait of a nice elderly gentleman. He may not have quite enough to do—which seems odd for a bishop, doesn't it?—but he undoubtedly means well. He likes cats, and he reacts angrily when Monsignor Holstein upsets his cat Tessie. He suffers no crisis of faith, battles no temptations, seems basically right about Holstein's blundering approach to public relations. . . . Then one notices that Father Gau, the man he puts in Holstein's place, is a flatterer and careerist. Did the Bishop make an unavoidable mistake, or was the appointment symbolic of some spiritual contradiction? Well, the Bishop is willing to be flattered. And look at the little things he does when he's alone. Look at his reading, for example. Instead of the Bible, he prefers the most this-worldly, time-bound volume one could imagine: a business appointment book, eagerly awaited, year by year. He "examine[s] his conscience" not by the Sermon on the Mount but by the appointment book's "Good Rules for Businessmen." He finds that he is "doing pretty well" according to those standards. Among the book's "good," though perhaps not golden rules, one finds the following: "Be wary of dealing with unsuccessful men."[6] That may be sensible advice, but it's not exactly Christian. Jesus wasn't the least bit "successful" in any terms that a contemporary businessman would recognize.

Perceptive readers will now be asking themselves what positive evidence there is that the Bishop is really a Christian. The answer is, None. There is a deep fissure between the inside and the outside of him. From here on, symbols of his self-divisions become more apparent, although he doesn't see them for what they are, and Powers refrains from easy explanations. (The Bible's rule of symbolism is, "The wise shall understand" [Daniel 12:10].) The Bishop is a traditionalist, but his protegé, Father Gau, easily obtains his permission for a program of modernization-for-the-sake-of-modernization. The program is to include a new cathedral. Several impious things take place, including the moving of graves out of consecrated ground to make room for a new building, along with a subdivision called Cathedral Heights, containing a street named after the Bishop. It is a symbol, if the Bishop could only read it, of how well this humble man has come to regard himself. The Bishop doesn't like everything that happens, but he goes along—with continuously unfortunate results. The new cathedral is a brutally modern structure, inadequately disguised by two inches of traditional stone: an ecclesiastical veneer, like the Bishop's own veneer of "religion." This architectural symbol of dishonesty, he is assured, will "be good for fifty, seventy-five—maybe a hundred—years," a poor prognosis for a structure that is meant to symbolize the eternal church. The architects claim that the building is shaped like a chasuble, a priestly robe; the contractors, who don't like the architects, think that it's shaped like a coffin.[7] Opinions, like motives, are divided; but apparently there's one thing it isn't shaped like. It isn't shaped like a cross.

The only thing the Bishop wants, the only thing he wishes to preserve out of the whole tradition of Christian symbolism, is a metaphor of his own significance. He considers a bishop the "keystone" of the church, so he wants to see real arches with real keystones. But arches aren't used in modern steel buildings, and when he inspects the purely ornamental arches that the architects have installed, he can't find a keystone: "In the middle of every arch there were *two* stones—*where the keystone should have been there was just a crack.*" The crack is supposed, somehow, to symbolize the presence of an "arch," while plainly showing that the arch isn't there.[8] The Bishop is horrified by the drabness and futility of the "crack," but he accepts it, just as he has accepted every other shabby failure in the church. He does not realize that he had the key to his own history, to his own inner life, when he identified the keystone as a symbol of himself. He should see the *absence* of a keystone as symbolic in the same way. He was supposed to be a keystone, but now he is only a crack, a division in the church's structure, the kind of crack one might expect to find in a building designed to last for only a generation or so. He occupies a religious office, but he is too self-divided to fulfill his religious role. He is *merely* symbolic; so instead of symbolizing the strength of the church, he symbolizes its weakness.

At the end of "Keystone," the Bishop is contemplating another symbol, a chart of the diocesan hierarchy, arranged in the form of a cross. It shows the bishop at the top, clergy to the left, nuns to the right, laity on the trunk, and the chancellor, Father Gau, at the center. Here is a symbol that the Bishop can understand, in a way: "[I]t seemed to him that it gave a distorted view of the spiritual plan of the diocese." It does indeed. Yet he sees only the fact that it gives undue prominence to Father Gau, whom he now knows is attempting to usurp his own role as the figure binding the church together. He doesn't see the impiety of placing the bishop at the head of the cross of Christ, or the larger impiety of using the cross as an organization chart. In his resentment, he removes the chart and hides it. "The next morning," however, "he noticed that the cross was still there, in outline, on the wall."[9] If only as a shadow, the Cross survives every bad usage of the church. But the Bishop doesn't see that meaning in the symbol, either, although it is easy enough to see. There is something inside him that keeps him from doing so, despite his obscure unhappiness with himself.

This is Powers's method throughout his work: he shows the quiet, unremarkable surface of everyday reality; and he lets you know that there is a more complex reality beneath—in this case, the fractures in the church and in the clergy whose job is to keep it whole. But this is not the end of the story. The defense of the church, and of Christianity, has already begun, with the discovery of the Cross as the symbol that cannot be removed. The defense continues in "Farewell," the second part of the tale of Bishop Dullinger.

Recovering the Faith

In this story, the Bishop has been retired and Father Gau—naturally—has taken his place. The external, official identity that Dullinger had confused with his whole self has been removed. Is there anything left of him? There is, and it is much more interesting and relevant to Christianity than the official self he has lost. What is left is the sinful but redeemable inner self, shadowed by the unremovable cross.

"Keystone" is a story like *Elmer Gantry*, the story of a clergyman's unnoticed deconversion from Christianity. Confronted with Bishop Dullinger, Lewis's candid village preacher would certainly ask him, "Why don't you believe in God?" But "Farewell" (ironically, in view of its title) is a story of revival, of a nominal Christian who is finally converting to real Christianity. The retired Bishop is not much better at analyzing himself than the active Bishop was, but he eventually sees that something has gone wrong, inside as well as outside. He notices that he has nothing to do but take the early masses at the (old) cathedral and read *Who's Who in the Midwest*. He occupies the remainder of his ample spare time with the pleasure of returning retirement gifts to everyone except the new bishop and his closest crony. That's his self-righteous form of revenge. Then he is visited by Monsignor Holstein, whose career in the church he has spoiled but who, surprisingly, has forgiven him. Holstein is there to discuss a woman in the diocese, Mrs. Nagel, who claims to have visions of the Virgin. His visit is followed by another surprising event. Strangely (as it seems) Bishop Dullinger is now inspired to forgive Bishop Gau and send him a message of reassurance. After that, the old Bishop "went to bed again, and this time he slept."[10] Once he has forgiven others, his conversion can proceed.

We see the outer symbols of inner volatility. The Bishop starts investigating Mrs. Nagel's visions, which suggest that the supernatural world may actually exist. Trying to learn more about the mysterious message that the Virgin may have vouchsafed to her, he visits her parish priest, a dweller in the unfashionable hinterland where "nothing special" is going on but there is evidence that "the diocese [is] still in good heart."[11] So, curiously, is the Bishop, now that he has lost his role in the story of diocesan material progress and has only New Testament roles to fall back on—the roles of repentant sinner, seeker of miracles, pilgrim on the road to God. He doesn't just fill these roles; he embraces them, transforming his external Christianity, which was as stolid and banal as his new cathedral, into a real and active faith.

Symbols of discipleship multiply fast. Mrs. Nagel's pastor is laid up with a bad back, so the Bishop moves in and does his work for him, bearing his burden as Christians are supposed to do for one another (Galatians 6:2). Jesus said, "Whosoever will be chief among you, let him be your servant" (Matthew 20:27). The Bishop now seems to understand that verse. He busies himself around the property, not just saying mass but sweeping the walk, buying food, and visiting the local jail (Matthew 25:34–36). Then he hears of illnesses elsewhere in the diocese and happily goes to substitute for clergy in other towns. In "Keystone," he had reacted to the report of a priest's fatal illness with distant resignation: "He figured to lose a couple of men every December."[12] Now he jumps at the chance to help whenever somebody comes down with the flu. Where there is a problem with a defecting priest, the Bishop takes over his duties and, leading by example, stages a miniature reformation:

> [H]e disposed of the amateurish posters (Peace, Joy, Love, and so on) in the churches, got the women to scrub the floors and pews, the men to wax and polish them, participating in these activities himself.[13]

That's an interesting passage. What's the matter with peace, joy, love, "and so on"? If the Bishop had dismissed these posters in his earlier life, it would have been an unconscious symbol of his lack of Christian "heart." But he is further along on his journey now, so the posters no longer seem the kind of thing in which New Testament Christianity should be interested. The Bishop is now feeling, and inspiring, real peace, joy, and love; by comparison, the posters are tawdry, external. Pasteboard exhortations to "love" in a church that needs to be cleaned are just so much *mere* symbolism, and the Bishop has gone beyond all that. When he participates in cleaning the church, he symbolizes qualities that really exist in him—competing with less Christian ones, but winning the fight. They include the quality of leadership that makes his role as bishop authentic—ironically, just when he is no longer officially functioning in that role. He thinks of the posters as "amateurish" because that's what they are, when viewed from the perspective of a man who has now become, in the good sense, a professional Christian.

The best indication of the Bishop's conversion is his eagerness to travel. Freed from gloomy isolation in the episcopal palace, he is both physically and spiritually on the road.

Powers's attitude is similar to Bishop Blougram's: the spiritual and the physical are distinct, but the spiritual reveals itself in the proper use of the physical. In this world, soul needs body; it needs all kinds of bodily tools. The principal tool of Bishop Dullinger, a modern American, is his car; and in his relationship to this vehicle one sees the revolution in his spiritual life. His Mercedes starts as a symbol of his office: a powerful, expensive, bishoplike car, but also, regrettably, a symbol of office that he mistakes for reality. He cares for the car as if it were an end in itself, even worrying about leaving it "out in the cold." But as his attitude toward Christian service changes, so does his attitude toward the car. He doesn't mind "driving twenty-eight miles over an unimproved road before breakfast, through ice and snow," because "the Mercedes [is] equipped" for it.[14] The car, like the Bishop, is now in its right place. There is no reason, Powers suggests, for the church not to be the Church, with bishops and expensive cars to do the bishops' work, so long as both the bishops and their cars are actually doing the work. A keystone—which is what Bishop Dullinger has become, however heavy and "dull" and old and retired he is—needs to be heavy. A Mercedes is a big, heavy car, very useful if you have to cope with ice and snow. It is an apt symbol of the Church and its power.

Bishop Dullinger's perspective at last converges with the author's, the inside view with the outside, the symbol with the reality: as Dullinger observes, the car (like the church and its bishop) is "still a great performer," despite its "looking older and grayer," with "ice on its roof" and "frozen glunk under its fenders."[15] At the end, it is the car that ennobles the Bishop by martyrdom. He is driving it when he suffers a traffic accident that claims his life. The church as a vehicle of martyrdom? Yes, for it is because of the church that martyrs die—often in such everyday events as automobile accidents. The open question is whether the other members of the church can correctly interpret the symbols that appear in the ordinary, "normal" course of its life.

However that question may be answered, Powers has taken the busy details of modern American life, those elements of the "real" world that constantly seem on the point of subverting the church, or rendering it ridiculous, and has demonstrated that they, too, can be instruments of grace. Meanwhile, by using the realistic details that flood the surface of his stories as signs and symbols of an underlying religious truth, he has achieved a deeper level of realism, a realism like that of biblical narrative, which recognizes that reality seldom comes with explanations conveniently attached to events. People who look for the psychology of conversion will not find it explained in so many words by the New Testament. Conversion, and the psychological conflicts leading up to it, are known by the effects that symbolize their presence. This symbolic method is much more "realistic" than ordinary novelistic "realism," which offers detailed explanations of psychological processes that no one has clear access to. Neither Powers nor Bishop Dullinger tries to explain exactly how the Bishop is converted to the Christianity he has always professed. Dullinger is too dull to do that, and Powers is too smart. The important thing is that such things happen, and that we can find out about them if we follow the complex symbolism hidden in the apparently simple, ordinary events of daily life. Powers leaves the "how" where it belongs, in darkness, which is the place of miracles.

But speaking of miracles, what happened to Mrs. Nagel's visions? They didn't get lost; they were thoroughly investigated by Bishop Dullinger and his colleagues. But they didn't amount to much. Mrs. Nagel turned out to be a nice woman who suffered from the misapprehension that the Virgin had given her an important message. The message was, sadly, "KEEP MINNESOTA GREEN."[16] It wasn't a gift from the Virgin, after all, at least probably not. If it had been, it would have been nothing but an encouragement to keep what you already have: the external world is already, quite visibly, very green, especially in Minnesota. The church is right to reject such a "miracle"; it is only a diversion. The real miracle has already happened, on the inside of Bishop Dullinger: he has recovered his faith. He has become a Christian. This transformation of reality was internal, and therefore only to be known by a careful reading of symbols.

Paradox and Simplicity

Nothing seems more obvious than the story of Bishop Dullinger when you first start to read it, but few stories in the English language seem more complicated, when you read it with New Testament ideas in mind. *Four Quartets* is different. Rare is the reader who opens this sequence of poems in free but carefully measured verse and says, "How simple it is!" In its methods—its relentless use of paradoxes and ironies, its constant hints of a revelation lurking behind or beneath its words, its insistence on reversal of meanings, on separating what is normally put together and uniting what is normally kept apart, on viewing time from the perspective of eternity and eternity from the perspective of time—*Four Quartets* is one of the most complex works of modern literature, and certainly one of the most complex explanations of Christianity. Yet its fundamental methods are simply New Testament methods, and its fundamental ideas are simply New Testament ideas. If we are guided through the poem by what we know about the New Testament, we will come to the end of the journey and "arrive," as Eliot says in conclusion, at the place "where we started"—at the basic New Testament view of the world. Is such a journey worthwhile? Yes, as Eliot also says, if it helps us to "know the place" better, or for "the first time."[17]

The composition of *Four Quartets* represented a considerable intellectual journey for the author himself. Like many intellectuals of his generation, Eliot (1888–1965) began his literary career as a religious skeptic. He was deeply dissatisfied with the "progressive" and rationalist "social gospel" Christianity of his upbringing. His poem *The Waste Land* (1922) depicts the contemporary world as a desert of used-up emotions and meaningless ways of life, with a few, evanescent hints of salvation appearing in stories and symbols from the past. Some of the stories and symbols in *The Waste Land* are Christian, but it is not clear that they are anything more than the kind of things about which one of the poem's voices says, "These fragments I have shored against my ruins."[18] Within a few years, however, the Christian story blossomed for Eliot into an idea and a way of life that he could accept as true. Although many aspects of his conversion remain mysterious, it was inspired in large part by his attachment to historic works of Christian literature.[19] In 1927, he symbolized his conversion by joining the Church of England. Publication of *Four Quartets*, his most considerable effort as a Christian poet, began in 1935, when the first part, "Burnt Norton," appeared in print.

The four poems in the sequence are named for places associated with the past: Burnt Norton, an old English country house; East Coker, the place in England from which an Eliot ancestor migrated to America in the seventeenth century; the Dry Salvages, a collection of rocks off the coast of New England that traditionally presented a hazard to fishermen; Little Gidding, the site of a seventeenth-century English religious community. In the completed work, published in 1943, this array of places and the complex meditations associated with them suggest, among many other things, the idea that the past (especially the Christian past), is still available and valuable as a source of inspiration, a sign that the world of time—the waste land of the modern world—can still touch the world of the timeless.

John Bunyan and Bishop Blougram viewed the Christian journey as an adventure that is always starting for eternity: the Christian's course, in Blougram's phrase, is "outward-bound." So does Eliot, but he also works from the opposite point of view. Much of his journey, in *Four Quartets*, is inward-bound, in its concern with exploring the inner world of human thoughts and emotions and in its attempt to see the journey from its end, to look back on time from the eternal perspective. That is a loftier but more difficult point of view. Indeed, it is one not literally possible to attain. Humans are bound by time, and time is the antithesis of eternity. From the perspective of eternity, all of time might appear "at once," as suggested by the book of Revelation, although that expression is inadequate, because it pictures everything as existing at the same *time*, not existing within a frame of timelessness.

Clearly, the effort to suggest the perspective of eternity is a challenging literary problem. But in *Four Quartets*, as in Christian literature generally, it is inseparably connected with the New Testament idea of the journey, and that is a very simple thing.

Humanity's journey began with God, at the moment of creation. Humanity's journey will return to God, at the end of time. The individual Christian's journey began with God, at the time when God first granted that person grace. The Christian's journey will return to God, at the time of the Christian's earthly end. So, paradoxically—but this is now easier to understand—the journey is both a voyage "out" and a voyage "back." It is a circling back to God, from whom we came, and to memories and stories of events in time, which give us symbolic indications that the journey is a progress, a spiraling return to an understanding of ourselves as pilgrims through time to eternity.

So let us begin the journey again (Christian literature is always a repetition, a return, and a revival), and begin at the end of Eliot's poem—because, as he says, "What we call the beginning is often the end / And to make an end is to make a beginning." Here is the Christian journey, as seen from the highest level of abstraction:

> We shall not cease from exploration
> And the end of all our exploring
> Will be to arrive where we started
> And know the place for the first time.[20]

From the eternal perspective, the journey is always starting, never "ceas[ing]"—and always returning to its "end." And from the eternal perspective, all times and places are knowable and reconcilable with God. This is simply to repeat what Christianity has always been about, the penetration of eternity into time, and the reconciliation of God with his creation. Earlier in the poem, Eliot said that prayer is "the intersection of the timeless moment," which can happen anywhere. From one's point of view at any one "place" in the Christian story, one can see in imagination all the other "places," from the Edenic "beginning" of human life,

> At the source of the longest river
> The voice of the hidden waterfall
> And the children in the apple-tree

to the journey's paradisal end, where "all shall be well and / All manner of thing shall be well." We know that—in terms of the world of time—any journey implies a change, and any change implies the abandonment of one "place" in the journey so that another "place" can be reached. From the eternal point of view, however, everything is part of the same pattern, a pattern in which "the rose" and "the fire" that seems to destroy the rose "are one."[21] That is a paradox. For this kind of literature, however, the vital consideration is to see, beneath the paradox, the simple Christian teaching about God's providence, exerting itself throughout the pattern of life.

"Good" Friday

Bishop Blougram argued for Christianity. Eliot is not so much arguing for it as presenting it, helping his readers to *see* its implications, showing how challenging its concepts can be. This has a great deal to do with his obvious desire to rehabilitate Christianity in the eyes of modern intellectuals who regard it as a childish and outmoded faith. *Four Quartets* was influenced by the preoccupations of such abstruse modern philosophers as F.H. Bradley, about whom Eliot had written a doctoral dissertation. Those preoccupations are not my subject, nor am I concerned with Eliot's many debts to philosophic writing in the Christian tradition. The truth is, *Four Quartets* needs none of that to explain it. It needs only the most basic understanding of New Testament ideas and literary methods, and an interest in seeing what can be done with them.

New Testament ideas and methods, and New Testament problems. One of the greatest problems that Eliot faces is the failure of so many Christians to act up to Christian teachings. This is simultaneously a theological difficulty and an obstacle to belief. Why should anyone believe in Christianity, considering the long history of Christians' strife with one another (let alone other people)? Eliot faces the problem by bringing up a particularly bad example, the bloody struggles of Christian against Christian in the Civil Wars in seventeenth-century England. His response, as I indicated in Chapter 11, is to admit what the New Testament itself says about Christians, that "all have sinned, and come short of the glory of God" (Romans 3:23), while emphasizing that the wars were, indeed, a conflict among brethren: "All touched by a common genius / United in the strife which divided them."[22] As the "place" for this part of his meditations in *Four Quartets*, Eliot chooses Little Gidding, a refuge for Christians of his own (Anglican) denomination, destroyed by the rival puritans. He stands, symbolically, at Little Gidding, remembers that John Milton, his predecessor in English poetry, was a leader of the puritans; and, like a brother, forgives him. The presence of Milton among the violent contenders suggests that it is appropriate to forgive fallen human genius, instead of using its fallenness as a reason to spurn the God of forgiveness. You are indebted to the shapers of your journey, to those (perhaps contentious) people who passed on their love and faith to you, are you not? Then the simple New Testament words apply: "Forgive us our debts, as we forgive our debtors" (Matthew 6:12).

The sins of Christians are an obvious instance of the larger problem of evil. Since the beginning of the intellectual rebellion against Christianity in the eighteenth century, God's "permission" of evil has been urged as a principal reason for unbelief. In 1943, at the depth of earth's greatest war, that argument had special urgency. Eliot gives credibility to his defense of the faith by facing the problem directly, staging one of his poem's most vivid discussions of evil in a "disfigured street" left by the German air force that was attempting to obliterate his country. The discussion (which repeats the method of Dante, recording the dialogues of hell in his *Divine Comedy*) makes the point that all merely human life, all life lived outside the prospect of eternity, tends to destruction. Even in the best of *times*, "the gifts reserved for age" are "the cold friction of expiring sense," "the rending pain of re-enactment / Of all that you have done, and been." This section of the poem is a brutally direct statement of the "natural" facts of life.[23] It is also Eliot's way of drawing a simple distinction, the distinction between God's "permitting" evil as if he wished for evil to take place, and God's permitting human existence to continue as it is, with all its harrowing demands and hidden possibilities.

Eliot, like Powers, suggests that human existence can be understood in terms of the basic Pauline distinction between the two selves and their two courses of life. The picture that Eliot projects is even more basic than that of Powers, and even more Pauline. The natural or fleshly self—German or British, it makes no difference—repeats the age-old deeds of the flesh, subtle or violent, and sees itself as bound to the wheel of time: "good for fifty, seventy-five—maybe a hundred—years." The spiritual self looks to eternity and (ideally) strives to repeat the pattern of its master, Christ. What Eliot hears on the bombed-out streets of London is a warning from the fleshly self about the impending doom of the fleshly self. He takes it as such.

Four Quartets is a modern apocalypse, an uncovering of the simple, often brutal, truth beneath the complexities of modern life and "advanced" thought. It is not surprising, therefore, that Eliot makes liberal use of the literary devices of the biblical Apocalypse. Like the author of Revelation, Eliot draws his images of evil not just from extraordinary events but from the common things of life, things that are superficially innocuous: "Because thou art lukewarm . . . Because thou sayest, I am rich, and increased with goods, and have need of nothing . . ." (Revelation 3:16–17). Eliot's lukewarm, mediocre human beings are the middle-class passengers seated comfortably on a train, "settled" pleasantly "[t]o fruit, periodicals and business letters." There are also people who are literally "rich, and increased with goods":

> The captains, merchant bankers, eminent men of letters,
> The generous patrons of art, the statesmen and the rulers,
> Distinguished civil servants, chairmen of many committees . . .

Viewed from the perspective of time, all alike "go into the dark / . . . And we all go with them, into the silent funeral."[24]

In *Four Quartets* the Christian idea of the journey appears in a multitude of little stories, like the multitude of little stories in Revelation. All these stories, happy or unhappy, are "places" that are seen from eternity; though where there is no consciousness of eternity, journeys can be imagined only as going "into the dark." So meeting the problem of evil does not mean denying its existence. Much less does it mean evading one's responsibility for it. Meeting the problem means seeking the shape and direction of life, recognizing that life is framed by eternity and that eternity is interested in giving the journey a proper direction. The discussion of evil that takes place on the war-ruined street ends with an admonition:

> From wrong to wrong the exasperated spirit
> Proceeds, unless restored by that refining fire

—the fire of God, the fire of the Holy Spirit, which purges and inspires, separating the soul from "self" and uniting the soul with God (compare Hebrews 4:12).[25]

In a daring moment, Eliot identifies even the German warplane—"the dark dove with the flickering tongue"—with this pentecostal visitor:

> The dove descending breaks the air
> With flame of incandescent terror

Of which the tongues declare
The one discharge from sin and error . . .
  To be redeemed from fire by fire.[26]

Eliot thus repeats the use of paradox in Donne's *Holy Sonnets*
("nor ever chaste, unless thou ravish me") and in the book of
Revelation, where the thing that ought to be damaging turns out
to be the thing that can repair the damage: "These are they
which came out of great tribulation, and have washed their
robes, and made them white in the blood of the Lamb"
(Revelation 7:14). A similar paradox was discovered by the
Christians whose story is told in the book of Acts, people who
were visited by the wonderful fiery dove and as a result endured
many painful adventures.

Eliot is not saying that the plane is literally the Holy Spirit.
He is saying that if God's providence is real, it must be total; it
must be able to proclaim itself in every way, in every thing. That
is his philosophical position. Ironically, for such a richly imagis-
tic poem as *Four Quartets*, it may seem too simple and abstract.
And its implications, as he pictures them, may seem cruel. What
recommends it, and humanizes it, is his emphasis on God's personal involvement in the story, as described by the New
Testament. The simple New Testament story is that the Son of
God entered the world of time to suffer its sins and cruelties, so
that the world might be redeemed from time. This is the old, old
story, the story already told many times in this book: "God was
in Christ, reconciling the world unto himself"; therefore "all
things are of God, who hath reconciled us to himself by Jesus
Christ" (2 Corinthians 5:18–19).

That, of course, is also abstract language, worthy of Eliot at
his most philosophical. But the idea can be repeated in other
ways. The least abstract, the most immediate literary imagery
is, perhaps, the kind derived from the body. This is the kind
of imagery that, according to the gospel of John, Jesus used
to represent God's full participation in the world of human
needs:

[M]y flesh is meat indeed, and my blood is drink indeed. He that
eateth my flesh, and drinketh my blood, dwelleth in me, and I in
him. As the living Father hath sent me, and I live by the Father: so
he that eateth me, even he shall live by me. (John 6:55–57)

Some of Jesus's disciples found his image far too fresh and vivid: "This is an hard saying; who can hear it?" (John 6:60). Certainly the disciples who witnessed Jesus's death must have found the saying especially painful to recall. After 1,900 years of communion services, the image has lost much of its original impact, but Eliot takes it out of the world of stained glass windows and restores its lurid emphasis: "The dripping blood our only drink, / The bloody flesh our only food." Only when the starkness of the original image is restored can one appreciate the drama of the Christian story as a whole, the story in which even the cruelest things are reversed and redeemed: "Again, in spite of that, we call this Friday good."[27] "Good" Friday celebrates Christ's crucifixion.

"And, Behold, We Live"

Eliot was known for his reserved manner and his emphasis on the intellectual, the formal, and the traditional in life and art. In his own way, however, he—like every other Christian writer, when you come down to it—was a revivalist, trying to recapture for his own time the intensity of the New Testament experience. *Four Quartets* is full of worries about *how* to do this, how to present the meaning of Christianity so that "the past experience" will be "revived in the meaning." Eliot sees the course of Christian literature as a journey in which the past must somehow be fully incorporated in the breaking moment. That idea returns him to his ruling image of repetition, of circling back, of a line of temporal events that eternity bends into a circle. When Christian literature finds new ways of reviving "the everlasting gospel," then the journey becomes a rounded "dance": "An easy commerce of the old and the new . . . / The complete consort dancing together."[28] It's a matter of finding and restoring the right pattern, of reproducing what I have called the New Testament's DNA.

But the specific words that the writer chooses must have the ability to extend New Testament meanings to modern people. That is what Eliot makes them do throughout his poem, and nowhere better than in the sequence of images that leads him to the flesh and blood of Good Friday. In modern Christian culture, one of the most popular images of Jesus is that of the Great Physician. The idea was introduced by Jesus himself, in a passage that appears in the three synoptic gospels (Matthew 9:12, Mark 2:17, Luke 5:31). It was repeated in a popular hymn, "My Faith Has Found a Resting Place" (1891) by Eliza Hewitt, the author of many revival songs:

> My great Physician heals the sick,
> The lost He came to save;
> For me His precious blood He shed,
> For me His life He gave.[29]

Two concepts come together here, the concept of the dying Christ and the concept of Christ the healer. Like other pairs of concepts that are favorites of Christian literature—time and eternity, forward movement and circular movement—this one is dramatically paradoxical. Hewitt mentions the Great Physician and then the dying Christ. Eliot heightens the drama by joining what she lists as parallels, and gives "physician" a modern specificity:

> The wounded surgeon plies the steel
> That questions the distempered part;
> Beneath the bleeding hands we feel
> The sharp compassion of the healer's art
> Resolving the enigma of the fever chart.[30]

The "fever chart" of a patient in a modern hospital represents the course of the patient's illness. The "enigma" derives from the paradox that "disease" and its treatment may be the route to health. Suffering becomes more comprehensible when one reflects that pain can result even from a doctor's compassionate desire to heal. But the suffering inflicted by a compassionate physician would be still more acceptable if one knew that the doctor had also suffered, had also been "wounded."

With the image of the suffering surgeon in mind, one is prepared for Eliot's vividly modern picture of God's world as an enormous "hospital"

> Endowed by the ruined millionaire,
> Wherein, if we do well, we shall
> Die of the absolute paternal care. . . . [31]

To be "reconciled" with God means to share the experience of the wounded Christ, to join his story of death and resurrection. "Know ye not," Paul says, "that so many of us as were baptized into Jesus Christ were baptized into his death?" You didn't know that? But Paul insists on it. He describes himself and his fellow Christians as being "buried" with Christ in order to attain his "newness of life." Death is part of the process of discipleship. Yet it is only one part. Death, literal or symbolic, is not the end of the journey: "as dying, and, behold, we live" (Romans 6:3–4, 2 Corinthians 6:9). Again, we call this Friday "good."

There is a strange passage, near the beginning of *Four Quartets*, that becomes much less strange when one has journeyed to the end of it, with Eliot's poetry in one hand and the New Testament in the other. The poet stands in a deserted garden and, in a moment of vision, sees it return to life. A bird calls "in response" to "unheard music"; the pool fills with water; the lotus blooms; the roses suddenly have "the look of flowers that are looked at." [32] As in Powers's stories, there is something going on beneath the surface of the reality we think we know. Reality is more complicated than we thought. But its complexity can be resolved back into the simple elements it contains: the world of God, the world of humanity, and the moments when they come together.

These moments happen whenever the DNA of the New Testament asserts itself, as it does in the ruined-garden passage, which contains all the traditional devices and emphases of Christian literature. Eternity joins the individual at a moment of time, a moment that is part of a long history of such moments, reaching back to the original garden that God "planted . . . in Eden" (Genesis 2:8). The moment is part of God's story, and the story of the person to whom he grants the revelation. The revelation is packed with paradoxes, because it shows the distinctness of time and eternity, past and present, God and humanity, while demonstrating their capacity for reconciliation. Its strangeness expresses itself in symbols and symbolic actions, not in analytical philosophy; and the symbols are those of a miraculous conversion, the transformation of death to life. The story suggests the central notion of Christian individualism, the idea that any individual can experience that transformation, and that every such individual's experience will therefore be important. It also suggests, ironically, that such transformations happen, not because of some great event in the outer world, but because of apparently small events, mere changes of perspective, in the inner one. The inside is more important than the outside; the small is more important than the great. And if these changes occur, then the journey back to the ruined garden will become, as it is always becoming, a journey forward into paradise, the repetition by Christ's disciple of Christ's own journey.

All these complicated things are happening in a few lines of verse, yet the effect is finally very simple: somehow "dry concrete" is "filled with water out of sunlight"; an "empty alley" fills with life and music. It is the kind of effect one remembers as one remembers a fellow human being, whether or not one understands the DNA inside that person, or even knows that it exists. But this is just the start of the reader's journey through the *Four Quartets*, poems that grow more powerful the more they are known and understood.

I hope it is also just the start of the reader's journey through Christian literature. To quote the title of another Christian poem[33]—much simpler in form, but with its own complex significance—"the half has never been told."

Part III

Texts

The Dream of the Rood

ANONYMOUS. TRANSLATED BY STEPHEN COX

Behold! I will tell you the best of dreams,
the dream that met me at midnight
when the speechbearers had gone to their sleep.
I thought that I saw a splendid tree
lifted in air and surrounded with light,
the brightest of beams. All that beacon was
covered with gold, crusted with gems
fair on the field. Five jewels gleamed
on the wide cross-span, while the angelbands watched,
fair through all ages. Nor was that a felon's
gallows on which those holy ones gazed,
or men on the earth, or this wondrous world:
it was the tree of triumph. And I torn by guilt,
stained with my sins, I saw its splendor.
Begirt with glory, shining with gold,
splendid with jewels stood the Overlord's tree.
Yet through the gold I could glimpse
the old torture: the right side of the tree
began to bleed. Sorrowing I beheld it
at times drenched with gore, at times decked with gold.
And there I lay for a long while grieving
beholding the hero-tree, the Lord's beacon,
till the best of woods its word began:

"It was long ago—and yet I remember—
the day I was hewed at the holt's end,
stirred from my roots. Strong foes took me,
made me a spectacle, bade me raise their sinners for them,
placed me upon their shoulders, planted me upon a hill,
fastened me fast. Then I saw the Lord of Men
hasten forward, full of zeal to mount upon me.
Though the earth trembled, against God's word
I dared neither to bend nor to break.
I might have felled every foe, but still I stood fast.

"Hardminded and strong, the young hero stripped himself
—he who was God Almighty—and climbed on the gallows,
the boldest of many, to redeem mankind.
I trembled when the warrior touched and embraced me,
nor was I bold to bow to the earth,
fall to the ground. I stood fast.
The rood was reared. Raised was the mighty King,
heaven's Lord, whom I could not help.
Dark nails they drove deep inside me;
on me are the wounds still seen, open malicious wounds.
Nor dared I any of them damage,
though they taunted us both together.
I was besmeared with blood,
covered with blood from the man's body
after he gave up the ghost.

"On that hill I endured horrible things;
I saw the God of Hosts sorely racked.
Darkness like clouds covered his shining;
a shadow went forth, black shade under sky.
All creation lamented, wept the Lord's death.
Christ was on cross.

"But to him hastened
men from afar—I saw it all—
and sore with much sorrow I bowed,
humbling myself to their hands.
They took from me God the Almighty
bore him away from his torment. But the guards
left me wet with blood, wounded with arrows.
They laid him down limb-weary,
they stood by his side,
heaven's ruler, and he rested awhile
weary from battle. They worked him his tomb
in his slayer's sight, carved it of shining stone,
set there the victorious Lord, began to sing dirges,
wretched at evening. Then they went away, weary,
and the sublime Lord stayed there alone.

"We three crosses stood weeping.
The voice of the warriors went away.

The body cooled, the fair corpse.
Then they felled us to earth, a fearful thing,
buried us deep in the darkened pit.
Still the Lord's friends found me,
his servants girt me with silver and gold.

"Now thou whom I love hast learned
the evil work that I endured,
my hard cares. But the time is come
when I am lauded in every land,
revered among men and by all creation
that prays to this sign. On me the Son of God
suffered. Therefore splendid I tower under heaven
and make holy whoever comes in awe of me.
The hardest of torments made me to men the most hateful,
but to them I pointed the path of life.
Lo! Just as his mother, Mary herself,
Almighty God for the sake of all men
made worthy above all women,
so heaven's Lord, the Prince of Glory, glorified me
over every wood in the world.

"I bid thee, beloved warrior,
to speak this sight to other men,
tell them in words of the wondrous tree
on which the Almighty suffered for man's many sins
and the deeds of Adam in days of old.
He tasted death, and from death he arose
in his might, mankind to aid.
He ascended to heaven, but hither he will return,
to this middle earth, mankind to seek—
on the last day, the Lord himself,
Almighty God, with all his angels.
Then he will deem, he who can doom,
what each man in this life has merited.
Nor may any fail then to fear
when he hears the Lord ask him
where in that multitude the man may be
who for the Savior's name would suffer death
bitter as he on the beam sustained.

"They will fear, and few will think
how they will come to answer Christ.
But no moment of fear need any man feel
who on his breast bears the best of signs,
for through the Rood shall each soul reach
its way to life with heaven's Lord."

Then prayed I to that beam with brightest mind
and deepest awe, there where I was, alone.
Impelled on its journey, my heart has endured
many longings. Yet to me life's bliss
is to visit still the victory beam
more often than any others
and eagerly worship. My will is warm;
my hope is resting upon the Rood.

I have no strong friends; all have gone forth,
left worldly joys, sought for themselves the Lord of Glory.
They live in heaven with the High Father,
dwelling in glory. And I look daily for the cross
that I here on earth once beheld
to bring me to bliss, to the banquet of heaven
where God's folk are seated forevermore,
that I with all saints may savor joy to the full.

May God befriend me, who on the gallows tree
suffered to redeem us from sin and give us life
in a heavenly home. Hope was renewed
with blessing and bliss to those who waited in burning.
On that raid the Son was successful,
ascending from hell with a host of spirits,
a joy to his angels and to all the saints
watching in glory. Almighty God, the King
of Heaven, returned where his homeland was.

Two Holy Sonnets

JOHN DONNE

V

I am a little world made cunningly
Of Elements, and an Angelike spright,
But black sinne hath betraid to endlesse night
My worlds, both parts, and (oh) both parts must die.
You which beyond that heaven which was most high
Have found new sphears, and of new lands can write,
Powre new seas in mine eyes, that so I might
Drowne my world with my weeping earnestly,
Or wash it if it must be drown'd no more:
But oh it must be burnt, alas the fire
Of lust and envie have burnt it heretofore,
And made it fouler, Let their flames retire,
And burne me ô Lord, with a fiery zeale
Of thee and thy house, which doth in eating heale.

XIV

Batter my hear, three person'd God; for, you
As yet but knock, breathe, shine, & seeke to mend;
That I may rise, and stand, o'rthrow mee, and bend
Your force, to break, blow, burn, & make me new.
I, like an usurpt towne, to another due,
Labour to admit you, but oh, to no end.
Reason your Viceroy in me, me should defend;
But is captiv'd, and proves weake or untrue.
Yet dearly I love you, and would be lov'd faine,
But am betroth'd unto your enemy,
Divorce mee, untie, or breake that knot againe,
Take me to you, imprison me, for I
Except you enthrall me, never shall be free,
Nor ever chaste, except you ravish mee.

The Collar

GEORGE HERBERT

I struck the board, and cry'd, No more;
                    I will abroad.
What? shall I ever sigh and pine?
My lines and life are free; free as the road,
    Loose as the wind, as large as store,
            Shall I be still in suit?
Have I no harvest but a thorn
To let me bloud, and not restore
What I have lost with Cordial fruit?
            Sure there was wine.
    Before my sighs did dry it: there was corn
        Before my tears did drown it.
Is the year only lost to me?
    Have I no bayes to crown it?
No flowers, no garlands gay! all blasted?
            All wasted?
    Not so, my heart: but there is fruit,
            And thou hast hands.
    Recover all thy sigh-blown age
On double pleasures: leave thy cold dispute
Of what is *fit, and not*; forsake thy cage,
            Thy rope of sands,
Which petty thoughts have made, and made to thee
Good cable, to enforce and draw,
            And be thy Law,
    Whilest thou didst wink and wouldst not see.
            Away; take heed.
            I will abroad.
Call in thy deaths head there: tie up thy fears.
            He that forbears
    To suit and serve his need,
            Deserves his load.
But as I rav'd and grew more fierce and wild
            At every word,
Me thoughts I heard one calling *Child*:
    And I repli'd, *My Lord*.

The Pilgrim's Progress from This World, to That Which Is to Come (Selections)

JOHN BUNYAN

The Opening Scene

As I walk'd through the Wilderness of this World, I lighted on a certain place, where was a Denn; And I laid me down in that place to sleep: And as I slept I dreamed a Dream. I dreamed, and behold I saw a Man cloathed with Rags, standing in a certain place, with his face from his own House, a Book in his hand, and a great burden upon his Back. I looked, and saw him open the Book, and read therein; and as he read, he wept and trembled: and not being able longer to contain, he brake out with a lamentable cry; saying, What shall I do?

In this plight therefore he went home, and refrained himself as long as he could, that his Wife and Children should not perceive his distress; but he could not be silent long, because that his trouble increased: wherefore at length he brake his mind to his Wife and Children; and thus he began to talk to them, O my dear Wife, saith he, and you the Children of my bowels, I your dear friend am in my self undone, by reason of a burden that lieth hard upon me: moreover, I am for certain informed, that this our City will be burned with fire from Heaven, in which fearful overthrow, both my self, with thee, my Wife, and you my sweet babes, shall miserably come to ruine; except (the which, yet I see not) some way of escape can be found, whereby we may be delivered. At this his Relations they were sore amazed; not for that they believed, that what he said to them was true, but because they thought, that some frenzy distemper had got into his head: therefore, it drawing towards night, and they hoping that sleep might settle his brains, with all hast they got him to bed; but the night was as troublesome to him as the day: wherefore instead of sleeping, he spent it in sighs and tears. So when the morning was come, they would know how he did;

and he told them worse and worse. He also set to talking to them again, but they began to be hardened[.] They also thought to drive away his distemper by harsh and surly carriages to him: Sometimes they would deride, sometimes they would chide, and sometimes they would quite neglect him: wherefore he began to retire himself to his Chamber to pray for, and pity them; and also to condole his own misery: he would also walk solitarily in the Fields, sometimes reading, and sometimes praying; and thus for some days he spent his time.

Now, I saw upon a time, when he was walking in the Fields, that he was (as he was wont) reading in his Book, and greatly distressed in his mind; and as he read, he burst out, as he had done before, crying, What shall I do to be saved?

I saw also that he looked this way, and that way, as if he would run; yet he stood still, because, (as I perceived) he could not tell which way to go. I looked then, and saw a man named Evangelist, coming to him, and asked, Wherefore dost thou cry? He answered, Sir, I perceive by the Book in my hand, that I am condemned to die, and after that, to come to Judgment; and I find that I am not willing to do the first, nor able to do the second.

Then said Evangelist, Why not willing to die? since this life is attended with so many evils? The Man answered, because I fear that this burden that is upon my back, will sink me lower than the Grave; and I shall fall into Tophet. And Sir, if I be not fit to go to Prison, I am not fit to go to Judgment, and from thence to Execution; and the thoughts of these things make me cry.

Then saith Evangelist, If this be thy condition, why standest thou still? He answered, because I know not whither to go. Then he gave him a Parchment-Roll, and there was written within, Fly from the wrath to come.

The Man therefore read it, and looking upon Evangelist very carefully; said, Whither must I fly? Then said Evangelist, pointing with his finger over a very wide Field, Do you see yonder Wicket-gate? The Man said, No. Then said the other, Do you see yonder shining light? He said, I think I do. Then said Evangelist, Keep that light in your eye, and go up directly thereto, so shalt thou see the Gate; at which when thou knockest, it shall be told thee what thou shalt do.

So I saw in my Dream, that the Man began to run; now he had not run far from his own door, but his Wife and Children perceiving it, began to cry after him to return: but the Man put his fingers in his Ears, and ran on, crying, Life, Life, Eternal Life: so he looked not behind him, but fled towards the middle of the Plain.

The Vanity Fair Episode

Then I saw in my Dream, that when they [Christian and Faithful] were got out of the Wilderness, they presently saw a Town before them, and the name of that Town is Vanity; and at the Town there is a Fair kept called Vanity-Fair: It is kept all the year long, it beareth the name of Vanity-Fair, because the Town where it is kept, is lighter than Vanity; and also, because all that is there sold, or that cometh thither, is Vanity. As is the saying of the wise, All that cometh is vanity.

This Fair is no new erected business, but a thing of Ancient standing; I will shew you the original of it.

Almost five thousand years agone, there were Pilgrims walking to the Cœlestial City, as these two honest persons are; and Beelzebub, Apollyon, and Legion, with their Companions, perceiving by the path that the Pilgrims made, that their way to the City lay through this Town of Vanity, they contrived here to set up a Fair; a Fair wherein should be sold of all sorts of Vanity, and that it should last all the year long. Therefore at this Fair are all such Merchandize sold, as Houses, Lands, Trades, Places, Honors, Preferments, Titles, Countries, Kingdoms, Lusts, Pleasures, and Delights of all sorts, as Whores, Bawds, Wives, Husbands, Children, Masters, Servants, Lives, Blood, Bodies, Souls, Silver, Gold, Pearls, Precious Stones, and what not?

And moreover, at this Fair there is at all times to be seen Juglings, Cheats, Games, Plays, Fools, Apes, Knaves, and Rogues, and that of every kind.

Here are to be seen too, and that for nothing, Thefts, Murders, Adultries, False-swearers, and that of a blood-red colour.

And as in other Fairs of less moment, there are the several rows & Streets under their proper names, where such and such Wares are vended: So here likewise, you have the proper places, Rows, Streets, (viz. Countreys, and Kingdoms) where the Wares of this Fair are soonest to be found: Here is the Britain Row, the French Row, the Italian Row, the Spanish Row, the German

Row, where several sorts of Vanities are to be sold. But as in other Fairs, some one Commodity is as the chief of all the fair, so the Ware of Rome and her Merchandize is greatly promoted in this fair: Only our English Nation, with some others, have taken a dislike thereat.

Now, as I said, the way to the Cœlestial City lies just through this Town, where this lusty Fair is kept; and he that will go to the City, and yet not go through this Town, must needs go out of the World. The Prince of Princes himself, when here, went through this Town to his own Country, and that upon a Fair-day too: Yea, and as I think it was Beelzebub, the chief Lord of this Fair, that invited him to buy of his Vanities; yea, would have made him Lord of the Fair, would he but have done him Reverence as he went through the Town. Yea, because he was such a person of Honor, Beelzebub had him from Street to Street, and shewed him all the Kingdoms of the World in a little time, that he might, (if possible) allure that Blessed One, to cheapen and buy some of his Vanities. But he had no mind to the Merchandize, and therefore left the Town; without laying out so much as one farthing upon these Vanities. This Fair therefore is an ancient thing, of long standing, and a very great Fair.

Now these Pilgrims, as I said, must needs go through this Fair: Well, so they did; but behold, even as they entred into the Fair, all the people in the Fair were moved, and the Town it self, as it were in a Hubbub about them; and that for several reasons: For,

First, The Pilgrims were cloathed with such kind of Raiment, as was diverse from the Raiment of any that traded in that Fair. The people therefore of the fair made a great gazing upon them: Some said they were Fools, some they were Bedlams, and some they are Outlandish-men.

Secondly, And as they wondred at their Apparel, so they did likewise at their Speech; for few could understand what they said; they naturally spoke the Language of Canaan; But they that kept the Fair, were the men of this World: So that from one end of the Fair to the other, they seemed Barbarians each to the other.

Thirdly, But that which did not a little amuse the Merchandizers, was, that these Pilgrims set very light by all their Wares, they cared not so much as to look upon them: and if they called upon them to buy, they would put their fingers in their ears, and cry, Turn away mine eyes from beholding vanity; and look upwards, signifying that their Trade and Traffick was in Heaven.

One chanced mockingly, beholding the carriages of the men, to say unto them, What will ye buy? but they, looking gravely upon him, said, We buy the Truth. At that, there was an occasion taken to despise the men the more; some mocking, some taunting, some speaking reproachfully, and some calling upon others to smite them. At last things came to an hubbub, and great stir in the Fair; insomuch that all order was confounded. Now was word presently brought to the great one of the Fair, who quickly came down, and deputed some of his most trusty friends to take these men into examination, about whom the fair was almost overturned. So the men were brought to examination; and they that sat upon them, asked them whence they came, whither they went, and what they did there in such an unusual Garb? The men told them, that they were Pilgrims and Strangers in the world, and that they were going to their own Country, which was the Heavenly Jerusalem; and that they had given no occasion to the men of the Town, nor yet to the Merchandizers, thus to abuse them, and to let them in their Journey. Except it was, for that, when one asked them what they would buy, they said, they would buy the Truth. But they that were appointed to examine them, did not believe them to be any other then Bedlams and Mad, or else such as came to put all things into a confusion in the Fair. Therefore they took them, and beat them, and besmeared them with dirt, and then put them into the Cage, that they might be made a Spectacle to all the men of the Fair. There therefore they lay for some time, and were made the objects of any mans sport, or malice, or revenge. The great one of the fair laughing still at all that befel them. But the men being patient, and not rendring railing for railing, but contrarywise blessing, and giving good words for bad, and kindness for injuries done: Some men in the fair that were more observing, and less prejudiced then the rest, began to check and blame the baser sort for their continual abuses done by them to the men: They therefore in angry manner let fly at them again, counting them as bad as the men in the Cage, and telling them that they seemed confederates, and should be made partakers of their misfortunes. The other replied, That for ought they could see, the men were quiet, and sober, and intended no body any harm; and that there were many that Traded in their Fair, that were more worthy to be put into the Cage, yea, and Pillory too, than were the men that they had abused. Thus, after divers words had passed on both sides, (the men behaving themselves all the while very wisely, and soberly before them) they fell to some blows, among themselves, and did harm one to another. Then were these two poor men brought before their Examiners again, and there charged as being guilty of the late Hubbub that had been in the Fair. So they beat them pitifully, and hanged Irons upon them, and led them in Chains up and down the Fair, for an example and terror to others, lest any should speak in their behalf, or joyn themselves unto them. But Christian and Faithful behaved themselves yet more wisely, and received the ignominy and shame that was cast upon them, with so much meekness and patience, that it won to their side (though but few in comparison of the rest) several of the men in the Fair. This put the other party yet into a greater rage, insomuch that they concluded the death of these two men. Wherefore they threatned that the Cage, nor Irons, should serve their turn, but that they should die, for the abuse they had done, and for deluding the men of the Fair.

Then were they re-manded to the Cage again, until further order should be taken with them. So they put them in, and made their feet fast in the Stocks.

Here also they called again to mind what they had heard from their faithful friend Evangelist, and was the more confirmed in their way and sufferings, by what he told them would happen to them. They also now comforted each other, that whose lot it was to suffer, even he should have the best on't; therefore each man secretly wished that he might have that preferment: but committing themselves to the All-wise dispose of him that rules all things, with much content they abode in the condition in which they were, until they should be otherwise disposed of.

Then a convenient time being appointed, they brought them forth to their Tryal in order to their Condemnation. When the time was come, they were brought before their Enemies and Arraigned; the Judges name was Lord Hategood. Their Indictment was one and the same in substance, though somewhat varying in form; the Contents whereof was this.

That they were enemies to, and disturbers of their Trade; that they had made Commotions and Divisions in the Town, and had won a party to their own most dangerous Opinions, in contempt of the Law of their Prince.

Then Faithful began to answer, That he had only set himself against that which had set it self against him that is higher then the highest. And, said he, As for disturbance, I make none, being my self a man of Peace; the Parties that were won to us, were won, by beholding our Truth and Innocence, and they are only turned from the worse to the better. And as to the King you talk of, since he is Beelzebub, the Enemy of our Lord, I defie him, and all his Angels.

Then Proclamation was made, that they that had ought to say for their Lord the King against the Prisoner at the Bar, should forthwith appear, and give in their evidence. So there came in three Witnesses, to wit, Envy, Superstition, and Pickthank. They was then asked, If they knew the Prisoner at the Bar? and what they had to say for their Lord the King against him.

Then stood forth Envy, and said to this effect; My Lord, I have known this man a long time, and will attest upon my Oath before this honourable Bench, That he is—

Judge. Hold, give him his Oath: So they swear him. Then he said, My Lord, this man, notwithstanding his plausible name, is one of the vilest men in our Countrey; he neither regardeth Prince nor People, Law nor Custom; but doth all that he can to possess all men with certain of his disloyal notions, which he in the general calls Principles of Faith and Holiness. And in particular, I heard him once my self affirm, That Christianity, and the Customs of our Town of Vanity, were Diametrically opposite, and could not be reconciled. By which saying, my Lord, he doth at once, not only condemn all our laudable doings, but us in the doing of them.

Judg. Then did the Judge say to him, Hast thou any more to say?

Envy. My Lord, I could say much more, only I would not be tedious to the Court. Yet if need be, when the other Gentlemen have given in their Evidence, rather then any thing shall be wanting that will dispatch him, I will enlarge my Testimony against him. So he was bid stand by. Then they called Superstition, and bid him look upon the Prisoner; they also asked, What he could say for their Lord the King against him? Then they sware him, so he began.

Super. My Lord, I have no great acquaintance with this man, nor do I desire to have further knowledge of him; However this I know, that he is a very pestilent fellow, from some discourse that the other day I had with him in this Town; for then talking with him, I heard him say, That our Religion was naught, and such by which a man could by no means please God: which sayings of his, my Lord, your Lordship very well knows, what necessarily thence will follow, to wit, That we still do worship in vain, are yet in our sins, and finally shall be damned; and this is that which I have to say.

Then was Pickthank sworn, and bid say what he knew, in behalf of their Lord the King against the Prisoner at the Bar.

Pick. My Lord, and you Gentlemen all, This fellow I have known of a long time, and have heard him speak things that ought not to be spoke. For he hath railed on our noble Prince Beelzebub, and hath spoke contemptibly of his honorable Friends, whose names are the Lord Old-man, the Lord Carnal-delight, the Lord Luxurious, the Lord Desire of Vain-glory, my old Lord Letchery, Sir Having Greedy, with all the rest of our Nobility; and he hath said moreover, that if all men were of his mind, if possible, there is not one of these Noble-men should have any longer a being in this Town; Besides, he hath not been afraid to rail on you, my Lord, who are now appointed to be his Judge, calling you an ungodly villain, with many other such like villifying terms, with which he hath bespattered most of the Gentry of our Town. When this Pickthank had told his tale, the Judge directed his speech to the Prisoner at the Bar, saying, Thou Runagate, Heretick, and Traitor, hast thou heard what these honest Gentlemen have witnessed against thee.

Faith. May I speak a few words in my own defence?

Judg. Sirrah, Sirrah, thou deservest to live no longer, but to be slain immediately upon the place; yet that all men may see our gentleness towards thee, let us hear what thou hast to say.

Faith. 1. I say then in answer to what Mr. Envy hath spoken, I never said ought but this, That what Rule, or Laws, or Custom, or People, were flat against the Word of God, are diametrically opposite to Christianity. If I have said amiss in this, convince me of my errour, and I am ready here before you to make my recantation.

2. As to the second, to wit, Mr. Superstition, and his charge against me, I said only this, That in the Worship of God there is

required a Divine Faith; but there can be no Divine Faith, without a Divine Revelation of the Will of God: therefore whatever is thrust into the worship of God, that is not agreeable to divine Revelation, cannot be done but by an humane Faith, which Faith will not be profit to Eternal Life.

3. As to what Mr. Pickthank hath said, I say, (avoiding terms, as that I am said to rail, and the like) That the Prince of this Town, with all the rablement his Attendants; by this Gentleman named, are more fit for a being in Hell, than in this Town and Country; and so the Lord have mercy upon me.

Then the Judge called to the Jury (who all this while stood by, to hear and observe;) Gentlemen of the Jury, you see this man about whom so great an uproar hath been made in this Town: you have also heard what these worthy Gentlemen have witnessed against him; also you have heard his reply and confession: It lieth now in your breasts to hang him, or save his life: but yet I think meet to instruct you into our Law.

There was an Act made in the days of Pharaoh the Great, Servant to our Prince, that, lest those of a contrary Religion should multiply and grow too strong for him, their Males should be thrown into the River. There was also an Act made in the days of Nebuchadnezzar the Great, another of his Servants, that whoever would not fall down and worship his Golden Image, should be thrown into a Fiery Furnace. There was also an Act made in the days of Darius, That who so, for some [time], called upon any God but him, should be cast into the Lions Den. Now the substance of these Laws this Rebel has broken, not only in thought, (which is not to be born) but also in word and deed; which must therefore needs be intolerable.

For that of Pharaoh, his Law was made upon a supposition, to prevent mischief, no Crime being yet apparent; but here is a Crime apparent. For the second and third, you see he disputeth against our Religion; and for the Treason he hath confessed, he deserveth to die the death.

Then went the Jury out, whose names were Mr. Blind-man, Mr. No-good, Mr. Malice, Mr. Love-lust, Mr. Live-loose, Mr. Heady, Mr. High-mind, Mr. Enmity, Mr. Lyar, Mr. Cruelty, Mr. Hate-light, and Mr. Implacable, who every one gave in his private Verdict against him among themselves, and afterwards unanimously concluded to bring him in guilty before the Judge. And first Mr. Blind-man, the Foreman, said, I see clearly that this man is an Heretick. Then said Mr. No-good, Away with such a fellow from the Earth. Ay, said Mr. Malice, for I hate the very looks of him. Then said Mr. Love-lust, I could never indure him. Nor I, said Mr. Live-loose, for he would always be condemning my way. Hang him, hang him, said Mr. Heady. A sorry Scrub, said Mr. High-mind. My heart riseth against him, said Mr. Enmity. He is a Rogue, said Mr. Lyar. Hanging is too good for him, said Mr. Cruelty; Let's dispatch him out of the way, said Mr. Hate-light. Then said Mr. Implacable, Might I have all the world given me, I could not be reconciled to him, therefore let us forthwith bring him in guilty of death. And so they did, therefore he was presently condemned, to be had from the place where he was, to the place from whence he came, and there to be put to the most cruel death that could be invented.

They therefore brought him out, to do with him according to their Law; and first they Scourged him, then they Buffeted him, then they Lanced his flesh with Knives; after that they Stoned him with Stones, then prickt him with their Swords, and last of all they burned him to Ashes at the Stake. Thus came Faithful to his end. Now, I saw that there stood behind the multitude a Chariot and a couple of Horses, waiting for Faithful, who (so soon as his Adversaries had dispatched him) was taken up into it, and straitway was carried up through the Clouds, with sound of Trumpet, the nearest way to the Cœlestial Gate. But as for Christian, he had some respite, and was re-manded back to prison; so he there remained for a space: But he that over-rules all things, having the power of their rage in his own hand, so wrought it about, that Christian for that time escaped them, and went his way.

Hymns and Gospel Songs

Am I a soldier of the cross,
A follower of the Lamb?
And shall I fear to own his cause,
Or blush to speak his name?

Must I be carried to the skies,
On flowery beds of ease;
While others fought to win the prize,
And sail'd thro' bloody seas?

Are there no foes for me to face?
Must I not stem the flood?
Is this vile world a friend to grace,
To help me on to God?

Sure I must fight, if I would reign;
Increase my courage, Lord!
I'll bear the toil, endure the pain,
Supported by thy word.

Thy saints, in all this glorious war,
Shall conquer tho' they die;
They see the triumph from afar,
And seize it with their eye.

When that illustrious day shall rise,
And all thy armies shine
In robes of victory thro' the skies,
The glory shall be thine.

—ISAAC WATTS

Come, thou fount of every blessing
Tune my heart to sing thy grace!
Streams of mercy never ceasing,
Call for songs of loudest praise;
Teach me some melodious sonnet,
Sung by flaming tongues above:
Praise the mount—O fix me on it,
Mount of God's unchanging love.

Here I raise my Ebenezer,
Hither by thy help I'm come:
And I hope, by thy good pleasure,
Safely to arrive at home:
Jesus sought me when a stranger,
Wandering from the fold of God;
He, to save my soul from danger,
Interpos'd his precious blood.

O! to grace how great a debtor
Daily I'm constrain'd to be!
Let that grace, Lord, like a fetter,
Bind my wandering heart to thee!
Prone to wander, Lord, I feel it;
Prone to leave the God I love—
Here's my heart, Lord, take and seal it,
Seal it from thy courts above.

—Robert Robinson

Amazing grace! (how sweet the sound,)
That sav'd a wretch like me!
I once was lost, but now am found,
Was blind, but now I see.

'Twas grace that taught my heart to fear,
And grace my fears reliev'd;
How precious did that grace appear
The hour I first believ'd!

Through many dangers, toils, and snares,
I have already come;
'Tis grace has brought me safe thus far,
And grace will lead me home.

The Lord has promis'd good to me,
His word my hope secures:
He will my shield and portion be,
As long as life endures.

Yes, when this flesh and heart shall fail,
And mortal life shall cease,
I shall possess, within the vail,
A life of joy and peace.

The earth shall soon dissolve like snow,
The sun forbear to shine;
But God, who call'd me here below,
Will be for ever mine.

—JOHN NEWTON

Glorious things of thee are spoken,
Zion, city of our God!
He, whose word cannot be broken,
Form'd thee for his own abode:
On the rock of ages founded,
What can shake thy sure repose;
With salvation's walls surrounded,
Thou mayst smile at all thy foes.

See the streams of living waters
Springing from eternal love,
Well supply thy sons and daughters,
And all fear of want remove:
Who can faint while such a river
Ever flows their thirst t'assuage?
Grace, which like the Lord, the giver,
Never fails from age to age.

Round each habitation hov'ring,
See the cloud and fire appear!
For a glory and a cov'ring,
Showing that the Lord is near;
Thus deriving from their banner
Light by night and shade by day;
Safe they feed upon the Manna
Which he gives them when they pray.

Blest inhabitants of Zion,
Wash'd in the Redeemer's blood!
Jesus, whom their souls rely on,
Makes them kings and priests to God:
'Tis his love his people raises
Over self to reign as kings,
And as priests, his solemn praises
Each for a thank-off'ring brings.

Saviour, if of Zion's city
I, through grace, a member am;
Let the world deride or pity,
I will glory in thy name:
Fading is the worldling's pleasure,
All his boasted pomp and show;
Solid joys and lasting treasure,
None but Zion's children know.

—John Newton

God moves in a mysterious way,
His wonders to perform;
He plants his footsteps in the sea,
And rides upon the storm.

Deep in unfathomable mines,
Of never failing skill;
He treasures up his bright designs,
And works his sov'reign will.

Ye fearful saints, fresh courage take,
The clouds ye so much dread

Are big with mercy, and shall break
In blessings on your head.

Judge not the Lord by feeble sense,
But trust him for his grace;
Behind a frowning providence,
He hides a smiling face.

His purposes will ripen fast,
Unfolding ev'ry hour;
The bud may have a bitter taste,
But sweet will be the flow'r.

Blind unbelief is sure to err,
And scan his work in vain;
God is his own interpreter,
And he will make it plain.

—WILLIAM COWPER

There is a fountain fill'd with blood
Drawn from Emmanuel's veins:
And sinners plung'd beneath that flood,
Lose all their guilty stains.

The dying thief rejoic'd to see
That fountain in his day;
And there have I, as vile as he,
Wash'd all my sins away.

Dear dying Lamb, thy precious blood
Shall never lose its pow'r;
Till all the ransom'd church of God
Be sav'd to sin no more.

E'er since, by faith, I saw the stream
Thy flowing wounds supply,
Redeeming Love has been my theme,
And shall be till I die.

Then in a nobler, sweeter song
I'll sing thy pow'r to save;
When this poor lisping stamm'ring tongue
Lies silent in the grave.

Lord, I believe thou hast prepar'd
(Unworthy though I be)
For me a blood-bought free reward,
A golden Harp for me!

'Tis strung, and tun'd, for endless years,
And form'd by pow'r divine;
To sound, in God the Father's ears,
No other name but thine.

—WILLIAM COWPER

Brethren, we have met to worship,
And adore the Lord our God;
Will you pray with all your power,
While we try to preach the word.
All is vain, unless the Spirit
Of the Holy One come down;
Brethren, pray, and holy manna
Will be shower'd all around.

Brethren, see poor sinners round you,
Trembling on the brink of wo;
Death is coming, hell is moving;
Can you bear to let them go?
See our fathers—see our mothers,
And our children sinking down;
Brethren, pray, and holy manna
Will be shower'd all around.

Sisters, will you join and help us?
Moses' sisters aided him;
Will you help the trembling mourners,
Who are struggling hard with sin?
Tell them all about the Saviour,

Tell them that he will be found;
Sisters, pray, and holy manna
Will be shower'd all around.

Is there here a trembling jailer,
Seeking grace, and fill'd with fears.
Is there here a weeping Mary,
Pouring forth a flood of tears?
Brethren, join your cries to help them;
Sisters, let your prayers abound;
Pray, O! pray, that holy manna
May be scatter'd all around.

Let us love our God supremely,
Let us love each other too;
Let us love and pray for sinners,
Till our God makes all things new.
Then he'll call us home to heaven,
At his table we'll sit down.
Christ will gird himself, and serve us
With sweet manna all around.

—GEORGE ATKINS

Pass me not, O gentle Saviour,
Hear my humble cry;
While on others Thou art smiling,
Do not pass me by.

Refrain:
Saviour, Saviour,
Hear my humble cry,
While on others Thou art calling,
Do not pass me by.

Let me at a throne of mercy
Find a sweet relief;
Kneeling there in deep contrition,
Help my unbelief.

Trusting only in Thy merit,
Would I seek Thy face;
Heal my wounded, broken spirit,
Save me by Thy Grace.

Thou the Spring of all my comfort
More than life to me,
Whom have I on earth beside Thee?
Whom in heav'n but Thee?

—FANNY CROSBY

Son of David! hear my cry;
Saviour, do not pass me by;
Touch these eyelids veiled in night,
Turn their darkness into light.
Son of David, hear my cry!
Saviour, do not pass me by.

Though the proud my voice would still,
They may chide me if they will,
Yet the more I'll pray for grace,
Only here shall be my place.
Son of David, hear my cry!
Saviour, do not pass me by.

Though despised by all but thee,
Thou a blessing hast for me:
Faith and prayer can never fail,
Lord, with thee I *must* prevail.
Son of David, hear my cry!
Saviour, do not pass me by.

Glorious vision! heavenly ray!
All my gloom has passed away;
Now my joyful eye doth see,
And my soul still clings to thee.
Thine the glory evermore,
Mine to worship and adore.

—FANNY CROSBY

General William Booth Enters into Heaven
(To be sung to the tune of *The Blood of the Lamb* with indicated instrument)

VACHEL LINDSAY

I.

(*Bass drum beaten loudly.*)
Booth led boldly with his big bass drum—
(Are you washed in the blood of the Lamb?)
The Saints smiled gravely and they said: "He's come."
(Are you washed in the blood of the Lamb?)
Walking lepers followed, rank on rank,
Lurching bravoes from the ditches dank,
Drabs from the alleyways and drug fiends pale—
Minds still passion-ridden, soul-powers frail:—
Vermin-eaten saints with mouldy breath,
Unwashed legions with the ways of Death—
(Are you washed in the blood of the Lamb?)

(*Banjos.*)
Every slum had sent its half-a-score
The round world over. (Booth had groaned for more.)
Every banner that the wide world flies
Bloomed with glory and transcendent dyes.
Big-voiced lasses made their banjos bang,
Tranced, fanatical they shrieked and sang:—
"Are you washed in the blood of the Lamb?"
Hallelujah! It was queer to see
Bull-necked convicts with that land make free.
Loons with trumpets blowed a blare, blare, blare
On, on upward thro' the golden air!
(Are you washed in the blood of the Lamb?)

II.

(Bass drum slower and softer.)
Booth died blind and still by Faith he trod,
Eyes still dazzled by the ways of God.
Booth led boldly, and he looked the chief
Eagle countenance in sharp relief,
Beard a-flying, air of high command
Unabated in that holy land.

(Sweet flute music.)
Jesus came from out the court-house door,
Stretched his hands above the passing poor.
Booth saw not, but led his queer ones there
Round and round the mighty court-house square.
Yet in an instant all that blear review
Marched on spotless, clad in raiment new.
The lame were straightened, withered limbs uncurled
And blind eyes opened on a new, sweet world.

(Bass drum louder.)
Drabs and vixens in a flash made whole!
Gone was the weasel-head, the snout, the jowl!
Sages and sibyls now, and athletes clean,
Rulers of empires and of forests green!

*(Grand chorus of all instruments. Tambourines to the
    foreground.)*
The hosts were sandalled, and their wings were fire!
(Are you washed in the blood of the Lamb?)
But their noise played havoc with the angel-choir.
(Are you washed in the blood of the Lamb?)
O, shout Salvation! It was good to see
Kings and Princes by the Lamb set free.
The banjos rattled and the tambourines
Jing-jing-jingled in the hands of Queens.

(Reverently sung, no instruments.)
And when Booth halted by the curb for prayer
He saw his Master thro' the flag-filled air.

Christ came gently with a robe and crown
For Booth the soldier, while the throng knelt down.
He saw King Jesus. They were face to face,
And he knelt a-weeping in that holy place.
Are you washed in the blood of the Lamb?

The Gardener

RUDYARD KIPLING

Every one in the village knew that Helen Turrell did her duty by all her world, and by none more honourably than by her only brother's unfortunate child. The village knew, too, that George Turrell had tried his family severely since early youth, and were not surprised to be told that, after many fresh starts given and thrown away, he, an Inspector of Indian Police, had entangled himself with the daughter of a retired non-commissioned officer, and had died of a fall from a horse a few weeks before his child was born. Mercifully, George's father and mother were both dead, and though Helen, thirty-five and independent, might well have washed her hands of the whole disgraceful affair, she most nobly took charge, though she was, at the time, under threat of lung trouble which had driven her to the South of France. She arranged for the passage of the child and a nurse from Bombay, met them at Marseilles, nursed the baby through an attack of infantile dysentery due to the carelessness of the nurse, whom she had had to dismiss, and at last, thin and worn but triumphant, brought the boy late in the autumn, wholly restored, to her Hampshire home.

All these details were public property, for Helen was as open as the day, and held that scandals are only increased by hushing them up. She admitted that George had always been rather a black sheep, but things might have been much worse if the mother had insisted on her right to keep the boy. Luckily, it seemed that people of that class would do almost anything for money, and, as George had always turned to her in his scrapes, she felt herself justified—her friends agreed with her—in cutting the whole non-commissioned officer connection, and giving the child every advantage. A christening, by the Rector, under the name of Michael, was the first step. So far as she knew herself, she was not, she said, a child-lover, but, for all his faults, she had been very fond of George, and she pointed out that little Michael had his father's mouth to a line; which made something to build upon.

As a matter of fact, it was the Turrell forehead, broad, low, and well-shaped, with the widely spaced eyes beneath it, that Michael had most faithfully reproduced. His mouth was somewhat better cut than the family type. But Helen, who would concede nothing good to his mother's side, vowed he was a Turrell all over, and, there being no one to contradict, the likeness was established.

In a few years Michael took his place, as accepted as Helen had always been—fearless, philosophical, and fairly good-looking. At six, he wished to know why he could not call her "Mummy," as other boys called their mothers. She explained that she was only his auntie, and that aunties were not quite the same as mummies, but that, if it gave him pleasure, he might call her "Mummy" at bedtime, for a pet-name between themselves.

Michael kept his secret most loyally, but Helen, as usual, explained the fact to her friends; which when Michael heard, he raged.

"Why did you tell? *Why* did you tell?" came at the end of the storm.

"Because it's always best to tell the truth," Helen answered, her arm round him as he shook in his cot.

"All right, but when the troof's ugly I don't think it's nice."

"Don't you, dear?"

"No, I don't, and"—she felt the small body stiffen—"now you've told, I won't call you 'Mummy' any more—not even at bedtimes."

"But isn't that rather unkind?" said Helen, softly.

"I don't care! I don't care! You've hurted me in my insides and I'll hurt you back. I'll hurt you as long as I live!"

"Don't, oh, don't talk like that, dear! You don't know what—"

"I will! And when I'm dead I'll hurt you worse!"

"Thank goodness, I shall be dead long before you, darling."

"Huh! Emma says, ''Never know your luck.'" (Michael had been talking to Helen's elderly, flatfaced maid.) "Lots of little boys die quite soon. So'll I. *Then* you'll see!"

Helen caught her breath and moved towards the door, but the wail of "Mummy! Mummy!" drew her back again, and the two wept together.

At ten years old, after two terms at a prep. school, something or somebody gave him the idea that his civil status was not quite regular. He attacked Helen on the subject, breaking down her stammered defences with the family directness.

" 'Don't believe a word of it," he said, cheerily, at the end. "People wouldn't have talked like they did if my people had been married. But don't you bother, Auntie. I've found out all about my sort in English Hist'ry and the Shakespeare bits. There was William the Conqueror to begin with, and—oh, heaps more, and they all got on first-rate. 'Twon't make any difference to you, my being *that*—will it?"

"As if anything could—" she began.

"All right. We won't talk about it any more if it makes you cry." He never mentioned the thing again of his own will, but when, two years later, he skilfully managed to have measles in the holidays, as his temperature went up to the appointed one hundred and four he muttered of nothing else, till Helen's voice, piercing at last his delirium, reached him with assurance that nothing on earth or beyond could make any difference between them.

The terms at his public school and the wonderful Christmas, Easter and Summer holidays followed each other, variegated and glorious as jewels on a string; and as jewels Helen treasured them. In due time Michael developed his own interests, which ran their courses and gave way to others; but his interest in Helen was constant and increasing throughout. She repaid it with all that she had of affection or could command of counsel and money; and since Michael was no fool, the War took him just before what was like to have been a most promising career.

He was to have gone up to Oxford, with a scholarship, in October. At the end of August he was on the edge of joining the first holocaust of public-school boys who threw themselves into the Line; but the captain of his O.T.C., where he had been sergeant for nearly a year, headed him off and steered him directly to a commission in a battalion so new that half of it still wore the old Army red, and the other half was breeding meningitis through living overcrowdedly in damp tents. Helen had been shocked at the idea of direct enlistment.

"But it's in the family," Michael laughed.

"You don't mean to tell me that you believed that old story all this time?" said Helen. (Emma, her maid, had been dead now several years.) "I gave you my word of honour—and I give it again—that—that it's all right. It is indeed."

"Oh, *that* doesn't worry me. It never did," he replied valiantly. "What I meant was, I should have got into the show earlier if I'd enlisted—like my grandfather."

"Don't talk like that! Are you afraid of its ending so soon, then?"

"No such luck. You know what K. says."

"Yes. But my banker told me last Monday it couldn't *possibly* last beyond Christmas—for financial reasons."

"Hope he's right, but our Colonel—and he's a Regular—says it's going to be a long job."

Michael's battalion was fortunate in that, by some chance which meant several "leaves," it was used for coast-defence among shallow trenches on the Norfolk coast; thence sent north to watch the mouth of a Scotch estuary, and, lastly, held for weeks on a baseless rumour of distant service. But, the very day that Michael was to have met Helen for four whole hours at a railway-junction up the line, it was hurled out, to help make good the wastage of Loos, and he had only just time to send her a wire of farewell.

In France luck again helped the battalion. It was put down near the Salient, where it led a meritorious and unexacting life, while the Somme was being manufactured; and enjoyed the peace of the Armentières and Laventie sectors when that battle began. Finding that it had sound views on protecting its own flanks and could dig, a prudent Commander stole it out of its own Division, under pretence of helping to lay telegraphs, and used it round Ypres at large.

A month later, and just after Michael had written Helen that there was nothing special doing and therefore no need to worry, a shell-splinter dropping out of a wet dawn killed him at once. The next shell uprooted and laid down over the body what had been the foundation of a barn wall, so neatly that none but an expert would have guessed that anything unpleasant had happened.

By this time the village was old in experience of war, and, English fashion, had evolved a ritual to meet it. When the postmistress handed her seven-year-old daughter the official telegram to take to Miss Turrell, she observed to the Rector's gardener: "It's Miss Helen's turn now." He replied, thinking of his own son: "Well, he's lasted longer than some." The child herself came to the front-door weeping aloud, because Master Michael had often given her sweets. Helen, presently, found herself pulling down the house-blinds one after one with great care, and saying earnestly to each: "Missing *always* means dead." Then she took her place in the dreary procession that was impelled to go through an inevitable series of unprofitable emotions. The Rector, of course, preached hope and prophesied word, very soon, from a prison camp. Several friends, too, told her perfectly truthful tales, but always about other women, to whom, after months and months of silence, their missing had been miraculously restored. Other people urged her to communicate with infallible Secretaries of organisations who could communicate with benevolent neutrals, who could extract accurate information from the most secretive of Hun prison commandants. Helen did and wrote and signed everything that was suggested or put before her.

Once, on one of Michael's leaves, he had taken her over a munition factory, where she saw the progress of a shell from blank-iron to the all but finished article. It struck her at the time that the wretched thing was never left alone for a single second; and "I'm being manufactured into a bereaved next-of-kin," she told herself, as she prepared her documents.

In due course, when all the organisations had deeply or sincerely regretted their inability to trace, etc., something gave way within her and all sensation—save of thankfulness for the release—came to an end in blessed passivity. Michael had died and her world had stood still and she had been one with the full shock of that arrest. Now she was standing still and the world was going forward, but it did not concern her—in no way or relation did it touch her. She knew this by the ease with which she could slip Michael's name into talk and incline her head to the proper angle, at the proper murmur of sympathy.

In the blessed realisation of that relief, the Armistice with all its bells broke over her and passed unheeded. At the end of another year she had overcome her physical loathing of the living and returned young, so that she could take them by the hand and almost sincerely wish them well. She had no interest in any aftermath, national or personal, of the War, but, moving at an immense distance, she sat on various relief committees and held strong views—she heard herself delivering them—about the site of the proposed village War Memorial.

Then there came to her, as next-of-kin, an official intimation, backed by a page of a letter to her in indelible pencil, a silver identity-disc, and a watch, to the effect that the body of Lieutenant Michael Turrell had been found, identified, and re-interred in Hagenzeele Third Military Cemetery—the letter of the row and the grave's number in that row duly given.

So Helen found herself moved on to another process of the manufacture—to a world full of exultant or broken relatives, now strong in the certainty that there was an altar upon earth where they might lay their love. These soon told her, and by means of time-tables made clear, how easy it was and how little it interfered with life's affairs to go and see one's grave.

"*So* different," as the Rector's wife said, "if he'd been killed in Mesopotamia, or even Gallipoli."

The agony of being waked up to some sort of second life drove Helen across the Channel, where, in a new world of abbreviated titles, she learnt that Hagenzeele Third could be comfortably reached by an afternoon train which fitted in with the morning boat, and that there was a comfortable little hotel not three kilometres from Hagenzeele itself, where one could spend quite a comfortable night and see one's grave next morning. All this she had from a Central Authority who lived in a board and tar-paper shed on the skirts of a razed city full of whirling lime-dust and blown papers.

"By the way," said he, "you know your grave, of course?"

"Yes, thank you," said Helen, and showed its row and number typed on Michael's own little typewriter. The officer would have checked it out of one of his many books; but a large Lancashire woman thrust between them and bade him tell her where she might find her son, who had been corporal in the A.S.C. His proper name, she sobbed, was Anderson, but, coming of respectable folk, he had of course enlisted under the name of Smith; and had been killed at Dickiebush, in early 'Fifteen. She had not his number nor did she know which of his two Christian names he might have used with his alias; but her Cook's tourist ticket expired at the end of Easter week, and if by then she could not find her child she should go mad. Whereupon she fell forward on Helen's breast; but the officer's wife came out quickly from a little bedroom behind the office, and the three of them lifted the woman on to the cot.

"They are often like this," said the officer's wife, loosening the tight bonnet-strings. "Yesterday she said he'd been killed at Hooge. Are you sure you know your grave? It makes such a difference."

"Yes, thank you," said Helen, and hurried out before the woman on the bed should begin to lament again.

Tea in a crowded mauve and blue striped wooden structure, with a false front, carried her still further into the nightmare. She paid her bill beside a stolid, plain-featured Englishwoman, who, hearing her inquire about the train to Hagenzeele, volunteered to come with her.

"I'm going to Hagenzeele myself," she explained. "Not to Hagenzeele Third; mine is Sugar Factory, but they call it La Rosière now. It's just south of Hagenzeele Three. Have you got your room at the hotel there?"

"Oh yes, thank you. I've wired."

"That's better. Sometimes the place is quite full, and at others there's hardly a soul. But they've put bathrooms into the old Lion d'Or—that's the hotel on the west side of Sugar Factory—and it draws off a lot of people, luckily."

"It's all new to me. This is the first time I've been over."

"Indeed! This is my ninth time since the Armistice. Not on my own account. *I* haven't lost anyone, thank God—but, like everyone else, I've a lot of friends at home who have. Coming over as often as I do, I find it helps them to have some one just look at the—the place and tell them about it afterwards. And one can take photos for them, too. I get quite a list of commissions to execute." She laughed nervously and tapped her slung Kodak. "There are two or three to see at Sugar Factory this time, and plenty of others in the cemeteries all about. My system is to save them up, and arrange them, you know. And when I've got enough commissions for one area to make it worth while, I pop over and execute them. It *does* comfort people."

"I suppose so," Helen answered, shivering as they entered the little train.

"Of course it does. (Isn't it lucky we've got window-seats?) It must do or they wouldn't ask one to do it, would they? I've a list of quite twelve or fifteen commissions here"—she tapped the Kodak again—"I must sort them out to-night. Oh, I forgot to ask you. What's yours?"

"My nephew," said Helen. "But I was very fond of him."

"Ah yes! I sometimes wonder whether *they* know after death? What do you think?"

"Oh, I don't—I haven't dared to think much about that sort of thing," said Helen, almost lifting her hands to keep her off.

"Perhaps that's better," the woman answered. "The sense of loss must be enough, I expect. Well, I won't worry you any more."

Helen was grateful, but when they reached the hotel Mrs. Scarsworth (they had exchanged names) insisted on dining at the same table with her, and after the meal, in the little, hideous salon full of low-voiced relatives, took Helen through her "commissions" with biographies of the. dead, where she happened to know them, and sketches of their next-of-kin. Helen endured till nearly half-past nine, ere she fled to her room.

Almost at once there was a knock at her door and Mrs. Scarsworth entered; her hands, holding the dreadful list, clasped before her.

"Yes—yes—*I* know," she began. "You're sick of me, but I want to tell you something. You—you aren't married are you? Then perhaps you won't. . . . But it doesn't matter. I've *got* to tell some one. I can't go on any longer like this."

"But please—" Mrs. Scarsworth had backed against the shut door, and her mouth worked dryly.

"In a minute," she said. "You—you know about these graves of mine I was telling you about downstairs, just now? They really *are* commissions. At least several of them are." Her eye wandered round the room. "What extraordinary wall-papers they have in Belgium, don't you think? . . . Yes. I swear they are commissions. But there's *one,* d'you see, and—and he was more to me than anything else in the world. Do you understand?"

Helen nodded.

"More than any one else. And, of course, he oughtn't to have been. He ought to have been nothing to me. But he *was*. He *is*. That's why I do the commissions, you see. That's all."

"But why do you tell me?" Helen asked desperately.

"Because I'm *so* tired of lying. Tired of lying—always lying—year in and year out. When I don't tell lies I've got to act 'em and I've got to think 'em, always. *You* don't know what that means. He was everything to me that he oughtn't to have been—the one real thing—the only thing that ever happened to

me in all my life; and I've had to pretend he wasn't. I've had to
watch every word I said, and think out what lie I'd tell next, for
years and years!"

"How many years?" Helen asked.

"Six years and four months before, and two and three-quar-
ters after. I've gone to him eight times, since. To-morrow'll make
the ninth, and—and I can't—I *can't* go to him again with nobody
in the world knowing. I want to be honest with some one before
I go. Do you understand? It doesn't matter about *me*. I was never
truthful, even as a girl. But it isn't worthy of *him*. So—so I—I had
to tell you. I can't keep it up any longer. Oh, I can't!"

She lifted her joined hands almost to the level of her mouth,
and brought them down sharply, still joined, to full arm's length
below her waist. Helen reached forward, caught them, bowed
her head over them, and murmured: "Oh, my dear! My dear!"
Mrs. Scarsworth stepped back, her face all mottled.

"My God!" said she. "Is *that* how you take it?"

Helen could not speak, the woman went out; but it was a
long while before Helen was able to sleep.

Next morning Mrs. Scarsworth left early on her round of commissions, and Helen walked alone to Hagenzeele Third. The
place was still in the making, and stood some five or six feet
above the metalled road, which it flanked for hundreds of yards.
Culverts across a deep ditch served for entrances through the
unfinished boundary wall. She climbed a few wooden-faced
earthen steps and then met the entire crowded level of the thing
in one held breath. She did not know that Hagenzeele Third
counted twenty-one thousand dead already. All she saw was a
merciless sea of black crosses, bearing little strips of stamped tin
at all angles across their faces. She could distinguish no order or
arrangement in their mass; nothing but a waist-high wilderness
as of weeds stricken dead, rushing at her. She went forward,
moved to the left and the right hopelessly, wondering by what
guidance she should ever come to her own. A great distance
away there was a line of whiteness. It proved to be a block of
some two or three hundred graves whose headstones had
already been set, whose flowers were planted out, and whose
new-sown grass showed green. Here she could see clear-cut letters at the ends of the rows, and, referring to her slip, realised
that it was not here she must look.

A man knelt behind a line of headstones—evidently a gardener, for he was firming a young plant in the soft earth. She went towards him, her paper in her hand. He rose at her approach and without prelude or salutation asked: "Who are you looking for?"

"Lieutenant Michael Turrell—my nephew," said Helen slowly and word for word, as she had many thousands of times in her life.

The man lifted his eyes and looked at her with infinite compassion before he turned from the fresh-sown grass towards the naked black crosses.

"Come with me," he said, "and I will show you where your son lies."

When Helen left the Cemetery she turned for a last look. In the distance she saw the man bending over his young plants; and she went away, supposing him to be the gardener.

Notes

1 "The Most Difficult Book in the World"?

1. Samuel Johnson, quoted in James Boswell, *Life of Johnson*, ed. George Birkbeck Hill, rev. by L.F. Powell (Oxford: Clarendon, 1934), 3:298.

2. Some Christian communities accept more books as part of the Old Testament.

3. It is not, to be sure, a new perspective on the history, sociology, or anthropology of the New Testament, but simply on its literary patterns. As a New Testament scholar has observed, "The NT is not usually treated literarily and thus descriptively, but rather historically and reconstructively. In other words, the documents are mined for information about the evolution of Christian beliefs"—Eugene E. Lemcio, *The Past of Jesus in the Gospels* (Cambridge: Cambridge University Press, 1991), p. 117. Literary patterns, however, are an objective, not a "reconstructive" issue. The question about them is merely: Do they exist or not, in the text before us? Yet that is the question on which most of the other debates are ultimately grounded, because the evidence of the New Testament text is the major evidence for Christian history in its earliest stages.

4. Augustine, *Confessions*, 8.29.

5. Genre is a special field of study for literary theorists and historians, and the debates that go on in that field are of very considerable interest; yet I am not trying to enter them here. As I indicate below, some of the New Testament books fit uneasily within the "genres" I have mentioned, and there are countless subsidiary "genres," even within the gospels: sermon, parable, dialogue, prayer, and so forth. A substantial account of genre would also reckon with the comparisons that can be made between New Testament writing and such extra-bib-

lical genres as biography, drama, and diatribe. Here, however, I merely wish to indicate the most basic possible classification of New Testament books into what Lemcio (118) and others call "canonical units." I do think it significant that those in the early church who arranged the New Testament books and gave them their headings or titles clearly thought of them as gospels, epistles, Acts, and Revelation (for a detailed treatment of this topic, see David Trobisch, *The First Edition of the New Testament* [New York: Oxford University Press, 2000]).

6. Some ancient authorities believed that the gospel of Matthew was originally written in "Hebrew," that is, Aramaic, the everyday language of Israel in Jesus's day. If so, the Aramaic text has not survived.

7. The major candidate is the second epistle of Peter.

8. J.A.T. Robinson, the most prominent "early dater" of the New Testament books, covers this ground thoroughly; see his *Redating the New Testament* (London: S.C.M. Press, 1976). Most scholars believe that Jesus's prophecies in Matthew 24, Mark 13, and Luke 21 refer to the catastrophe of A.D. 70, whether they accept them as true prophecies or suggest that they were composed in such a way as to suggest an event that had already taken place when the gospels were written. Yet nothing is said, there or elsewhere in the New Testament, to confirm that the event has taken place; and even New Testament books, such as the gospel of John, that emphasize differences between Jesus's followers and more traditional Jews are silent about the devastation of the Jewish religious capital.

9. Papias's comments are preserved in Eusebius's early-fourth-century *Ecclesiastical History*, 3.39.

10. D. Moody Smith, "When Did the Gospels Become Scripture?", *Journal of Biblical Literature* 119.1 (2000), pp. 3–20, presents a stimulating reassessment of the common critical assumption that the gospels are "documents generated in specific times and places to address issues of such times and places" rather than attempts to write generally and authoritatively to the church or the world at large. He calls attention to Luke 1:1–3 and the last chapter of John as witnesses to gospel intentions. For a clear (and unskeptical) statement of the opposing view, asserting the parochial origin, interests, and first authority of the gospels, see Harry Y. Gamble, Jr., "Christianity: Scripture and Canon," *The Holy Book in Comparative Perspective*, ed. Frederick M. Denny and Rodney L. Taylor (Columbia: University of South Carolina Press, 1985), pp. 36–62, especially pp. 41–42.

11. This is one of the problems addressed by Donald Guthrie, reviewing the nature and difficulties of modern "form criticism," particularly that of the very influential Rudolf Bultmann (1884–1976): Guthrie, *New Testament Introduction*, 4th ed. (Leicester, England: Apollos, 1990), pp. 209–247; see especially 222–23.

12. Like Lemcio, pp. 1–29, I find it ironic that some scholars who are skeptical about the gospels' ability to reveal the historical Jesus are confident about the gospels' ability to reveal the conflicts of the first-century church. On each question, the evidence is drawn from the same texts.

13. I follow Joseph B. Tyson and Thomas R.W. Longstaff, *Synoptic Abstract* (Wooster: Biblical Research Associates, 1978) and Tyson, *The New Testament and Early Christianity* (New York: Macmillan, 1984), pp. 150–57. About one-sixth of the total number of pericopes (which is 586, by Tyson's count, including repetitions from gospel to gospel) are not rigorously classifiable because they "have partial or overlapping parallels" (*New Testament*, p. 151). Figure 2 relies on Tyson's total of 501 pericopes that can be distinctly assigned to various gospels. As Tyson warns, "pericopes are of unequal length, and sometimes they vary considerably in wording" (*New Testament*, p. 151). For this reason, although Luke shares about seventy percent of Mark's pericopes, most scholars prefer to say that he has taken "more than half" of Mark's material.

14. I quote an author otherwise famous for his religious skepticism, "modernism," and "liberalism"—J.A.T. Robinson, *Can We Trust the New Testament?* (Grand Rapids: Eerdmans, 1977), p. 54.

15. A second-century Christian named Tatian constructed a clever "harmony" of the four gospels that filled some people's desire for just one narrative. In the long run, however, Christians preferred the originals. For an account of the many, mostly small, editorial changes that did occur in certain manuscript families of the New Testament, see Frederic G. Kenyon, *The Text of the Greek Bible*, rev. ed. (London: Duckworth, 1949).

16. Unfortunately, that is what frequently happens when scholars talk about gospel origins as if they were the sole "literary" topics to be addressed—a point made by Lemcio, p. 107, and Norman R. Petersen, *Literary Criticism for New Testament Critics* (Philadelphia: Fortress, 1978), p. 10. The question is often asked by people not directly involved in biblical studies, Why is so little literary criticism, of the familiar sort, available about the New Testament? One reason for this is modern intellectual skepticism about Christianity and an associated lack of interest in assessing its literary contributions. Another reason is the special character of the New Testament literature. Thus Petersen (pp. 10–11, 18), who is surprised by the identification of "origins" scholarship with "literary criticism," nevertheless claims that "historical critics have rightly concluded that biblical writings are not literary because they do not conform to ancient canons of literature." (He says this even while applying his own literary criticism to the supposedly nonliterary documents.) Still another reason

can be found in the ability of some prominent methods of New Testament study to reduce the text, especially that of the gospels, to the status of something less than literature. The text may be reduced to its innumerable reputed sources in documents or sayings; or to stories thought to have been invented by first-century communities of believers, expressing their views of Jesus and his teaching; or to the editorial methods of "redactors" (writers and editors) expressing their own theology, generally in opposition to that of others—the three tendencies often characteristic, respectively, of "source criticism," "form criticism," and "redaction criticism." Finally, New Testament criticism is ordinarily conducted in institutional settings that reward either investigation of the text's historical contexts or investigation and teaching of its religious implications. The middle ground, the ground of the text and its overt literary patterns, often lacks professional encouragement.

17. For a clear summary of the reasons for and against Pauline authorship of 1 and 2 Timothy and Titus, see Luke Timothy Johnson, *The Writings of the New Testament: An Interpretation*, revised edition (Minneapolis: Fortress, 1999), pp. 423–431. Johnson is largely favorable to Paul. See also his account (pp. 393–95, 407–412) of questions arising about Paul's epistles to the Ephesians and Colossians, two other works whose authorship has been challenged, though on insufficient grounds, as Johnson indicates.

18. Dorothy Sayers, "A Vote of Thanks to Cyrus," *Christian Letters to a Post-Christian World: A Selection of Essays* (Grand Rapids: Eerdmans, 1969), p. 53.

19. On the effects and implications of this idea, see *The New Testament as Canon: A Reader in Canonical Criticism*, ed. Robert W. Wall and Eugene E. Lemcio (Sheffield: Sheffield Academic Press, 1992).

20. Samuel John Stone, "The Church's One Foundation," *Poems and Hymns* (London: Methuen, 1903), pp. 28, 239–240. I reproduce the poem, first published in 1866, as it appeared in revised form in 1868, with the restoration of stanza 3, omitted from the revision.

21. Trobisch, *First Edition*. "Edition" need not imply that the internal features of New Testament books were "edited" in the sense of "revised"; a better word might be "prepared for publication." On canon formation generally, see the elegant essay by F.F. Bruce, "Tradition and the Canon of Scripture," *The Authoritative Word: Essays on the Nature of Scripture*, ed. Donald K. McKim (Grand Rapids: Eerdmans, 1983), pp. 59–84. An exceptionally clear and comprehensive account of the subject is offered by Bruce M. Metzger, *The Canon of the New Testament: Its Origin, Development, and Significance* (Oxford: Clarendon, 1997). The most difficult books to "canonize" were Hebrews, James, 2 John, 3 John, Jude, and Revelation; for a variety of

reasons, varying from book to book, they seemed sufficiently unlike other New Testament books to cause some Christians of the third and fourth (and even sixteenth) centuries to question them. Authors who provide late dates for the settlement of the canon ordinarily have this in mind. The six books were impossible to exclude, however, because they were too well rooted in the church's history of reception and too well connected to the ideas and literary methods of the universally accepted books.

22. The importance of broadly literary criteria in canon formation appears in Eusebius, 3.25, and in the late-second-century work of Irenaeus, *Against Heresies*, 1.8.

23. Some recent authors have presented much more favorable views of the Gospel of Thomas and other "apocryphal" books. For many readers, the most attractive introduction to these views is that of Elaine Pagels in *Beyond Belief: The Secret Gospel of Thomas* (New York: Vintage, 2003). Pagels suggests that (1) because the gospel of Thomas (allegedly) differs from the gospel of John about the special character of Jesus's divinity, John was written in opposition to Thomas; that (2) the teachings of the gospel of Thomas were "venerated by 'Thomas Christians,' apparently an early group . . . like those devoted to Luke, Matthew, and John"; and that (3) Christianity would be very different if Thomas had been incorporated into the New Testament, as it might well have been (see especially pp. 38–39, 57–58). But (1), besides being a non sequitur, ignores the lack of any external evidence for an early date for Thomas, which is not named by any source or presented in any manuscript fragments before the start of the third century; (2) the idea that each gospel was appropriated by a distinct group is merely a speculative deduction from the existence of each gospel; and (3) the sayings unique to Thomas, some beautiful and profound, some vague and confused, are general enough to be adapted to virtually any set of doctrines. Pagels's discussion lacks serious attention to the difference in literary character between canonical and apocryphal books, which habitually add grossly fanciful or polemical material to New Testament stories, or use New Testament incidents or ideas as gateways to abstract speculation—a tendency that flourished during the formative period of the canon (as shown by Irenaeus, e.g. 2.20–27) but did not flourish in the canonized works.

24. Elisha Hoffman, "Are You Washed in the Blood?" (1878), *Tabernacle Hymns No. 2* (Chicago: Tabernacle, 1921), no. 121.

25. Isabel Paterson, *New York Herald Tribune "Books,"* (January 10, 1937), 14.

26. In quoting from the KJV, I do not consider myself bound by the typographical conventions of its current printings, or by the practice of printing every verse as a separate paragraph.

2 The DNA of the New Testament

1. Leopold Damrosch, Jr., *Symbol and Truth in Blake's Myth* (Princeton: Princeton University Press, 1980), 8. On the history of studies of the Bible as literature, and on some of the difficulties involved, see David Norton, *A History of the Bible as Literature*, 2 vols. (Cambridge: Cambridge University Press, 1993).

2. I believe this contention is roughly similar to that of the biblical scholar Robert Alter, who emphasizes the ability of literary forms or methods to embody religious ideas. Writing of the Hebrew Scriptures, Alter suggests that "it is important to move from the analysis of formal structures to a deeper understanding of the values, the moral vision embodied in a particular kind of narrative." Alter also maintains (correctly, in my view) that the New Testament was written, "by and large, according to different literary assumptions" from those of the Hebrew Scriptures (*The Art of Biblical Narrative* [New York: Basic Books, 1981], pp. ix, x). This does not mean, of course, that the New Testament has no intellectual or literary debt to the Old. It simply means that they are different kinds of literary works, using different patterns of ideas and methods.

3. "Methods" or "devices"? Either word might be appropriate here. In a work of literary theory, much could properly be made of differences among "methods," "devices," "strategies," "tactics," and other ways of working with words; but in literary practice, these modes of verbal action tend to shade into one another, depending, for example, on their use on either a small or a large scale. In this book, the use of just one such term would represent a false precision, and the continual listing of several—"methods, devices, and strategies or tactics"— would be tedious. The remaining option is to alternate among a diversity of closely related terms, and that is what I do.

4. As Robert Louis Wilken has said, "The Christian gospel was not an idea but a certain kind of story, a narrative about a person and things that had actually happened in space and time" (*The Spirit of Early Christian Thought: Seeking the Face of God* [New Haven: Yale University Press, 2003], p. 15). On the idea of Christianity as "historical," and some of its applications, see Stephen Cox, "Theory, Experience and 'The American Religion'," *Journal of the Evangelical Theological Society* 36 (1993), pp. 363–373.

5. Flannery O'Connor, "The Church and the Fiction Writer" (1957), *Collected Works* (New York: Library of America, 1988), p. 810.

6. Robert Browning, *Bishop Blougram's Apology, Poems of Robert Browning*, ed. Donald Smalley (Boston: Houghton Mifflin, 1956), lines 197–202. For further discussion of this poem, see Chapter 15, below.

7. Wilken, p. 106.

8. See Chapter 5, below.

9. Augustine, *Confessions,* 8.29.

10. Another possible translation is "reflecting as a glass . . ." The element that remains the same is the idea of progress that happens by means of a likeness or image (εἰκών, "eikon").

11. John Milton, *Paradise Lost* (New York: Norton, 1993), p. 299 (Book 12, lines 583–87).

12. Martin Luther King, Jr., "Our God Is Able," *Strength to Love* (New York: Harper and Row, 1963), p. 102.

13. C.S. Lewis, *The Screwtape Letters* (San Francisco: HarperCollins, 2001), p. 65.

14. Examples will emerge later in this book, especially in Chapter 10. For a particularly interesting example, see Wilken, pp. 110–135, on the way in which even a great theologian and a pope were martyred for taking an individual stand against a Christian emperor. Berndt Moeller, "Scripture, Tradition and Sacrament in the Middle Ages and in Luther," *Holy Book and Holy Tradition,* ed. F.F. Bruce and E.G. Rupp (Manchester: Manchester University Press, 1968), pp. 113–135, shows how appreciation for Christianity as a historical religion diminished and then returned, in the later Middle Ages, with the return to a "literal" reading of the Bible. Such a reading revived older concepts of Christian history as a sequence of unique events and, with those concepts, the Christian emphasis on the history of the individual as one "stand[ing] before God" (p. 129).

15. The quoted phrase and general concept are derived from Robert W. Wall, "The Acts of the Apostles in Canonical Context," *The New Testament as Canon: A Reader in Canonical Criticism,* ed. Robert W. Wall and Eugene E. Lemcio (Sheffield: Sheffield Academic Press, 1992), p. 127.

16. As Harry Y. Gamble, Jr., points out, the Christian focus on Jesus affected the way in which the Old Testament would be read by Christians; see Gamble, "Christianity: Scripture and Canon," *The Holy Book in Comparative Perspective,* ed. Frederick M. Denny and Rodney L. Taylor (Columbia: University of South Carolina Press, 1985), pp. 37–38. Christians may not always realize the ways in which their methods of reading locate within the Old Testament literary characteristics that it might not possess in other readings.

17. See, for example, 2 Corinthians 6:4–10, 7:11, 11:20–28; Revelation 7:4–12,11:18, 18:11–24.

18. A. Katherine Hankey, "Tell Me the Old, Old Story" (1866), *Gospel Hymns: Nos. 1 to 6,* ed. Ira D. Sankey *et alia* (Chicago: Biglow and Main, 1894), no. 28. "Early dew" repeats the admonition of Hosea 6:4, 13:3 in the Old Testament.

19. James Wood, *The Book Against God* (London: Jonathan Cape, 2003), p. 164.

20. Wood, p. 161.

21. On this "doctrine of the two selves," see especially Chapter 7, below.

3 The Gospel of Luke

1. For a similar contradiction, apparent though reconcilable, compare Luke 17:20–21 with Luke 17:24.

2. Matthew 18:12–14 also has the lost sheep story.

3. Thomas Jefferson, letter to William Short, October 31, 1819, *The Writings of Thomas Jefferson*, ed. Andrew A. Lipscomb and Albert Ellery Bergh (Washington: Thomas Jefferson Memorial Association), 15.221.

4. In the King James version, Matthew quotes Jesus as using the word "hypocrites," but the most trustworthy manuscripts omit this similarity to Luke.

5. Jesus's statement about saving rather than destroying is not well attested among the oldest manuscripts, although his rebuke is.

6. The reference is to Isaiah 53.

4 The Gospel of John

1. The evidence is more complicated than I have so far indicated. John 21:24 ("This is the disciple . . . we know that his testimony is true") is an addition to the gospel proper, but the use of the first person in the next (and final) verse may represent a climactic return to "the author's version." John 20:30–31, the final verses of the preceding chapter, may once have been intended as the gospel's conclusion, as many scholars assume, but John's repetitive style could easily have allowed for two "conclusions." The verbal evidence is not decisive, and there is no other evidence. Supposing that John 21 does represent the continuation of a first or "original" version, either with or without an accompanying change of writership, are its final passages (starting with verse 15? or verse 23? or verse 24?) an additional continuation, or part of the same? There is even the possibility that the "we" in "we know" is simply a dramatic shift in the one author's rhetorical point of view. In any event, if Chapter 21 is a continuation, it is clearly a continuation in the same style as the earlier chapters, with no overt suggestion of a different voice until verse 24. Certainly, a work may be "continued" without a change in authorship.

2. Somewhat exaggerating the extent of agreement within the scholarly community, Donald Guthrie says, "Few scholars would dispute that the fourth gospel presupposes that the readers are acquainted with the synoptic tradition. To cite one example, the apos-

tles are abruptly introduced as 'the twelve' without further definition, and it is clearly assumed that the readers will know who they were"— Donald Guthrie, *New Testament Introduction*, 4th ed. (Leicester: Apollos, 1990), p. 265. In addition to more obvious differences, John's chronology of events departs from the synoptics'. It does not seem designed to contradict them, but it mentions different time markers.

3. Leland Ryken, *The Literature of the Bible* (Grand Rapids: Zondervan, 1974), p. 281.

4. Hyde W. Beadon, "Glory to Thee, O Lord" (1863), *The Church Hymnal: Revised and Enlarged . . . 1892* (Episcopal), Edition A, ed. Charles L. Hutchins (Boston: The Parish Choir, 1918), no. 70.

5. The King James Version translates ἀρχὴν τῶν σημείων ("archèn tôn semeíon") as "this beginning of miracles"; I follow Ryken 281 and the Revised Standard Version in reading "semeíon" literally as "signs."

6. Ryken, p. 279.

7. T.S. Eliot, *The Love Song of J. Alfred Prufrock* (1915), *The Waste Land and Other Poems* (New York: Harcourt, 1962), lines 90–95.

8. Augustine, *Confessions,* 11.11–14, 12.15; *The City of God,* 11.5–6.

9. See also Paul: "By him [Christ] were all things created . . . And he is before all things, and by him all things consist" (Colossians 1:16–17).

5 Making a Church

1. See also the double narrative of events at Acts 25:1–21, and the triple recounting of Paul's conversion experience (Acts 9, 22, 26).

2. "Western" manuscripts of Acts vary in many passages from manuscripts of Acts that belong to other textual "families," but the variations probably do not reflect revision by the author. See Frederic G. Kenyon, *The Text of the Greek Bible*, rev. ed. (London: Duckworth, 1949), pp. 232–36; Bruce M. Metzger, *A Textual Commentary on the Greek New Testament* (London: United Bible Societies, 1971), pp. 259–277.

3. I am giving *kerygma* a more general meaning than Eugene E. Lemcio gives it, in his incisive discussion of the subject: *The Past of Jesus in the Gospels* (Cambridge: Cambridge University Press, 1991), 115–131. Nevertheless, I believe he is right in finding a "core" *kerygma* broadly displayed in the New Testament. His brief history of scholarly attitudes toward the *kerygma* is very apt and useful.

4. Compare the "gather[ing] together" of "the gentiles, and the people of Israel" to oppose Jesus, as seen from the perspective of Acts 4:27.

5. The King James version says "too superstitious," which makes the wrong suggestion to modern readers, as if Paul were actually trying to insult his audience.

6. On Acts 26:28, which often supplies a theme for later Christian literature, Metzger (p. 496) comments, "The difficulty of capturing the nuances intended in the verse is notorious." It is not entirely clear whether Agrippa is telling Paul that he may soon win him over or commenting on Paul's own idea that he may do so. What is clear is that Agrippa is not yet where Paul wants him to be.

7. The change of name begins at Acts 13:9.

6 Paul the Thinker

1. The idea is perhaps most entertainingly represented by George Bernard Shaw in his Preface to *Androcles and the Lion* (1915).

2. We know that he sometimes cites from memory because of slight variations from his written sources.

3. Even Paul's one-page epistle to Philemon addresses both a practical problem of slavery and the larger problem of the church as a web of relationships.

4. At Romans 15:25–26 Paul indicates that he is collecting such contributions.

5. John Oxenham (pseudonym of William A. Dunkerley), "In Christ There Is No East or West" (1908), *Great Hymns of the Faith*, ed. John W. Peterson (Grand Rapids: Zondervan, 1968), no. 417.

7 Paul the Leader

1. John Garrett, *Roger Williams: Witness Beyond Christendom 1603–1683* (London: Macmillan, 1970), pp. 159–175.

2. Donald Guthrie, *New Testament Introduction*, 4th edition, 1990 (Leicester: Apollos, 1990), p. 438.

3. There is strong dispute about the additional advice (1 Corinthians 14:34–35) that "women keep silence in the churches." To many scholars, these verses seem an interpolation by another hand, because they brusquely interrupt two comments that fit together perfectly well without them, and because 1 Corinthians 11:5 refers to women praying and prophesying in public.

4. The image is used also by Paul, at Ephesians 2:20–22.

5. For an accessible review of the complex issues of sequencing in 1 and 2 Corinthians, see Guthrie, pp. 437–459. There is a good deal of speculation that 1 or 2 Corinthians, or both, may consist of multiple letters copied together as one (Guthrie, pp. 453–57). The evidence, which is largely impressionistic, seems insufficient to challenge the literary integrity of the books as received.

6. T.S. Eliot, "Little Gidding," *Four Quartets* (San Diego: Harcourt, n.d.), lines 239–242.

8 The Art of Revelation

1. See Chapter 2, above, on the two functions of prophecy.

2. William Blake, annotations to Bishop Watson's *Apology for the Bible*, *The Complete Poetry and Prose of William Blake*, newly revised ed., ed. David V. Erdman, (Garden City: Doubleday-Anchor, 1982), 617. On the opening of eyes, compare John 9.

3. Tradition has associated the four beasts with the four written gospels. The Old Testament reference is Ezekiel 1:10.

4. Stephen Cox, *Love and Logic: The Evolution of Blake's Thought* (Ann Arbor: University of Michigan Press, 1992), especially pp. 31–33, 205–09. Richard Bauckham, *The Climax of Prophecy: Studies on the Book of Revelation* (Edinburgh: Clark, 1993), pp. 150–173, examines the special quality, among works of ancient literature, of John's revelation "in the spirit" (Revelation 1:10) and makes acute comments (158–59) on its relationship to the book's literary complexities.

5. Acts 1:9. This is one of the many points of contact between Revelation and the first five books of the New Testament.

6. Like the earthquake at Jesus's crucifixion, apparently the worst moment of the life-death-triumph story (Matthew 27:51).

7. This is the majority scholarly opinion, supported by numerological comparisons between 666 and the numbers that can be assigned to the letters of Nero's name, as represented in various ways in various symbolic systems. See Bauckham's account (especially pp. 384–452) of numbers and their possible implications in Revelation. Skeptics will suggest that one can find any name in 666, if one is allowed to use any formulation of the name and any interpretive system one chooses, and that the very extensive use of mathematics that Bauckham finds in Revelation would be lost on any audience lacking the scholarly knowledge that Bauckham himself exhibits. Nevertheless, one cannot deny that there are "technique(s) of numerical composition" in the book (p. 3) or that John may have assumed that *some* in his audience would appreciate all its complexities (p. 30).

9 Early and Late

1. Anon., *The Dream of the Rood*, trans. Stephen Cox, based on the text in Frederic G. Cassidy and Richard N. Ringler, ed., *Bright's Old English* (New York: Holt, 1971), pp. 310–17. I have attempted a faithful but not a literal translation. Literal translation does not allow a plausible recreation of Old English poetry's alliterative style and distinctive formality.

2. See, for example, *Beowulf,* lines 901–915, 1700–1768.

3. Literally, "he stayed there with small company," a typically Anglo-Saxon use of ironic understatement.

4. Rudyard Kipling, "The Gardener," *The Writings in Prose and Verse of Rudyard Kipling* (New York: Scribner's, 1926), pp. 433–450.

5. Though there is a perhaps unrelated trail to be followed in Luke 7:37–50, John 11:2, and John 12:4–8.

6. The classic instances are the pear tree passage in Book 2 of Augustine's *Confessions* and the account of the malicious things that children "naturally" do in Book 2, Chapter 1 of Swift's *Gulliver's Travels.*

10 Revive Us Again

1. William Blake, *Jerusalem*, plate 53, line 19, *The Complete Poetry and Prose of William Blake*, newly revised edition, ed. David V. Erdman (Garden City: Doubleday-Anchor, 1982), p. 203.

2. William Paton Mackay, "Revive Us Again" (1863), *Gospel Hymns: Nos. 1 to 6*, ed. Ira D. Sankey *et alia* (Chicago: Biglow and Main, 1894), no. 20.

3. David Daniell, *The Bible in English: Its History and Influence* (New Haven: Yale University Press, 2003), p. 142.

4. The story of Master Wisehart appears in John Foxe, *Actes and Monumentes* (London: John Daye, 1570), 2.1444-48.

5. It should be noted that many early texts omit those words of Jesus, which are so much a part of the subsequent tradition of Christian literature.

6. The story of these martyrs appears in Foxe, 2.1443–44.

7. Acts 24:25; Philip P. Bliss, "Almost Persuaded" (1871), *The Music Men of Rome*, ed. Alfred B. Smith (Greenville, South Carolina: Al Smith Ministries, 1997), p. 31.

8. Ira D. Sankey, *My Life and the Story of the Gospel Hymns* (Philadelphia: The Sunday School Times Company, 1907), pp. 168–170; photo, author's collection; Bliss, "Hold the Fort," *Music Men*, p. 17. In one adaptation, "Hold the Fort" became a popular anthem of American trade unionists.

9. Bliss, "Man of Sorrows" (1875), *Music Men*, pp. 22–23. The song is based on Isaiah 53:3, which Christians traditionally regard as a prophetic reference to Jesus.

10. Sinclair Lewis, *Elmer Gantry*, in *Sinclair Lewis: Arrowsmith, Elmer Gantry, Dodsworth* (New York: Library of America, 2002), pp. 547; 676–77, 754, etc.; Peter Harvey, *Reminiscences and Anecdotes of Daniel Webster* (Boston: Little, Brown, 1877), pp. 409–410. The song was "Welcome, Sweet Day of Rest," which alludes to the pleasure of singing hymns on the Lord's day. The self-referential allusion had been omitted in the hymn book.

11. "Must Jesus Bear the Cross Alone?", now a popular gospel song, was written in four stages, from the late seventeenth to the mid-

nineteenth century. "Amazing Grace" was written in 1779 in six stanzas; fifty years later, another verse appeared; this endured, but by the 1980s, when the song achieved its current, immense popularity, two of the original verses had been dropped. An example of songs written about other Christian songs is Albert E. Brumley's popular "Amazing Grace Is the Sweetest Song I Know," which mentions five other hymns besides "Amazing Grace."

12. Bernard Ruffin, *Fanny Crosby* (n.p.: United Church, 1976), p. 68. For an account by the subject herself, see Fanny J. Crosby, *An Autobiography*, originally *Memories of Eighty Years* (1906; reprint Grand Rapids: Baker Book House, 1986), pp. 111–12.

13. Frances Crosby, "Blind Bartimeus," in Philip Phillips, *The Gospel Singer, For Sabbath Schools, Etc.* (Philadelphia: Lee and Walker, 1874), no. 96.

14. Crosby, "Pass Me Not," *Gospel Hymns: Nos. 1 to 6*, ed. Ira D. Sankey *et alia* (Chicago: Biglow and Main, 1894), no. 585.

15. Ruffin, p. 102.

16. Fanny Crosby, "All the Way My Savior Leads Me," *Gospel Hymns*, no. 42. Jesus said, "Your fathers did eat manna in the wilderness, and are dead. . . . I am the living bread which came down from heaven: if any man eat of this bread, he shall live for ever" (John 6:49–51).

17. William Cowper, "God Moves in a Mysterious Way" (1773), Cowper and John Newton, *Olney Hymns, in Three Books* (New York: Hodge, Allen, and Campbell, 1790), pp. 267–68. "Cowper" is pronounced "Cooper."

18. John Newton, "Amazing Grace," *The Works of the Rev. John Newton* (New York: Williams and Whiting, 1810), 3.353–54. The current last verse ("When we've been there ten thousand years") was composed by an unknown author after Newton's death.

19. John Newton, "Glorious Things of Thee Are Spoken," *Works*, 3:372–73.

20. William Cowper, "There Is a Fountain," *Olney Hymns*, pp. 84–85. Almost universally associated with this hymn, which the author entitled "Praise for the Fountain Opened," is the mysterious music of "Cleansing Fountain," an American camp-meeting tune that Mr. Cowper, a cultivated English gentleman, might not have approved. But hymns and hymn tunes conduct their own journeys, and sometimes cross one another at the proper points.

21. On Crosby: Ruffin, pp. 69, 158. On Watts: Theron Brown and Hezekiah Butterworth, *The Story of the Hymns and Tunes* (New York: American Tract Society, 1906), p. 43. The most convenient source on Watts is currently *Oxford Dictionary of National Biography*, ed. H.C.G. Matthew and Brian Harrison (Oxford: Oxford University Press, 2004), 57.725–30.

22. Ruffin, pp. 167, 180.

23. Brown and Butterworth, p. 284; see also the *Oxford Dictionary*, 47.398–400. Text of Robert Robinson, "Come, Thou Fount," from John Rippon, *A Selection of Hymns, from the Best Authors . . .* (Chillicothe: J. Hellings *et al.*, 1815), no. 509.

24. Isaac Watts, "Am I a Soldier of the Cross?", Rippon, no. 228.

25. George Atkins, "Holy Manna," *The Southern Harmony, and Musical Companion*, revised edition., ed. William Walker (New York: Hastings House, 1854), no. 103.

11 The Christian Life

1. T.S. Eliot, "Little Gidding," *Four Quartets* (San Diego: Harcourt, n.d.), lines 169–199.

2. Samuel Johnson, "Life of Cowley," *Samuel Johnson*, ed. Donald Greene (Oxford: Oxford University Press, 1984), p. 677.

3. John Donne, *Holy Sonnets, Poems by J. D., with Elegies on the Authors Death* (London: By M.F. for John Marriot, 1635), pp. 331–342. All quotations from Donne are from this edition.

4. Donne is citing John 2:17, which in turn cites Psalm 69:9 in the Old Testament.

5. What is crisis in the poems, however, may have been more like seriousness in the life. On Donne the poet and Donne the religious man, see Helen Gardner, ed., John Donne, *The Divine Poems* (Oxford: Clarendon, 1966), pp. xv–xxxvii. Gardner dates the *Holy Sonnets* to around 1609, before Donne became a priest (pp. xlix–l).

6. George Herbert, "The Collar," *The Temple* (London: T.R. for Philemon Stephens, 1656), p. 147.

7. There is an analogue in Paul's speech to the men of Athens, in which he says that God wants them to "seek the Lord, if haply they might feel after him, and find him, though he be not far from every one of us" (Acts 17:27).

8. Here it does not seem to imply, as is commonly thought, a clergyman's collar. Anglican priests did not wear distinctive collars until much later in history.

9. John Bunyan, *The Pilgrims Progress from This World, to That Which Is to Come* (London: Nath. Ponder, 1679), 1. Subsequent page references will appear in parentheses in my text. This edition includes substantial changes to the first edition.

10. Bunyan, *The Pilgrim's Progress . . .* (London: Nath. Ponder, 1678).

11. Modeled on the chariot and horses that, in the Old Testament, conveyed the prophet Elijah to heaven (2 Kings 2:11–12).

12. For elaboration of this idea, see Elder Olson, *The Theory of Comedy* (Bloomington: Indiana University Press, 1968).

12 A Tradition of Individualism

1. John Newton, Preface, William Cowper, *Poetical Works*, ed. H.S. Milford, 4th edition, corrected by Norma Russell (London: Oxford University Press, 1971), p. 650.

2. Henry Crabb Robinson, *Henry Crabb Robinson on Books and Their Writers*, ed. Edith J. Morley (London: Dent, 1938), 1:325.

3. William Blake, annotations to Bishop Watson's *Apology for the Bible*, *The Complete Poetry and Prose of William Blake*, newly revised ed., ed. David V. Erdman, newly revised ed. (Garden City: Doubleday-Anchor, 1982), p. 617.

4. Blake, *The Marriage of Heaven and Hell*, plates 11–13, *Poetry and Prose*, pp. 38–39.

5. Blake, "The Shepherd," "The Lamb," *Poetry and Prose*, pp. 7–9.

6. Blake, "The Little Boy Lost," "The Little Boy Found," *Poetry and Prose*, p. 11.

7. Blake, "The Chimney Sweeper," *Poetry and Prose*, p. 10.

8. Blake, *Marriage*, plates 3, 14 (with Blake's characteristically eccentric punctuation), *Poetry and Prose*, 34, 39. Compare Genesis 3:24 and Luke 23:43.

9. Blake, "A Vision of the Last Judgment," *Poetry and Prose*, p. 564.

10. For a detailed account, see Stephen Cox, *Love and Logic: The Evolution of Blake's Thought* (Ann Arbor: University of Michigan Press, 1992).

11. A convenient source for Blake's ideas is his poem *Milton*, plates 39–43, *Poetry and Prose*, pp. 140–44.

12. Blake, *The Four Zoas*, ms. p. 104, lines 5–9, *Poetry and Prose*, p. 376. Compare Revelation 4:8, 5:9–13.

13. Blake, *The Gates of Paradise*, *Poetry and Prose*, p. 259.

14. Blake, "To Tirzah," *Poetry and Prose*, p. 30. Some complexities of the poem not discussed here are noticed in Cox, pp. 197–98.

15. Sometimes this is virtually all that critics discuss. Even standard reference works sometimes refuse to accept *prima facie* evidence of Dickinson's favorable views toward Christian ideas; see Beth Maclay Doriani's flat pronouncement that Dickinson's poem 525 (see below) projects "a faceless, silent 'infinitude' who, although he does not lash out at [the speaker], nevertheless silences her; the speaker 'worshipped—did not 'pray'": *An Emily Dickinson Encyclopedia*, ed. Jane Donahue Eberwein (Westport: Greenwood, 1998), p. 127. My own discussion emphasizes the wealth of Christian interpretations of the universe in Dickinson's poems, including and especially poem 525. For an exhaustively contrary view to my own, one that to me seems interesting but greatly overstated, see Cynthia Griffin Wolff, *Emily Dickinson* (New York: Knopf, 1986), especially pp. 261–282. A helpful survey of

Dickinson's religious attitudes is provided by Roger Lundin, *Emily Dickinson and the Art of Belief* (Grand Rapids: Eerdmans, 1998).

16. Emily Dickinson, poem 236, "Some keep the Sabbath" (1861 or 1862), *The Poems of Emily Dickinson: Variorum Edition*, ed. R.W. Franklin (Cambridge, Massachusetts: Harvard University Press, 1998). Subsequent references to Dickinson's poems will cite them parenthetically, by their approximately chronological numbering in this edition. Dickinson did not name her poems.

17. Lundin, 166.

18. Wolff, however (cf. note 14, above), concedes that Dickinson was a committed Christian at the end of her life; see especially pp. 504–07, 518–19.

13 The Glory Part

1. Emily Dickinson, poem 353, *The Poems of Emily Dickinson: Variorum Edition*, ed. R.W. Franklin (Cambridge, Massachusetts: Harvard University Press, 1998).

2. Theodore Roosevelt, June 17, 1912, in *The Autobiography of Theodore Roosevelt*, ed. with supplements by Wayne Andrews (New York: Scribner's, 1958), p. 345.

3. Katharine Lee Bates, "America the Beautiful," *Great Hymns of the Faith*, ed. John W. Peterson (Grand Rapids: Zondervan, 1968), no. 531. I rely on the version that is popularly preserved and used, ignoring the author's many, often remarkably maladroit verbal variations.

4. Julia Ward Howe, *Reminiscences* (Boston: Houghton Mifflin, 1900), pp. 274–75. I quote the finished version of the poem as printed in the *Atlantic Monthly* 9 (February 1862), p. 145.

5. Howe's first draft is close to the poem as we know it, but "transfigures" was originally "shines out on" (Howe, insert following p. 276). The change is a good example of re-intensification of Christian revelation by return to the New Testament source.

6. James Baldwin, *Go Tell It on the Mountain, James Baldwin: Early Novels and Stories* (New York: Library of America, 1998), p. 183. Compare Revelation 21:4.

7. Baldwin, p. 198.

8. Baldwin, p. 214–15.

9. Baldwin, p. 215. Compare 1 Corinthians 9:24–27, Philippians 2:16, and still more appositely to Baldwin, p. 204, Hebrews 12:1–2.

10. Nicholas Vachel Lindsay, *General William Booth Enters into Heaven and Other Poems* (London: Chatto and Windus, 1919), pp. 1–4.

11. Elisha Hoffman, "Are You Washed in the Blood?" (1878), *Tabernacle Hymns No. 2* (Chicago: Tabernacle Publishing Co., 1921), no. 121. Compare Revelation 7:14.

14 Scornful Wonder

1. For a very helpful survey of anti-Christian attitudes in literature, see D. Bruce Lockerbie, *Dismissing God: Modern Writers' Struggle against Religion* (Grand Rapids: Baker Books, 1998).

2. On the issues raised by Frazer in *The Golden Bough* (1890 and following), see Tryggve N.D. Mettinger, *The Riddle of Resurrection: "Dying and Rising Gods" in the Ancient Near East* (Stockholm: Almqvist and Wiksell, 2001). The classic response of Christian scholarship to the reduction of Christianity to its "sources" and "analogues" is J. Gresham Machen, *The Origin of Paul's Religion* (1925; reprint Grand Rapids: Eerdmans, 2003).

3. Samuel John Stone, "The Church's One Foundation," *Poems and Hymns* (London: Methuen, 1903), pp. 28, 239–240 (see Chapter 1, Figure 3, above). For the work's intellectual background, see the *Oxford Dictionary of National Biography*, ed. H.C.G. Matthew and Brian Harrison (Oxford: Oxford University Press, 2004), 52.910, on Stone, and 12.552-55, on John William Colenso, provoker of the proximate Higher Critical controversy.

4. Harold Frederic, *The Damnation of Theron Ware* (New York: Holt, Rinehart, and Winston, 1958), pp. 70, 73. Subsequent page references will appear in parentheses in my text.

5. Sinclair Lewis, *Elmer Gantry*, in *Sinclair Lewis: Arrowsmith, Elmer Gantry, Dodsworth* (New York: Library of America, 2002), p. 547. Subsequent page references will appear in parentheses in my text.

6. William Faulkner, *Light in August*, corrected text (New York: Vintage-Random House, 1985), p. 487.

7. John Adams to Thomas Jefferson, July 16, 1813; Thomas Jefferson to John Adams, July 5, 1814, *The Adams-Jefferson Letters*, ed. Lester J. Cappon (Chapel Hill: University of California Press, 1959), pp. 360, 432–33. Adams was on record as having "no objection . . . to the miracles of Jesus Christ," on the assumption that the "author of nature" could "suspend" the natural laws he had made: see Adams's Diary, March 1, 1756, in *The Works of John Adams, Second President of the United States*, ed. Charles Francis Adams (Boston: Little, Brown, 1856), 1.7–8. Sixty years later, he calls Jesus "benevolence personified," echoing the deist idea of Jesus as a human moralist, and says that his own "Creed" is "contained in four short words '*Be just and good*'" (in which Jefferson concurs); yet he denies that supernatural "revelation is impossible or improbable" (Adams to Jefferson, December 12, 1816, Jefferson to Adams, January 11, 1817, *Letters*, pp. 499, 506; Adams to F.A. Vanderkamp, December 27, 1816, *Works*, 10.234–35). Adams is hopeful that the "mischief" he made as a revolutionist was intended by providence as productive of an "ultimate good" (Adams to Benjamin Rush, August 28, 1811, *Works*, 9.635). As for revelation, he believes

that "[t]he human Understanding is a revelation from its Maker which can never be disputed or doubted" (Adams to Thomas Jefferson, September 14, 1813, *Letters*, p. 373).

8. Thomas Jefferson, quoted in John Adams to Thomas Jefferson, July 16, 1813, *Adams-Jefferson Letters*, pp. 359–360.

9. Thomas Jefferson, letter to William Short, October 31, 1819, *The Writings of Thomas Jefferson*, ed. Andrew A. Lipscomb and Albert Ellery Bergh (Washington: Thomas Jefferson Memorial Association), 15.221.

10. John Adams to Thomas Jefferson, March 2, 1816, *Adams–Jefferson Letters*, pp. 464–65.

11. Percy Bysshe Shelley, chorus from *Hellas* (1821), *Percy Bysshe Shelley: The Major Works*, ed. Zachary Leader and Michael O'Neill (Oxford: Oxford University Press, 2003), pp. 558–59.

12. A.E. Housman, "Bredon Hill," *A Shropshire Lad*, *The Poems of A.E. Housman*, ed. Archie Burnett (Oxford: Clarendon, 1997), *Poems*, pp. 22–24.

13. A.E. Housman, "The Carpenter's Son," Poems, pp. 50–51.

14. D.H. Lawrence, *The Man Who Died*, *The Complete Short Novels*, ed. Keith Sagar and Melissa Partridge (Harmondsworth: Penguin, 1982), p. 564. The editors use Lawrence's original title for the story, *The Escaped Cock*. A similar tale, with similar ironies and paradoxes, is told by Lawrence's contemporary George Moore, in *The Brook Kerith* (1916).

15. Lawrence, especially pp. 595–96.

16. Lawrence, pp. 570–71.

17. Isabel Paterson, *New York Herald Tribune "Books"* (February 19, 1933), p. 12; John Henry Raleigh, "Biographical Note," in Frederic, p. xxviii.

18. The outraged commenter was Minnie Kennedy, Sister Aimee's own mother. See Lately Thomas (pseudonym of Robert V.P. Steele), *Storming Heaven: The Lives and Turmoils of Minnie Kennedy and Aimee Semple McPherson* (New York: Morrow, 1970), p. 100; emphasis added.

19. The reference is to the hymn by Lewis E. Jones, "There Is Power in the Blood" (1899), *Great Hymns of the Faith*, ed. John W. Peterson (Grand Rapids: Zondervan, 1968), no. 198.

20. Contrast Paul at Galatians 5:16–25.

15 Keeping Watch

1. Thornton Wilder, *Heaven's My Destination* (New York: Harper and Brothers, 1935), pp. 17–31, imitating Mark 11:15–17, John 2:14–17. Subsequent page references to this work will appear in parentheses in the text.

2. Thornton Wilder, *The Bridge of San Luis Rey* (New York: Albert and Charles Boni, 1928), p. 85.

3. Lew Wallace describes his original attitude toward religion as one of "absolute indifference" until a conversation with Robert G. Ingersoll, the skeptic (see p. 268, above), made him "ashamed of [his] ignorance." He resolved to write a novel that would allow him to "study the subject," and the result was that he "became a believer in God and Christ." His three overlapping accounts are in some ways of more interest than *Ben-Hur. Lew Wallace: An Autobiography* (New York: Harper and Brothers, 1906), pp. 926–937 (reprinting his article, "How I Came to Write *Ben-Hur*," *The Youths' Companion* [February 2, 1893]); "How Ben-Hur Was Written," *The Chariot* (November 1895), pp. 3, 6; *The First Christmas* (New York: Harper and Brothers, 1899), pp. v–ix.

4. Ernest Hemingway, *The Old Man and the Sea* (New York: Scribner's, 1952), p. 166. Subsequent page references will appear in parentheses in the text.

5. William Faulkner, *Faulkner in the University: Class Conferences at the University of Virginia 1957–1958*, ed. Frederick L. Gwynn and Joseph L. Blotner (Charlottesville: University of Virginia Press, 1959), pp. 167–68.

6. This is despite Faulkner's partiality to certain emphases, mentioned in the discussion of his character Reverend Gail Hightower in Chapter 14, above, and despite (or because of) his sympathy with his characters' feeble ways of doing their best.

7. Phillip E. Johnson, *Reason in the Balance* (Downers Grove: InterVarsity Press, 1995).

8. Pierre Lecomte du Noüy, *Human Destiny* (New York: Longmans, Green, 1947). For a more recent work that regards biological evolution as well attested, see Stephen M. Barr, *Modern Physics and Ancient Faith* (Notre Dame: University of Notre Dame Press, 2003), a physicist's account of science's compatibility with Christianity.

9. John Betjeman, "The Conversion of St. Paul," *Uncollected Poems* (London: John Murray, 1982), pp. 67–70.

10. The great evangelical scholar J. Gresham Machen (*The Origin of Paul's Religion* [Grand Rapids: Eerdmans, 1925]) also took Paul's conversion as the beginning of the argument for Christianity.

11. Compare William Blake: "If Morality was Christianity[,] Socrates was The Savior"—annotations to Thornton's *The Lord's Prayer, Newly Translated* (1827), *The Complete Poetry and Prose of William Blake*, newly revised ed., ed. David V. Erdman (Garden City: Doubleday-Anchor, 1982), p. 667.

12. Martin Luther King, Jr., "Transformed Nonconformist," *Strength to Love* (New York: Harper and Row, 1963), pp. 8–15. King's comment about rewriting appears in his Preface (p. x). A clear account of King's

formative literary influences, especially the preaching of the word as practiced in the African American church, is offered by Richard Lischer, "The Word That Moves: The Preaching of Martin Luther King, Jr.," *Theology Today* 46 (1989), pp. 169–182.

13. C.S. Lewis, *The Screwtape Letters* (San Francisco: HarperCollins, 2001), 60–61.

14. T.S. Eliot, "Burnt Norton," *Four Quartets* (San Diego: Harcourt, n.d.), lines 99–105.

15. James Wood, *The Book Against God* (London: Cape, 2003), pp. 214, 200.

16. Wood, pp. 178–79. See also p. 39, above, on Bunting's inability to stop arguing against God and detach himself from the Christian story.

17. Robert Browning, *Bishop Blougram's Apology*, *Poems of Robert Browning*, ed. Donald Smalley (Boston: Houghton Mifflin, 1956), pp. 188–212; lines 58, 50–51. Subsequent line numbers appear parenthetically in the text. I have compared this text with that of Frank Charles Allen, *A Critical Edition of Robert Browning's "Bishop Blougram's Apology"* (Salzburg: Institut für Englishe Sprache und Literatur, 1976).

18. Not much, according to Browning's "Christmas-Eve and Easter Day" (1850) and his later poem "A Death in the Desert" (1864), a vigorous attack on the Higher Critics' historical and philosophical assumptions.

19. G.K. Chesterton, *Robert Browning* (1903) (London: Macmillan, 1961), pp. 189, 200–01. Browning's editor is not so gloomy, but after stipulating that "most interpretations disregard [Blougram's] worldliness in order to give high marks for his Christian beliefs," he states his own opinion that the Bishop "masks his devotion to worldly values in a show of faith and can only resort to the deceptive half-truths of the intellect for his self-justification" (Allen, p. ii). One reference work calls Bishop Blougram a skeptic who "continues to stand before the world as an exponent of doctrines he no longer holds"—William Rose Benét, ed., *The Reader's Encyclopedia: An Encyclopedia of World Literature and the Arts* (New York: Crowell, 1948), p. 112. *Blougram* is the *kerygma* for intellectuals, but only for intellectuals who are willing to read it closely.

20. Smalley, ed., in *Poems of Robert Browning*, p. 505.

16 Difficult—and Easy

1. J.F. Powers, *Wheat that Springeth Green* (New York: Knopf, 1988), p. 133.

2. Powers, *Wheat*, p. 117.

3. Powers, *Wheat*, pp. 136–37, 131.

4. J.F. Powers, "Keystone," *Look How the Fish Live* (New York: Knopf, 1975), pp. 55, 58.

5. Powers, *Wheat*, pp. 117, 118.

6. Powers, "Keystone," pp. 46–47.

7. Powers, "Keystone," pp. 69, 67.

8. Powers, "Keystone," p. 70.

9. Powers, "Keystone," p. 76.

10. Powers, "Farewell," *Look How the Fish Live*, p. 152.

11. Powers, "Farewell," p. 158.

12. Powers, "Keystone," p. 45.

13. Powers, "Farewell," p. 163.

14. Powers, "Farewell," pp. 158–59, 163.

15. Powers, "Farewell," p. 163.

16. Powers, "Farewell," p. 166.

17. T.S. Eliot, "Little Gidding," *Four Quartets* (San Diego: Harcourt, n.d.), line 242.

18. T.S. Eliot, *The Waste Land*, *The Waste Land and Other Poems* (New York: Harcourt, 1962), line 431.

19. For a lucid account of Eliot's religious development, see Lyndall Gordon, *T.S. Eliot: An Imperfect Life* (New York: Norton, 1999). On the development of *Four Quartets*, see especially Helen Gardner, *The Composition of Four Quartets* (London: Faber and Faber, 1978).

20. Eliot, "Little Gidding," lines 214–15, 239–242.

21. Eliot, "Little Gidding," lines 52, 245–48, 255–56, 259.

22. Eliot, "Little Gidding," lines 173–74.

23. Eliot, "Little Gidding," lines 78–149.

24. Eliot, "The Dry Salvages," *Four Quartets*, lines 132–36, "East Coker," *Four Quartets*, lines 101–110.

25. Eliot, "Little Gidding," lines 144–45.

26. Eliot, "Little Gidding," lines 81, 200–06.

27. Eliot, "East Coker," lines 167–171.

28. Revelation 14:6; Eliot, "The Dry Salvages," line 97; "Little Gidding," lines 220–23.

29. Lidie H. Edmunds [pseud. of Eliza Hewitt], "My Faith Has Found a Resting Place" (1891), *Great Hymns of the Faith* (Grand Rapids: Zondervan, 1970), no. 228. Other popular hymns in this tradition include "The Great Physician Now Is Near" (1859), by William Hunter; "Jesus Heals Today" (1894), by James M. Kirk; and George F. Root's "The Hem of His Garment" (1906), based on the gospel story discussed in Chapter 3, p. 52, above. See also John Newton's Olney hymn "The Good Physician," with its emphasis on healing by transformation of vision: "He makes no hard condition, / 'Tis only—look and live": *The Works of the Rev. John Newton* (New York: Williams and Whiting, 1810), pp. 375–76.

30. Eliot, "East Coker," lines 147–151.

31. Eliot, "East Coker," lines 157–160.

32. Eliot, "Burnt Norton," *Four Quartets*, lines 23–39. Although the most obvious "lookers" in this passage are the shades of people from the past, 1 Corinthians 13:12 is also relevant.

33. Frances Havergal, "The Half Has Never Been Told" (1878), *Coronation Hymns*, ed. E.O. Excell (Chicago: E.O. Excell, 1910), no. 151.

Scripture Index

General Index

Abraham, 112–13
Acts of the Apostles, writing, 82–85;
    literary methods, 82–100
Adams, John, 256–59
Agrippa (Herod Agrippa II), 98, 182
Alighieri, Dante, 315
Alter, Robert, 368n.2
Anglicanism, 197–200
apocryphal books, 16, 367n.23
Aratus, 96
Arius, 79
Athanasius, 79
Atkins, George, quoted, 194–96
Augustine, 4, 29, 80, 169

Baldwin, James, 242–44
Bartim[a]eus, 186, 187
Barton, Bruce, 280
Bates, Katharine Lee, 240
Beowulf, 161
Betjeman, John, 284–86
Blake,William, 36, 140, 175,
    219–226
Bliss, Philip P., 180–83
Booth, William, General, 244–250
Bradley, Francis Herbert, 314
Browning, Robert, 25, 291–99, 309,
    312
Buffon, Georges–Louis Leclerc,
    Comte de, 257–58
Bunyan, John, 209–217, 229, 312

Caiaphas, 73
Calvin, John, 182
Charles I, King of England, 198–99
Chesterton, G.K., 275, 297–98
Christianity: —attacked, 251–274; —
    defended, 275–299, 314–321; —as
    historical religion, 22, 24, 369n.14;
    —institutional, 86–92, 118–135,
    138–140, 189–190, 223–24,
    227–28; —"primitive," 118–19,
    135, 197; —revivals of, 175–196,
    226–27, 239–240, 244–45; —
    spread of, 157–58
Colenso, John William, 379n.3
Constantine, Emperor, 168
Constantinople, First Council of, 80
Cornelius, 84
Cowper, William, 188, 190–91, 192
Cromwell, Oliver, 198
Crosby, Frances Jane, 185–88, 191,
    192

D'Alembert, Jean le Rond, 257–58
Damrosch, Leopold, Jr., 21
Daniel, prophet, 137–38
Darwin, Charles, 253
David, King, 36, 45
deism, 222, 227, 230, 252–53,
    256–59
Dickinson, Emily, 219, 225–35,
    237–39, 276

ALSO FROM OPEN COURT

The Rise of Tolkienian Fantasy

JARED LOBDELL

When Tolkien's *Lord of the Rings* appeared in 1954, it was eagerly sought by a rapidly widening community of readers while snootily dismissed by eminent critics as juvenile escapism. For many years most literary scholars refused to take Tolkien seriously, but today they reluctantly admit that he is indeed one of the greatest of writers.

Jared Lobdell contends that Tolkien's literary achievement actually constitutes a new mainstream of literary development. The future of fiction lies in fantasy, and Tolkien is part of a vital organic growth with roots in the past.

Celtic revival, medieval revival, "feigned history," the Edwardian adventure story—many tributaries flow into the swelling stream of Tolkienian fantasy. Professor Lobdell (author of *The World of the Rings*) traces Tolkien's most important precursors and influences. Some are familiar figures: Rudyard Kipling, William Morris, Kenneth Grahame, and H. Rider Haggard. Others, such as R.S. Surtees and George MacDonald, have been neglected lately.

Finally, Lobdell looks at some of the ablest heirs of the master: contemporary fantasists Ursula LeGuin, Stephen King (in the *Dark Tower* series), and J.K. Rowling.

"avoids the limitations of most books on Tolkien. Where critics generally squeeze him into a single mold, Lobdell gives the reader a rich, sweeping, and far more valid picture of the inspirations and sources that lie behind Tolkien's work."

— MARJORIE J. BURNS, author of *Perilous Realms: Celtic and Norse in Tolkien's Middle-earth*

AVAILABLE FROM BOOKSTORES OR BY CALLING 1-800-815-2280

For more information on Open Court books, go to
www.opencourtbooks.com.